THE 11:11 CODE

THE GREAT AWAKENING BY THE NUMBERS

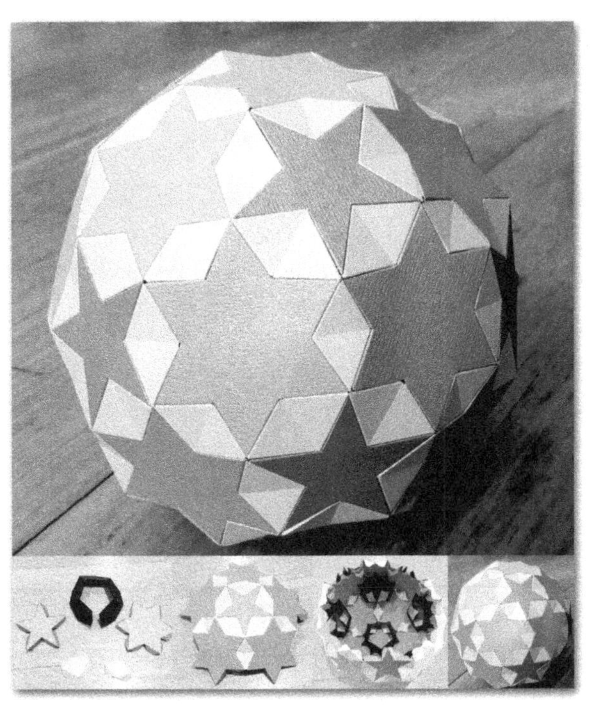

CHARLES J. WOLFE, BSEE, M.ENG

The 11:11 Code: The Great Awakening by the Numbers

For more about this author please visit www.1111code.com

Ordering Information: Quantity sales. Special discounts are available on quantity purchases by corporations, associations, and others. Orders by US trade bookstores and wholesalers. For details, contact the publisher at the address above.

Front Cover Photography by Jacque Brund, photomodes.com
Polyhedron (on title page) Photography & Assembly Credit to Robert Webb, software3d.com
Photography and graphics by Charles J. Wolfe, BSEE, M.Eng unless otherwise credited
Editing by The Pro Book Editor
Interior and Cover Design by IAPS.rocks

ISBN: 978-1-7346218-2-2

1. Main category—Philosophy/Good & Evil
2. Other category—Body, Mind & Spirit/Numerology

First Edition

TABLE OF CONTENTS

Numbers are the highest degree of knowledge. It is knowledge itself.

—Plato[1]

The most beautiful thing we can experience is the mysterious.

—Albert Einstein[2]

There are many who will dub me a "nut" for what I have written in this book. My reply is this, from author David Icke: Today's mighty oak is just yesterday's nut that held its ground.[3]

We are the gods of the atoms that make up ourselves, but we are also the atoms of the gods that make up the universe.

—Brother Manly P. Hall[4]

Bill & Kathe:
I really hope you enjoy reading my book. Have fun! Talk to you soon!

1 http://platonicrealms.com/quotes/Plato.
2 https://www.forbes.com/quotes/190/.
3 https://www.goodreads.com/quotes/71619-today-s-mighty-oak-is-just-yesterday-s-nut-that-held-its.
4 https://www.azquotes.com/quote/944031

I am not unaware, Lucilius, excellent man, of how great is the enterprise whose foundations I am laying in my old age, now that I have decided to traverse the world, to seek out its causes and secrets, and to present them for others to learn about.

—Seneca, circa AD 65, addressing Lucilius Junior in his Latin book on philosophy, *Naturales Suaestiones*[5]

It had long since come to my attention that people of accomplishment rarely sit back and let things happen to them. They went out and happened to things.

—Leonardo da Vinci[6]

5 https://www.worldcat.org/wcpa/servlet/org.oclc.lac.ui.DialABookServlet?oclcnum=642208470
6 https://www.positivityblog.com/leonardo-da-vincis-top-six-tips-for-getting-things-done/

PROLOGUE

The average world traveler visits popular "glossy brochure" places such as London, Paris, Rome, Venice, and Prague as well as countries with nice beaches, and gathers a nice portfolio of photos in front of famous statues and churches—which is all great—travel is wonderful. As a specialist performing testing and repairs on large electric power turbine equipment, my assignments have sent me to far-flung reaches of the Earth, often ending with *-stan* or *-ia*. Having traveled to more than 228 territories[7] worldwide, I've had the privilege of experiencing many cultures at a depth most will never have the opportunity to access and spent time in very difficult places many people have never heard of, much less visited, like Azerbaijan, Algeria, Chad, Turkmenistan, and Indonesia. I have the dubious honor of having visited the emergency room on every continent but Antarctica. One of my fellow field engineers who was more than seventy years old once told me over cocktails in Madrid that "we may not be millionaires, but we are cultural billionaires because of our deeply immersive global travel experiences." These words resonate with me to this day. I've worked on every electric power grid on the planet with the exception of Australia. If you live in Asia, Africa, Europe, North or South America, I have worked on a large power generator connected to your power grid and then to your house. I've included Appendix 5 with a list of major world cities where I have worked.

Rarely was I placed in fine accommodations like the average business traveler would be entitled to. Many times I stayed in remote working

7 By territories I am counting individual states, provinces, welayats, oblasts, cantons, etc. of various countries visited

camps in the middle of the desert, hours from the nearest city. Some of these experiences were oddly reminiscent of the gulags of the old Soviet Union, with tightly controlled access in and out, ubiquitous barbed wire fences topped with concertina wire, and WWII-era trains that resembled something from *Dr. Zhivago*. Oftentimes, upon landing in a foreign country, a security team picked me up at the main airport and whisked me away in a van that would take me many hours out into the country, usually to small towns where most residents had little or no prior contact with outsiders. I worked where the locals worked. I ate where they ate. I shopped for groceries and got haircuts where they did. I made an effort to learn two to three words of their language every day. I studied the local religious practices and cultural customs. For a short period of time, I did my best to act like a chameleon and integrate myself into the host culture. In a couple of situations while working in the former Soviet Union, people suspected me of being a covert agent for the US government, and I was once followed around town by a large man in a black suit and sunglasses on a cloudy day while I was living in Turkmenistan where you had to have police permission to be out in public after the nightly 11:00 PM curfew that applies to all citizens, on pain of arrest and prosecution. For that brief period of time, I learned what it was to truly live in a country run by an autocratic leader. In this sense, I feel that I have lived many lifetimes within the space of the past forty-plus years.

Throughout my world travels, I've logged more than a million miles of air travel. Assuming the average speed of an international airliner is 600 miles per hour, that is about 2,500 hours of sitting on a plane and staring out at the clouds, stars, and the land below, wondering what life is *really* all about. I've spent literally *years* sitting in hotels, remote desert camps, and subarctic work compounds, completely alone and thousands of miles from everyone and everything that was important to me while working on the world's electric power grid systems. Despite the soul-crushing loneliness and complete lack of human affection, these assignments built character and gave me the time for deep introspection and soul-searching so that I could contemplate the purpose of existence and try to understand my role in the whole show. I'd been virtually everywhere, and I'd seen and done almost everything I'd ever wanted to do. Now what?

Until deciding to write this book, I had been waiting for the right person to ask the right question that would prompt me to explain what it all meant.

But that never happened. No one ever asked the magic question because it doesn't exist. I needed to dig deeper.

It was a quarter to six in the evening on Wednesday, October 15, 2008, when I was working at a turbine overhaul project in Bonny Island, Nigeria, and heard the sharp, unmistakable staccato bursts of automatic weapons being emptied of ammunition. We were just packing up our tools and test equipment and planning on enjoying dinner and beers when the largest petrochemical facility on the African continent came under attack. A total of eight men were killed—five rebels from MEND[8] and three Nigerian Navy officers who were safeguarding the jetty used to load $40 million per day of liquefied natural gas onto ships bound for destinations around the world.

My forward security detail in Nigeria. Another military team followed behind my convoy.

My security detail while on the project.

8 MEND stands for Movement for the Emancipation of the Niger Delta. (For clarity, Niger is pronounced *nye-jer.*)

During the attack, my team and I were kept under armed guard and locked in the control room of the power station from 5:45 until 11 in the evening, after the situation had stabilized. That night, I experienced a dream that went far beyond just a dream. I don't know how to explain what happened, but I sat upright and went through a harrowing experience of terror and impending death, the likes of which I had never felt before and have never again since. I had an out-of-body experience that literally took my breath away. This was a truly terrifying and disturbing experience which haunted me for many months afterward. In retrospect, it also served as the beginning of my spiritual awakening. This onslaught put the fear of God into every bone in my body, and for the first time, I truly came to terms with my temporal, mortal nature. This was the sharp beginning of my path toward spiritual awakening. The attack was a real wake-up call in many respects.

On my last day as I was leaving camp and heading to the airport to depart Lagos, Nigeria, and on my journey back home to my frantic fiancée who today is my wife and best friend, Britta. I was in the back seat of the Toyota Hilux pickup truck with my military escort when I noticed what appeared to be a large dead animal in the center of the road—a deer maybe? As we got closer, I realized it was a dead *person*. As we passed the corpse, I saw that it was a young man of maybe eighteen or twenty years of age. One of his legs was torn open, and flesh was hanging out from people having driven over him repeatedly. In complete shock and horror, I asked the driver why someone hadn't stopped and at least pulled the body to the side of the road. The answer was simple: if anyone dared touch the man's corpse, they would likely be treated as murder suspects. As I pondered this horrifying loss of human life, I felt terrible for the parents, siblings, and children who had lost their son, brother, or father. Life in Nigeria is as raw and unfiltered as it gets. You can have someone assassinated and dumped in a swamp for just $50, according to one of the local engineers I had become good friends with on the project.

Another hair-raising ordeal happened one morning as I was entering the Russian-owned RusAl, an aluminum-smelting plant near Calabar, Nigeria, and my security convoy stopped at the gate security checkpoint. Normally, the convoy drivers just flash their military credentials, and the security guards wave us through to the power station. This morning was very different. The driver displayed identification, but the RusAl guards got in a very heated but short-lived argument with my forward security detail. In the flash of an instant, all four soldiers jumped out of the truck with their AK-47s drawn and rushed the security shack. I have no idea what was said between the two parties, but the security gate *immediately* opened, and we went straight to the plant after that. I was so terrified that I thought I was going to turn into a pillar of salt! Nigeria, as with most countries I've lived and worked in, could occupy the pages of its own book.

As I mentally unpacked from these experiences, I struggled to understand what had happened to me during the night of my out-of-body experience. By random chance or divine serendipity, by a friend's recommendation I happened upon a book titled *DMT: The Spirit Molecule* by Rick Strassman, MD, which happened to go through the biochemical basis for out-of-body and near-death experiences. One of the core tenets of physics is that energy cannot be created or destroyed; it can only change form. In the human body, we have various forms of energy that make us alive—electrical, chemical, thermal, and mechanical. I wanted to know what form of energy our consciousness converts to at death. Strassman's book really opened a Pandora's box of curiosity and investigation into the realms beyond the basic human experience.

Most scientists seem to share the notion that understanding human consciousness is one of the hardest problems humanity has ever attempted to solve, and, worse, we are scarcely any closer to solving this great mystery now than we were at any point in the past. I would even go so far as to suggest that the ancient civilizations—Mayans, Aztecs, Incas, Egyptians, and others—may have known much more than we do today.

The mysteries of religion and science make up some of the most difficult and controversial unanswered questions that humankind has ever pondered as the subjects seek to get to the root of who we are and where we came from and to discover the secrets of the physical universe, respectively. No two subjects have created as much mystery and intrigue as these have. In the paradigm of modern education, scientists, engineers, and mathematicians, among others, are taught to almost exclusively operate from a purely rational, left-brain standpoint and reject any information that cannot be rigorously proven using scientific principles. Conversely, scholars of religion are not trained to give much weight to scientific or mathematical facts when delving into the spiritual domain. Instead, they base much of their doctrine on faith.

The main purpose of this book is to take these two separate circles of thought and overlap them in an attempt to make the case for the existence of God by seeing what can be found in the union of the two seemingly disparate subjects. The physics aspect will be demonstrated mathematically, while the spiritual side will be proved empirically through presenting an exhaustive amount of data I accumulated while traveling the world and studying. My hope is that by the end of the book, the reader will understand better how science and spirituality are complementary, not opposites, and have a deeper appreciation for all forms of life. The book aims to enlighten the reader about the greater framework of sacred numbers hidden in plain sight that have left their unmistakable stamp on many of mankind's greatest and most influential events throughout time and across all cultures, irrespective of geographic and cultural boundaries.

Another aspiration of this work is to give some context to the Great Awakening and the QAnon movement, which I am convinced is the greatest communication event in human history. In the end, I hope you walk away with a deeper appreciation for the creator of the universe and all of his handiwork and find comfort in knowing that he has a plan in place for saving humanity from self-destruction.

It is also my hope that this book will help atheists, agnostics, and doubters take a fresh look at spirituality. It's meant to help people who are struggling with their faith in a higher being and strengthen the faith of those who are already believers. The end goal is to bring about love and peace in a world that needs it now more desperately than ever before. This book will guide the reader to find beauty and love in nature and within themselves and perhaps gain a deeper understanding of the universe in the process. This book was written with the intention of helping the reader in building a relationship with the essence of the creative spirit of the cosmos within yourself, helping you realize that you are part of the divine consciousness at large.

I will attempt to play with the quirkiest inner workings of the scientific mind in an effort to get through to even the most hardened, educated scientist by using our common language and utilizing logical, analytical, and mathematical thought processes while placing historical and current events within numerological contexts that may give clues to the future. I use mathematics as the overarching principle—the one and only truly timeless and universal language.

Take a moment to ponder the following duality concept:

> Grammar is the mathematics of the right hemisphere. Mathematics is the grammar of the left.

Mathematics is the one language that transcends all barriers, including time, age, race, political viewpoints, geography, color, gender, and even religion. It is one of the greatest gifts from God, for it provides the keys to understanding the universe and all its inner workings. It's the one and perhaps only subject that people of all religions on Earth agree on. Ponder that!

I got my first deep exposure to university level mathematics in first grade when I noticed that the neighboring electrical engineering student had tossed out some textbooks in a huge mountain of trash. While I was waiting for the school bus to pick me up, I went over and grabbed a textbook on advanced calculus and proceeded to obsessively study every single page of that book. It was as if I was an archaeologist who had stumbled upon some sort of Rosetta Stone of sorts, chocked full of cool diagrams, elegant equations, and really awesome sounding words like eigenvector, holomorphic, and the secret magic of imaginary numbers. I studied that textbook so much that my mother ended up throwing it out because I wasn't interested in my schoolwork. I never really understood much of it until about 12 years later, but it was enough to light the spark of curiosity and imagination that would stay lit for the remainder of my life. I spent the next 20 years struggling through a new math course every semester of university study in my quest to get to the bottom of how everything works.

While it wasn't my primary goal when I started this project, numerology ended up becoming a sort of "super science" with which I was able to draw fascinating and completely unexpected connections between unrelated fields. *The 11:11 Code* will provide detailed proof of why and how it represents a code of light (physics) and enlightenment (spirituality), to help my fellow humans gain a broader and more profound perspective on life and what it's all about and maybe even find a connection to the creative spirit that put everything into orderly existence. It is my hope that by the end of this book, you'll realize there is a profoundly rich body of evidence in the physical universe that has been left as well-hidden cosmic Easter eggs for us to discover in the form of numbers.

In the first stages of compilation, I was primarily dedicated to collecting pieces of information that were mostly unrelated as a detective or sleuth picking up pieces of evidence that he may or may not need in order to crack the case. Writing this book was a similar process, during which I collected any and all information I could get my hands on; then, as time went on, I jettisoned earlier material for more interesting stuff discovered later. At least 90 percent of what you're about to read is composed of things that I myself learned, as I sat down to write about other things. Life is what happens to us while we are busy making other plans, as the old adage goes. The latter half of the writing process is what I call the synthesis phase, where I reviewed my collection of dots and worked on drawing lines to connect between them.

Inevitably, the synthesis process generated many new unexpected dots of its own, causing me to continue iterating on the line-drawing process, further generating new dots, and so on. The process seemed like it could go on infinitely. I had voluminous extra material that I had planned to add to the book, but when I saw the page count rising to great length, I had to call it quits at some point. The body of material I delved into has taken on a mind of its own and ballooned into something that is at least ten times bigger than what I had envisioned. The term *divine inspiration* is an often-overused term, but it feels very applicable here.

Many books and websites talk about sacred geometry and its connection to spirituality, but one of the aims of this work is to explain how they are connected. No single example can explain it, but through repetition and great diversity of examples, it is my hope to make this topic intuitively clear to the reader by the time you are finished reading.

> For a sample of some enjoyable Nigerian music, the reader is encouraged to search YouTube for the artist Banky W. and the tracks "Capable" and "You Really Don't Know Me." Another artist called 9ice and his song "Street Credibility" will give you a nice sample of the genuine sounds of Africa.

Before you jump into the text, I'd urge you to open up YouTube and search for the video of Shpongle's "Around the World in a Tea Daze."

This will set the mood for the around-the-world trip you're about to embark on.[9] If a picture is worth a thousand words, then a video is worth a thousand pictures, thus a million words. My lovely wife, Britta, found this entrancing video that captures the essence of world travel so wonderfully.

> Recommended background music: Try "September—Deep Chill Mix" by Alone on YouTube. Tune in and fasten your seat belt.

Now would be a great time for you to grab a nice cup of hot tea and get comfortable. Prepare to dig into what I believe is one of the most mysterious riddles of all time.[10]

9 https://youtube/PP2hWvVyyUM
10 The sun's diameter is 864,000 miles.

Mathematics is the queen of the sciences and number theory is the queen of mathematics. She often condescends to render service to astronomy and other natural science, but in all relationships she is entitled to first rank.

—Carl Friedrich Gauss, German mathematician[11]

You can't connect the dots looking forward; you can only connect them looking backwards. So you have to trust that the dots will somehow connect in your future. You have to trust in something—your gut, destiny, life, karma, whatever.

—Steve Jobs[12]

Who looks outside, dreams;
Who looks inside, awakens.

—Carl G. Jung[13]

Mathematicians grow very old; it is a healthy profession. The reason you live long is that you have pleasant thoughts. Math and physics are very pleasant things to do.

—Dirk Jan Struik[14]

The Laws of nature are but the mathematical thoughts of God.

—Euclid[15]

---

11 https://proftomcrick.com/2011/12/06/the-queen-of-mathematics/.

12 https://www.brainyquote.com/quotes/steve_jobs_416875.

13 https://philosiblog.com/2011/09/05/your-vision-will-become-clear-only-when-you-can-look-into-your-own-heart-who-looks-outside-dreams-who-looks-inside-awakes/.

14 MAA Focus, vol. 20, no. 9, pg. 16, December 2000.

15 https://www.brainyquote.com/quotes/euclid_126362.

There are problems to whose solution I would attach an infinitely greater importance than to those of mathematics, for example touching ethics, or our relation to God, or concerning our destiny and our future; but their solution lies wholly beyond us and completely outside the province of science.

—Carl Friedrich Gauss[16]

God used beautiful mathematics in creating the world.

—Paul A. M. Dirac[17]

Mathematics is the alphabet with which God has written the universe.

—Galileo Galilei[18]

The diversity of the phenomena of nature is so great, and the treasures hidden in the heavens so rich, precisely in order that the human mind shall never be lacking in fresh nourishment.

—Johannes Kepler[19]

---

16 https://en.wikiquote.org/wiki/Carl_Friedrich_Gauss.
17 https://www.brainyquote.com/quotes/paul_dirac_279316.
18 http://holytrinity.academy/wp-content/uploads/2016/04/Maths.pdf.
19 https://en.wikiquote.org/wiki/Johannes_Kepler.

CHAPTER 1

WORKING AND PLAYING WITH NUMBERS

"The firm belief that symbolism and numerology cannot have power is what ensures that they are the hidden language of power."

—Martin Geddes,
via Twitter (used with written permission)

Let's bite the bullet and get the harder stuff over early in the book. I'll make it worth your while later—this is the contract I make with the reader. The average reader probably found this book because of an inherent interest in numerology, so a certain amount of mathematics is appropriate.

Numbers and the language of mathematics are among the most profound mysteries and rank among the greatest gifts to mankind. They are tools we can use to figure out how the universe works, what we are made of, and what we are doing here on Earth. Numbers allow us to make concrete sense and order out of an otherwise seemingly chaotic and mysterious universe. Knock, and the door shall be opened. And there is no bigger door than mathematics, commonly known as the *queen of the sciences*. As a scientist, for me to imagine not understanding mathematics would be the same level of confusion as being a stranger in a foreign country and not understanding the local language. You can survive, but you'll likely be somewhat confused and dependent on others for navigation and survival.

Numbers form an alphabet. Equations are mathematical sentences. Operators (for example, basic arithmetical operations: +, -, x, and /) are akin to punctuation. Rules of operations are the grammar, and theories are the stories.

Numbers conceal a veiled language that transcends time and culture, telling an incorruptible message that time cannot alter. Theorems from 3,000 years ago are just as valid and incontestable today as they were in the time of the ancient Egyptians. The laws and theorems of mathematics, the eternal property of the universe, are merely on loan to us once we discover them. Kepler's laws of planetary motion, Newton's laws of physics, and Euclid's concepts of geometry are but a few examples of timeless statements written many centuries ago that we can comprehend today without any aid of translation. Between career and pleasure, I have traveled to more than 228 territories worldwide and encountered many different languages and cultures. I always found it enjoyable that I could explain a technical concept to a person in China, for example, by drawing a circuit diagram or a phasing vector diagram backed up with relational equations to explain a concept to someone who doesn't understand English. If I get the message wrong, I could die from an 18,000-volt shock. Pictures speak a thousand words, and more importantly they transcend culture and language in most cases.

While mathematical equations can be understood readily, written language has certainly changed over time. Spoken language tends to evolve and change with each generation. Today's spoken English would be unintelligible to someone who spoke Middle English nearly a thousand years ago. Old English from 1,500 years ago is essentially a completely foreign language. Language changes with time. Language evolves and grows with technology. Concepts such as modems, WiFi, Bluetooth, and countless other modern terms would be incomprehensible if spoken about just a hundred years ago, so despite it not being everyone's favorite thing to use or learn, it is an incredibly important thread showing how we have advanced over the ages.

On 11/11/1675, one of the most revolutionary and widely utilized branches of mathematics was born when German mathematician Wilhelm Gottfried Leibniz published his discoveries, which heralded the birth of integral calculus. While this subject strikes terror into millions of high school and college students, we would simply not have been able to invent many of the conveniences of the modern world, including electronics and complicated machinery, without this pivotal development.[20] In this sense, 11/11 represents a huge source of enlightenment for humanity—a new set of mathematical power tools to drive technological and scientific progress.

Deep understanding of the core fundamentals of mathematics is a deeply guarded secret revealed only to those brave enough and persistent enough to work through it long enough for the punch line. Every child in school asks, "When will I ever use this stuff anyway?" But the fact that no one ever tells you is that mathematics becomes a subconscious part of our machinery of thought. It operates quietly in the background at the deepest levels of our human operating system—at the level of intuition. Kind of like a new app for a cellphone, or a new program for your laptop. After enough courses on mathematics, scholars obtain a level of intuition that allows them to comprehend how virtually everything works. It's honestly magic of the purest form. Technology such as computers, mobile phones, 3-D movies, television, radio, nuclear power, space travel, medical imaging, and holography (to name a few) are all direct results of mathematical understanding of the physical laws of how those systems work. There are countless claims citing the power of numbers but very few concrete explanations or examples to back them up as to the deeper reasons *why*. You and I are here to change that. By the time you're finished reading, you will hopefully have a much deeper fundamental appreciation of the role that these and other powerful numbers play in the lives of those *whose mind permits that possibility*. The only things in life that have power are the things we give power to by believing in them.

Language of the Right Side of the Brain

I would like to lead into the subject of language with a fun fact. The sentence "The quick brown fox jumped over the lazy brown dog" is famously used as a training tool in typing classes because it uses every letter of the English alphabet in one sentence and with the minimum number of characters. But did you know that this string of words is also useful in cryptography for testing out the effectiveness of code-breaking algorithms?

As English is the language of the British Empire, one of the most globally widespread empires in Earth's history, and the United States, a former British colony, has attracted millions of immigrants from across the world

20 http://scihi.org/leibniz-and-the-integral-calculus/.

for decades, the English language has made an unmatched level of contact with other languages around the world. Words like *punch* and *pajamas* come from India, for example. Where I grew up, there had been a large influx of Swedish immigrants who settled in the Chicago area beginning in 1846, including several of my father's ancestors who arrived from Sweden in the late 1890s.[21] The English language inherited many words from Swedish, like the word *resort,* which is a portmanteau of Swedish *resa* (to travel) and *ort* (place), which makes "travel place." Around Christmas, many songs and cards use the expression "yule tide." This is a deterioration of the original Swedish term *jultid*, which is pronounced "yool-teed," where *jul* is Swedish for Christmas and *tid* means time.

Some other fun Swedish words are *fart* (*speed* in English), *sex* (the number six), *gift* (married)[22], *bra* (good), *kiss* (urine), *puss* (kiss), *smoking* (tuxedo), and *kock* (chef). As a young boy, I often recall my great-grandmother using the phrases "this here" or "that there" when pointing or referring to an object nearby. I always chalked it up to poor grammar or lacking education, but in fact, the terms *den här* and *det där* are perfectly valid expressions in Swedish, which literally translate to *this here* and *that there*. Great-Grandma said some seriously funny stuff. If the dog was doing something bad, such as digging into the trash, she would say, "ish kabiddle," borrowed from old Yiddish. Most young children get a "boo-boo" when they fall down, a term inherited from lesions or enlarged lymph nodes attributed to bubonic plague, referred to as a *bubo*.[23]

While working in Turkmenistan, I noticed a Russian-manufactured Kamaz military transport truck carrying about twenty to thirty soldiers standing up in the back of the truck. On the side of the truck, there was a large stencil-painted word "ADAMLAR." I asked my local translator what that word meant, and he answered, "Men." In Turkic languages, the *-ler* and *-lar* suffixes denote a plural form of the base word. Therefore, *adamlar* is the plural of *Adam* or men. Turkish and other Turkic languages are among the oldest languages on the planet and were certainly spoken back in biblical times. In Turkish, multiple suffixes can be tacked on to the end of a base word to reflect ideas such as gender, quantity, possession, and many other linguistic factors.

Many people ask me where is the most interesting place I've been in

21 http://www.encyclopedia.chicagohistory.org/pages/1222.html.

22 The Swedish word *gift* has a second meaning: *poison*, and is a funny inside joke in Sweden that *marriage* equals *poison*.

23 https://www.medicinenet.com/script/main/art.asp?articlekey=2542.

the world. I'd have to say Kazakhstan. Why? First off, it's a name that scares away all but the most hard-core tourist. But it's one of my favorites because of its exotic mix of people, languages, culture, and geography. It is a former Soviet republic, so virtually everyone speaks Russian. So too, most speak Kazakh, a Turkic language written with modified Cyrillic (Russian) characters. The average ethnic Kazakh has a very Asian appearance, but it is not uncommon to see someone with green or blue eyes and/or reddish hair and eastern "Vostochniy" eyes (the root Vostok means *east* in Russian). The prevailing religion is Islam, and the cuisine includes features from Turkey, the Caucasus, Russia, India, China, and Korea (among others). It is not uncommon to see native women cooking up *burak* bread in a *tamdoor*, clearly borrowing from the *tandoor* clay oven in India to the far south. Kazakhstan is at the heart of the traditional Silk Road, a key nexus between customers in Europe and producers in the Far East. The country has varied geography, including desert, forests, and mountains, not to mention a downhill ski area called Chymbulak, which I visited in Alma-ata, the country's old capital nestled at the foothills of the Tian Shan mountains (Chinese for *heaven mountain*). The photo in this chapter shows me posing with the border guards and holding a Kalashnikov rifle after making a land crossing from Bekdash, Turkmenistan near Zhangaozen, Kazakhstan. It wasn't until I looked at the photo on the following day that I noticed the soldier had his hand on his pistol, ready to dispatch me if I had made one false move! Yikes…

Music Break: Kazakh music video: "NN-Bek—Kyzdar-ay" (Кыздар ай)

A couple more interesting connections with extremely old languages occurred when I was in Athens, Greece, on a brief two-day visit between work assignments in Turkey and Israel. I was going down the stairs from the Acropolis and saw an arrow pointing down that said κάθοδος (*kathodos*) with the English inscription "Way Down." Recalling my days in high school chemistry, I thought of the positive electrode in electrochemistry being named the cathode. Aha! Got it! This referred to "the way down" for electrons. On my *way down*, I noticed all the street signs had the word οδος (*odos*) on them. I pondered that for a moment. Then it dawned on me. It meant *street*. Then I realized where the peculiar word *odometer* came from. It means *street meter*! Then it all came together. *Kath* and *odos* meant "the road down." People often ask how I was able to pick up several languages—and the answer is in large part owing to taking in clues from my surroundings and then drawing connections and recognizing patterns, much the same way a young child learns his or her native tongue.

Language is as complex as we need it to be to explain our environment. Native cultures living in the Arctic deal with snow and ice more than any other culture. For example, Canadians in the Nunavik region have at least fifty-three words to describe different types of ice and snow depending on physical characteristics. One type of ice may be strong enough to support humans and animals, whereas thin ice that could break and cause someone to fall through would have another name. The word *matsaaruti* is a type of easily packed snow that it is easy to ride a sleigh over. *Pukak* denotes a soft, powdery snow. According to Clifford Pickover, West Greenlanders have more than forty words for various types of ice, such as *siku* (sea ice), *nilak* (chunks of freshwater ice), and *nittaalaaqqat* (hard grains of snow).[24]

When I worked in the Middle Eastern country of Jordan, one of my corporate hosts at the project taught me that there are seven different words in Arabic to communicate their level of thirst. No one knows thirst better than someone who lives in a desert climate. These seven words range from being just a little bit thirsty to being on the verge of death, and everything in between.

As an electrical engineer, I deal with many types of electricity—digital signals, analog signals, control signals, power circuits, sensing circuits, AC, DC, single-phase, three-phase, high-frequency, low-frequency, modulated, multiplex, simplex, etc. The average person who doesn't work in

24 Clifford Pickover, *Sex, Drugs, Einstein, & Elves: Sushi, Psychedelics, Parallel Universes, and the Quest for Transcendence* (Petaluma, CA: Smart Publications, 2005).

my industry just knows it all as simply *electricity*. The deeper we go into any subject, the richer our vocabulary must become. A criminal defense attorney's vocabulary will be chock-full of words of varying intensity for concepts such as innocence, guilt, and all the tiers of punishment. A butcher has dozens of words for the specific cuts of what the rest of us might just call meat. A surgeon will have numerous different types of suture knots for closing up a wound. To the rest of us, it's all just *stitches*. Every profession has its own jargon or industry-specific lingo, which is not necessarily meant to be understood outside the members' circle.

Language provides a lot of clues about what's important to a culture. For example, Greek has at least seven words for love. These are very specific and can distinguish brotherly love, romantic love, divine love, and so forth. Spanish is the same way. In fact, all the Romance languages (of which French, Italian, Spanish, Portuguese, and Romanian are the five most widely spoken) do a much better job than their Germanic counterparts. With English, Swedish, German, and all Germanic languages in general, the list for emotionally descriptive words is shorter, making it more difficult to communicate the exact nature of our emotions. In English, for example, we don't have many words between *like* and *love*. We have to improvise with amplifiers such as *somewhat*, *really,* or *kind of* to inflate or deflate the level of our feelings.

In my experience, the farther north you go, the colder it gets and the more important productivity becomes, generally speaking. A person living in the tropics can find something to eat all year on fruit trees, whereas the people in Canada, Russia, or Mongolia must plan much of the year to ensure that they have enough supplies for the cold winter months, and practices such as pickling meats and vegetables as well as making preserves from fruit become strategic matters of sustenance. I have found that the colder the climate, the more the culture and language are geared toward productivity as a matter of survival, often at the expense of taking more time to enjoy life and feel emotions. Life in the northern climates is harder, and the languages generally reflect a survival-over-pleasure mentality.

When I lived in China for six months while working for General Electric, I learned how to read and write about fifty Mandarin characters. Considering the complexity of the characters and the fact that the English alphabet is comprised of only twenty-six letters, that may seem impressive at first. But fifty characters is barely 2 percent of the Chinese set with its 3,000 characters! I honestly cannot imagine how much mental capacity it must require to learn all of the Chinese characters.

One time I was practicing my meager Mandarin writing skills with one of the people I was working with. As I was writing down the strokes for the character combination for electricity, the coworker said, “That’s not correct!”

I said, “What do you mean that’s not correct? It looks right, doesn’t it?”

He said, “Yes, but you wrote the strokes in the wrong order!”

I was perplexed about this, but after some research, I learned that stroke order matters in Chinese. Each of the twenty-something strokes in the words has a predetermined sequence that is drilled into every Chinese pupil during their schooling. In engineering school, there was an immensely high proportion of East Asian students, particularly in my undergraduate discipline, electrical engineering. The common myth was that Asian students were smarter and inherently better at academics. Excelling at school is less about raw intelligence and more about one’s ability to focus their attention and work really hard for extended periods of time. East Asian children learn incredible levels of mental discipline from a very young age as they master the complexity and nuance of their written language, and I would argue that this is in large part responsible for their apparent excellence in academics as a whole and mathematics in particular. They also have a much more competitive society, with little or no safety net if they fail.

In English, we write from left to right. Hebrew and Arabic languages are written right to left, and certain East Asian languages, such as Japanese and Mandarin, are often written in vertical columns. Certainly, in Chinese, performing the strokes in the correct sequence is of great importance.

I always enjoy portmanteau words whenever I come across them. Portmanteaus are words cobbled together as combinations of parts from other words. For example, Delmarva is a region where the states Delaware, Maryland, and Virginia meet. Similarly, Texarkana is near the confluence of Texas, Arkansas, and Louisiana. An interesting portmanteau pair are the cities Calexico and Mexicali, predictably located at the border between Southern California and Mexico’s Baja Norte. I worked in Mexicali four times for a total of about five months, and in fact, witnessed a broad-daylight kidnapping there. That's another story for another time.

LANGUAGE OF THE LEFT SIDE OF THE BRAIN

There is a certain timelessness associated with the language of numbers. The rules and laws of how they interact are not subject to change or revision with few exceptions. Once a rule or theorem is developed and proven, it almost always stands the test of time and holds true for the indefinite future. Five fingers on the human hand carries the same meaning as it would have 40,000 years ago. Five alien fingers held up in the air on a planet in a distant galaxy would still carry the same immutable concept of "five-ness" that it conveys here on Earth. The concept of number is incorruptible. For example, the Pythagorean theorem states that the sum of squares of the adjacent and opposite sides of a right triangle is equal to the square of the hypotenuse. Pythagoras lived from 570 to 495 BC, more than 2,500 years ago, and to this day, his ubiquitous formula for computing distance between two points is used in virtually all areas of math, science, architecture, electronics, engineering, and software. Radar systems that assisted in the lunar landings used this timeless relation to execute safe landings. All GPS calculations involve this ancient formula for calculating distances. It is noteworthy that an ancient Babylonian clay tablet known as Plimpton 322[25], which was owned by the G. A. Plimpton collection at Columbia University, contains a list of numbers that obey the Pythagorean theorem and is believed to be as old as 1800 BC, long before Pythagoras's time! The fact that it is tablet #322 in the collection is interesting to me for reasons that will become clear as this story develops.[26]

Pythagoras's theorem is just as true today as it was thousands of years ago. Mathematical truths are truths that exist outside of the limitations of time; thus, mathematics is the preferred language scientists use to record observations and lessons of the laws of nature. Many times the math is developed as a result of a discovery, and in other cases, the math exists without application for hundreds of years prior to discovery of the problem that it would eventually be used to solve.

25 The number 322 will be extremely important in later pages.

26 http://www.columbia.edu/cu/lweb/eresources/exhibitions/treasures/html/158.html.

RETHINKING NUMEROLOGY

Numerology has languished alongside some of the other metasciences, such as astrology and sacred geometry, which struggle to find proof and analytical structure to back up their claims. What if we renamed Numerology something slightly more dignified sounding, such as *Numeristics*? Would people take it more seriously then? Would that begin to dispel the stigma that the subject and its adherents have endured all these years?

Equations describe relationships between groups of numbers, but the actual numbers themselves can be intrinsically interesting as well. This book will delve into the private lives of the numbers themselves and see what, if any, meaning can be derived from that study. Illustrious German mathematician Carl Friedrich Gauss famously stated that mathematics is the "queen of the sciences." Gauss further elaborated his belief that the branch of math known as number theory is the "queen of mathematics." Gauss was born in 1777 and died at age 77 on 2/ 23/1855, fitting numerological markers at the beginning and end of the life of one of the planet's greatest mathematical minds.[27] The digits of the year 1777 add up to 22 or 11+11. If you add 1111 + 666 you arrive at 1777. According to the overview of Stein's *Elementary Number Theory: Primes, Congruences, and Secrets*, "The systematic study of number theory was initiated around 300 BC when Euclid proved there are infinitely many prime numbers. At the same time, he also cleverly deduced ... that every positive integer factors uniquely as a product of primes."[28] The fundamental theorem of arithmetic states, "Every natural number can be written as a product of primes uniquely"[29]

This seemingly simple statement will be an extremely powerful tool as we unlock the mysteries of numerology and dig into the 11:11 code.

Before embarking on this project, my understanding of the numbers presented in this book was akin to a shoebox full of random photographs from various stages of my life. There were so many really interesting things I wanted to talk about, but it was all stored in my mind with very little organization. As I penned this document, a wonderful and not entirely unexpected side effect was that it helped me organize my thoughts

27 https://www.encyclopedia.com/people/science-and-technology/mathematics-biographies/carl-friedrich-gauss#2830901590.

28 https://www.springer.com/gp/book/9780387855240.

29 William Stein, *Elementary Number Theory: Primes, Congruences, and Secrets* (New York: Springer, 2009).

in a similar manner. It was as if the solution was embedded into the problem—it simply needed to be tackled through the process of writing. This effect upon my memories was akin to the process of organizing old photos into a highly organized and annotated album. Prior to these investigations, I never understood why someone would think the yawn-inducing topic of number theory would be one of the most interesting subfields of mathematics, but the deeper I delved into the topic, the richer it got. Expecting it to eventually become boring, I've often been surprised that this never happened. Instead, it blossomed into an interesting and rewarding topic of inquiry.

An unlimited plethora of books are available to undertake a rigorous study of mathematics. That's not my goal here. The aim of this book is to look for philosophical and spiritual meaning in the numbers themselves and unveil the story that they seem to be subtly trying to communicate to those of us who are receptive and interested.

I scoured countless websites and read numerous books on numerology, and while I found many of them intriguing, I was left wanting much more. According to author Underwood Dudley, "Modern numerology is fairly uniform and one numerology book will, for the most part, be like another. They are like calculus books, though with slightly more variety. They will tell you how to find your number, or numbers—name number and birthdate numbers are standard, but there is also the life-path number, karma number, and others—give the properties of the numbers, and then proceed to fill the remaining space with examples."[30] For example, I went to the numerology.com website and found it had a section on the numbers 11, 22, and 33. Like virtually all numerology sites, the numbers 11, 22, and 33 are listed as master builder numbers. But why? No one has yet been able to explain why. That's why I'm here writing this book. I've got the mystery cracked! And you will too by the time you reach the back cover!

While writing this book, I noticed a news story about 22 illegal immigrants who scurried out of a single vehicle, all in the space of 11 seconds, as captured on video in the link in the footnotes.[31] Sometimes, I just sit back and ask myself, "Why 11 and 22?" And other times, I can dig deeper and get answers based on scientific principles.

30 Underwood Dudley, *Numerology: Or, What Pythagoras Wrought* (Washington, DC: The Mathematical Association of America, 1997).

31 http://www.theamericanmirror.com/video-22-illegals-pour-out-of-pickup-truck-in-11-seconds-after-fleeing-tx-traffic-stop/.

The vast majority of authors simply state that these numbers are master numbers with little more explanation than simply saying they have high vibrations. Why does it have a high vibration? Because it's an angel number and all angel numbers are master numbers. And so on, with more circular reasoning. As a scientist, that explanation leaves me wanting something deeper and more complete. I study vibrations and waves of energy as an electrical engineer and physicist. I need to see some concrete, provable information. At the same time, I have become convinced that these numbers are powerful because of the countless situations in my life where they have manifested themselves.

It was my initial idea to write about the occurrences of these master numbers at key points in my life and how they steered me toward my eventual awakening. As time went on and I started to research historical events, I was astonished to see that these master numbers were imbedded into many of the world's most important events, discoveries, achievements, and catastrophes, as well as being scattered throughout the numbers we use to measure the cosmos and the heavenly bodies that inhabit space. These occurrences are scattered across centuries and millennia, and they span the globe, the solar system, and even into the limitless reaches of the universe. Virtually everywhere I have looked, I found these unmistakable fingerprints, which seem suggestive of some sort of higher cosmic intelligence. Many of the occurrences of these master numbers were tied to good events, but there are many examples associated with catastrophic occurrences as well. The principal unifying theme is that the events were usually of importance to me personally or to society as a whole. As I realized how widespread the phenomena were, I widened my search into the sciences and looked for the numbers imbedded in the laws of biology, physics, and chemistry. Again, I was pleasantly shocked. Similarly, when I freed my inquiry from the limitations of Earth, I found these magic numbers sprinkled all over the solar system, galaxies, and the universe as a whole. This subject matter started out as something much smaller and limited in scope, but it took on a life and quite literally, an *intelligence* of its own. The piece of literature that resulted is much more substantial than I could have ever imagined. The book you're reading now doesn't even remotely resemble the book I started to write when I first sat down.

Einstein famously stated, "Science without religion is lame, religion without science is blind."[32] All aspects of spirituality cannot be readily apprehended without purposeful, dedicated study and introspection directed toward that specific purpose. Intentions matter. I seek to use numbers to unveil universal truths. These truths, when properly considered, can unify concepts found in religion and science. I agree with Einstein that a person needs to comprehend both religion and science to truly understand what we are and why we are here. A deep appreciation for both will symbiotically reinforce one's understanding and belief in both if applied correctly.

Philosopher and entheogenic explorer Terence McKenna cleverly stated, "The most astonishing coincidence of all which is that mathematics describes nature—that's a coincidence as far as I can tell—why should it? No philosopher I have ever read, no mathematician has ever been able to make any cogent sense … that the abstract operations of the human mind should somehow map over the core dynamics of nature. *It's a coincidence.*" (*emphasis mine*)[33]

In George Orwell's famous book *1984*, two of the major forms of societal rot foretold included warnings that our language and mathematics would be purposely watered down in an effort to make us dumber and thus easier to manipulate. The terms *goodspeak* and *goodthink* referred to the ill-fated political correctness movement. Orwell referred to the mathematical dumbing-down process in a chapter titled "2 + 2 = 5," where Big Brother seeks to brainwash students and stupefy them by purposely teaching incorrect mathematics. This is a truly visionary idea for a book written in 1949, the year both of my parents were born, as it predicted the Common Core math curriculum that I believe is one of the biggest educational travesties ever perpetrated on the young minds of our country, interfering with a child's ability to properly perform basic arithmetic operations by making it unnecessarily complicated. For fun, add up the digits of 1984: 1 + 9 + 8 + 4 = 22 or 11 + 11.

With Google searches of the term 11:11 turning up more than 864,000,000 times at the time of writing, I know I am not alone in my interest in this concept. Perhaps someone much smarter and more motivated than me, with much more sophisticated computer abilities, could perform a massive survey of the entire internet and see what comes up and analyze connections within those findings!

32 https://newrepublic.com/article/115821/einsteins-famous-quote-science-religion-didnt-mean-taught.

33 https://www.yousubtitles.com/Terence-McKenna-Describing-the-Nature-of-Synchronicity-Lecture-id-2393693.

THE 11:11 CODE IN THE METRIC SYSTEM

In the very late stages of finalizing this work, I was reading an article about the definition of one second of time. Nothing interesting or surprising turned up, but it did lead me to visit Wikipedia's page on the Système international (d'unités) or simply the SI system of units, also known as the metric system. I was doing what I believed to be final editing on the book and had sworn that I would not be adding any new information to the book. Then this bombshell arrived. I was completely blown away to see that there are exactly 22 units used in science and engineering, which are derived from 7 fundamental units. The most basic units that we use to measure all scientific quantities are as follows:

Unit:	Abbreviation:	Measures:
Kilogram	kg	mass
Ampere	A	electric current
Second	s	time
Candela	cd	luminous intensity
Meter	m	length
Mole	mol	amount of a substance
Kelvin	K	temperature

All the 22 derived units are created based on combinations of these 7 fundamental units. For example, the newton, a unit of force, is defined as a kilogram-meter per second-squared or ($kg*m/s^2$). Velocity or speed is measured in meters per second (m/s). Frequency is simply defined in terms of reciprocal time (1/s).[34] I do believe that the ampere was incorrectly listed as a fundamental unit as it is derived as a coulomb per second, with the coulomb and second being fundamental units. The corrected version should have the coulomb replace the ampere in the chart previously outlined, but I recorded it as found. This in no way diminishes this discovery!

These 22 derived units are by no means the only units in usage in science and engineering, but they represent the fundamental set of units upon

34 https://www.bipm.org/utils/common/pdf/si_brochure_8_en.pdf.

which all other units of measure are derived. This is a remarkable discovery as it puts a bedrock foundation under the key points of this book by showing that the numbers 7 and 22 underpin virtually everything that we know or measure about our physical universe from quantum physics, electricity, magnetism, chemistry, thermodynamics, astronomy, and virtually all other areas of science and engineering where we measure *anything*. These 22 units (11 + 11) give us a standard amount of a quantity such that everyone in the world measures it exactly the same. Furthermore, if we take the number of derived SI units (22) divided by the number of fundamental SI units (7), we get 22/7 = 3.142, which is equal to pi within 0.4 percent accuracy.

In all my extensive research over the past several years, I have seen no one else make this connection. In this book, I made the claim that pi is one of the fundamental numbers that dictates physical form in the universe and enters into virtually all scientific calculations in some way or another, including energy transmission and the laws of probability from the quantum scale to the cosmic scale. Pi, 7, and 22 are among a few truly universal numbers that have now been shown to be part of the fabric of our universe and reality as we know it. To discover these very special numbers hiding within the fundamental units of scientific measure was an incredible confirmation of my earlier claim, which to be honest was completely unexpected but was a delight for me to discover.

But wait. There's more unexpected excitement. While penning this section, I discovered that in the year 1822, year "11 + 11" of the nineteenth century, the famous French mathematician Joseph Fourier was the first to create a system of dimensional analysis that laid the groundwork for how we manipulate scientific units within calculations.[35] The year 1822 was a very fruitful year for Fourier because he published his treatise *Théorie analytique de la chaleur* on the theory of heat flow utilizing differential equations.[36]

As a fun bit of trivia, the American Standards Association officially set the inch as being equal to 2.54 centimeters in 1933.[37]

35 https://books.google.com/books?id=TDQJAAAAIAAJ&pg=PR3&hl=en#v=onepage&q&f=false.

36 https://www.maths.tcd.ie/pub/HistMath/People/Fourier/RouseBall/RB_Fourier.html.

37 https://books.google.com/books?id=WDgJAQAAMAAJ&pg=RA3-PA4#v=onepage&q&f=false.

LIFE NUMBER CONCEPT

A popular movie *The Number 23* starring Jim Carrey starts with him reading a book about the number 23 and becoming convinced it was written about *his* life. He becomes obsessed with the idea that all incidents and events are directly connected to the number 23. He starts noticing the number on clocks, calendars, street signs, license plates, dates, and countless other seemingly random things. These ostensibly random occurrences happen with such frequency and direct applicability to events going on in his past and present life that he begins to view occurrences of that number as harbingers of what is to come in his future. Created as a thriller film, the movie's plot has a dark, foreboding message. But in my own personal story of my life number, 22 has (so far!) been part of a very positive story of me and my family ascending the ladder of enlightenment and spiritual growth and a bellwether of good things to come.

Maybe your interest in this book was sparked by having seen repeating numbers throughout your life, having not really paid attention before but now wondering if there is some meaning to it all. You're not alone! To those of us who have experienced the 11:11 synchronicity phenomenon either directly, or through other repeated digit numbers, we are now beginning to realize that these numbers have been following us all of our lives. We haven't been imagining things after all, and between here and the back cover, you'll come to understand exactly why. Discovering that my life number has been leading me throughout my life is the closest I'll ever come to knowing what it feels like to discover a guardian angel who has been protecting me all along.

MY LIFE NUMBER: 22

Recommended music: VonnBoyd's "Overcast"

As a large portion of this book deals with numerology, it is important to define two important words.

1. Pareidolia is defined as follows: "the tendency to perceive a specific, often meaningful image in a random or ambiguous visual pattern." The scientific explanation for some people is pareidolia, or the human ability to see shapes or make pictures out of randomness.

2. Apophenia is defined as "the tendency to perceive a connection or meaningful pattern between unrelated or random things (such as objects or ideas)."[38]

As an engineer and applied mathematician, I've always tended to be very logical, requiring proof before I buy into anything. Until fairly recently, I thought numerology was interesting but still regarded it as a fringe subject, not worthy of being considered a science. Numerology was to mathematics what astrology is to astronomy in my mind. It was a fascinating "little brother" subject that hadn't reached its prime (pun intended)...just yet. I'm not looking at the back of cereal boxes or the 800-222-2222 divorce attorney phone numbers on highway billboards and getting excited every time I see the number 22. A toddler accidentally ingests an unknown poison while exploring the garage. What do you do? You call the Poison Control Center at 1-800-222-1222, right? Numbers with repeated digits are very easy to remember over number sequences that lack a clear and simple pattern, so it makes sense that things like advertising and urgent care and so forth would intentionally use repeating digits. I don't read anything mystical into cases like this where the number was deliberately chosen. Noticing numeric patterns in the unintentional things that are out of our control is what finally caught my attention and made me look closer at numerology. Is there something deeper than just the ease of remembering one digit four times?

This chapter seeks to tell the continuously unfolding story of what I would later come to see as my *life number*. The number 22 has been an auspicious marker at many key milestones in my life, starting from *day one* when I took my very first breath on March 22. This didn't occur to me until I reached age 40. Until about 2015, I had just chalked up occurrences of the number 22 to being neat coincidences, never really reading anything deeper into them. I just sort of thought to myself, "Hmmmph...22 again..." I didn't know how to go deeper (a *lot* deeper)—that is, not until recently. When my son Erik was born, I found it incredibly interesting to hear the doctor inform us that he measured 22 inches in length, which is documented on his birth certificate. That's 11 + 11. That was the tipping point for me, of what would become a deep quest for answers as to why the number 22 keeps popping into my life at the most inexplicably perfect moments. Erik's birth caused me to deeply reflect on my life, who I am,

38 www.merriam-webster.com.

and what kind of father I wanted to be to this beautiful child. I had to make some difficult choices.

Four years after the birth of our son, I had had enough of alcoholism and sought the help of the local chapter of Alcoholics Anonymous where I lived in Door County, Wisconsin, and was shocked to see that AA district 22 was ready and able to assist in my recovery.[39] The 11 + 11 code was coming to my aid in my deepest time of need. This is an example of my master number showing up at a key time, a pivotal and difficult time in my life—my rock bottom.

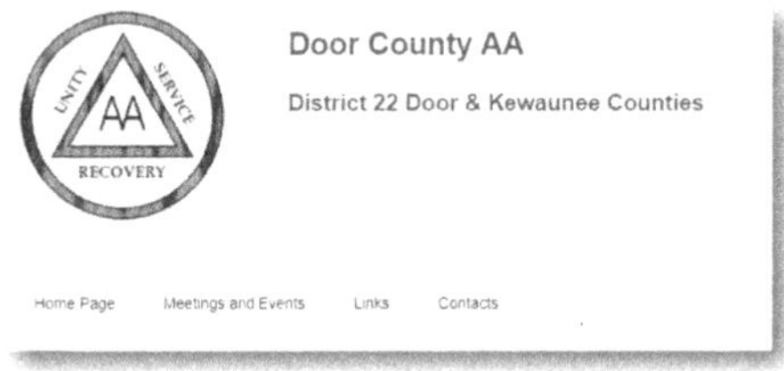

That subject could fill the space of its own book, but in the end, I am thankful for having experienced the hardship of alcoholism because it made my life afterward seem so much more miraculous and showed me the Creator's infinite capacity to forgive and wipe the slate clean again with grace. Nothing else could have brought me to my knees to seek God's grace the way alcohol did. I've been absolutely sober ever since and have zero desire to ever turn back. I haven't had a single drip, drop, or dram since that fateful St. Patrick's Day three years ago. To any readers who may be facing their own struggles with alcoholism or other chemical addiction, stand by. I am currently 106 pages into writing a book about fighting addictions and still winning. In fact, I'm beginning my fourth year of complete sobriety at the time of publishing! Alcoholism is the only form of incarceration where you are both warden *and* inmate, and the only key to escape is through abstinence and helping other people who still suffer with addiction in their recovery. Killing the inner beast by deprivation and starvation is the only method that works. I have shared my email address at the end of the book for anyone who would like to learn more about how I tackled my compulsion to drink.

Repeated occurrences of the number 22 in the most uncanny and meaningful situations caused me to scratch my head and ask if there might be

39 http://doorcountyaa.org/.

something deeper that the universe was trying to show me. Perhaps an ancestor such as my deceased father was on the other side, subtly but persistently attempting to communicate with me. With a bit of faith and an open mind, I discovered an unmistakable pattern that really amazed me and increased my belief in the presence of an all-knowing, loving, universal, and creative spirit that had already mapped out virtually all my life's key steps. As you progress through the pages of this work, always bear in mind that 22 = 11 + 11, and the 11:11 code is not a new concept I came up with. Many unexpected revelations about these numbers will unfold as you continue to turn the pages.

THE NUMBER 3

The fundamentals of Christianity are built upon the foundation of the Holy Trinity, composed of the Father, the Son, and the Holy Spirit. The Holy Trinity may also be symbolic of the past (father), the present (you), and the future (your children). Understanding our place in the universe requires a sense of perspective about where we are in life's grand time line as we act as a vital link between past and future generations, participating in an unbroken chain of life stretching back possibly millions or billions of years.

The US government is composed of three independent branches—judicial, legislative, and executive. Our home planet, Earth, is the third planet from the sun. Our eyes have specialized sensors called rods and cones that encode light intensity and color respectively. The cone cells have three types of receptors that are sensitive to red, green, or blue, as described by the Young-Helmholtz theory.[40] In many ways, we humans consider ourselves superior to insects, but consider that while we have three types of color receptors, butterflies are said to have as many as fifteen types of cones that allow them to see the full human spectrum as well as deep into the infrared and ultraviolet ranges. I can scarcely imagine how beautiful the world must appear to a butterfly![41] The world's electric power system is built upon three phase power circuits as well.

Sigmund Freud defined the structure of the human psyche as being composed of three distinct components—the ego, the id, and the superego.[42]

40 Thomas Young, 1802. *Bakerian Lecture: On the Theory of Light and Colours*. Phil. Trans. R. Soc. Lond. 92:12–48. doi: 10.1098/rstl. 1802.0004.

41 http://www.sciencemag.org/news/2016/03/butterfly-has-extreme-color-vision.

42 https://www.ncbi.nlm.nih.gov/pmc/articles/PMC4076885/.

These essentially correlate to the conscious, subconscious, and unconscious mind. Time is divided into three essential epochs: past, present, and future. These concepts give us our perception of time, as well as our position in time relative to other events.

All matter is composed of three fundamental building blocks—protons, electrons, and neutrons. All matter (at least on Earth) exists in one of three physical phases—solid, liquid, or gas. A fourth phase (plasma) exists in stars and during nuclear reactions and electric arcs, but it is not present under the otherwise normal steady-state conditions commonly encountered on Earth.

Our lives appear to be imbedded in a three-dimensional world where we have a sense of left-right, forward-backward, and up-down. I mentioned that we have *at least* six senses, meaning that aside from sight, hearing, taste, touch, smell, and orientation, we also have an unprovable but no less real *spiritual sense*. That's right—the sixth is our sense of which is up and down. Our inner ear has three partially fluid-filled loops known as semicircular canals that tell us which way is up, acting as our own intrinsic inertial guidance and control system. As we tilt our heads, the fluid in the three loops shifts slightly and activates tiny sensitive hair cells inside the canals, notifying our brains of the change in orientation with respect to the local gravity vector. If you close your eyes, plug your ears, ignore all other senses, and tip your head by a certain angle, you would certainly have a sensation that you were no longer vertical.

As an applied mathematician, I marvel at the fact that the three loops effectively form an X-Y-Z coordinate system within each of our ears, and all three loops are at approximately 90 degrees to one another, which my fellow math geeks will recognize as an orthonormal coordinate system. These three principal axes can be likened to the three orthogonal[43] basis vectors T, N, and B, which form the basis of the study of differential geometry (i.e., the study of the curvature of space).

THE DIVINE NUMBER 7

Like many of the important numbers discussed in this work, 7 is a prime number, divisible only by one and itself. Some interesting facts about the occurrence of the number 7 in the book of Revelation are as follows:

43 Orthogonality conveys the sense of independence and perpendicularity, much the same way as vertical and horizontal directions are both independent and oriented at ninety degrees to each other.

- In Revelation 1:20 alone, it mentions 7 golden candlesticks, 7 stars, 7 angels, 7 churches, and 7 lampstands.
- The number 7 occurs fifty times in the book of Revelation.
- There were 7 letters written to the 7 churches.
- Seven angels stood before the Lord with 7 trumpets.
- There were 7 thunders and 7 last plagues.

The ancient Pythagorean society of mathematicians and philosophers attached deep significance to numbers and their esoteric meanings in life. In respect to life and its divisions, they remarked the ages are measured by the number seven as follows (as written by Westcott):

> In the first seven years (1 x 7 = 7), the teeth are erupted.
>
> Second seven years (2 x 7 = 14), comes an ability to emit prolific seed.
>
> Third seven years (3 x 7 = 21), the growth of the beard is manhood.
>
> Fourth seven years (4 x 7 = 28), strength reaches its maximum.
>
> Fifth seven years (5 x 7 = 35) is the season for marriage.
>
> Sixth seven years (6 x 7 = 42), the height of intelligence arrives.
>
> Seventh seven years (7 x 7 = 49), the maturity of reason.
>
> Eighth seven years (8 x 7 = 56), perfection of both.
>
> Ninth seven years (9 x 7 = 63), equity and mildness, passions become gentle.
>
> Tenth seven years (10 x 7 = 70), the end of desirable life.[44]

44 https://archive.org/details/numberstheiroccu1911west/page/n4.

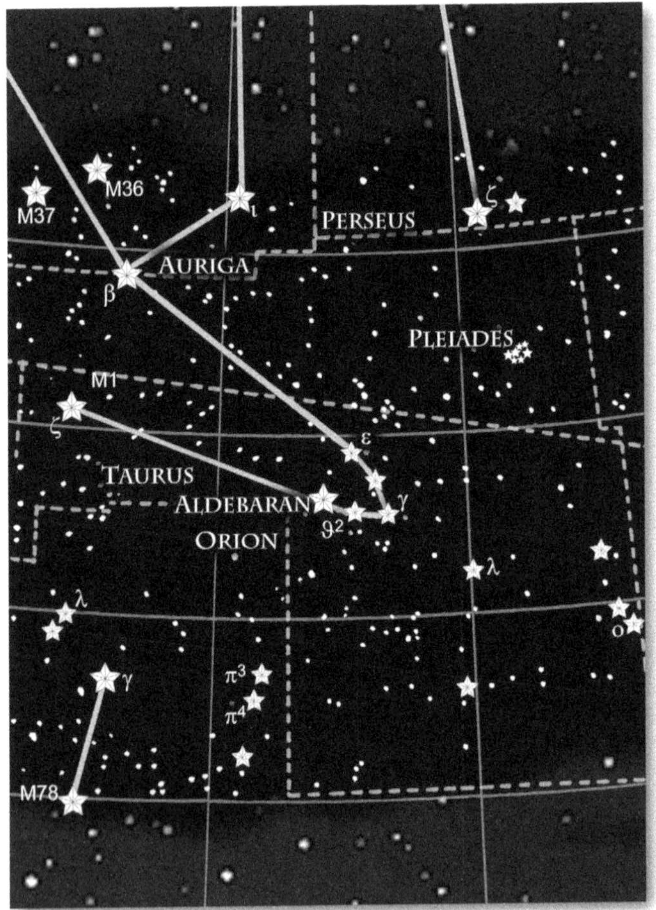

The constellation of Taurus[45]

First Kings 7:25 says, "The Sea stood on twelve oxen, three facing north, three facing west, three facing south, and three facing east. The Sea rested on them, with all their hindquarters toward the center." This is a puzzling verse—that is, unless we read it intently and connect this with the fact that the planet Earth is composed of 12 tectonic plates. These plates are normally in a quiescent state, but whenever they do move, it usually results in earthquakes and volcanic activity. Why am I mentioning this here? The 7 stars and 7 angels in Revelation 1:20 may be referring to the star cluster known since ancient times as the Pleiades, which are located in the constellation of Taurus, the bull. The stars that make up the Pleiades

45 https://en.m.wikipedia.org/wiki/Taurus_(constellation).

are estimated to be at an average distance of 444 light-years (or 12 x 37, where 37 is a star number) from Earth.[46]

King Solomon's temple with the 12 bulls[47]

The world is composed of 7 continents, and the human body is composed of seven vital organs, without which life cannot be supported. They are the brain, heart, two lungs, a pair of kidneys, and the liver. As a prime number, seven is of vital importance to life as we know it. Earth has 7 vital "organs," and so do we!

The difference between good and evil usually comes down to intentions. For example, a hammer is just a tool. In the hands of a murderer, it can be turned into a deadly assault weapon. In the hands of a skilled carpenter, that same hammer can be used to build a stately, beautiful church. It's

46 https://www.space.com/26976-pleiades-star-cluster-distance-quasars.html.
47 http://blogs.umb.edu/buildingtheworld/iconic-monuments/solomons-temple-israel/.

the same hammer, but there are different intentions. Water is just water. It can be used to drown someone or to make iced tea or baptize a child. The number 666 may be taken to represent the intentions of man, which are often flawed by sin, and 777 may be seen as the intentions of God, which of course are always good. Our intentions essentially choose the moral polarity (good or evil) that will direct the intrinsic power of the 111 core toward the direction of our willing. Electricity can be used to kill a criminal in the electric chair, or it can be used to restart someone's heart through a defibrillator. It all comes down to the intentions of the user. It is just energy waiting to be converted into the form desired by the person controlling it.

Once a mystery is solved, it usually becomes another boring fact to get buried in a textbook. An unsolved mystery brings a sense of wonder and intrigue to many generations and can serve to direct humanity's attention upward and away from ourselves as we seek credit for solving it. A mystery gives us a focal point on which we can admire the symmetries, harmonies, and patterns that the divine mind has programmed into numerical form. Sometimes we learn more from pondering the question than we do from receiving the answer because of the time and effort we expend trying to comprehend the mystery. In mathematics, the benefit doesn't always come from arriving at the answer. The learning happens during the *process* of arriving at a final solution. A similar metaphor applies to life. In life, our joy is found along the journey, not just at the destination.

CURIOSITIES OF NUMBER 11

Many people I have known or spoken to have reported that they see the number 11 and multiples of it (22 and 33) showing up in the most uncanny situations. There are entire groups on social media and private websites dedicated to investigating the mystery of these and other magic numbers and why they show up at various times and situations in our lives. Schimmel explains that the number 11 is a sacred marriage of the microcosm and the macrocosm that is the combination of 5 (which is 2 + 3) and 6 (which is 2 x 3).[48] Later you will see the interplay between the numbers 5 and 6 discussed at a deep level, in particular in pentagons and hexagons found in nature.

48 Annemarie Schimmel, The *Mystery of Numbers* (Oxford: Oxford University Press, 1993), 191.

In Buddhism, the number 11 has deep significance. The 11 groups of kindnesses include the following:

1. a man entered the way,
2. the two truths,
3. the three gates of delivery,
4. the four truths of the correct law,
5. the five faculties,
6. the six authorities,
7. the seven members of the illumination,
8. the eight members of the path,
9. the nine residences of the being,
10. the ten forces of the realized, and
11. the eleven deliverances of the heart full of love.[49]

Aquarius is the 11th sign of the zodiac. Around the turn of the millennium, by most accounts the world officially entered into the age of Aquarius, which the ancients foretold to be a period of enlightenment, peace, and love. Earth precesses on its axis in much the same way as a spinning top does around its axis as it wobbles, circumscribing a cone in the space above it. Earth's precession completes a full cycle every 25,772 years, meaning the planet's north pole is aligned with each of the twelve zodiac sectors of the heavens for about 2,147 years or one-twelfth of a precessional period. The study of astrology attributes various powers and themes to each of the twelve zodiac zones. The ancient Egyptians said, "As above, so below."

Are events on Earth somehow tied to events in the heavens? Why shouldn't they be?

World War I ended on Armistice Day, 11/11/1919. The signing of the peace treaty at the 11th hour on the 11th day of the 11th month was a hurried process that occurred at the very last moment.

The US House of Representatives Bill HR-1111, which was introduced

49 https://www.virtuescience.com/11.html.

before Congress on February 16, 2017, and titled "Department of Peacebuilding Act of 2017," set forth the establishment of the following offices:

1. The Office of Peace Education and Training,
2. The Office of Domestic Peacebuilding Activities,
3. The Office of International Peacebuilding Activities,
4. The Office of Technology for Peace,
5. The Office of Arms Control and Disarmament,
6. The Office of Peacebuilding Information and Research,
7. The Office of Human Rights and Economic Rights, and
8. The Intergovernmental Advisory Council on Peace.

The act also says, "The department shall encourage citizens to observe and celebrate the blessings of peace and endeavor to create peace on Peace Days, which shall include discussions of the professional activities and achievements in the lives of peacemakers."[50] Apparently, the number 1111 also represents a vision of world peace.

Thirty-three is widely regarded in numerology as a number of perfection or completion, as previously explained in this book. An internet search of the number 33 will yield a plethora of sites talking about 11, 22, and 33 as angel numbers, master builder numbers, enlightenment codes, and awakening codes. Google it! Try searching "11 22 33."

The UN logo has eight angular sectors, and each has four zones for a total of 32 curved rectangles with a circular 33rd zone in the center.

50 https://www.congress.gov/bill/115th-congress/house-bill/1111.

Geometry is interesting because it is the nexus between numbers and physical form. A cube with the side length of 11 will have a volume of 1,331 cubic units, as $11^3 = 1,331$. I find it most gratifying to observe that 1,331 seconds works out to 22 minutes and 11 seconds as 1,331 = (22 x 60) + 11, a nifty little equation that has my three favorite numbers (11, 22, and 33) imbedded within.

Readers who have traveled to Asia or visited Asian grocery stores may be familiar with the Japanese candy named *Pocky*. They are essentially long, slender breadsticks made of cookie material and can be dipped in chocolate sauce as a snack for children. November 11 is the annual national Japanese Pocky and Pretz Day, and the date is a reference to the long, slender 1 shape of the sticks.[51]

In China, November 11 is a popular holiday known as Singles Day.[52] On 11/11/2017, the retail sales because of Singles Day in China smashed the all-time record for biggest shopping expenditures in one day with a staggering $33 billion in sales![53] That's 11+11+11 billion dollars on 11/11/17.

In the German Rhineland, the carnival season begins at 11:11 a.m. on 11/11 every year.[54]

The human skull is composed of 22 or 11+11 bone plates that are initially separate and floating at birth, later fusing to form the complete cranium.

Repeated Digit Numbers

Numerology and gematria play a very important if somewhat cloaked role in the Bible. Gematria is the ancient technique whereby a numerical value is assigned to each letter of the alphabet, and then the gematria value of a word is determined by adding the values of the individual letters up. Proponents of gematria claim that mystical or spiritual meanings are imbedded into certain words and phrases. The core of the 11:11 Code is built upon an awareness and understanding of repeated digit numbers, especially 11, 22, and 33. I will begin with some examples from the Bible. Due to the profusion of books available on gematria, I will not dedicate very much space in this book to the topic. This is a very well-documented topic to which I have very little to contribute.

51 https://www.glico.co.jp/info/kinenbi/1111.html.
52 https://blogs.wsj.com/chinarealtime/2011/11/11/chinese-couples-rush-to-the-altar-on-111111/.
53 https://amp.abc.net.au/article/9144040.
54 Annemarie Schimmel, The *Mystery of Numbers* (Oxford: Oxford University Press, 1993), 191.

The Bible is composed of 66 books. Note that 66 = 3 x 22 or 3 x (11 + 11).) The Bible was written by a total of 33 writers. The word *amen* is stated 99 times in the Bible.

It is also noteworthy that if you take all the numbers between 1 and 11 and add them up, you get 66, as in 1 + 2 + 3 + ... + 10 + 11 = 66. Sixty-six is a triangular number because if you start with a row of 11 logs on the ground, stack a layer of 10 logs on top of the 11, and then another row of 9 on top of the 10, and so on until you place one log on top of two, you will have a triangular pile of 66 logs. Triangular numbers are special and a topic of curiosity in number theory and recreational mathematics.

The human spinal column is composed of 33 vertebrae.

In Freemasonry, there are a total of 33 degrees of initiation.

Jesus is said to have lived to the age of 33 years.

The rosary or Anglican prayer beads are composed of 33 beads.[55]

The Olympic Games are composed of a total of 33 sports.[56]

The US Constitution was amended 11 + 11 + 11, or 33 times. Twenty-seven (3^3 = 3x3x3 = 27) of the amendments were ratified. The remaining six failed to get enough states' votes to become fully official. Amendment 22 states that a president shall not serve more than 2 terms.[57]

The white supremacist hate group known as the Ku Klux Klan is often abbreviated KKK, which cross-references to 11-11-11 if you set K equal to its rank in the alphabet, the 11th letter: (11 + 11 + 11 = 33). This is quite possibly another case of a sinister organization on the dark side hijacking beautiful symbolism from Christianity for their own nefarious purposes. The devil is extremely clever! I'm not proud to say this is part of *The 11:11 Code* too. As you can see, the number 11 doesn't always necessarily represent something good, or bad for that matter. It seems to show up when something is important or influential in the overall human story of ascendance toward eventual perfection. The good events teach us how to be, and the bad ones how *not* to be. Both lessons are equally important.

Researching the number 33 will take you down an endless rabbit hole, though we'll focus primarily on its role in the Bible and religious/spiri-

55 http://www.kingofpeace.org/prayerbeads.htm.
56 https://www.olympic.org/.
57 http://www.whitehousetransitionproject.org/wp-content/uploads/2016/04/Terms-Tenure_101909-1.pdf.

tual impacts. The majority of numerology books cover gematria and the significance of certain key numbers in greater depth than we have space for here. My goal is to give brief introductions to the reader so that we all have a basic appreciation for common numerology. After establishing some numerology fundamentals, the remainder of the book will focus on the numerology of 11 and its multiples.

I'd like to give a huge kudos to author Richard Amiel McGough on his book titled *The Bible Wheel*. I learned a lot of fascinating information from his book and website and recommend his book to anyone wanting to dig even deeper into the mathematical structure of the Bible as well as a profound lesson in gematria.[58]

According to the Bible Wheel site,

> The structure consists of a circular matrix of sixty-six cells on a wheel of twenty-two spokes. The sixty-six cells form three wheels within the wheel called cycles. Each cycle spans a continuous sequence of twenty-two books: The outer wheel starts with Genesis and ends on the 22nd book, Song of Solomon. The middle wheel goes from Isaiah to Jeremiah. The innermost wheel spans Romans to Revelation.
>
> With the completion of the Bible Wheel, we now have a fully unified view of the whole Bible as a symmetrical, mathematically structured two-dimensional object. The increase from the traditional one-dimensional list of books to the two-dimensional Bible Wheel immediately reveals a host of unanticipated correlations between the three books on each spoke with one another and the corresponding Hebrew Letter. [59]

Genesis 4:22 talks about Tubal-Cain, who was an eighth-generation descendant of Adam and Eve. The verse reads, "Zillah also had a son, Tubal-Cain, who forged all kinds of tools out of bronze and iron. Tubal-Cain's sister was Naamah."[60]

Here we have the 22nd verse of the fourth (2 x 2 = 4) chapter of the first book of the Bible talking about a man who may have been the world's first tool and die maker, metallurgist, and engineer—a man after my own

58 Richard Gough, *The Bible Wheel: A Revelation of the Divine Unity of the Holy Bible* (Yakima, WA: Bible Wheel Book House, 2006).

59 https://www.biblewheel.com/Wheel/Spokes/tav_seal.php.

60 https://www.biblegateway.com/passage/?search=Genesis+4%3A22&version=NIV.

heart! The story of Tubal-Cain plays an important symbolic role in certain secret societies.

The Bible has 22 books that have 22 or more chapters.[61] In my opinion, one of the most mysterious and obscure verses in the Bible is Isaiah 22:22. It states, "The key of the house of David I will lay on his shoulder; So he shall open, and no one shall shut; And he shall shut, and no one shall open."[62]

This verse is particularly special in that it is said to be the only verse in the entire Bible that is quoted directly in another verse. It is repeated in Revelation 3:7, which says, "To the angel of the church in Philadelphia write: These are the words of him who is holy and true, who holds the key of David. What he opens no one can shut, and what he shuts no one can open."[63]

These two verses make a direct *key* connection to the middle and outer wheels of the Bible Wheel. Again, I must give credit to Richard Gough for this astute observation![64] One of the greatest lessons in virtually all religions is the message that God is love. Love for all life-forms is the key to restoring the world to peace and harmony. (The topic of the *key* will be brought up again when we get to DNA and chlorophyll.)

Here are some more interesting facts on the number 22. The Hebrew alphabet is composed of 22 letters. The Bible's 66th book, Revelation, has 22 chapters, and the last chapter has 21 verses. They stopped writing one verse short of 22. Why? If they had written a 22nd verse, what might it have said? Was it deleted by some king, pope, or other elite power at some point in the last two thousand years of history? What might it have said? Or is it an intentional signal of incompletion, leaving the final capstone of perfection for humankind to enact at a later date?

Additionally, did you know that the word *alphabet* comes from the first two letters of the Greek alphabet, *alpha* and *beta*? Similarly, the Hebrew character set gets its name from the first two letters, *aleph* and *beth*.

Numbers 22:22 (King James Version) states, "And God's anger was kindled because he went: and the angel of the Lord stood in the way for an

61 http://www.isee22.com/22_and_the_bible.html.

62 https://www.biblegateway.com/passage/?search=Isaiah+22%3A22&version=NIV.

63 https://www.biblegateway.com/passage/?search=Revelation+3%3A7&version=NIV.

64 Richard Gough, *The Bible Wheel: A Revelation of the Divine Unity of the Holy Bible* (Yakima, WA: Bible Wheel Book House, 2006).

adversary against him. Now he was riding upon his ass, and his two servants were with him."[65] This term for *donkey* is used a total of ten times in chapter 22 of the book of Numbers.

Of the three Abrahamic religions—Christianity, Judaism, and Islam—each has an arcane, mystical, spiritual tradition that studies the deeper, hidden meanings of their respective religion. In Christianity, Gnostics investigate the esoteric mysteries of the religion. In Islam, the Sufists (students of Sufism) are the cabalistic branch. In Judaism, the study of Kabbalah does the deeper digging. In Kabbalah, the Tree of Life has ten spherical nodes called sephirot, which is linguistically similar to the word *sphere*. There are 22 mystical paths making all possible connections between adjacent sephirot. (Note that in Hebrew the *-ot* ending denotes plural of the singular sephar*im*.) Ancient Kabbalists created this diagram as a map of human spiritual awakening and moral development whereby each path was assigned one of the 22 letters of the Hebrew alphabet, each with a deep spiritual significance.

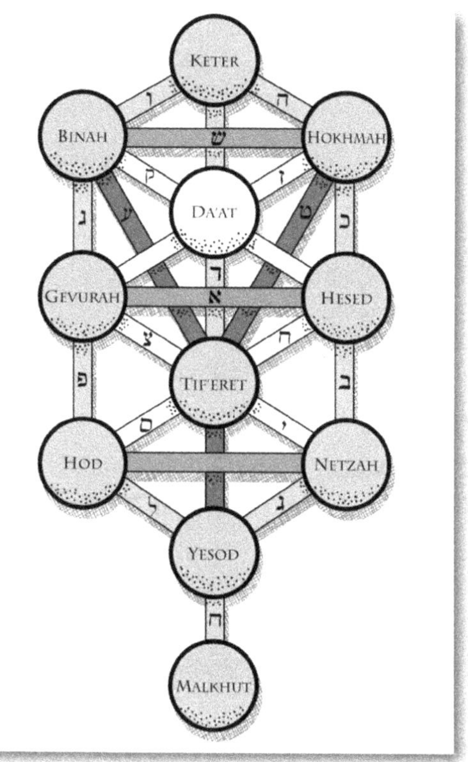

65 https://www.biblegateway.com/passage/?search=Numbers+22%3A22+&version=KJV.

On a chance investigation using Google Earth, out of pure curiosity, I entered the GPS coordinates of 33°*N* - 33°*E*, and much to my surprise, it was a point in the eastern Mediterranean Sea just 125 miles northwest of Jerusalem. Remembering that Jesus is said to have lived to the age of 33, this is interesting to me. I also find it interesting that the 33rd parallel passes through ***Phoeni***x, Arizona, and ancient ***Phoeni***cia, which is now known as Lebanon. With so many other deep connections having been made in my life, I have trained my mind to look for connections rather than take the easy way out and chalk things up to mere coincidence. What's the deeper message here?

THE NUMBERS 12 AND 13

The number 12 plays a particularly interesting role when analyzed from a mystical perspective. How many disciples did Jesus have? Twelve. The ancient Zoroastrian religion believed there were 12 gods. Buddhism teaches the 12 paths of life. How many systems are in the human body? Twelve. How many pairs of cranial nerves emanate from the brain? Twelve. The human body has twelve principal systems—circulatory, reproductive, nervous, skeletal, and digestive, to name just a few.

The heavens are divided into 12 main zodiac constellations, each occupying 30 degrees of arc in the night sky. The horoscope is based on the main 12 zodiac signs; however, very little is said about the constellation Draco, *the dragon*, considered to be the thirteenth zodiac symbol. *Drakon* or dragon occurs 13 times in the Bible.

The year is divided into 12 months.

The clock is composed of 12 hours.

There are 12 members of a standard jury trial.

There are 24 jurors in a grand jury trial (2 x 12).

There are 12 troy ounces in a pound of gold or silver.

There are 12 days of Christmas.

There are 12 steps in Alcoholics Anonymous, and all other addiction support groups.

There are 12 inches in a foot.

There are 12 Roman tablets of law.

Israel had 12 tribes.

The Dalai Lama has 12 advisors.

Twelve generals surrounded George Washington.

There are 12 notes of the chromatic musical scale.

In geometry, 12 equal-sized spheres will completely surround one at its center.

There are 12 compulsory grade levels in the American school system (or 13 if you count kindergarten).

There are 12 dots on a domino tile.

There are 12 spaces per side of a backgammon board.

A bar code (UPC or universal product code) is composed of 12 digits.

Boy Scout law is composed of 12 principle attributes that a Scout should aspire to achieve. A scout is trustworthy, loyal, helpful, friendly, courteous, kind, obedient, cheerful, thrifty, brave, clean, and reverent.

There were 12 Caesars (first 12 emperors of Rome).

There are 12 face cards in a standard deck.

The Federal Reserve system is composed of 12 banks.

There are 12 historical books of the Old Testament (books 6–17).

There are 12 labors of Hercules.

There are 12 minor prophets of the Old Testament (last 12 books of the Old Testament).

There were 12 Olympians (Greek and Roman deities).

There are 12 softball player positions.[66]

The number 12 shows up often in the grocery store—a dozen eggs, a dozen dinner rolls, a dozen doughnuts. A *baker's dozen* is 13.

On the back of the US dollar, the pyramid has 13 layers of stones.

I believe that the man Jesus really did have 12 men as his disciples, but what if the 12 disciples are also a metaphor for the 12 systems of the body and/or the 12 pairs of cranial nerves that effectively connect our computer

66 http://www.michaelleehill.net.

(brain) to all its sensors? All the sensory information that goes into or out of the brain takes place through those cranial nerves. Vision, audition (hearing), gustation (taste), touch, and smell all take place via the cranial nerves. Speech, movements of the eyes, and facial expressions are all projected out to the world via the cranial nerves as well.

What if Christ doubled as a metaphor for the pineal gland, which is supported and served by the 12 functional systems of the body and informed by the 12 cranial nerve inputs? This proposal merits more than just a passing glance. This may be one of the greatest kept mysteries of all Christianity! I'll delve much deeper into this concept later on, but for now I just wanted to plant the seed, give it some sunlight, and let it germinate for a while. Soon we will be up to our eyeballs studying the sun, the provider of all earthly life. I'm taking a layered and phased approach to some of humanity's deepest mysteries.

In Revelation 12:1, it states, "And there appeared a great wonder in heaven; a woman clothed with the sun, and the moon under her feet, and upon her head a crown of twelve stars." This refers to the woman of the apocalypse. Where else have we seen a crown of 12 stars? The European Union flag, of course! This may be a coincidence, or maybe not. A crown of 12 stars may also refer to the 12 houses of the zodiac. In any case, I can't pretend to know the exact meaning of this passage, but I add these ideas here for your consideration. Sometimes there is value in simply observing and pondering things like this.

Many airplanes have the seat rows numbered without a 13th row. A lot of tall buildings do not label the 13th floor as 13 but instead skip to 14. The horror film series *Friday the 13th* is famous in its own right with 11 horror films as well as an eponymous television series with 12 episodes. The movie series was based on the setting at Camp Crystal Lake. When I met my wife, she lived in Crystal Lake, Illinois. The majority of this book was written from our home in Crystal River, Florida—11 years since we met.

Here's an interesting piece of trivia. Over a very long period of time, we see Friday falling on the 13th day of the month every 212 days on average.[67] The number 212 will be discussed at length later in this book, but for now, accept that it is a significant number.

The year can be divided into four seasons, each with 91.25 days, for a total of almost exactly 13 weeks per season (as 4 x 13 = 52 weeks in a year).

The moon actually orbits around the Earth 13 times per year—once every 28 days. The number 28 is considered to be a *perfect* number because it is the sum of all numbers that can be multiplied together to make it—28 = 1 + 2 + 4 + 7 + 14.

If we discard the Gregorian calendar currently in use for timekeeping around the world in favor of a 13-month calendar with every month having 28 days, we are left with a 364-day year. The Eastman Company, in fact, lobbied for the adoption of the 13-month calendar to greatly simplify the reckoning of dates.

Here's another mathematical curiosity. We can arrive at the number 365 (days in the year) in the following two ways: $365 = 10^2 + 11^2 + 12^2$, but even more curiously, $365 = 13^2 + 14^2$. Looking at this another way, we notice that: $10^2 + 11^2 + 12^2 = 13^2 + 14^2$. Notice these are consecutive numbers from 10 to 14, each squared. Normally, these coincidental tricks are fun, but the fact that these relationships relate to a key characteristic of our planet (length of the year) leads me to question if possibly these little mathematical Easter eggs were hidden within the secret fabric of our reality. This begs the question of intentionality: were these little nuggets left for us on purpose, or are they purely accidental? In grade school, I was always taught to go with your first answer; follow your gut.

Now back to the numerology fun! While we are at it, $1 + 3^3 = 28$, $1 + 2 + 3 + 4 = 10$, and $1^3 + 2^3 + 3^3 + 4^3 = 100$.[62] Taking this a step further, we can write

67 https://en.wikipedia.org/wiki/Friday_the_13th.

$10^2 = (1 + 2 + 3 + 4)^2 = 1^3 + 2^3 + 3^3 + 4^3 = 100$. This can be beautifully imagined if we picture a cube with side length of 1 inch, another cube with side length of 2, and two more cubes each with side lengths of 3 and 4 respectively. The volume of the first box will be 1 x 1 x 1 = 1 cubic inch. The second will have volume 2 x 2 x 2 = 8 cubic inches. The third will have a volume of 3 x 3 x 3 = 27 cubic inches. The fourth will have a volume of 4 x 4 x 4 = 64 cubic inches. The combined volume comes out sublimely to 1 + 8 + 27 + 64 = 100. Numbers are but one of the many languages of the gods, but in my opinion, it could be the favorite.

As long as we are digging into the clever relationships between the numbers 1, 2, 3, and 4, I wanted to share a discovery I made. I wondered what would happen if I added up the sum of the factorials of the first four numbers. Later on we will go into the factorial function in more detail, but for now, suffice it to say that the factorial (denoted by !) multiplies a number by all whole numbers below itself. For example, four factorial, written as "4!" tells us to multiply 4 x 3 x 2 x 1 = 24. Similarly, 3! = 3 x 2 x 1 = 6, 2! = 2 x 1 = 2, and of course, 1! = 1. Now add the four results together, and we get 1! + 2! + 3! + 4! = 1 + 2 + 6 + 24 = 33.

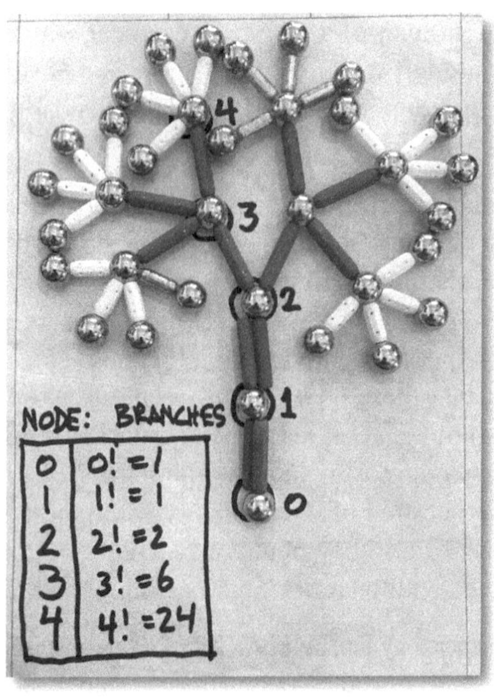

In the photo above, I constructed a tree by using the factorial function. The bottom ball is free, node n=0 is like ground zero, or the acorn that starts the tree. The factorial of zero is designated as 1 from the gamma function. This 1 means I add one stick to that ball, then place another ball. The next ball is ball #1, so I put one stick on the next level, followed by one ball. Next ball is #2. Now I apply two sticks to the last ball. The factorial of 2 is 2x1=2, which tells the total number of branches at the current level. Now I have the first branching point. The next level is level #3, and we put 3 sticks on each of the two balls from the previous step. Now we are up to 6 branches total at the highest level, because 3 factorial is 3x2x1=6. Now I put 4 sticks on each of the six lower nodes and voila, we have a total of 24 branches at the outermost level because 4! = 4x3x2x1=24. I have just demonstrated that the factorial function is built into nature's topology of trees whether we are talking about lungs, veins, arteries, or something from the forest. In the factorial tree depicted above, if you add the number of total branches from node 1 through 4, you get a total of 33 branches, graphically summing up all of the numbers that I just worked through. If you continue this process out to 5 nodes, you get 120 branches. Six gives 720, seven for 5,040, and eight balloons out to 40,320, which is about as many leaves as you would expect on a mature tree! The factorial function blows up more rapidly than almost any other function.

Mathematics operates at the fundamental core of all aspects of nature. In Swedish, the word for science is *naturvetenskap*. *Natur*=nature, *veta*=to know (like to *vet* someone for hire), and *skap* = -ship / -ness. In other words, in Swedish, a scientist is one who studys "nature-ness." I really prefer the Swedish word over its English cousin because the latter is sterile and anodyne, whereas the Viking term gives direct credit to nature. I always looked at science as first and foremost a way to comprehend the mind of God, and to a slightly lesser degree, an interesting path to earning a satisfying wage in the world.

While we are having fun adding up numbers, let's see what other interesting items can be found within the first ten whole numbers (1–10). We already know that 6-factorial or 6! is equal to 6! = 6 x 5 x 4 x 3 x 2 x 1 = 720. Suppose we ignore the number 7 and do the same for the other numbers 8 through 10 (10 x 9 x 8 = 720). Isn't that interesting? If we omit 7, it becomes a sort of balancing point for the product of the numbers to its left and right! In the same vein, what if we compare the products on both sides of 7 that *include* 7?

So 1 x 2 x 3 x 4 x 5 x 6 x 7 = 5,040. Now try the right side, which would be 7 x 8 x 9 = 5,040. As has been shown two different ways, the number 7 occupies a spot of balance and equilibrium within the hierarchy of the first ten numbers within the product space or realm of multiplication. I'd love to pretend that I came up with this, but I would rather give credit to Michael Schneider, who wrote *A Beginner's Guide to Constructing the Universe,* as this is the first and only place I've seen this neat set of mathematical tricks.[68]

When I see such harmonious relationships between numbers, I don't necessarily try to infer meaning, but I do appreciate that these little numerical treats have been imbedded into the numbers that map our matrix of reality and measurement as a reminder of the intelligence of the divine mind that set it all in motion. There are no coincidences—only connected events and concepts. It's incumbent upon us to search for the deeper connections. Numbers have a much deeper, richer, and more interesting life than just tallying up taxes and counting widgets in factories. They have a secret and sacred inner world waiting to be explored.

BIG NUMBERS

Given that this is a numerology book at its core and we will be tackling some very big numbers later in the text, let's explore some ways to wrap our minds around—or visualize—the magnitude of the numbers we'll need to be adept at working with and conceptualizing. The entire purpose of what you're about to read is to hopefully expand your mind's ability to comprehend exceptionally large numbers. It will be very helpful later on, when we look into astronomical distances, to really have a feeling of how vast space really is.

Even a small pack of playing cards can reach deep into infinity if we look into all of the possible ways to arrange a full deck of 52 cards. There are 52! = 52 x 51 x 50 x 49 x … x 3 x 2 x 1 = 8.058×10^{67} (8 with 67 trailing zeroes!) unique ways to sort the deck. There are about 250 billion stars in the Milky Way galaxy. In order to have 8.058×10^{67} stars, you would have to have 250 billion Milky Way galaxies (*each* with 250 billion stars)

68 Michael Schneider, *A Beginner's Guide to Constructing the Universe: The Mathematical Archetypes of Nature, Art, and Science* (New York: Harper Perennial, 1995).

inside of a cluster, 250 billion of these clusters within a super cluster, 250 billion super clusters within whatever you would call this space, and so on for a total of five levels up.

Here is another way to visualize just how big a number with 67 zeroes to the right is. Assuming that a grain of sand is 1 millimeter in diameter, you could fit about 7,000 grains of sand in a 1-ounce shot glass. If you were to dump 8,000,000,000{+ *58 more zeroes!*} grains of sand on the Earth's surface, the layer of sand would be at a depth of 10.7 billion light-years. This means that it would take 10.7 billion years for a beam of light to shine from the surface of the Earth to the outer surface of the sand pile while traveling at 186,000 miles *per second.* That's incomprehensibly large! That's just from looking at all possible arrangements of just 52 items. Trying to calculate the number of ways to arrange all 3.5 billion base pairs in the human DNA chain would be the closest approximation of infinity that I could imagine, and I believe this would be well outside of the capabilities of the greatest supercomputer to calculate.

DNA is quite possibly the most ingenious innovation in the history of the universe. According to Dr. Jeremy Narby:

> It is a molecule which is highly specialized in storing and duplicating information. Proteins do this, but they are incapable of reproducing themselves without the information contained in DNA. Life, therefore, is a seemingly inescapable synthesis of these two molecular systems.
>
> It is a molecule which is highly specialized to storing and duplicating information. Proteins do this, but they are incapable of reproducing themselves without the information contained in DNA. Life, therefore, is a seemingly inescapable synthesis of these two molecular systems.
>
> Crick calculates the probability of the chance emergence of one single protein (which would go on to build the first DNA molecule). In all living species, proteins are made up of the exact same 20 amino acids, which are small molecules. The average protein is a long chain made up of approximately 200 amino acids, chosen from those 20, and strung together in the right order. According to the laws of combinatorials, there is a 1 chance in 20 multiplied by itself 200 times for a single specific protein to emerge fortuitously. This

> figure, which can be written 10^{260}, is enormously greater than the number of atoms in the observable universe (estimated at 10^{80}).[69]

Ten billion multiplied times itself eight times! Think of a tree with ten billion branches. Each sub-branch has ten billion sub-branches. And on, and on, six more levels out—all eight expansions go up by a factor of ten billion.

Really Big Numbers

To get a feeling for extremely large numbers of extremely small objects, like molecules of water, I find the following quote by physicist Lord Kelvin quite interesting:

> Suppose that you could mark the molecules in a glass of water, then pour the contents of the glass into the ocean and stir the latter thoroughly so as to distribute the marked molecules uniformly throughout the seven seas; if you then took a glass of water anywhere out of the ocean, you would find in it about a hundred of your marked molecules.[70]

In another mind-bending explanation of how inconceivably small the atom is, it is estimated that the average snowflake has around 10 quintillion (10 with 19 zeroes!) worth of water molecules contained in its structure. To give the reader a frame of reference, the combination of all the oceans of the world collectively hold 3.53 quintillion gallons of water.[71] A quintillion is what you get when you take one trillion of something and copy it one million times, and a trillion is a million times a million. The typical snowflake has more atoms in it than three times the number of gallons in all the planet's oceans.

Anyone interested in unfathomably gargantuan numbers may be familiar with the term *googol*. The spelling of the internet search giant Google was the result of a mistake in the founders' original intention to use Googol to signify that the company provides a virtually infinite amount of information to its users. The googol (10^{100}) can be written out as: 10,000,000,00 0,000,000,000,000,000,000,000,000,000,000,000,000,000,000,000,000,0

69 Jeremy Narby, *The Cosmic Serpent: DNA and the Origins of Knowledge* (New York: Jeremy P. Tarcher/Putnam, 1998).

70 Erwin Schrodinger, *What Is Life?* (Cambridge: Cambridge University Press, 2015).

71 https://oceanservice.noaa.gov/facts/oceanwater.html.

00,000,000,000,000,000,000,000,000,000,000,000,000,000 (10 followed by 100 zeroes!).

The term was coined in 1920 by nine-year-old Milton Sirotta (1911–1981), nephew of US mathematician Edward Kasner. Kasner popularized the concept in his 1940 book *Mathematics and the Imagination*. Other names for googol include *ten duotrigintillion* on the short scale, *ten thousand sexdecillion* on the long scale, or ten *sexdecilliard* on the Peletier long scale. When I lived in Sweden, I always wondered why they said "miljon" for million, but the word for billion was "miljard" based on the Peletier.

The symbol for infinity, ∞, which resembles the numeral 8 sideways, has the mathematical name *lemniscate*. According to Wikipedia, in algebraic geometry, a lemniscate is any of several figure 8 or ∞-shaped curves. The word comes from the Latin *lemniscatus*, meaning "decorated with ribbons," from the Greek λημνίσκος (*lemniskos*), which means ribbons, or alternatively, it may refer to the wool from which the ribbons were made.[72] Have you ever noticed the little figure 8 on the globe? Have you ever wondered what it's there for and looked into it? The *analemma* is one of God's fine signature strokes on our skies, whereby the sun traces out an infinity symbol throughout the course of a year.

Stop!
Do a YouTube search for "A Year in the Life of the Sun"
Whoa. Pretty awesome, huh?

Googol has no special significance in mathematics but is useful when comparing with other very large quantities, such as the number of subatomic particles in the visible universe or the number of hypothetical possibilities in a chess game. Kasner used it to illustrate the difference between an unimaginably large number and infinity, and in this role it is sometimes used in teaching mathematics. To give a sense of how big a googol really is, the mass of an electron, which is just under 10^{-30} kg, can be compared to the mass of the visible universe, estimated at between 10^{50} and 10^{60} kg. It is a ratio in the order of about 10^{80} to 10^{90} or only about one ten-billionth of a googol (0.00000001 percent of a googol).

The highest numerical value banknote ever printed was a note for 1 sextillionpengo (10^{21} or 1 milliard bilpengo as printed) printed in Hungary in

72 Martin J. Erickson, *Beautiful Mathematics*, (Washington, DC: Mathematical Association of America, 2011), 1–3.

1946. In 2009, Zimbabwe printed a 100 trillion (10^{18}) Zimbabwean dollar note, which at the time of printing was worth about $30 US.[73]

> Take a few moments and search YouTube for: "Symphony of Science—We Are All Connected".

LARGE EXPANSES OF TIME

In the modern world, we calculate time based on a system where the smallest whole unit is the second and the largest common unit is the millennium. Of course, the second is divided down into smaller units that are fractions of the second (e.g., microseconds and nanoseconds), but the smallest whole unit is the second. In between those two extremes, we have minutes, hours, days, weeks, months, years, decades, and centuries.

Ancient Eastern civilizations worked with much bigger units of time. For example, in Hinduism, one day of Brahma is defined as 4.32 billion years. This enormous block of time is subdivided into a thousand maha-yugas at 4.32 million years each. Incidentally, this is within 5.1 percent of the Earth's estimated age of 4.54 billion years, based on radiometric dating techniques.[74] The Hindu philosophers went even further. A year of Brahma is defined as 3.11 trillion years. According to Y'Viavia, time can be expressed in 22 different powers of 10, 10^{22} years being the largest imaginable period of time in the Hindu scale, referred to as a cycle of Brahma.[75]

The Buddhist faith also reckons time on massive time scales. A *kalpa* is a great measure of time, defined as 16 million years. A medium kalpa is 320 billion years. A great kalpa is an astonishing 1.3 trillion years.

Science creates units to meet the needs of the subject being studied. Clearly, these ancient mystics and philosophers were studying the universe on an intractable time scale and putting together the bigger picture. In Japanese, I find it fascinating that they have a system of extremely large numbers going up as high as *muryotaisu* (無量大数), which is 10^{88} or 1 with 88 zeroes to the right. According to *Universe Today* magazine, there are approximately 10^{82} atoms in the observable universe.[76] *Muryotaisu* is

73 https://en.wikipedia.org/wiki/Names_of_large_numbers#The_googol_family.
74 https://www.universetoday.com/75805/how-old-is-the-earth/.
75 Signet II Y'Viavia, *The Akshaya Patra Series* (Bloomington, IN: Xlibris, 2015).
76 https://www.universetoday.com/36302/atoms-in-the-universe/.

one million times greater than the number of atoms in the universe. What in the universe would the ancient Japanese scholars be using such truly astronomical numbers for?

In geological time scales, the Earth's life is divided into 22 different periods, such as the widely-recognized Jurassic period made famous by Hollywood. The Jurassic period was approximately 200 million years ago and lasted 56.3 million years. But why 22 periods? Why not 20 or 25? Why do almost all of life's big control knobs seem to stop at 22? Who or what keeps sending out these coded 11 + 11 messages?

The ancient Maya also had a rich system of reckoning time over vast scales. The Mayan calendar used *tun* to equal one year. Katun equals 20 years. Baktun equals 394 years. Piktun equals 7,885. Kalabtun equals 157,704. Kinchiltun equals 3,154,071. And finally, the alautun was defined as 63,081,429 years. Notice that each number is a multiple of 20 times the number that preceded it.

The Mayan counting system was base-twenty, unlike the modern base-ten system. They counted time in this manner since at least 5000 BC. Around the year 3114 BC, they developed a calendar that seemed to stop on the date of December 21, 2012, or 12/21/12.

You can see the numbers 11 and 22 in that date. Add up the digits of that date, 12/21/2012 and you get (1 + 2) + (2 + 1) + (2 + 0 + 1 + 2) = 11. It's also fun to notice how 12 + 21 = 33.

The Mayans believed that something of immense consequence would happen on or about that date. Many people took this to mean the world would end, so a widespread conspiracy that the world might end on that date developed. The Mayan calendar seemed to predict that the world would end after the 13th baktun, which 13 x 394 = 5,122 years later. I find it utterly fantastic that the Higgs boson from particle physics was discovered in 2012 as well! The Higgs boson is a classic example of the mathematics showing up long before physics discovering something in the physical world. The Higgs boson is also known as the God particle, and it gave scientists what was believed to be the final missing piece to the puzzle of how our universe is held together. Think about it. The same year the Mayan calendar ends, humankind discovers the most fundamental physical particle of our universe. The God particle is a very short-lived particle with a mean life of just $\sim 1.6 \times 10^{22}$ seconds.[77]

That's 1.6 with the decimal point moved 22 places to the left. That's very close to the value of the golden ratio, don't you think?

I doubt that any of this is a coincidence, not in the scale of thousands of years or infinitesimally small shaves of a second. Everything is connected, and everything has meaning. I don't believe in coincidences. Our universe is a collection of interconnected events. One of our jobs is to look carefully for the connections. The connections are almost always there if you look for them hard enough.

THE GOLDEN RATIO

One of the most fascinating and perplexing numbers ever discovered by man and found ubiquitously in nature is the golden ratio, often known as phi (*fee* or sometimes *fye* in the Greek ϕ). Any book on numerology that doesn't discuss this number should be viewed with skepticism, and should make you wonder what other vital numbers they neglected to include. This number has fascinated humankind ever since its discovery in nature more than 2,400 years ago, and it has been applied in art, science, and architecture. Before I go into why it's such an amazing number, let's first understand its basic principles.

> Search YouTube for a video titled "Great Demo on Fibonacci Sequence Spirals in Nature—The Golden Ratio." It's just under four minutes in length, and I am sure you'll find it enjoyable.[78]

Throughout history, rectangles with a length-to-width ratio of 1.618 have been considered the most subjectively pleasing to the eye. This ratio was named the golden ratio by the Greeks. In the world of mathematics, the numeric value is called phi, named for the Greek sculptor Phidias.[79]

The famous Italian mathematician Leonardo de Pisa (1170–1250), who was better known as Fibonacci, is credited with the eponymous Fibonacci sequence, which is a progression of numbers in which each number in a sequence is the sum of the two numbers before it.

77 https://atlas.cern/updates/physics-briefing/higgs-boson-s-shadow.
78 .
79 http://www.geom.uiuc.edu/~demo5337/s97b/art.htm.

Imagine we are at T = zero, which would signal the moment the physical universe was spoken into existence by the mind of God. At this moment, there is nothing. Then *the One* speaks. Nothing plus one equals one. Now add that answer plus one again. Now we have two. Add the second and third terms 1 + 2 = 3. Now add 2 + 3 = 5 and 3 + 5 = 8. And on and on—1, 1, 2, 3, 5, 8, 13, 21, 34, 55, 89. Try doing this yourself, and stop when you're tired or otherwise satisfied. Then divide your last term by your second-to-last number, and you have an approximate value of phi!

Also take this moment to notice that the golden ratio, 1.618, can be derived from the most basic numbers zero (0) and one (1) and requires no other numbers. Isn't it remarkable? Consider that virtually every type of electronic information is stored entirely digitally in the form of ones and zeroes in binary code—every phone call, email, text message, tweet, Instagram, Facebook posting, video, or song now is encoded into binary and transmitted and stored as ones and zeroes. As I type into my word processing software right now, all of my ramblings and graphics are being encoded into millions of little bits of *something*, and tiny spaces of *nothing*. If you're reading this work on a tablet, then 100 percent of this book is being stored as ones and zeroes.

An excellent article on the mystical and spiritual aspects of the golden ratio was written by a very good friend of mine and fellow author, P.D. Newman, and the link is provided in the footnotes.[80]

PHI IN NATURE

The golden ratio is also commonly called the divine proportion because of its prevalence in nature. The phenomenon of *phyllotaxis* is derived from the ancient Greek *phýllon* (leaf) and *táxis* (arrangement). Phyllotaxis is the phenomenon that can be seen by counting the number of clockwise spirals and counterclockwise spirals on objects such as pine cones, pineapples, and sunflowers. The number of spiral paths in one direction will be approximately 1.618 (phi) times the number of spirals in the opposite direction!

As suggested earlier in this book, there seems to be some spiritual significance to numbers with repeating digits, such as 222. Let's see what

80 http://tupelomason.blogspot.com/2013/10/the-divine-proportion-tracing-nature.html.

happens if we divide the 360 degrees of a circle by ϕ: 360 / 1.618 = 222.5 degrees.

Subtracting this from 360, we are left with a complementary angle of 137.5 degrees, which is known as the *golden angle*. The number 137 is very special and quite probably the most perplexing and mysterious number in the universe.

In the study of phyllotaxis, it has been found that successive leaves on a plant tend to exhibit this angle between them. In botany, the Fibonacci sequence is seen in branching networks, such as roots and branches of a tree. This has fascinated mathematicians, biologists, and botanists alike for centuries. The spiral shape of a snail shell exhibits the divine ratio. The proportions of the arms of spiral galaxies also embody the golden ratio.

A wonderful book on this topic is called *The Golden Ratio* by Mario Livio. This is one of the most interesting and thought-provoking books I have ever read, and I would strongly encourage the reader to get a copy of it as well as Livio's other book, *Is God a Mathematician?*

MORE FUN WITH NUMBERS

For readers not interested in mathematics, you could skip this section without losing any continuity. For the rest of you that found me in the Numerology section of the bookstore, let's get into it!

While writing this book, I was playing around with the different operations on my scientific calculator. I discovered that if you take the cube root of 11, you get 2.22. This means that if you have a cube with side lengths of 2.22 inches, the volume will be almost exactly 11 cubic inches. Stated compactly, $\sqrt[3]{11} \approx 2.224$. Another fact I discovered is if you take the square root of 11.112233445566778899, you get approximately 3.333. Even more interestingly, if you take 3.333333 (repeating) and square it, you get 11.1111111. Similarly, $3.333^3 = 37.037037037\ldots$, which is essentially a fractal recipe for the sum of smaller and smaller copies of the star umber 37. Why? Also, $11.11^2 = 123.4321$.

It is also interesting from a mathematical standpoint to notice what happens when we divide small whole numbers by 9. Taking 1/9, we get

0.11111 with 1 repeating infinitely to the right of the decimal. This can be represented as an infinite sum of

$$\frac{1}{10}+\frac{1}{100}+\frac{1}{1{,}000}+\frac{1}{10{,}000}+\ldots=0.1111111\ldots$$

So too, 2/9 = 0.22222. The same pattern is true out to 8/9=0.88888. Computing 20/9 gives 2.2222 repeating. And 30/9 = 3.33333. I don't go much deeper into this beyond just admiring this brief glimpse into infinity (infinite number of terms) and the domain of the infinitesimal (infinitely small contributions to the sum as the number of terms, n, tends toward infinity).

Similarly, if we take the first four positive powers of 10 and add them, we get the following:

$$10^0 + 10^1 + 10^2 + 10^3 = 1 + 10 + 100 + 1{,}000 = 1{,}111$$

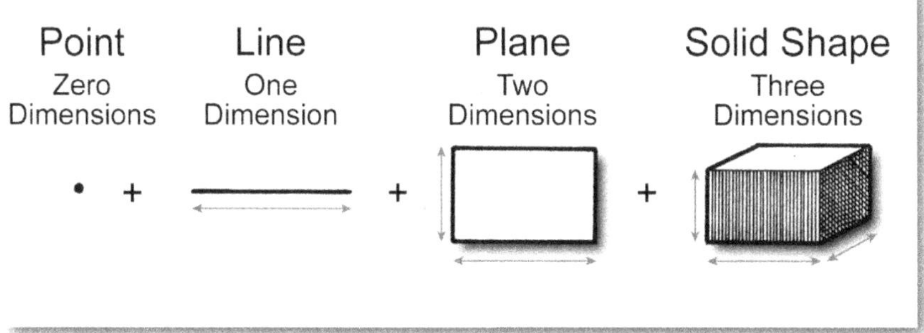

Geometrically, this is equivalent to taking the value of a point (zero dimension), plus the length of a line of 10 units, plus the area of a square with side length of 10, plus the volume of a cube with side length of 10 (and ignoring units, of course).

For readers who really enjoyed this chapter and would like more, please take the time to visit the link in the footnote. It takes about 30 minutes to read but was well worth it.[81] Thank you to my good friend Marlene Wheeler for the recommendation!

81 https://www.kryon.com/k_chanelhandbook03.html

CHAPTER 2
FROM HUMBLE BEGINNINGS

My life started when I was born in the northern Chicago-area, blue-collar, working-class lakefront suburb of Waukegan, Illinois, on March 22. My first home was at 322 Hull Court. The digits of my birth year add up to 22. My birth date, which is 3/22, is of course 322 without the separator.

My neighborhood buddy Bob "Bobby" Kretz (at right) and myself (Left) at about age 5 on the front porch of 322 Hull Court (you can see half of the house number above me)

My father, who passed away in 2005, had taken an educational voyage around the world with a program called World Campus Afloat when he was eighteen and nineteen years of age, right after high school. For a period of about three months, he traveled on a ship that made ports of call at various points across east, west, and southern Africa as well as India, Ceylon, and all over Asia. During his visit to India, he met with a fortune-teller who counseled him that he would get married to his childhood love and absolutely must ensure that the wedding date fall on February 23. The guru didn't tell him why other than saying it was very important.

After proposing to his childhood sweetheart, my father insisted that their wedding date had to be 2/23. Note that this is my birthday, 3/22, backward. Their wedding took place on a Friday, very uncustomary for a wedding as most take place on a weekend because of work and school schedules. It bears mentioning that both of my parents were age twenty-three at the time of their wedding.

My beloved sister, Suzanne was born on 10/13, which of course adds up to 23. Although there is no way to prove it, I firmly believe the adherence to the guru's advice set the course for my magical dance with the numbers 3 and 22 over the next forty-plus years of my life and played a large role in my spiritual awakening and realization of the secretive role that some higher power must have played in charting my life's overall movie script. My father's birth date, 10/12, has digits that sum to 22, and the digits of his birth year 1949 sum to 23. Perhaps all that wise guru in India did was just add together the numbers to get 23 and take the 2 from the 12 of his day of birth. Then maybe he told my dad it was this magical key to the heavens, and he might have been none the wiser.

Or had the guru actually found his connection to the creative spirit of the universe through a spiritual understanding of numbers? Did he know how to interpret the story numbers are capable of telling through coincidences too serendipitous to be random?

One of Dad's Greatest Gifts

Growing up, I remember sitting on the couch next to my dad, and he would bring out his coin and paper money collection that he had amassed during his overseas travels. I loved seeing the different alphabets and number systems and was captivated by the variation in coin size, thickness, color, metallic composition, edge geometry, holes through the center, and other features. But looking through his collection of paper money told an even more beautiful story. What each country put on their money told me a lot about what is important to that society. The colors, faces, scenes of life in that country, and key human achievements shown on these bills told a wonderful but mysterious story about its own part of the world. I felt a deep desire to learn as much as I could about our world, and my interest in collecting foreign money has become a lifetime passion for me. To this day, I continue to collect samples of the currency from every country I visit.

One of the greatest secrets my dad ever gave me was his own personal trick. He said, "Make a point to learn how to say hello, please, thank you, and I'm sorry in *every* single language that you come into contact with. Learn these four phrases, and the natives will forgive nearly all other cultural missteps virtually anywhere you go on Earth."

A happy family of seven on a motorbike in Leyte, Philippines

As a child, I always had an innate love and curiosity for nature and science. The symmetry, harmony, and beauty of nature always captivated my attention. As a child, my summers were spent with my grandparents at their summer home on Washington Island, above the tip of Wisconsin's thumb that juts out into Lake Michigan. This quaint little slice of heaven has the rough dimensions of eight miles by five miles, which works out to **8/5 = 1.60**, which is close enough (1.1 percent) to the golden ratio 1.618 for me to call it good. The island is located eleven kilometers from the mainland and lies at 45 degrees and 22 minutes of arc north of the equator, placing it 22 minutes[82] north of the halfway point between the north pole and equator. This fact gives the island four perfectly distinct seasons.[83]

Some of my fondest memories were taking boat rides and exploring the other uninhabited islands and peninsulas, hiking in the forest with my grandmother, and chasing butterflies in the meadows. During my third year of high school, my grandparents sold their island home. It was 1993, a year whose digits sum to 22. I was crushed, realizing this wonderful chapter of cherished memories was coming to an abrupt close. But the memories are mine to keep. Every summer after that, until my college years, I embarked on my annual pilgrimage and took the forty-five-minute ferry ride from the tip of the Door Peninsula across to Washington Island to drive around and replay the fond memories of my childhood. I always drove past my grandparents' house and admired its lovely alpine lodge structure and perfect location on the shores of the quaint Figenschau Bay, an immaculate, silent little place straight out of a story book. Washington Island maintains the distinction of being the largest Icelandic settlement in the United States, thanks to the original settlers who arrived in the 1800s from Eyrarbakki, Iceland. About three years ago, I returned and just happened to notice for the very first time that the address was 2241 Green Bay Road. Here is the number 22 showing up again, at a very important place in my life. I had driven past that sign literally hundreds of times during the previous forty-plus years, but it wasn't until this time that I realized the 22 had been there all along.

According to the Washington Island Ferry Line website, the Island has a total surface area of 22 square miles.[84] The absolute last address on Wisconsin state highway 42 before the ferry dock to Washington Island is 220 State Hwy 42. This scenic byway has a total length of 222 kilometers, beginning in Sheboygan, WI (where we lived for 4 years) and ending at the ferry dock.[85]

---

82 A degree of angular measure can be subdivided into 60 minutes.
83 http://washingtonisland.com/washington-island/.
84 https://wisferry.com/.
85 https://www.revolvy.com/page/Highway-156-(Wisconsin).

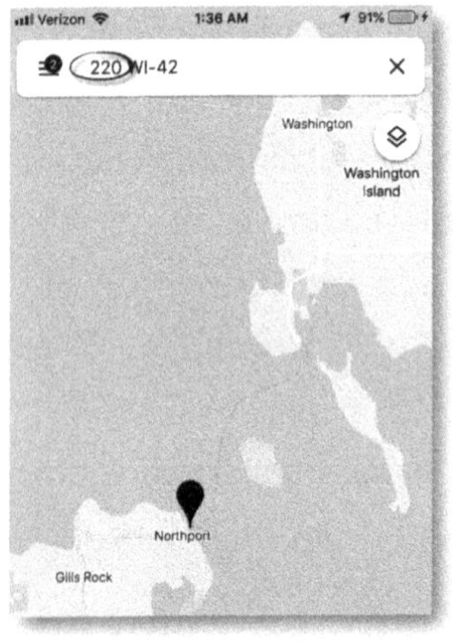

The universe seemed to be trying to tell me something. At this point, I received another extremely clear sign that many of the important stages of my life were preplanned by some great cosmic mind and stamped with the 22 marker of authenticity and the quality of being preordained or deterministic. This could not all be a coincidence. I think the term *synchronicity* is a much better choice, as it implies being synchronized with some entity that's separate from me. My first girlfriend lived at an address of 2207 Russell Road, which is something that I didn't realize until I started writing this book and thinking back about all the most influential people and places that have been a part of my life at some point. The 22 code seems to be less about good or bad and more about how deeply something imprinted on my life.

FASCINATION WITH ANCIENT ENERGY

While I was growing up in the charming but tough, working-class Chicago suburb of Waukegan, the local electric utility had a coal-fired power plant just over a mile from our house that has been in continuous operation since

1905.[86] I could see the red chimney lights blinking dutifully through the night from their perch 450 feet up the smokestacks from my backyard as the smoke rolled out merrily into the night sky. I could hear the occasional loud and distant *boom* sounds as the 110-ton railcars of coal were being unloaded. My great-grandmother used to get fuming mad as she bitterly complained about how the *'lectric* plant would wait 'til after dark to belch out the worst of their ash and soot! Everybody seemed to hate the place, but hated it even more when the power was out, so I had to investigate.

This provoked my curiosity to the point that I would, at the age of four, beg my mom to drive me down to the power plant to see what all the racket was about.

I was mystified and fascinated by the huge, tangled electric jungle of powerlines, transformers, relays, lightning arrestors, and switches in the high-voltage yard. I admired the 1920-era masonry details and huge, arching, neoclassical windows that encased the turbine hall. It was all so amazing for my young eyes to see.

Street view of the Waukegan power station turbine hall

When I was in fourth grade, my mother arranged for me and all my

86 http://lakecountyhistory.blogspot.com/2010/03/power-plant-of-waukegan.html

friends to take a tour of the coal plant as part of my tenth birthday party. I remember my excitement as I first passed through the gate and signed in at the security guard building. I could hear the transformers humming away as 138,000 volts and hundreds of millions of watts of power sizzled through them invisibly. I could hear the whine of the turbines off in the distance, dutifully churning out as much power as the city and surrounding area could handle. As we entered the vast turbine hall, I remember the low, droning sound of the massive machines getting louder, and we could feel the heat of the boiler. You could just feel the floor shaking as if you were inside of a very large ocean-going ship. The sensation of power was palpable everywhere. I was inside one of planet Earth's awesome engine rooms! It was like stepping back a hundred years in time, as the original General Electric turbines from the early 1900s were still in place but sitting idly in the silence of retirement. As we made progress from north to south, the machines got successively bigger and more powerful, beginning with ten megawatt machines from 1905, to 100 megawatts (MW) in 1949, to 320 MW in the late sixties. It was amazing to think that Thomas Edison was still alive when this place was built! Looking at the antique GE and Westinghouse workhorses, I never thought that one day I would be working at the same factories where these machines were made in Schenectady, New York (General Electric), and Charlotte, North Carolina (Westinghouse).[87]

The smell of burning coal reminded me that the era of modern progress was being made possible by electricity produced by burning a truly ancient fuel that had been hidden in the Earth's crust for hundreds of millions, if not *billions*, of years. I imagined a time when my ancient ancestors sat gathered around a firepit and used the same fossil fuel—fuel that was formed hundreds of millions or even billions of years ago from dead biological material pressed together under tremendous heat and pressure for intractable periods of time, leaving behind virtually pure carbon. And this carbon was ready to surrender its energy in exchange for being liberated to the gaseous phase in the form of carbon dioxide and eventually reenter the carbon cycle by being absorbed in a leaf, where it would eventually return to the soil to repeat the process. But for a few seconds, the coal's

87 Schenectady was where Thomas Edison and George Westinghouse duked out the classic *war of the currents*. The interested reader is encouraged to look up *the war of the currents* for a fascinating account of the most influential battles of the entire industrial revolution. Wikipedia has an excellent article on the subject, but space and scope do not permit its inclusion within this book.

energy would be free to travel at the speed of light from the generators to the customers' appliances.

At that moment in my life, I was amazed to see that the power station was making electricity by burning fossils of plants and animals that had lived so very long ago. In essence, we were unlocking stored sunlight energy collected by plants from a time that existed long before humans. It's comforting to know that the Creator started planning for the humanity experiment many hundreds of millions of years ago, knowing one day we would need and make good usage of these fuels. One thing is clear to me. These fossil fuels are not here by accident or luck, but rather by divine providence of an intelligent and caring Creator. Don't you think it's a bit of a miracle that crude oil can be separated into hundreds of products, including gasoline, diesel, butane, asphalt, kerosene, jet fuel, heating oil, motor oil, butane, octane, and natural gas, among others?[88] Does anyone honestly think these resources were left in the Earth as an accident or co-incidence, or it was just a stroke of random luck?

I remember our affable, intrepid escort, Mr. Bob Burkett, opening one of the inspection hatches to look inside one of the operating coal furnaces. I recall the searing heat and blinding white-orange light escaping from the five-inch hole, leaving spots on my retina for the next several minutes. It was almost as if we were looking at the sun itself while watching some billion-year-old stored solar energy being released from the prison of carbon bonds. Looking inside the bottom of the boiler was like looking straight into the inferno of hell. Stalactites of black, molten lava dripped down from the inner guts of the boiler as the noncombustible silicate portions of the coal melted and fused into a sort of shiny, opaque volcanic glass resembling obsidian. Eventually, this gets ground up in hydraulic crushers and flushed out as slag into settling ponds outdoors. Every few hours the boiler operator (who would be *me* sixteen years later) would have to come by and use a 25-foot-long steel pole as a battering ram against the stalactites to knock them off so they'd fall into a giant hydraulic grinder at the bottom of the boiler. This process was affectionately dubbed "poking the monkey's tail."

In any event, this tour was like stepping back into antiquity. The plant was dark, loud, and dusty with shadowy spaces punctuated by bursts of intense light from the furnace and the thousand-watt mercury vapor dis-

88 Did you know that one gallon of gasoline contains more than thirty-three kilowatt-hours of energy?

charge lamps overhead. There was a definite sense of working with the Earth's most basic alchemistic elements—earth, wind, fire, and water. I felt a sense of awe as I witnessed humankind working with ancient fossil fuels to convert all that stored energy into bringing light and happiness to our modern society. I couldn't escape the feeling that my young eyes were witnessing one of humankind's greatest innovations at work.

Exactly twenty-two years since the previous photo at age four, during one of the high points of my career. I am changing the FAA aircraft warning lights at the Waukegan plant, exceptionally proud to be 450 feet above my birthplace, the Chicago skyline visible in the background. Photo taken on August 3, 2001.

As a young, impressionable boy, I was awestruck to learn about the conversion of energy that took place in a power station. Going back hundreds of millions of years, the sun's mass was converted via nuclear fusion into optical energy. A portion of the sun's mass is constantly being converted into energy following Einstein's ubiquitous equation $e=mc^2$, whereby the energy density of matter (e/m) is equal to the speed of light squared. Later on, I'll show you where 1111 is actually lurking inside this little equation! The light energy traveled the 93 million miles through empty space for eight minutes and twenty seconds (500 seconds in total!) before reaching the Earth and being converted into chemical energy in the leaves of plants through the miracle of photosynthesis, upon which all earthly life-forms depend. The plants died, stacked up, and eventually were subducted under the ground during tectonic plate movements, burying the vegetation deep underground. The immense pressure compacted the plant matter into a denser energy form—coal.

In the power station, the coal is milled down to the consistency of talcum powder before being blown into the furnaces with huge 4,160-volt motor-driven fans. This aspect of grinding the fuel down to the consistency of facial powder increases the ratio of surface area to volume, making virtually 100 percent of the carbon available for combustion immediately. The chemical energy is converted into thermal energy in the boiler. This heat converts water to steam, which causes the pressure that makes the turbine rotate, converting the thermal energy to mechanical energy. The last step is to convert the rotating mechanical energy into electrical energy. At this point, the energy gets transmitted out into the power grid, where customers are free to convert the electricity back into virtually *any form* they choose!

Electricity is a unique resource in that it can be converted into virtually any purpose we seek. We use cell phones to convert electric power into radio signals to speak with people somewhere else on the planet at the speed of light. We convert it into light, into sound energy through radios, into images and sound via television, and into hot and cold air via heaters, air conditioners, and refrigerators. We convert it into motion with motors and information via computers. Dentists use electricity to create X-rays. We use electricity to probe the structure of matter with electron microscopes. Medical specialists locate tumors with MRI machines. Cinemas project three-dimensional movies for us to watch. Supercomputers figure out your DNA sequence electronically. And on and on, the uses of electricity are as limitless as the human imagination, to the point that electricity has become one of the greatest extensions of the human mind.

The overall point here is that the discovery of electricity was one of the universe's greatest gifts to humankind, allowing us to harness the truly magical power of the electron. To this day, I think electricity and electromagnetics represent magic in its purest form. The reader may question why I'm devoting so much space to this topic, but I feel it serves as a great focal point to draw attention to the power that the master architect of the universe has left for us to discover and harness for the betterment of humanity. No other single invention in the history of humankind even comes close in comparison in terms of improving the quality of human life and spurring global industrial revolution.

Electricity has also gotten me in trouble. I was booted from church camp in fourth grade for showing another camper how to short out the power to the entire camp. I told him to put a glove on, put a plastic bag over it, put one end of a wire on the neutral bus, and then look away while touching the other end to the 240-volt rail of a circuit-breaker panel. The camp director (whom I am good friends with to this day) had us both stacking firewood until they could contact our parents to notify them of our impending expulsion and arrange for someone to take us on the four-hour drive home! (Kids, don't try this at home.)

FASCINATION WITH MODERN ENERGY

Just five miles north in the town of Zion, Illinois, there was a nuclear power plant with two 1,040-megawatt Westinghouse pressurized water reactors, commissioned in 1973, breaking the 1 billion watt threshold for a single generator. Let's not forget that just two years earlier, Gene Cernan and Jack Schmidt were the last men to walk on the moon's surface. These must surely have been heady times with both the space age and the nuclear age simultaneously peaking! Much of this excitement about the present and high hopes for the future still persisted well into my childhood. Even at my young age, I knew that at more than 2 billion watts of output, it was nearly three times as powerful as its coal-burning counterpart and produced more than one-third of Chicago's electric power needs. I knew nuclear energy was the most modern form of energy, and with it came a certain mystique that provoked immeasurable curiosity in me.

The now demolished Zion Nuclear Station's Unit 2 generator rotor, a 200,000-pound electromagnet that spun at thirty times per second inside the blue generator behind me, supplied electricity to the Chicago metropolitan area for three decades. At 1.04 billion watts, this single machine produced the power of the world's largest locomotive engines 211 times over, or enough power for about half a million homes.

On the playground at school after touring the coal plant, I asked other children where their parents worked. I had hoped that one day I would find someone whose dad worked at the secretive, strictly off-limits Zion nuclear plant so I could get an insider's tour of the gargantuan facility. Honestly, I was somewhat scared of the place, as the average Zion resident was. I never knew if it was going to blow up one night and shoot out radiation that would kill me and my family, but my curiosity was much too strong. During school, we had to go through evacuation drills and memorize protocol in the event of a nuclear disaster. This added to the sense of intrigue about the facility. A fellow fourth grade student named Charles Fossler had a dad who was an instrumentation technician at the plant. His father, Al, was also a patient of my grandfather, a well-respected chiropractor in the community. After getting to know Charles better, I was able to charm him into asking his dad to give us fourth-grade boys a tour. It was one of the most amazing experiences of my life to go inside of this massive facility and experience two 1.5-million-horsepower machines screaming away, producing enough power for a large portion of downtown Chicago. My mind was blown and the stage set for what would become a deeply satisfying career in the electric power industry.

The utility that owned the Zion plant, Commonwealth Edison, had about fourteen or fifteen power stations throughout the state of Illinois. For some reason, they assigned the designation of "Station 22" to the Zion plant. I never really understood why they'd chosen that number, but knowing what I know today, I suppose the architects who designed the facility may have made the mystic connection between the holy city of Zion in Israel. There was the fact that the Hebrew alphabet has twenty-two characters and that people of the Jewish faith were very prevalent in the architecture, physics, and engineering professions. At the time of its debut in 1973, this plant was the biggest nuclear plant on the planet, comprising the largest piece of turbomachinery ever produced, stretching Westinghouse Electric Corporation's capabilities to their maximum at the East Pittsburgh electric works. This achievement came with great fanfare and prestige to a small bedroom suburb of Chicago that also (ironically) holds the dubious distinction of having been the world headquarters of the Flat Earth Society. I can imagine the designers would want to give it some sort of spiritual fingerprint and a nod to the original Zion in Israel by way of the number 22. Remember 11 + 11 = 22.

While finishing up writing, I was assigned to a project at the Quad Cities atomic power station exactly twenty-two years after I was badged as an intern at the Zion nuclear plant. The security staff member in charge of minting my new badge for unescorted access was ready to have me pose for a headshot but told me, "Wait! I've already got your picture in the system!"

I said, "How is that possible? I haven't worked for this company since I was a university student!"

He replied that he had a photo of me from when I was badged for Zion as a college intern. I was twenty-two years of age in the photo. Adding further to my astonishment, the Quad Cities plant had an address of 22710 and was at mile marker 22 on Highway 84. The next street north of the plant is 222nd Street. I love synchronicities like this.

I realized from a very young age that when the power went out, all life came to a screeching halt. The toaster no longer toasted. The freezer no longer froze. The air conditioner stopped conditioning. The TV stopped producing images and sounds. The radio ceased to produce music. It was lights out. Game over. Light some candles and pray the power comes back on soon. *Electricity must be some pretty important stuff*, I concluded. And it became my life's mission to figure out how it worked, and then I navigated through some of the world's toughest engineering schools on my path to becoming a globally respected expert on the subject matter. Now I continue to travel worldwide, fixing and installing power turbine-generator equipment. My childhood fascination with electricity made me appear as a bit of a strange kid, but my unusual obsession has led me into an educational and working path that would allow me to see and learn about the whole planet in a way that no other career could have possibly done for me.

Music Break: Give a listen to "Sae It"
by VonnBoyd on YouTube.

PERSONAL CONNECTIONS WITH NUMBERS

When my then-fiancée, Britta, and I were planning our wedding in 2009, we had already chosen as our venue the Gordon Lodge in Baileys Harbor, Wisconsin, because of its gorgeous location and ample facilities, making it perfect for the dream wedding. We wanted to have the wedding in the early summer, but because of high demand, were given one option in August, two options in September, and one option in October. Everything else was completely booked for the summer. August 22 was the earliest date and, having already realized the extensive chain of very positive events in my life that contained the number 22, we seized this auspicious date without delay.

A few years later, our only child, Erik, was born. He was 22 inches in length at birth. Neither the date Britta's water broke nor our son's length at birth could have been determined by us, so we took this undeniable appearance of the number 22 as still further validation that a higher power was active in directing the most important aspects of our lives. My son's kindergarten class was in room 222, a decision on which we had zero input or influence of any sort. His first-grade class had 22 students, including him. You just can't make this stuff up. We took this continuing accumulation of signs as a message, almost daring me to start documenting it. Life throws down the dots, and it's up to us to draw the lines connecting them.

This book is dedicated to understanding the antithesis of Socrates's famous quote, "The unexamined life is not worth living." You're reading about my method of appreciating life through deep, intense examination.

Soda advertisement using 11:11 Code concepts to sell product at a gas station in Wisconsin

During a business trip in 2016, I landed in Houston on a Friday night and reached my hotel at 10:45, just in time to get a seat at the hotel restaurant bar and order some dinner. As I waited for my food, I decided to fall prey to my nerd instincts and Google the prime factorization of the number 322, the month and day I was born, to see if by chance it held any hidden meaning. As a refresher to the reader, prime factorization takes a number and strips it down to all the prime numbers, which when multiplied, equal the number in question. For example, the number 221 breaks down to simply 13 x 17. There are no two whole numbers that when multiplied together, equal either 13 or 17. My birth date 322 breaks down to 2 x 23 x 7. I also noted that the sum of the digits 3 + 2 + 2 = 7. To me, this was a euphoric moment. Since antiquity, the number 7 has been regarded as a holy number, the number representing divine perfection. Seven is one of the most frequently used numbers in the Bible—the 7 days of creation of the Earth and heavens, and the 7 seals of revelation, among others. In fact, Psalm 12:6 talks about the number 7 as a number of purity.

"The words of the LORD are pure words: as silver tried in a furnace of earth, purified seven times."[89]

There are 7 *entrances* to the human head—two eyes, two ears, two nostrils, and the mouth. That's 2+2+2+1=7. From biology, we know that the human genome contains 46 chromosomes and a child receives 23 chromosomes from each parent in order to obtain a complete set of instructions for building a person.

In the autumn of 2017, I was invited to give an informal presentation to the math club at the College of Lake County (CLC) just outside of Chicago. I had earned my associate's degree in engineering at CLC, graduating in 1996. I presented on many of the mathematical topics in this book but with much less emphasis on the spiritual aspect. As it is a public institution, I had to keep it at least somewhat free of spiritual or religious messages. On my way to the campus, which is located off Washington Street, I noticed the street also has signs calling it County Road A-22. I never really thought about this or made any connections back in the 1990s, but this time I realized this was yet another literal and metaphorical sign along my life's path, my life's number 22, serving as my guide. So in line with my first school being located at 522 Belvidere Road, my first college also had 22 prominently in its address.

89 https://www.biblegateway.com/passage/?search=Psalm+12%3A6&version=NIV.

Photo of the "A22" sign directly across the street from the college. Address information taken from the CLC website.[90]

In the summer of 2016, we moved two hours north. My wife also spent her childhood in this very special and enchanting part of the world, so this was a very auspicious move for us, the culmination of a dream for both of us. During the closing of the purchase, we were of course signing stack after stack of papers. When presented with the plat of survey, I happened to notice that the property parcel number was a fifteen-digit number starting with 22-03 followed by eleven more digits. This was very symbolic to me as my birthday is 3/22, and because I had recognized 22 as my life number, this served as a surprise confirmation that this was the right move for us. We took it as God's blessing that we had made the right decision. Nearly three years later, we still feel that this was a great move.

In the fall of 2017, Gary, a friend and former mentor from my time working at General Electric, called me up and asked if I was available to run a project for him at a power station in Florida. After some discussion, I spoke with my employer and we agreed on contractual terms, which resulted in my going to work for two months on that project in Crystal River. I was working ten-hour night shifts for nine weeks away from my family in Wisconsin. It was a very lonely and depressing time for me, but financially and strategically, it ended up being one of the most important opportunities of my entire twenty-year-plus career. There were six turbine units being installed at a new power station, and the planned capacity was more than 1.68 billion watts of electricity, or enough power for more than 925,000 homes. I was assigned to work on steam turbine #1, and in order

90 https://www.clcillinois.edu/aboutclc.

to access the turbine, I had to ascend eight flights of stairs to an elevation of about fifty feet above ground. At each landing, the structural steel beams were joined together by eight bolts. Each bolt had been torqued to specifications, and the iron worker had put his or her initials and date next to each set. The worker had written, "DC 3-22-17," at least forty-five times on the entire structure. At that time, I was growing dissatisfied with my then-current employer and actively investigating opportunities elsewhere. Seeing my birthday so many times was quite *literally* the writing on the wall that it was time to leave my job and go to work permanently on this project.

One day after completing my initial assignment, the company contacted me and asked me to return to the project as a full-time Lead Engineer of electrical construction. Remembering the repeated occurrence of 3/22 on the staircase, I took this as a coded signature that this was meant to become part of my life path and somehow intuitively *knew* that if I took the risk to start my own company and accept this challenging assignment, I would be protected my spirit guides, whoever they are. I bravely, albeit tentatively, tendered my resignation from my previous company and started my own consulting business, vastly increasing my income (and risk). I also obtained a level of freedom and independence that would forever change my life. My first client was a global Japanese giant whose logo is a pyramid formed by three diamonds—Mitsubishi! The company logo is composed of three four-sided diamonds, for a total of 3 x 2 x 2 = 12 sides. All the equipment supplied to the project had the project number 00033 or just 33 emblazoned on the nameplate. The number 33 (11 + 11 + 11) will become increasingly relevant as the book progresses.

After accepting this assignment and forming my own consulting company, I moved my family down to Crystal River, Florida, into a house ten miles from the plant. Several weeks after settling in, we were walking the dog, and he stopped to do his doggie business in our front yard. I noticed a light green phone terminal box in our front yard with stickers designating it as box number 22387. Here we go again. The number 22 gave us a confirmation stamp that we were in the right place and gave me a sense that I was being watched over and protected. Every phone box on our entire street began with 22. None of the other streets in the 200-plus home subdivision had boxes beginning with 22. There are no coincidences. Delighted with our move to Florida, I sat in church one Sunday and picked up the Bible, and I happened to open up to Revelation 22:1, which says,

"Then the angel showed me the *river* of the water of life, as clear as *crystal*, flowing from the throne of God and of the Lamb."[91]

Remembering that 22 is my life number, I also noted that the words *crystal* and *river* were in the first verse of the last chapter of the last book of scripture. The city of Crystal River attracts tourists from around the world to admire the Eden-like, pristine natural springs of seventy-two-degree (that's equivalent to 22 degrees Celsius) fresh groundwater that surges out of the Earth from cerulean and turquoise springs and attracts the gentle manatees by the hundreds.

In 2017, I was casually browsing through my newsfeed on Facebook and noticed one of my friends from grade school named Melissa had posted a photo of herself and three other former classmates standing in front of Andrew Cooke Elementary School, where I had attended kindergarten through second grade. I happened to notice the number 522 above their heads as the address number on the side of the school building. At that point, I realized my first school had also contained my lucky number 22 in its address.

Again, yet another sign that my life's plan just might possibly have been carefully preplanned and scripted by *someone*. By itself, this discovery would have been written off as no big deal, but when taken together with the preponderance of other dots and after synthesizing all the interconnections between the dots, this took on a far deeper significance.

Six years prior to writing this book, I had just gone to work for a company where I ended up working with a guy named Mike. We really hit it off wonderfully, and to this day, we are very close friends. It wasn't until our

91 https://www.biblegateway.com/passage/?search=Revelation+22%3A1&version=NIV.

third year of working together that I happened to notice his birth date on his driver's license when we were at a bar in Texas and were carded by the bartender. His birthday was also March 22, but exactly ten years after I was born. Naturally, a long conversation ensued regarding this serendipitous discovery. As it would turn out, we were born ten years apart to the *hour*. I was born at noon central standard time, and Mike was born in the eastern time zone at one in the afternoon on 3/22, exactly ten years later. From this point forward, our friendship took a deeper turn, and it became apparent to us both that we were put in each other's lives not by chance but by a higher purpose.

There are far too many instances of randomly assigned airplane seats and hotel rooms being given to me by computers, without my input. In at least 40 to 50 percent of the instances, my seat numbers are in row 22, and at least 60 percent of the hotel rooms I get assigned to are a three- or four-digit number containing the number 22 or even 222. This has been happening at such a high frequency that it is almost comical. American Airline's computers randomly assigned 22B22M2 as my frequent flyer number. Note that B is the second letter of the alphabet as well. It's actually gotten to the point that my wife and I get surprised when this *doesn't* happen.

Two days after I started writing this chapter, I had to fly from Chicago to Ho Chi Minh City, Vietnam for a project. When the airline agent weighed my bag, it came to 22.1 kilograms, even though I did not weigh it prior to leaving home. My first flight had me seated in seat 22H, and my second flight from Taipei, Taiwan, to Ho Chi Minh City had me assigned to seat 22G. Both were assigned randomly by the airline computer. As I sat at the gate looking at the plane I would be flying on from Chicago to Taipei, I noticed the number 22 was emblazoned on the flap for the front wheel of the landing gear. I simply couldn't see such synchronicities without having the unmistakable sensation that some invisible power was trying to indicate its presence to me—to the point of showing off. I took these numerological coincidences as a sign that my higher power was watching over me during this trip and that I was going to exactly the place I needed to be at that time. It also gave me a deeply comforting sense that the trip I was about to embark upon would have a deeper purpose than *just* going to work on electrical equipment. I began to shift my thoughts toward the divine purpose, carrying a sense of optimism and love to share with all whom I would come into contact with on the other side of the world. This was going to be a different kind of trip overseas.

My boarding pass for the trip from Taipei, Taiwan, to Ho Chi Minh City, Vietnam

In another mind-blowing synchronicity, I was working on the other side of the planet in Indonesia and felt an urge to just text Mike and ask how things were going. He texted me back and said, "Dude, look what time it is." I saw that it was 10:22 p.m. my time, which corresponded to 8:22 a.m. his time back in the United States. I told him about the grade school I had gone to in the Chicago area and having noticed the 522 on a sign in the group photo, above the three ladies' heads. He told me to call him immediately. When I called, he was clearly shaken. He said that I wouldn't believe this but that he also went to a school that was on Belvidere Road (1,200 miles away from my school and ten years after I was in grade school) and that the address was also 522. Cue the *Twilight Zone* music.

So there I was, 9,000 miles away from Mike, thought of him and texted at 10:22 without ever considering the time. Then Mike reported he had been thinking of me at that exact moment also, but I had beaten him to the punch on texting. Then we discovered that we had gone to separate grade schools ten years and 1,200 miles apart. He also told me that he spent the vast majority of his childhood at a house located at 1111 Hickory Way, which was in an area with a zip code of 33327. This is interesting to me for three reasons. First, many of my childhood years were spent at my great-grandmother's house at 813 Hickory Street in Waukegan, Illinois. Second, his street address was 1111. Third, Mike's childhood zip code, 33327, is mathematically interesting in that the product of the first three digits equals the last two (3 x 3 x 3 = 27), which can be visualized as a three-by-three Rubik's cube with twenty-seven cubic cells. And don't forget we both share 3/22 as our birthday. At this point, we were both convinced that we had been put in each other's lives by some sort of higher providence and a deeper, richer story was unfolding each time we had one of our longer talks.

In another recent synchronicity event, I had been sent to Texas for business meetings. During my meetings, I was told I needed to immediately pack up and travel to Colorado to attend to an emergency work project where a customer had experienced the failure of a major piece of electrical equipment. As I got within five miles of the hotel, I noticed the mile marker signs were increasing with each mile (as one might logically expect)—217, 218, 219, etc. Right after I passed mile marker 222, I pulled into my hotel. Numbers with repeated digits seem to be a mode of communication between me and something else. I thought that was pretty awesome. But the next day at the plant, I was waiting in the maintenance manager's office to discuss the project with him and casually looking at the various glossy charts and posters on his wall. One of the posters was a map of all the ethanol-producing plants in the United States. I looked for the plant where I currently was and found the map had it numbered as 222 on the list. Seriously. So I am staying at a hotel at mile marker 222 and working at plant 222 out of all 241 possible ethanol plants in the United States. What are the chances of this happening? Computing 1/241 works out to about 0.4% probability.

I am now convinced that there are certain rules of conduct on *the other side* (heaven) where our ancestors and passed loved ones are desperately but patiently working to get our attention; however, the rules must state that the messages have to be both subtle and symbolic.

11:11 Synchronicity—The Beginning

Merriam-Webster's online dictionary defines the term synchronicity as:

> "the coincidental occurrence of events and especially psychic events (such as similar thoughts in widely separated persons or a mental image of an unexpected event before it happens) that seem related but are not explained by conventional mechanisms of causality—used especially in the psychology of C. G. Jung."92

Have you ever noticed certain events in your life that seemed a bit serendipitous in terms of their timing, location, or applicability to something

92 https://www.merriam-webster.com/dictionary/synchronicity.

that's going on in your life? Do you notice certain numbers keep showing up in your life in the oddest of circumstances?

I received my formal initiation into the 11:11 phenomenon when I was at a youth camp in second grade; the cabin leader, Kent McIlhany, wrote "11:11" on small pieces of tape and stuck them on the trash can, above the light switch, in the bathroom stall, on the top rail of the bunk beds, on the mirror, and generally all over the place. At the end of the eight-day camping period, virtually everyone in my cabin was noticing 11:11 all over the place at peculiar times. Many of us found ourselves looking at the clock at exactly 11:11 virtually every day, even waking up from a deep sleep only to notice the clock at 11:11. At the time, it seemed like a really cool trick, but we had no reason to think anything deeper was going on, or that it would reactivate a major phenomenon later in life. Ever since that time, I still catch myself looking at the clock at exactly 11:11. In the process of writing this book, I was talking to my best friend, Wesley, who was in the same cabin more than thirty years ago and, to this day, fondly remembers the cabin leader's experiment on us young guinea pigs. On Facebook and other social media platforms, there are entire groups dedicated to sharing and discussing occurrences of 11:11, 22, 33, and other multiples of 11 and what it all means. I would find out during the process of writing this book that the man who got my cabin leader's generation started was a psychology teacher named Frank Milkent who had retired by the time I went through the same high school. He had told his students they would thank him in 40 years. That was about 37 years ago.

Don't believe me? Perform an internet search for "11:11 enlightenment" or "master numbers" and see what comes up in the top ten results! Here's a bit of trivia. As of January 2018, Facebook had more than 2.2 billion (or 22×10^8) active monthly users according to Wikipedia.[93] Facebook's net income for the year 2018 was $22.111 billion.[94]

Now that I am in my forties, I have come to realize that this was the start of a long and unabated series of events during which multiples of 11, such as 22 and 33, which are commonly referred to as master numbers in numerology, would become my awakening codes, and I had to embrace 22 in particular as my life number and enlightenment code. I never understood why until I wrote this book. The conclusions were *not*

93 https://newsroom.fb.com/company-info/.
94 https://www.macrotrends.net/stocks/charts/FB/facebook/net-income.

known prior to writing this piece. Virtually all discoveries were made during the writing process. It's hard to believe, but this is the absolute truth. Although the minor occurrences of 22 and other multiples of 11 in daily life are too numerous to recount here, I have made a point to leave out the minor occurrences such as receipts or car license tags with multiple master numbers on them and instead only list the major occurrences that cannot be categorized as random coincidence. Some readers may question my apparent obsession with these numbers showing up in my life, but I am more focused on finding out why *these numbers* appear obsessed with *my life*. Perspective matters.

CHAPTER 3
LIFE HACKING

Seasons of Life—Lessons from Real Trees

Okay, that's enough math for a while. Let's talk about the seasons. In places in the world where there are four distinct seasons, we can gain a lot of insight into our own life cycle by observing the cycle trees go through during the course of a year. In the spring, the trees sprout buds, which is a sign of birth. Summer represents youth and fertility, with leaves, flowers, fruits, and nuts being produced to attract pollinators and to scatter their seeds to give life to the next generation of trees. Autumn represents old age as the deciduous or broadleaf trees shed their leaves. It's similar to how we start to lose our hair and teeth in our golden years as death looms in the future. As the tree is at the peak of its life for the year, it puts on a beautiful grand finale of glorious fall colors, turning the forest into a virtual canvas of the great cosmic painter. Winter represents death. The tree goes into a dormant stage and growth either slows down or pauses altogether. The white snow reminds us of the silver hair of later life as well. Watching the cycle of broadleaf trees and plants in general gives us a beautiful reminder that we too have a finite life cycle and should cherish each season of our lives.

Trees represent one of Earth's most important resources. We derive lumber, fruit, nuts, firewood, and paper from them. We depend on them for pulp for making toilet tissue as well as the paper for this book. It comes down to what our intentions are. We depend to a large extent on trees for the vital oxygen we breathe as well as the removal of the toxic carbon dioxide we expel. Few things in this world have more diverse uses than trees. Everyone is familiar with trees of the forest variety, but they occur much more widely in real life, in places where we may not think of them as such.

Our nervous system is also similar to a tree. The trunk is the brain stem/spinal cord, and each of the 33 pairs (11 + 11 + 11) of vertebral nerves act as branches going out to communicate with the various regions of the body, branching off into smaller and smaller bundles of nerves, finally ending in sensory neurons distributed throughout the tissues and organs of the body.

Pay attention and make mental notes every time you see the number 33. By the time you reach the Appendix, you'll be amazed by where else this number shows up and the deeper implications of this phenomenon.

Similar analogies can be made to the other major systems of the body, such as the urinary, circulatory, respiratory, and lymphatic systems. All these systems utilize the tree as one of the most efficient distribution topologies known to nature. If you analyze the structure of a tree as compared to that of a lung, there are remarkable similarities—a trunk, branches (bronchi), twigs (bronchioles), and leaves (alveoli). Like virtually all processes in nature, there is a yin and yang, a balance and symmetry to be admired. The wooden tree inhales the carbon dioxide we exhale as waste while exhaling the oxygen that all animal life depends on, while our lung-tree performs the reciprocal process. This represents symbiosis at its finest—a perfectly designed system or balance and reciprocity. The lung is a tree fractal where the internal surface area (of the alveoli) is maximized, whereas a wooden tree is a tree fractal that maximizes the area of an external surface (the leaves), allowing the tree to harvest as much solar energy as possible while expending a minimum of the tree's resources. The exchange of carbon takes place between two trees—one rooted in the plant kingdom and the other in the animal kingdom. Nature loves trees.

If a Tree Falls in the Woods

In one of my favorite books, *Biocentrism*, by Robert Lanza, MD, he poses the age-old question, If a tree falls in the woods, does it make a sound? Lanza is asking a philosophical question as well as a question rooted firmly in physics. Our first visceral reaction is to say, "Yes, of course, it makes a sound, because every tree you've ever watched fall also made a sound." But on second thought, what really is *sound*? What if there was no ear within a thousand miles of the tree falling? Not the ear of an insect, an owl, snake, human, or any animal with the ability to hear. Does it still make a *sound* then?

The answer is very clever. It does not make a sound. Rather it simply creates a time-varying fluctuation in air pressure. Chew on that for a moment. Without an ear to convert the pressure oscillations into an electrical signal to send to a brain to interpret it as the experience of hearing a sound, the tree falling simply creates a wave of acoustic pressure variations.

According to Lanza:

> When someone dismissively answers, 'of course a tree makes a sound if no-one's nearby,' they are merely demonstrating their inability to ponder an event that nobody attended. They are finding it too difficult to take themselves out of the equation. They somehow continue to imagine themselves present when they are absent.[95]

Lanza makes a similar argument for the idea that the perception of light as having color is purely the result of consciousness. Without an eye to observe light, it is simply electromagnetic energy composed of a magnetic wave and an electric wave, traveling together in lockstep. Only through the mechanism of hitting a retina and being encoded into electrochemical nerve signals and then processed by the brain is this electromagnetic energy perceived as light. What we perceive as color is simply the eye's interpretation of the different frequencies of electromagnetic energy impinging upon the retina. To a dog, the human color spectrum is probably just a black-and-white grayscale palette. To the butterfly, it's probably something more beautiful than we can imagine since they have fifteen different types of color receptors versus our meager *three*! The electromagnetic spectrum is virtually infinite in its spread. The tiny snippet we are able to observe from 390 to 700 nanometers is such an incredibly small slice of the overall energy spectrum that it is essentially 0 percent of what is available to be observed. Even one million is still *exactly zero* percent of infinity. Repeat that to yourself a couple of times. Our visual spectrum is but the tiniest sliver of the overall electromagnetic spectrum, which seems virtually filled to overflowing with information at all frequencies.

95 Robert Lanza, *Biocentrism* (Dallas: Benbella Books, 2009).

What else is happening in the universe at all the other frequencies that we cannot see? This is why astronomers look at all frequencies, including infrared, visible light, ultraviolet, radio frequency, microwave, gamma wave, cosmic wave, and beyond. The tiny glimpse that we are able to see through our visible bandwidth is but a peep through the keyhole of the door to our universe.

Dr. Lanza's two books, *Biocentrism* and *Beyond Biocentrism,* are two of my favorites, and I would highly recommend them to anyone who enjoyed the current section as a discussion on the senses and how we perceive our external environment as our reality. I was surprised how a medical doctor was able to teach me more about understanding quantum physics than seven years of engineering school was able to do.

ELECTRICAL TREES

As an engineer and a lover of nature, I enjoy explaining how electrical energy flows in terms of tree topologies. Humankind has taken nature's lesson of efficiency and optimal distribution networks and designed many systems that follow a treelike design. Power leaves the beating hearts of our planet—the massive generators at our various types of power plants with electricity flowing through the power lines. These act as the vital arteries of our nation, as typically 138,000 to 765,000 volts of electricity get transmitted hundreds of miles across the country. The amount of voltage difference between any two wires of the three phases of these circuits is high enough to break down (ionize) the air and literally jump several feet, and thus, these must be kept many feet apart from each other and isolated from the tower structure.

When one state is lacking in power, electric power from a stronger neighboring region of the power grid surges through the wires to assist the neighboring region experiencing the deficit. We can envision the grid voltage as being represented by the depth of water in a large tank. The power generators are like pumps adding water to the tank, and the power users are the drains. If more power is being produced than used, the voltage rises. Similarly, the water level of the tank would likewise rise if the pumps contributed water at a faster rate than it was being drained off. As the water level rises, so does the pressure at the bottom of the tank. The higher the pressure, the higher the water's tendency to leak (at a higher flow rate too). A power outage in New York City would be akin to a major hole in the bottom of one side of the tank, and initially, a large wave of water from one side of the tank would rush to fill the void left near the leak. The power grid works in a similar fashion, with current always flowing from areas of higher voltage (electrical "pressure") to areas of lower voltage. Energy always seeks to find the lowest possible potential energy state whether we are talking about water, heat, electricity, or virtually any other form of energy.

But how can a power grid be like a tree? The extra-high-voltage (345–765 kV) wires stop at substations near major industrial and population centers, where it gets broken down via transformers to lower (but still *lethally high*) voltages such as 14,400–34,500–138,000 volts. Split into multiple circuits, it branches out dozens of miles farther to the nation's factories, cities, and towns. At the next stop, the power is broken down to lower voltages, such as 4,160 to 34,500 volts and branches into still more distribution feeder circuits to supply specific neighborhoods or industrial areas. Near these consumers, those voltages are broken down still farther into 120 to 480 volts so it can be utilized safely within homes and businesses. As you're probably realizing, each time voltage gets broken down to another lower level, the number of branch circuits increases dramatically! Inside the homes and businesses, these voltages are sent to various appliances and broken down to even lower voltages, such as 1 to 24 volts for usage at the circuit board level within specific appliances, computers, and cell phones. This remaining voltage is branched farther out into many more smaller networks at the circuit board level. On the circuit board, at the chip level the voltage gets broken down to even lower levels, going as low as tenths to hundredths of a volt where the power branches out into *thousands*, *millions*, or even *billions* more circuits within integrated circuits and microprocessors at a nano level where *machine thinking* is performed.

Electric power in the United States and the rest of the Americas fluctuates from positive to negative polarity sixty times every second because the rotating magnetic fields in the power plant generators flip from north to south and back again sixty times per second, giving rise to the term *alternating* current. Europe, Asia, Africa, and most of the remaining countries employ a fifty-cycle power grid frequency. Japan is the only country I am aware of that has portions of its power grid operating at either of the two frequencies, depending on geography. Computers and smart appliances need to *think* at a much higher frequency than fifty or sixty decision cycles per second. A deeper theme of this book is the fundamental nature of the numbers 5 and 6, and in the world's power grids, we see these numbers showing up as 5 x 10 and 6 x 10 for a 5-to-6 ratio between grid frequencies. For the moment, I'll draw your attention to the 5- and 6-pointed stars on the ball sculpture on the title page at the opening of the book, and we'll address this in deeper detail later. Toward the end, we will also look into pentagons and hexagons in the most basic molecular structures that are used to assemble DNA, the software program of life. Could it be that we are made of pentagons and hexagons at the molecular scale? Keep reading!

In most cases, the alternating power at the circuit board level is rectified to zero frequency (direct current or DC as found in a battery), and this DC power then goes on to excite a quartz jewel oscillator known in electrical engineering as a *clock*, which oscillates at billions of times per second and well into the gigahertz range. This clock is not used to tell time (at least not directly). Rather, this clock is used as a synchronizing metronome of sorts to tell logic circuits such as logic gates, registers, multiplexers, and flip-flops when to perform a calculation step, and the next click tells it to proceed to the next calculation and so on. It has the same role as the person on the rowing team to tell the team when to pull the oars simultaneously. When all the logic is complete and the problem is solved, the signals return back *up* through the series of network levels just the same as how our circulatory tree works. In the human body, the heart corresponds to the power generator, which is like a pump for electrons. The high-voltage transmission lines correspond to the aorta and other main arteries of the heart. The lower-voltage distribution networks represent our arterial capillaries. The microprocessor relates to the sophisticated internal processing that takes place at the cellular level in our bodies where DNA is the master software. The venous capillaries take the blood back through the vein tree, eventually returning to the heart through the vena cavae, completing the circuit, and the cycle continually repeats for the rest of your life.

OTHER NATURAL TREES

Trees occur in hydrology as well. Tiny streams of rainwater collect and form tiny creeks that join to form larger tributary streams and then small rivers, joining into major rivers such as the lengthy Mississippi or the mighty Amazon, and then the water returns back to the ocean. Did you know the Amazon River pushes out 216,000 cubic meters of water per second? Recall that 216,000 = 6 x 6 x 6 x 1,000. Keep this fact in mind. We will be delving deeper than virtually anyone else has gone into the mysterious number 666 later in this book, and it turns out that it may not be entirely evil as we have been conditioned to believe.[96]

Electrical currents also tend to follow treelike paths. When a high-voltage electrode is attached to a specimen of insulating material, such as a piece of wood, and the power is turned on, the electricity will follow a tree-like path, simultaneously probing all possible paths to ground, eventually burning through on the most efficient route. Nature defaults to tree-shaped networks as an optimal solution to distribution problems. Lightning strikes follow treelike paths through the sky as well. An internet search of the term "Lichtenberg figure" turns up some interesting examples of electrical trees in physics.

The old axiom that electricity always takes the easiest path is only partially true. Electricity takes *all* paths simultaneously, *all* the time, every time it's applied to a circuit. Think of a bucket with two leaks—one large and one small. Of course, water would leak through both holes, not just the bigger one. Clearly, more water will intrude through the bigger hole, but the point is that all holes cause leakage. The correct statement would be more as follows: Electricity takes *all* paths to ground, but the majority will follow the easiest path.

Long Circuits

Since the dawn of the electric age, we have been taught to avoid short circuits. After all, cartoons have shown Tom the cat getting smoked when Jerry the mouse puts the wrong two wires together, and this image is indelibly etched into the consciousness of virtually every kid who grew up looking forward to Saturday morning cartoons every week. And in the real world, there has been much unfortunate experience teaching us short circuits are bad. They happen in a flash. They cause fires and melt appliances. They kill people, and consequently, they allow electrical energy to pass from the high-voltage conductor to the neutral conductor without producing any useful work. All that is produced is a flash of light, a ball of

96 https://en.m.wikipedia.org/wiki/List_of_unusual_units_of_measurement.

fire, and usually some level of destruction—nothing beneficial happens. The trick with electricity is to trick it into taking longer, more complex and convoluted paths to get as much useful work out of it as possible, without letting the "magic smoke" out.[97]

In electrical engineering we started out with just simple circuits, such as a battery connected to a lamp. We obtained useful light, which helped humankind along on the path of life. But as we got cleverer and technology continued to develop, we learned to make our circuits more and more intricate. As the intricacy of electrical circuits increases, the more functionality we can pack into a given space. The point is that it would be easy to throw a wrench across the positive (+) and negative (-) terminals of a car battery, but what would that accomplish beyond a destructive flash that is over within microseconds? Then you're left with a melted wrench and a destroyed battery. We get the most out of circuits by lengthening the path between positive (+) and negative (-) as much and as elegantly as possible. Make your electrons jump through as many hoops as possible during their life—that wondrous trip from the positive (+) electrode of the battery back to the negative (-) one.

Why just toss biscuits at your dogs without first getting them to do tricks when you can make them sit up, shake, roll over, and give high fives first? This comes down to the fundamental concept of efficiency—getting the most out of the energy available from *any* given system while minimizing parasitic losses such as Ohmic heating because of current flowing through resistive circuit elements. Such is life.

FAMILY TREES

The decoding of the human genome around the turn of the millennium was easily one of the most important and profound of all humanity's greatest achievements as it finally gave us the ability to literally read our human software that had been a secret for all prior eternity as far as we know. Exploring one's own family tree and ethnic heritage can be one of the most rewarding experiences in life. As with most other things in life, the harder you work on it, the more you get out of the experience.

During my senior year of engineering school at the University of Illinois

97 In the power industry, we have a saying that when something blows up, it stops working because the magic smoke was let out. Everything electrical runs on this magic smoke. Our job is to keep the magic smoke inside the machines.

at Urbana-Champaign, I spent eight months as a foreign exchange student at the University of Örebro in Örebro, Sweden. About three hours west of Stockholm and two hours east of Värmland, it was also the county where my Swedish ancestors had once lived. Many of the place names in Sweden are descriptive. Örebro translates to "penny bridge," and Värmland works out intuitively to "warm land." In the late 1800s, a group of nine of my ancestors in my father's bloodline emigrated from Sweden to the United States, processed through Ellis Island, and ended up in the industrial city of Waukegan, Illinois. Oskar Söderquist, one of my dad's great-uncles, had tremendous foresight. Before he died, he wrote a twenty-page story about his life growing up in Sweden, taking the trip across the Atlantic, and starting their new lives in the United States. In his story he included hand-drawn maps of the village where he lived and dropped lots of small details and clues that would later be extremely helpful to me.

After a couple of months in my new host country, I had adjusted to the culture and my Swedish language skills were solid enough that I undertook genealogical research to track down any living relatives in the country and figure out where my ancestors' village was located so I could visit. The path was long and arduous, fraught with many disappointments and struggles, though punctuated by several massive breakthroughs that made it worth the burn. While many of my fellow exchange students spent their evenings and weekends partying and drinking, (I did my fair share of that too, don't worry!) I spent much of my free time at the local libraries and historical societies researching thousands of pages of books and countless files of microfiche records. My efforts were not in vain. As it turned out, in certain rural areas of Sweden there was a tradition of naming homes. One of the key details my ancestor Oskar had left was the name of their log cabin, *Lillerud*. During an appointment I had scheduled with a historian Orebro Stadsbibliotek library, I explained to him that the house was named Lillerud. After a few minutes, he excused himself from his office, asking me to wait patiently as he walked away. He returned about five minutes later with an old dusty book in his hands and blew a few decades worth of dust off the top. The book was a comprehensive compilation of all the homes in Sweden from that era. It had that classic "old book" smell and feel. The good news was that Lillerud was on the list. The not-so-good news was that there were a total of seven homes with that same name scattered in various areas around the country. The other positive news was that five of the seven were in Värmland, where my ancestors hailed from, so I knew I was getting warmer. Now the task was to determine which of the five Lilleruds in Värmland was the correct one!

Another key clue from the story was the name of the creek that supplied water to the wooden flour mill where my ancestors dragged sleds of grain to be milled into flour. I studied hundreds of detailed topographical maps at the city library, looking for clues on the same maps that the military uses for planning field exercises. By this method, I was able to pinpoint the village to be Ostra Glänne.

At this point, I sought to connect with genealogical and historical experts in Karlstad, the county seat of Värmland county, and was eventually placed in contact with the right people. I took a train to Karlstad one weekend and spent a couple of days doing genealogy research, and with the help of a good Samaritan named Barbro Södersten, I was able to add more than two hundred names to my family tree. Barbro turned up relatives going back as far as the year 1560! One of the great discoveries was a letter that the historian had filed under my family's last name. In the year 1976, a lady by the name of Ingrid Ehmer wrote a letter to my ancestors in Waukegan, seeking to learn what had happened to them after they emigrated to the United States. Her letter was turned back as *undeliverable* because my ancestors had moved from that address, and the letter was returned and filed at the county historical society in Sweden.

On a lark, I decided to make a phone call to the phone number listed on Mrs. Ehmer's letterhead, fully expecting to get someone else on the other end of the line. Much to my astonishment, Ingrid answered my call! As I explained who I was, why we were here, and how we were related, she was absolutely speechless. I tried in my best Swedish to explain to her that it was true and that we were indeed cousins, working up the family tree while rattling off all our common ancestors, starting back from our first common ancestor before the family was split across the Atlantic. To greatly compress a very rich and detailed story and not detract from the core narrative here, I traveled to Stockholm to meet her, her daughter, and all their children. It was such a wonderful experience, and her daughter, Kajsa, and her husband, Ulf, later attended my wedding in the United States in 2009. By now, you're familiar with how the numbers 22 and 23 have shown up at important points and places in my life. As it turns out, my cousin Kajsa has 22 in the last two digits of her mobile phone number and the house she lives in has a street address of simply "23."

Separately, I was able to get in touch with a man named Inge Nylin, who was approaching ninety years of age and had lived his entire life in Ostra Glänne. Inge was considered the most respected historian in the area where my ancestors had lived, and he was familiar with several of the families and geographic locations detailed in my ancestor's typewritten story. He recognized all of the names of the families listed in my ancestor's story and told me tales of many of the people my forefathers had known. He took me on a tour of the entire village, and I was able to visit Lillerud, my ancestors' humble abode. In Oskar's story the family home was described as a log cabin. When we stopped the car and knocked on the door, we explained to the startled homeowner who we were and why we had stopped by. We showed her the story written by Oskar and explained that this house used to be a log cabin. She excused herself for a moment and then returned with a photograph taken halfway through a renovation several years prior. At that point, half of the house had its current modern siding, and the other half was the original log cabin exterior! The property lines, apple trees, hills, forest lines—virtually everything matched the hand-drawn map from almost a hundred years prior. Inge continued down the road and took me to the old flour mill, which was in very dilapidated condition. One of the windows was broken out, and I was able to squeeze myself in. I toured around and admired the wooden wheels and cogs that had turned the huge millstone that had made the flour that fed my ancestors in the 1800s.

With deeper research twenty years later with my cousin Kajsa's help, I discovered that the flour mill was known as Mill 33, and the GPS coordinates were 59.6033 N + 13.2232 E.[98] Keep the number 33 under your hat. This substory is rich enough to warrant its own book, but there is a reason I am taking the time to tell this much of the story. I was very sad to hear that the mill had been razed a few years ago due to its dilapidated condition. I had always hoped to return one day and help finance its restoration and preservation, but I guess that just wasn't in the cards…

To review, we found my most distant relative who was born in the year 1560. It said in the church records that he immigrated to Sweden from Russia via Finland. This fact stuck with me for twenty years as being quite perplexing. In 2017, I ordered DNA testing through Ancestry.com, and the report confirmed much of the oral history of my family tree—showing

98 http://www.bygdeband.se/plats/63624/sverige/varmlands-lan/kil/frykerud/glanne-ostra/glanne-kvarn/.

large percentages of Scandinavian, British, German, and Czechoslovakian blood. Making the connections with my living Swedish cousins ushered in a new era of excitement for me, my family, and the cousins as we reconnected across the Atlantic. We are looking forward to when my young son Erik gets to meet his Swedish cousins who are very nearly the same age. What a wonderful legacy this is, one that I hope will continue indefinitely.

MELTING SAND

Silicon is one of the most useful elements to mankind and the second most abundant on Earth. Following the discovery that we could melt silica sands to produce glass, we learned how to create lenses with which we built the microscope to probe the microscopic domain, and similarly, the telescope to help us comprehend the infinitesimal mysteries of the macroscopic realms as well as the infinite grandeur of the cosmos. We also melted the sands of our planet to create silicon wafers with which we created artificial intelligence by means of the transistor and integrated circuits such as the central processing unit of a computer. We literally took raw materials of the Earth and created artificial intelligence that is potentially billions of times more intelligent than humans in terms of raw processing power and speed. Though as of this moment, while we have not been able to replicate sentience, emotion, true imagination, and spirituality, we have literally taught dirt how to think. Let that set in. Years ago, every molecule of the smart phone in your possession was nothing but a deposit in the planet's crust!

From melting sand, we have been able to create digital cameras that capture the moments of our lives as well as surveillance cameras that watch our every move and send those images to be stored (remembered!) on computer hard drives possibly hundreds of miles away. And the worst of them automatically mail you a $200 speeding ticket with a picture of you and your car. Silicon-based intelligence already regulates certain human behaviors and enforces broken laws. The concerns of privacy in the era of the police surveillance state are very concerning.

Just as the microscope has allowed us to visualize molecules, we built up our scientific knowledge to a certain level, and then we improved the microscope so we could see atoms. We answered a lot of questions but created many more once we learned to smash atoms and study subatomic particles. Then our ability to probe the structure of matter at the subatomic level got stronger, answered more questions, and created still more questions. This highlights the fractal nature of our physical universe. There probably is no lower limit to how finely we can divide matter. The deeper we probe, the more questions than answers we create. Humankind experiences a similar problem as we continuously expand our abilities to probe the boundaries of our universe. Stronger telescopes always show the universe is infinitely bigger than previously thought. God has purposely left the smallest and greatest mysteries of creation beyond our ability to satisfy our obsession to be able to measure or quantify the micro- and macroscopic mysteries and limits of our existence.

As we probe the structure of matter with ever-increasing microscope power, we discovered that all atoms consist of a nucleus at the center and electrons orbiting it. As we explored the cosmos with the telescope, we discovered that planets orbit a sun. There seems to be a fundamental structural order that pervades the universe at these two extremes of scale.

As I admire these similarities, I ask the following question:

Is this just by chance, or is the universe trying to exhibit a silent but omnipresent intelligence?

If we have intelligence and we came from the universe, then logically, the universe must *itself* possess an inherent intelligence, right?

As above, so below. As within, so without.

CHAPTER 4

SEEING 22 EVERYWHERE

Following discussions with both Albert Einstein and Wolfgang Pauli, psychologist Carl Jung believed there were parallels between synchronicity and aspects of relativity theory and mechanics. Jung believed life was not a series of random events but rather an expression of a deeper order, which he and Pauli referred to as *unus mundus*. This deeper order led to insights that a person was both embedded in a universal wholeness and that the realization of this was more than just an intellectual exercise but also had elements of a spiritual awakening. From the religious perspective, synchronicity shares similar characteristics with an intervention of grace. Jung also believed that in a person's life, synchronicity served a role similar to that of dreams, shifting a person's egocentric conscious thinking to greater wholeness.[99]

As defined by the *Oxford English Dictionary*, catch-22 means "a supposed law or regulation containing provisions which are mutually frustrating; a set of circumstances in which one requirement, etc., is dependent upon another, which is in turn dependent upon the first." One example that popped into my mind when I first explained catch-22 was the need to have a driver's license in order to get to the Department of Motor Vehicles to take your driver's license exam. Another example is the desire to be rich in order to hire enough lawyers to avoid paying taxes. Although catch-22 has come to be used in a more general sense to mean "an absurd predicament" or "a tricky and frustrating rule or restriction" (such as having to

99 Igor Limar, "Carl G. Jung's Synchronicity and Quantum Entanglement: Schrödinger's Cat 'Wanders' Between Chromosomes," *NeuroQuantology* 9, no. 2 (2011): 313.

pay taxes on money you withdraw from your retirement fund in order to pay taxes), the true catch-22 presents not just an annoying impediment but a solid brick wall.[100]

Catch-22 is one of those rare colloquial phrases whose origin is known with absolute certainty. It was coined by the American novelist Joseph Heller in 1961 as the title of his novel *Catch-22*, based on his experiences as a US bomber pilot in Europe in World War II. The central character in the book is the B-25 bombardier Yossarian, whose all-too-accurate perception of the futility and insanity of war introduces him to what Heller dubbed catch-22 (*catch* being used here in the sense of a *snag* or *hidden trap* in military regulations).

The novel *Catch 22* was a huge hit in the 1960s and remains one of the seminal late-twentieth-century works of literature. The phrase catch-22 immediately entered the lexicon of a society beset by an increasingly Kafkaesque bureaucracy.

Interestingly, the number 22 in the title was not Heller's original choice. An early excerpt of the novel published in a magazine was actually titled "Catch 18," but the publication of the very popular novel *Mila 18* by Leon Uris during the same period necessitated the change to *Catch-22*. Even more interestingly—or perhaps most interestingly of all—Heller's book was released on 11/11/1961.[101]

Have you ever noticed that any time you see a new clock for sale, the hands are almost always in the 10:10 position? Pause for a moment and perform an internet search for the word *clock*. Select *images*. What do you see?

Now try this. Grab your smart phone and start to compose a text message. Scroll through and find a clock or alarm clock emoji. Does it have a clock with the hands at the 10:10 position? All the clock emojis on my iPhone have 10:10 indicated! Virtually all the clocks in any sort of advertisement or other application for the general public to view invariably have hands placed in the 10:10 position with very few counterexamples. Why? I don't have an authoritative answer, but my gut tells me that it's for good psychological reason. The hands resemble a smile on the clock face! This works upon our subconscious human attraction toward *happy* things.

100 http://www.word-detective.com/2011/10/catch-22/.
101 https://www.onthisday.com/events/november/11.

Remember this next time you're shopping for a new clock or wristwatch or composing a text message!

During the course of a twelve-hour period, how many times do the minute and hour hands cross? For the average person, the answer isn't as obvious as it may seem! Most people would think they would cross 24 times since there are 24 hours in a day, right? The answer is that the minute hand and hour hand cross eleven times every twelve hours, so in a twenty-four-hour day, they cross 11 + 11 times for a total of 22. The mathematical explanation can be found in Appendix C.

The number 322 is quite an interesting number to me on a personal level as well as in many other instances.

Light from one of the main stars in Draco, specifically Omicron Draconis, takes 322 years to reach our planet. The shape of the Draco constellation closely resembles a snake in an S shape with a clearly discernable head.

The highly secretive fraternity at Yale University known as Skull and Bones has a skull and crossbones as its logo with the number 322 inscribed below the bones. The fraternity meets in room 322 at the university. In the context of the Skull and Bones fraternity, the number 322 is thought to refer to 322 BC, the year that the Greek orator Demosthenes died, a milestone that signaled ancient Athens beginning its transition from democracy to plutocracy or rule by the wealthy minority. There may be an implication of the group's belief that America should follow a similar course and surrender the responsibilities of government exclusively to the wealthy.

Further fascinating information about the secret fraternity is how significant numbers that we have also discussed (aside from 322) can be seen in relation. George W. Bush is a member of Skull and Bones (a spin-off of the Brotherhood). July 6, 1946 was his birthday. It can be reduced to the power number 33 (7 + 6 + 1 + 9 + 4 + 6 = 33), which is thrice eleven. The following four names are composed of eleven letters: George W. Bush, Adolf Hitler, World War I, and World War II.[102]

Swinging back to 322, the ancient Greek philosopher Aristotle died in the year 322 BC. In the same year, Ptolemy brought Alexander the Great's body to Memphis, Egypt, and buried him in a golden sarcophagus.

102 http://www.dimension1111.com/1111-numbers-9-11-wtc.html.

President Obama elected to have a nonstandard presidential portrait with him situated in a garden. A close inspection of his watch seems to reveal a time of 3:22. I wonder what meaning if any is associated with this symbology, or was it just a randomly chosen time?

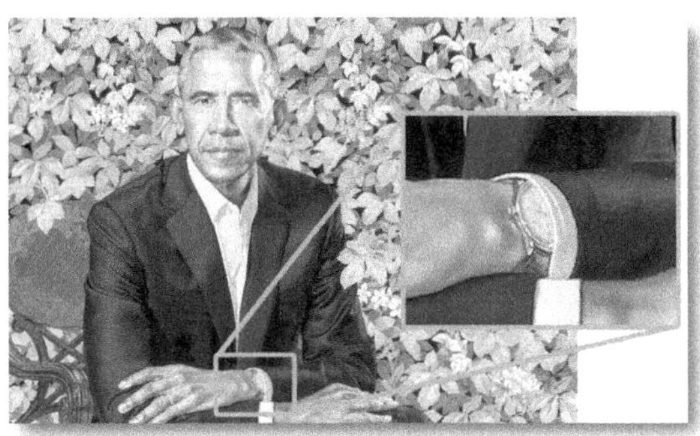

The *Georgia Guidestones* is a granite-stone monument erected on 3/22/1980 by a man operating under the pseudonym of Robert C. Christian, sometimes affectionately referred to as the American Stonehenge. Rumors abound regarding his true identity and affiliation, many conjecturing that he was part of a secret society such as Skull and Bones and/or the Illuminati, both Luciferian secret societies commonly ascribed to by the elite ruling class. Skull and Bones would be a logical fit, given the erection date of 3/22. Otherwise, it was a 1/365 = 0.27% probability of the event randomly falling on that day of the year. The monument has inscriptions in eight different languages and attempts to advise humanity on how to save the planet, which includes—perhaps disturbingly so—the concept of population control. It also clearly advocates the completion of the New World Order. Interestingly, the monument has a 7/8-inch hole drilled through the capstone that focuses a sunbeam on the center column and, at noon, pinpoints the day of the year.[103] By itself, that's not too remarkable, until you convert 7/8" to metric, where you find the wonderful result that the hole is 22.22 millimeters in diameter, or 2 x 11.11 mm. Similarly, a 7/16" hole works out to 11.11 mm.

The inscription on the monument reads as follows:

1. Maintain humanity under 500,000,000 in perpetual balance with nature.
2. Guide reproduction wisely—improving fitness and diversity.

103 https://www.wired.com/2009/04/ff-guidestones/?currentPage=1

3. Unite humanity with a living new language.
4. Rule passion—faith—tradition—and all things with tempered reason.
5. Protect people and nations with fair laws and just courts.
6. Let all nations rule internally resolving external disputes in a world court.
7. Avoid petty laws and useless officials.
8. Balance personal rights with social duties.
9. Prize truth—beauty—love—seeking harmony with the infinite.
10. Be not a cancer on the Earth—Leave room for nature—Leave room for nature.

Recommended listening: "Vibration of the Fifth Dimension" by Vesna Dharma

Occurrences of 22 in Popular Culture

While this book is dedicated to expounding on deeply significant aspects of numbers and numerology, I think it is important to have a little bit of fun as well. In that spirit, I wanted to include some trivia tidbits for your amusement and/or amazement. This section is simply a tabulation of random facts about the number 22, borrowed from Wikipedia:[104]

In Jay-Z's song "22 Two's," he rhymes the words too, to, and two 22 times in the first verse.

- The element osmium is the densest naturally occurring element, with a density of just more than 22 grams per cubic centimeter.
- "22" is a song by Lily Allen on the album *It's Not Me, It's You.*
- *22 Dreams* is a song and album by Paul Weller. The album contains 22 songs on it.
- The Norwegian electronica project *Ugress* uses 22 as a

104 https://en.m.wikipedia.org/wiki/22_(number).

recurring theme. All four albums feature a track with 22 in the title.

- "22" is a song by Taylor Swift on her fourth album, *Red.*
- "The Number 22" is a song by Ashbury Heights on the album *The Looking Glass Society*.
- Cubic 22 was a Belgian techno duo.
- "22" is a song by the English alternative rock band Deaf Havana on their album *Old Souls.*
- In British bingo calling tradition, 22 is referred to as "Two Little Ducks."
- *Revista 22* is a magazine published in Romania.
- "Twenty Two" (February 10, 1961) is episode 17 of season 2 (February 10, 1961) of the 1959–64 TV series *The Twilight Zone*, in which a hospitalized dancer has nightmares about a sinister nurse inviting her to room 22, the hospital morgue.
- The Canadian comedy series *This Hour Has 22 Minutes* is described as "an iconic comedy show armed with sardonic sketches, biting parodies, and an unrelenting skewering of the weekly news. Starring Mark Critch, Cathy Jones, Susan Kent, and Trent McClellan, *22 MINUTES* has been at the forefront of provocative satire for more than a quarter of a century, targeting politics, culture, and world events."[105]
- Traditional tarot decks have 22 cards with allegorical subjects. These serve as trump cards in the game. (Note the Trump reference.) The Fool is usually a kind of wild card among the trumps and unnumbered, so the highest trump is numbered 21. Occult tarot decks usually have 22 similar cards that are called Major Arcana by fortune-tellers. Occultists have related this number to the 22 letters of the Hebrew alphabet and the 22 paths in the Kabbalistic Tree of Life.
- The movie *Mile 22* debuted on the silver screen later in the month of August 2018. The movie plot features an elite paramilitary team called Overwatch that is tasked with

105 https://www.cbc.ca/22minutes/.

transporting a police officer named Iko Uwais with vital information about a potential terrorist attack 22 miles across Southeast Asia from the American embassy to an airfield.[106]

- Mafia boss James "Whitey" Bulger was arrested on June 22, 2011 and imprisoned for his role in the murder of 11 people.[107]
- San Francisco-based rap artist Berner released an album titled *11/11* in 2018.[108]
- Garry Kasparov is widely considered to be the greatest chess player of all time. He was crowned the thirteenth World Chess Champion in 1985 at age 22, the youngest in history to hold the global crown, and he held the title for fifteen years until 2000.[109]
- Hillary Clinton's personal email address, which got her a large amount of undesired attention, was hdr22@clintonemail.com. She testified in front of the Benghazi commission on October 22, 2015, to discuss the September 11, 2012, attack. The number 22 doesn't always portend good things.
- The .22-caliber long rifle, often simply referred to as a 22, is the most popular caliber of ammunition in the world, according to Wikipedia. The first gun I ever fired was my grandfather's .22 rifle during target practice on an array of empty soda cans when I was just eight years old. The bullet diameter is actually 0.223 inches, and the round owes its origin to the Flobert BB caps of 1845 through the .22 Smith & Wesson cartridge of 1857.[110]

As a general rule of thumb in American society, the average student graduates high school at age 18 and completes their bachelor degree in 4 years, typically ready to enter the work force at about age 22.

106 https://www.imdb.com/title/tt4560436/plotsummary?ref_=tt_ql_stry_2.
107 https://www.chicagotribune.com/news/nationworld/ct-whitey-bulger-girlfriend-sentencing-20160428-story.html.
108 https://en.wikipedia.org/wiki/Berner_(rapper)#cite_note-Discogs_rec-16.
109 https://www.uschesschamps.com/battle-legends-kasparov-vs-short/information/meet-legends.
110 https://www.range365.com/22-rimfire#page-4.

THE NUMBER 22 IN SPORTS

In the process of writing, I discovered that both international football (soccer) and American football have 11 players per team for a total of 22 people on the field.[111] But wait! There's more. The international regulation size soccer ball is 69 cm in circumference.[112] Divide this by pi (π = 3.1415), and you will see that the diameter is 22 centimeters. Now we see that one of the most popular sports on the planet has 22 players and a ball that is 22 cm across. Germans refer to a penalty kick as the *Elfmeter* (eleven-meter) kick.[113] Nothing to see here. I'm sure it's just another random coincidence. You may disagree with this dismissal by the time you're done reading this.

Atlanta Hawks wingman Vincent Carter became the 22nd player in NBA history to reach the 25,000-point threshold in his career on 11/22/2018 during Atlanta's 124–108 loss to the Toronto Raptors.[114] Carter again made history in January 2019 when he announced his plans to continue playing into his 22nd season, which would be the longest continuous NBA career in league history.

Tiger Woods jumped back into the headlines on April 14, 2019, when he won his first major golf event in 11 years, and it had been 22 years since he'd won a Masters tournament. His win resulted in a $22 million sponsorship contract with Nike.[115]

On Friday August 9, 2019, at the age of 22, gymnast Simone Biles became the first athlete in history to successfully land a "double-double dismount." The word "double" implies the number two, and here we have it twice, effectively making a "2-2" dismount as the 22-year-old became the first to pull off this feat of acrobatic agility.[116] August 9th was the 221st day of the year in 2019.[117]

Super Bowl LIV (54) took place on 2/2/2020 and the Kansas City Chiefs enjoyed victory as their coach Andy Reid celebrated his 222nd career win. Furthermore, this was his 2nd time with his team playing in the super

111 https://ussoccer.app.box.com/s/xx3byxqgodqtl1h15865/file/296741999141.
112 https://resources.fifa.com/mm/document/footballdevelopment/refereeing/02/90/11/67/lawsofthegame2017-2018-en_neutral.pdf.
113 Annemarie Schimmel, The *Mystery of Numbers* (Oxford: Oxford University Press 1993), 191.
114 http://www.espn.com/nba/story/_/id/25344641/vince-carter-atlanta-hawks-reaches-25000-career-points.
115 https://www.sunjournal.com/2019/04/14/tiger-woods-makes-masters-15th-and-most-improbable-major/.
116 https://www.dailymail.co.uk/news/article-7346135/Simone-Biles-22-gymnast-land-double-double-dismount-balance-beam.html.
117 https://www.calendar-365.com/day-numbers/2019.html.

bowl—the first time was in 2005. This date gathered a lot of attention on social media due to the profusion of "2222" and the fact that 02/02/2020 is palindromic, meaning the number is the same whether you read it left to right or the reverse.[118]

Before shifting gears from the subject of sports, I'd like to leave you with some interesting facts about baseball legend Babe Ruth, who is widely regarded as one of the greatest baseball players of all time. Would it shock the reader to know that his career spanned 22 seasons and tallied 2,214 runs batted in (RBIs)?[119] Ruth also had a career-earned run average of 2.28.[120] Where I have found greatness, I have often found the number 22. Closing out the subject of baseball, a bit of trivia is in order. The longest baseball game in history spanned a total of 33 innings. The record-setting game in 1981 between the Rochester Red Wings and the Pawtucket Red Sox took a total of eight hours spread across two days to complete.[121]

Fun fact: (and this is the absolute *last* fact that was added to the book on 2/17/20 just before surrendering my manuscript to the book design team) The winner of the Daytona 500 race that took place on 2/16/20 was won by Denny Hamlin driving car #11. As if that wasn't awesome enough, recall that on 11/11/19 he dominated the NASCAR Cup Series race at Phoenix Raceway to clinch a berth in the following weekend's championship finale. His Phoenix win tied him with NASCAR Hall of Famer Bobby Isaac for 22nd on the all-time wins list at stock car racing's highest level.[122] Well done, sir!

11+11 IN HOLLYWOOD AND TELEVISION

Watching a movie one night, it struck me to rewind and pause it at the opening screen with the Paramount Pictures logo. I'd noticed the arc of stars above the mountain and, on a whim, decided to count them. Since I began writing, I started counting virtually everything. Would you believe that there are 22 stars? Think about it. A very large portion of the films you have watched and enjoyed during your life started with this banner of 22 stars. What does it mean? Pure coincidence? Synchronicity? Something deeper?

118 https://en.wikipedia.org/wiki/Andy_Reid
119 https://www.baseball-reference.com/players/r/ruthba01.shtml.
120 http://www.baberuthcentral.com/babe-ruth-statistics/babe-ruth-the-pitcher/.
121 https://www.milb.com/pawtucket/ballpark/longest-game.
122 https://dennyhamlin.com/

Go ahead. Count them!

In 1916, film producer Adolph Zukor put 22 actors and actresses under contract and honored each with a star on the logo.[123]

I was casually researching the history of the red carpet used in Hollywood when I made another fascinating discovery: the red carpet tradition began in 1922 (22 = 11 + 11) at the Egyptian Theater when Sid Grauman hosted the debut of *Robin Hood*, starring Douglas Fairbanks, the "First King of Hollywood." Today, the red carpet is probably the most widely-recognized symbol of the Academy Awards.[124] Who would have guessed there would be a connection to the 11:11 Code? Certainly not me.

In the 2004 movie *National Treasure*, I was completely shocked during the scene where one of the actors analyzed the clock on Independence Hall on the backside of a $100 bill. The clock reads 2:22. This is only true on the series-2003 $100 bills. The current $100 bill shows a time of 10:30.[125] According to Uri Geller's website, if you look at the back of a $100 bill, you will notice that the windows on each side of Independence Hall have 11 windows on each side for a total of 22 windows—the 11:11 Code.[126] I strongly urge the interested reader to read through Geller's website. It's a gold mine of information for any 11:11 enthusiast.

123 http://ocgirl.net/wp-content/uploads/image/paramount/paramount-2.jpg.
124 http://behindthescenes.nyhistory.org/red-carpet/.
125 http://mentalfloss.com/article/533668/facts-about-national-treasure-movie-nicolas-cage.
126 https://www.urigeller.com/are-your-eyes-attracted-to-11-11/.

HAPPY BIRTHDAY, TWO-TWO!

The ubiquitous song "Happy Birthday to You" first appeared in print in 1911 in the book *The Elementary Worker and His Work.* One of the most widely recognized songs on the planet was published in 1922 in a book titled *The Everyday Song Book,* copyrighted by Warner-Chappell Music company, and it is estimated that they collected $2 million per year in royalties. On September 22, 2015, Judge George H. King ruled that the song was no longer eligible for copyright protections, placing it in the public domain for free usage. The copyright was born with a 22 and died with a 22.[127]

And what good is a birthday party without ice cream? Is there anyone on Earth who doesn't love a Klondike ice cream bar? What would you do for one?? As it turns out, the Klondike bar was invented in 1922 and for years could only be enjoyed at Isaly's grocery markets in Pittsburgh and Ohio. The blue star seal on the logo has, believe it or not, 22 points. This is very similar to what we saw in the number of stars in the Paramount Pictures logo.[128] But why 11 + 11? My research was unable to unearth the reason!

MICHAEL JACKSON

Michael Jackson was awarded Artist of the Century on his 22nd American Music Award on January 22, 2002.[129] His third child, Prince Michael Jackson II (a.k.a. Blanket) was born on February 22, 2002 (2/22/2) at Sharp Grossmont Hospital in La Mesa, which is near San Diego in Southern California, through surrogacy.[130] The King of Pop released a film *Moonwalker* in 1989, which was made on a $22 million budget and remained number one on Billboard's Video Chart for 22 weeks.[131] On December 22, 1993, Jackson professed his innocence against charges that he sexually abused Jordan Chandler. One month later on January 22, 1994, Jackson agreed to pay the Chandlers $22 million in restitution for the alleged abuse.[132]

On June 25, 2009, the Los Angeles Fire Department received a 911 call at

127 http://copyright.nova.edu/happy-birthday/.
128 https://www.ydr.com/story/life/2018/05/19/unwrapping-klondike-bars-history-pittsburgh/625843002/.
129 https://kidskonnect.com/people/michael-jackson/.
130 https://www.burrosabio.net/michael-blanket-jackson-short-biography/.
131 https://en.wikipedia.org/wiki/Moonwalker.
132 https://www.rollingstone.com/culture/culture-features/michael-jackson-child-sexual-abuse-allegations-timeline-785746/.

12:22 p.m. stating that Jackson was unconscious and had stopped breathing. The musical icon who defined my generation never again woke up.[133] For Michael Jackson, the number 22 seemed to follow him when he was at his best and at his worst. It seems to be a number that is attracted to extremes as well as to people and events that have had a powerful influence on humanity for better or for worse. In Jackson's case, it was both.

In another tragic end to an extremely talented and beloved artist, Whitney Houston's eponymous album was one of the top-selling albums of all time with sales exceeding 22 million copies. That's 11+11 million.[134]

Iron Maiden

In their album *The Number of the Beast*, Iron Maiden has a song titled "22 Acacia Avenue." The album was released on 3/22, my birthday.[135] Music press reports told stories of unexplained phenomena occurring during the sessions at Battery Studios, such as lights turning on and off by their own accord and recording gear mysteriously breaking down. These odd occurrences climaxed when album producer Martin Birch was involved in a car accident with a minibus transporting a group of nuns, after which he was presented with a repair bill for £666.[136] I researched far and wide to try to understand if there was a deeper significance to the choice of 22 Acacia Avenue for track #4, but all I could find was that 22 Acacia Avenue in England is similar to 123 Main Street in the United States. The idea was that it was just a typical, unremarkable suburban address of which there are at least sixty instances throughout cities in the United Kingdom.[137]

BBC News posted an article summarizing the results of a study of fifteen Acacia Avenues in England, where hundreds of people were interviewed. The road name has become a byword for suburban life after use in sitcoms, films, song titles, and cartoons. The survey found Acacia Avenue workers on average kept the same job for 11 years, earned around the national average wage of £22,500, and took 21 minutes to get to work.[138]

As we will discuss next, I have evidence to suggest that the acacia tree may very well be the Tree of Life mentioned in Genesis 3:22, which says:

133 http://articles.latimes.com/2013/apr/30/local/la-me-ln-michael-jackson-cancer-patient-20130430.
134 https://en.wikipedia.org/wiki/Whitney_Houston_(album)
135 https://ultimateclassicrock.com/iron-maiden-number-of-the-beast-album/.
136 https://en.m.wikipedia.org/wiki/The_Number_of_the_Beast_(album).
137 https://en.wikipedia.org/wiki/Acacia_Avenue.
138 http://news.bbc.co.uk/2/hi/uk_news/england/5198502.stm.

> And the Lord God said, Behold, the man is become as one of us, to know good and evil: and now, lest he put forth his hand, and take also of the Tree of Life, and eat, and live forever.

The ancient Egyptians regarded the acacia tree as the vessel that contained the spirit of the god Osiris.[139] A concoction similar to the Amazonian entheogenic tea known as ayahuasca was made from the roots of the acacia tree and mixed with the crushed seeds of the Syrian rue bush. In the twentieth century, modern science revealed that the acacia roots contained high concentrations of the *human* neurotransmitter dimethyltryptamine (DMT), which is an entheogenic (psychedelic) compound believed to be responsible for supernatural visions experienced in dreams, near-death experiences, actual death, and extreme trauma (as well as some normal states of consciousness). DMT has been found to occur naturally in virtually all living organisms, including humans. In his book *DMT: The Spirit Molecule*, Rick Strassman, MD, states that DMT is produced in the pineal gland as well as the lungs and is believed to be responsible for human experiences of the spiritual and supernatural.[140] The reader is encouraged to read Dr. Strassman's book to delve into the mysteries of the role that the natural neurotransmitter DMT plays in the context of human consciousness and spirituality. Maybe some of my readers have experienced DMT or ayahuasca; I'd love to hear from you via email. Maybe one day I'll get the courage to try it out for myself…

In his book *Alchemically Stoned*, P. D. Newman writes:

> DMT happens to be inside of every human being. For, DMT is actually manufactured by the human organism, and high amounts of the same have been found in the urine and bloodstream of meditating monks, praying nuns, and even schizophrenics Endogenous DMT production is therefore believed by many scientists to be the physiological basis for mystical experiences, near-death and out of body experiences, and a whole host of subjective phenomena that cannot otherwise be explained or even begin to be explored by modern science.[141]

In *The Synchronicity Key*, Wilcock speaks of an elixir of immortality which a hero finds during his or her quest which makes the whole en-

139 https://www.collective-evolution.com/2014/05/31/the-tree-of-life-acacia-nilotica/.

140 Personal communication: Rick Strassman email 7/17/2017.

141 Newman, P D. *Alchemically Stoned – The Psychedelic Secret of Freemasonry* (The Laudable Pursuit, 2017).

deavor worth while. Wilcock explains that the elixir need not necessarily be a liquid, but can be any sort of magical substance that gives the beholder the power to change the world. Wilcock goes on to explain that the more struggles the hero encounters along his quest, the greater the positive change he will achieve in the universe.

THE 11:11 CODE IN FUN TV SHOWS

One of my all-time-favorite television programs as a child was *The Three Stooges* in black-and-white. The slapstick comedy series began in 1922. My favorite character, Curly, was born Jerome Horwitz on October 22, 1903, in New York City.[142] Shemp died of a heart attack on 11/22/1955. The trio were picked up by Metro-Goldwyn-Mayer (MGM) in 1933 to produce a series of short movies, effectively ushering them into Hollywood.[143] Now we have uncovered 11, 22, and 33 lurking in one of the funniest shows of all time.

I discovered that the children's cartoon *SpongeBob SquarePants* had run for 11 seasons at the time of writing. Each regular episode was 11 minutes in duration, and the special episodes ran for 22 minutes.[144] Even Squidward Tentacles and Patrick Star have been in on *The 11:11 Code*. Nice.

South Park, one of my other favorite cartoons during high school and university years, was in its 22nd season as of the time of writing, and each episode lasts 22 minutes.[145] As it turns out, television shows are often packaged into seasons with at least 22 episodes.[146]

Comedy icon Johnny Carson's last broadcast of *The Late Show* was on May 22, 1992, after thirty years of running one of the most successful late-night comedy shows in television history.[147] *The Late Show* was ranked #22 in the 2013 edition of *TV Guide Magazine's* "60 Best Series of All Time" rankings.[148]

Jay Leno was on the air for 22 years and enjoyed a peak audience of 22.4 million viewers.

Conan O'Brien called it quits on January 22, 2010.

142 https://www.britannica.com/topic/the-Three-Stooges.
143 https://www.myjewishlearning.com/article/the-three-stooges/.
144 https://en.m.wikipedia.org/wiki/SpongeBob_SquarePants.
145 https://en.wikipedia.org/wiki/South_Park.
146 https://www.denofgeek.com/tv/us-tv/29834/the-problem-with-22-episode-seasons.
147 https://www.metv.com/stories/looking-back-on-johnny-carsons-last-episodes-of-the-tonight-show.
148 https://www.tvguide.com/news/tv-guide-magazine-60-best-series-1074962/.

David Letterman was on the air for 33 years.

The most popular game show of all time, *Wheel of Fortune*, was originally filmed in Studio 4 at NBC Studios in Burbank, California. After NBC canceled the popular show in 1989, filming resumed at CBS Television City's Studio 33 in Los Angeles, which continued until 1995. Then the show moved to Sony Pictures Studio 11, where it currently remains. The game show episodes are 22 minutes in length. There you go—the combination 11-22-33.[149]

All of these examples for fun in TV represent multiples of 11. Humor is clearly an essential element of the 11:11 Code.

The interested reader can dig even deeper into occurrences of the number 22 by visiting the Virtuescience website.[150] Uri Geller's site is also quite excellent and is worth a visit.[151]

STAR WARS AND THE 11:11 CODE

As a kid who grew up in the late '70s and the '80s, few movies had a greater impact on my generation than the original *Star Wars* trilogy. The original *Star Wars* movie was released in 1977 and produced on a budget of just $11 million.[152] It raked in a total of $775 million with $314 million (think *pi* million) worth of the revenue generated outside of the United States.[153] It replaced *Jaws* as the highest-earning film in North America just six months into release, eventually earning more than $220 million during its initial theatrical run ($888 million in 2017 dollars). The original first film had a playtime of 121 minutes (or 11 x 11).[154] Here we see 11, 22, 77, and 888 showing up in relation to one of the most influential movies of all time.[155]

149 https://en.m.wikipedia.org/wiki/Wheel_of_Fortune_(U.S._game_show).
150 https://www.virtuescience.com/22.html.
151 https://www.urigeller.com/are-your-eyes-attracted-to-11-11/.
152 https://www.simplemost.com/star-wars-facts/.
153 https://factsd.com/star-wars-facts/.
154 http://www.bbfc.co.uk/releases/star-wars-film.
155 https://en.wikipedia.org/wiki/Star_Wars_(film).

Me visiting Luke Skywalker's childhood home *planet, Tatooine* ***[sic] in the Sahara Desert in Matmata, Tunisia, during a day off of work in Bouchemma in 2006. We passed the actual town of Tataouine [spelling corrected] on the way to Matmata. Director George Lucas was reported to have chosen Tataouine because of the exotic sounding name instead of the actual geographic location of Matmata during his November (11th month) 1975 trip to Tunisia. (1 + 9 + 7 + 5 = 22.)*** [156]

Outside Tataouine, Tunisia

Soylent Green

The 1973 movie *Soylent Green* portrayed a dystopian version of the future set in the year 2022 (fifty years in the future during production), in which the population of New York City has grown to forty million. Most housing is dilapidated and overcrowded, and homeless people fill the streets and line the fire escapes, stairways of buildings, abandoned cars, subway platforms, etc. Unemployment is at around 50 percent. Summers are oppressively hot and humid with temperatures higher than ninety degrees Fahrenheit because of the planet's recent climate change, which is the result of the greenhouse effect. Food as we know it in this present

156 https://www.cntraveler.com/stories/2016-05-02/tatooine-exists-on-earth.

time is a rare and expensive commodity. Most of the world's population survives on processed rations produced by the massive Soylent Corporation, including Soylent Red and Soylent Yellow, which are advertised as "high-energy vegetable concentrates." The newest product is Soylent Green—small green wafers advertised as being produced from "high-energy plankton." It is much more nutritious and palatable than the red and yellow varieties, but like most other foods, it's in short supply, which often leads to weekly food riots.

Without going into the entire plot, it is interesting to see the police discovered the body of murder victim William R. Simonson (Joseph Cotten), a sixty-eight-year-old wealthy lawyer living in a luxury high-rise apartment building called Chelsea Towers West. Simonson lived on the 22nd floor in apartment 22A.

Here we go again—a culturally significant movie with multiple 22 signatures.[157]

INDIANA JONES AND THE LAST CRUSADE

During a project in Israel in 2006, I took the day off to tour the archaeological site at Petra, Jordan, another of George Lucas's filming sites where *Indiana Jones and the Last Crusade* was filmed. The film earned 22 nominations and 8 awards.[158] The filming of the temple interior was completed on July 22, 1988.[159]

The author at Petra's iconic treasury

157 https://m.imdb.com/title/tt0070723/synopsis?ref_=m_tt_stry_pl.
158 https://www.imdb.com/title/tt0097576/awards?ref_=tt_awd.
159 https://infogalactic.com/info/Indiana_Jones_and_the_Last_Crusade.

STAR TREK

The television series *Star Trek* has an absolute treasure trove of 22-isms. For starters, the series averaged 22 episodes per season. Montgomery Scott (a.k.a. Scotty) was born in Scotland in the fictitious year 2222 and was in Aberdeen on 3/3/2222. Leonard McCoy was born in the state of Georgia in 2227. Mr. Spock was born on the planet Vulcan in 2230, the same year Mr. Sulu was portrayed to have been born on Earth. Captain James T. Kirk was born in Iowa in the year 2233, and his father was killed that same year. Mr. Chekov was born in Russia in 2241. The *USS Enterprise* was launched on her maiden voyage in 2245. The events of *Star Trek: The Original Series* took place during the years 2266 through 2269. There are a great deal more *events* that took place in the twenty-third-century *Star Trek*, but these are a few of the most prominent highlights for my fellow Trekkies. Much more can be found in the *Star Trek Officers Manual.*[160]

The movie *Star Trek: First Contact* made its debut in theaters on 11/22/1996 and had a total playtime of 111 minutes.[161] With both *Star Trek* and *Star Wars* bearing undeniable 11/11 numerological signals, doesn't it make you wonder if any 11:11 artifacts can be found if we investigate the stars in the heavens?

Keep reading. There are no rhetorical questions in this book, just answers.

E.T. THE EXTRA-TERRESTRIAL AND THE 11:11 CODE

Steven Spielberg's movie *E.T.* was another movie that defined childhood for most of us who grew up in the '70s and '80s. The film was released on June 11, 1982, and shown in slightly more than 1,100 theaters. It grossed $11.8 million in its debut week alone while averaging nearly $11,000 per theater.[162] It went on to become the top-ranking film of all time, a title that it held for 11 years until 1993, when *Jurassic Park*, another Spielberg film, displaced it for the top spot. There you have it—five instances of 11 relating to *E.T.* the movie. To boot, *Jurassic Park* was released on June 11, 1993, and the digits of 1993 add up to 22.

Update: I watched *E.T. The Extra-Terrestrial* about 10 months after writ-

160 https://www.cygnus-x1.net/links/lcars/USS-Enterprise-Officers-Manual.php.
161 https://www.imdb.com/title/tt0117731/.
162 https://www.boxofficemojo.com/movies/?id=et.htm.

ing the previous paragraph. I sit here typing on the day after Christmas 2019, after showing my eight-year-old son Erik (that handsome little guy on the cover!) one of my favorite childhood movies. I always thought the little girl in the movie, *Gertie,* was such a cute little sweetheart when I was Erik's age, watching this film in 1982 when I, myself, was seven years of age. On a whim, as with the vast majority of the material in this book, I Googled "Gertie E.T." and was gobsmacked to discover that Drew Barrymore, who played Gertie, was born on 2/22/1975.[163] Think about that for a moment: the 22nd day of the 2nd month, of a year whose digits sum to 22. Numerologically equivalent to 2/22/22. WHOA... Just WHOA.

THE AVENGERS

The highest grossing movie of all time (as of early 2020) was *Avengers: Endgame*, which debuted on April 22, 2019, in the Los Angeles market. The film was the culmination of a series of a 22-film superhero series.[164] *Endgame* sales eclipsed the previous record-holder, *Titanic*, in just 11 days after release, becoming one of only five movies to ever surpass the $2 billion level, joining the company of *Avatar* ($2.78 billion), *Titanic* ($2.187 billion), *Star Wars: The Force Awakens* ($2.06 billion), and *Avengers: Infinity War* ($2.04 billion). After only 47 days in theaters, the film attained the honor of largest-selling movie of all time.[165]

OTHER EXAMPLES IN ENTERTAINMENT

The 11:11 code can be found on television, as well as the silver screen. I'll start with this gem as the former VP inappropriately kisses his teenage granddaughter on the lips on national TV. Note the date on the background!

163 https://www.imdb.com/name/nm0000106/.
164 https://en.wikipedia.org/wiki/Avengers:_Endgame.
165 https://www.boxofficemojo.com/chart/top_lifetime_gross/?area=XWW.

In the movie *I Origins*, the lead character buys a lottery ticket with the date 11/11/06 and time stamp of 11:11:11. Similarly, the movie *11-11-11* is a 2011 supernatural horror film written and directed by Darren Lynn Bousman. The film is set at 11:11 on the 11th day of the 11th month, and it concerns an entity from another world that enters the earthly realm through heaven's 11th gate. The film was released on November 11, 2011, in 17 theaters domestically. It was distributed by Columbia Pictures in North America, though most of its revenue was generated from foreign showings. Finally, the film runs for 1 hour and 22 minutes.[166]

During the movie *The Martian*, as the lead actor is configuring his spacecraft for liftoff from the surface of Mars, his computer screen flashes through a program routine and displays a clock time of 22:22:208375.

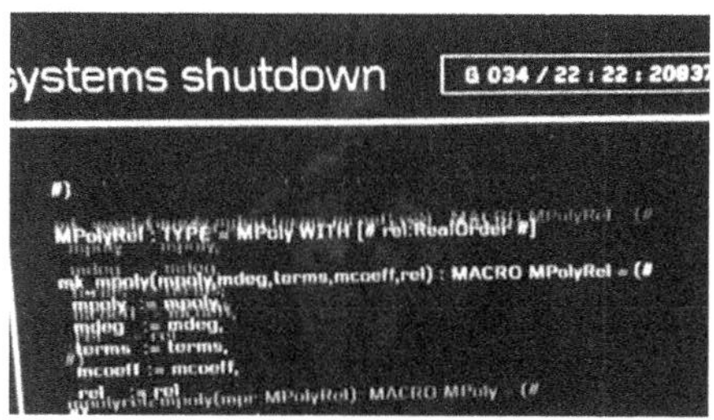

Mini-fact: The fictional superhero Superman was first conceived in 1933.[167]

166 https://www.boxofficemojo.com/movies/?id=111111.htm.
167 https://en.m.wikipedia.org/wiki/Superman.

The sun will be turned to darkness and the moon to blood before the coming of the great and dreadful day of the Lord.

—Joel 2:31[168]

There is geometry in the humming of the strings, there is music in the spacing of the spheres.

—Pythagoras[169]

Our Universe is a sorry little affair unless it has in it something for every age to investigate.

—Seneca[170]

Everyone who is seriously involved in the pursuit of science becomes convinced that a spirit is manifest in the laws of the universe—a spirit vastly superior to that of man… In this way the pursuit of science leads to a religious feeling of a special sort, which is indeed quite different from the religiosity of someone more naïve.

—Albert Einstein, letter to a child who asked if scientists pray, January 24, 1936 (Einstein Archive 42-601)[171]

168 https://biblehub.com/niv/joel/2.htm

169 https://www.brainyquote.com/quotes/pythagoras_386262

170 https://www.goodreads.com/quotes/7675751-our-universe-is-a-sorry-little-affair-unless-it-has

171 John DePillis, *777 Mathematical Conversation Starters* (Washington, DC: The Mathematical Association of America, 2002).

CHAPTER 5

THE UNIVERSE

Solar Eclipse of 2017

> For some nice background music, give "Lifeblood" by Grandyzer a listen.

On August 21, 2017, there was a complete solar eclipse, as many American readers may well recall. Having never experienced the totality of a full eclipse, I decided to take the family to Paducah, Kentucky, to experience the totality, during which 100 percent of the sun is obscured by the moon for a short period of time. We drove down, pulling a rented camper trailer. The only camper that was available at the last minute from our RV dealer was a triangle-shaped pop-up camper. We sort of winged it and just drove south without making any advance reservations for a campsite. That probably wasn't my smartest move. The day before we needed to have a campsite, we pulled over at a gas station and searched the internet for campgrounds. We called seventeen or eighteen different campgrounds and discovered that all of them were completely sold out because of the incredible number of people who had migrated to the region to witness this historic eclipse. Luckily, we made one phone call to a campground that was also full, but they gave us a referral to a nearby campground where they believed one site might be left to rent. So I called that campground, and lo and behold, they had exactly one campsite left!

When we arrived at the Triangle Fishing Club and Campground, we were shocked to learn that the last remaining site was a corner lot on a bluff with a commanding view over the marina and lake! We were fully expecting to get the worst site in the entire campground, perhaps behind a trash dumpster next to a septic tank at the back of the lot. We were completely blown away by our good fortune. On top of that, we found out it was a members-only community, so I am still humbled to this day that we as outsiders were welcomed into the community for our two-night visit. These forced occurrences of the three-sided pyramids (the trailer shape and the name of campground) gave me pause, and I thought about the Holy Trinity of the Father, Son, and Holy Spirit and what message they might be trying to send me.

Now here comes the interesting part. About two hours before the eclipse, I googled the time of onset and duration of the totality of the eclipse—the time when the moon would completely block the sun. I was astonished to see that the complete totality of the eclipse started at exactly 1:22 p.m. and lasted for exactly 2 minutes and 21 seconds. Think of the numbers, starting at 1:22 and going for 2:21 minutes.[172] The date of this eclipse and Veterans Day 11/11/2017 were exactly 2 months and 22 days apart.[173] These numbers and the double occurrence of 22 sandwiched between the ones were astonishing for several reasons. The time of onset and duration of the totality both vary for every location in the country. No two places have the exact same onset and duration, owing to the complex geometric interaction of the sun-moon-Earth system and local angles of incidence depending upon latitude and time zone. Secondly, there is no way to influence or change these times as they are set firmly by the motions of the heavenly bodies. There's no way for humankind to influence it.

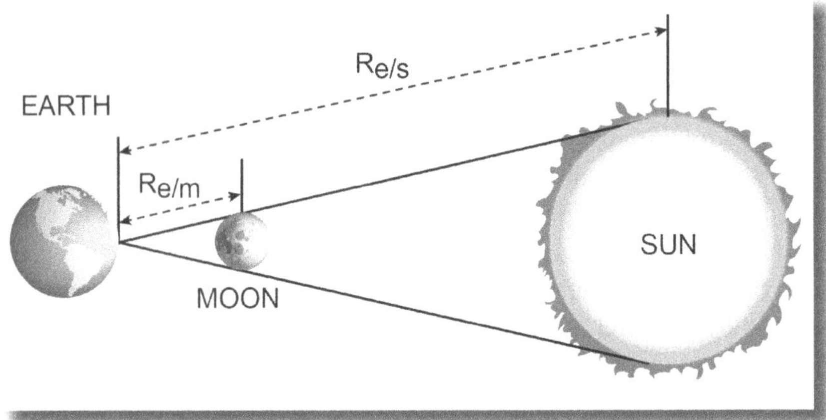

172 http://paducahky.gov/solar-eclipse-2017.
173 https://www.timeanddate.com/date/durationresult.html?m1=8&d1=21&y1=2017&m2=11&d2=11&y2=2017&ti=on

It is truly remarkable that the moon almost *exactly* covers the sun—nothing more, nothing less. Why should it? In a random system devoid of divine, intelligent design, the moon would either overlap or underlap the sun's disc, but the chances of it being nearly exact are, well, *astronomical.* That pun was very much intended. Geometry reveals the reason.

The average distance from Earth to the moon is 238,855 miles. Average Earth-sun distance is 92,900,000 miles. Divide the two numbers, and you get a ratio of 389. Now the sun's diameter is 864,337 miles, and the moon's diameter is 2,159 miles. Divide the two, and you get almost exactly 400. These two ratios are within 2.3 percent of being identical. Again, is this random serendipity or a deliberate act of divine design? How close the moon is to Earth in its elliptical orbit determines whether the eclipse will be complete blockage, or if a thin fiery ring of the sun will still get past the moon. The complete eclipse occurs when the moon is at its closest to Earth (perigee) and the annular (ring) eclipse occurs at its farthest, at apogee.[174]

How about the number of seconds in a day? Try 24 hours times 60 minutes per hour times 60 seconds per hour. You get 86,400, which is one-tenth of the Sun's 864,000-mile diameter or equivalently a radius of 432,000 miles. Take 432 x 432 = 186,624, which is within 0.2 percent of the actual speed of light, 186,000 miles per second. Adding 432 to its mirror image, 234, totals 666. Did you know that 666 minutes corresponds to 11.11 hours?

Lastly, our location for viewing the eclipse was not of our choosing. It was determined to be the only campground available in the entire region after nearly two hours of Google searches and calling an exhaustive number of campgrounds—fourteen to be exact. The campsite name was *Triangle Resort*, and our camper, which again was the only camper available at our dealer, was triangle-shaped. This is a possible symbol of a pyramid or the triangle of the Trinity—the Father, Son, and Spirit, which are the entities responsible for everything that happens in the universe. This is how we interpreted it—as divine fingerprints. Maybe it was just a lucky coincidence.

Luke 21:25 says:

> And there will be strange signs in the sun, moon, and stars. And

174 https://www.space.com/annular-solar-eclipse-after-christmas-2019.html.

> here on earth the nations will be in turmoil, perplexed by the roaring seas and strange tides.[175]

In my opinion, this verse clearly seems to make a connection between the 8/21/17 eclipse and the historic events that would follow in 2018 worldwide. The peak eclipse experience was near Cairo, Illinois. In the year 2024 (seven years later), the next complete eclipse will occur with a maximum point almost exactly at the same point, and the paths of the 2017 and 2024 eclipses will have made a cross right over the southern tip of Illinois. Think *cross* in a biblical context, and they are seven years apart. Why *seven*? Why a cross?? Why in the state of my birth, Illinois? Is there a deeper message being communicated by the geometric alignments of the heavenly bodies?

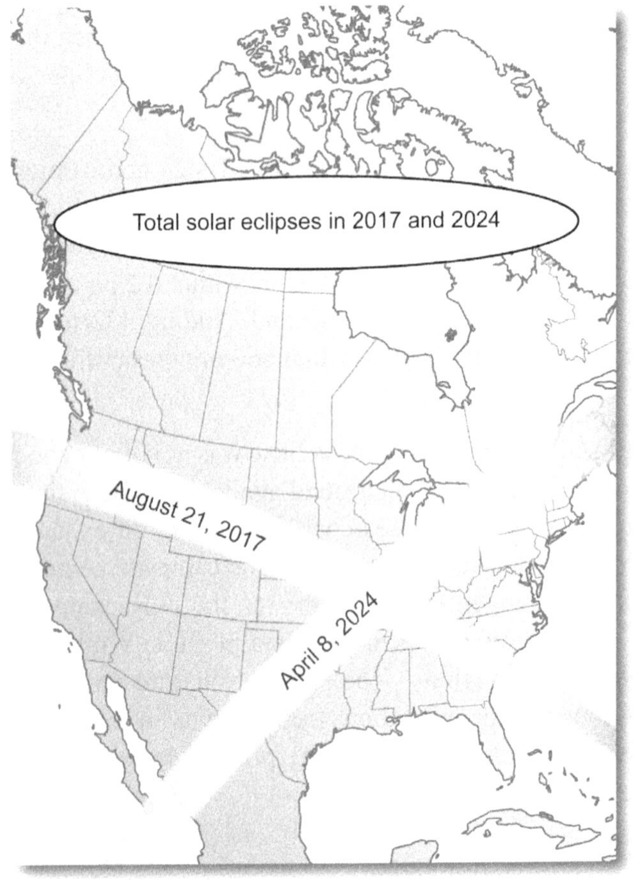

175 https://www.biblegateway.com/passage/?search=Luke+21%3A25&version=NIV.

The previous millennium's last complete solar eclipse occurred on August 11, 1999. It was the most-viewed total solar eclipse in human history. The track of this eclipse began in the Atlantic a few hundred miles east of Boston, Massachusetts, and swept northeast across the ocean, reaching totality in Cornell, England, at 11:11 a.m. It swept across Europe to the Black Sea, Turkey, Iraq, Iran, Pakistan, and India, ending in the Bay of Bengal.[176]

Comet Shoemaker-Levy 9

Comet Shoemaker-Levy 9 was a comet that broke apart in July 1992 and collided with Jupiter in July 1994, providing the first direct observation of an extraterrestrial collision of solar system objects. Astronomers observed at least 21 pieces of the comet fall into Jupiter's atmosphere at a speed of 37 kilometers per second. The spiritual significance and mathematical properties of 37 have already been well established.

The largest chunk hit Jupiter on July 18 at 07:33 UTC when Fragment G struck. This impact created a giant dark spot more than 12,000 kilometers (7,500 miles) across, estimated to have released an energy equivalent to 6,000,000 megatons of TNT (600 times the world's nuclear arsenal).

The last fragment, referred to as Fragment W, impacted the planet on July 22, 1994. The letter W is the 23rd letter of the alphabet, which makes me wonder if there weren't 22 or 23 pieces in total![177]

The topic of Jupiter wouldn't be complete without a brief mention of the most prominent feature of the largest planet in our solar system, the Great Red Spot. The storm has been raging for at least as long as the time of its first discovery in 1664 by Robert Hooke. The storm measures approximately 10.000 miles across or 1.3 times the diameter of Earth. Winds as high as 432 kilometers per hour have been measured near the outer boundary of the storm, while the center is relatively calm.[178] The number 432 is noteworthy because if you add its mirror image, 432 + 234 = 666. Fascinatingly, the storm is located at 22 degrees south of the Jovian equator.[179] Adding further to the numerological mysteries of the largest planet, in 1955, Bernard Burke and Kenneth Franklin measured

176 http://www.dimension1111.com/the-number-11-celestial-events-and-calendars.html.

177 https://en.wikipedia.org/wiki/Comet_Shoemaker%E2%80%93Levy_9.

178 https://www.universetoday.com/136402/get-closest-look-jupiters-great-red-spot/.

179 https://www.britannica.com/place/Great-Red-Spot.

radio frequency bursts from the big planet broadcasting to the universe at 22.2 megahertz.[180]

Finally, the planet Jupiter has a diameter of 88,846 miles, which is approximately 11 times that of Earth's 7,918 miles—11.22 times, to be exact.[181]

SKULL ASTEROID

On November 11, 2018 (yes, that's 11/11 in a year whose digits sum to 2 + 0 + 1 + 8 = 11), an asteroid made a close shave past Earth. At a comfy distance of 24 million miles, this is still a close scrape in astronomical terms.

The astronomical name for the asteroid is 2015TB145, and it made its last Earth approach on October 31, coinciding with Halloween in 2015.[182] The media nicknamed the asteroid the Great Pumpkin as a nod to the beloved Charlie Brown Halloween special cartoon. It is also widely nicknamed the Skull because of its striking resemblance to a human cranium as seen in the artist's impression that follows. Additionally, the asteroid has an "arc of observation of 22 days, which represents the total amount of time that the asteroid can be seen from its first approach, until its final departure from view."[183] The comet's encounter velocity was estimated to be 22 miles per second.[184] Lastly, the asteroid's orbital period is 1,112 days, which is close enough to 1111 to mention here.[185]

180 https://www.researchgate.net/publication/260246095_DETECTION_OF_RADIO_EMISSIONS_FROM_JUPITER.
181 https://www.space.com/33553-biggest-thing-universe.html.
182 https://www.space.com/42315-halloween-asteroid-skull-earth-flyby-november-2018.html.
183 https://en.wikipedia.org/wiki/2015_TB145#cite_note-jpldata-2.
184 https://earthsky.org/space/big-asteroid-will-safely-pass-earth-on-halloween-october-31-2015.
185 https://www.businessinsider.com/a-skull-shaped-asteroid-will-make-its-way-to-earth-around-halloween-2017-12.

Remembering that 11 + 11 is 22, we have a double reference here to the book's title. Is the solar system trying to tell us something? To me, it seems to be saying that all of the heavens were designed by the same great architect and crafted by the same master builder.

The Number of the Sun

The ancients believed that the sun *was* God. What if they were right all along? What if this is what the Bible has been trying to tell us through scripture? I'm of the belief that God manifests his presence through *all* things, and the sun should be no exception.

Psalm 84:11 reads, "For the Lord God is a sun and shield."[186]

Malachi 4:2 states, "But to you who fear My name, the Sun of Righteousness shall arise with healing in His wings."[187] Notice the spelling is *Sun*, not son in this verse.

What is the connection between God and the sun? I think it goes much deeper than modern religion would have us believe. Or maybe there is secret, cryptic knowledge that has been lost during the passage of the millennia.

Let's revisit the polar circles from the previous chapter now. As the reader is probably aware, the arctic (and Antarctic) circles have the special property of being the lowest latitudes where the sun can be seen 24 hours a day in the peak of summer as well as experiencing 24 hours of darkness during the nadir of winter. Think about what this means in terms of the latitude of this phenomenon. We are able to observe the sun 24 hours a day once we reach a latitude of exactly $66° - 33' - 44''$ (66.6 degrees) north or south of the equator! (Notice that all three numbers are multiples of 11!) Furthermore, the phenomenon of the midnight sun happens at the summer solstice, which is around June 22 in the northern hemisphere and December 22 in the southern hemisphere.[188] Similarly, the equinoxes, or the days when the hours of daylight equal the amount of night, also occur on or about the 22nd of March and September.

The brilliance of the master architect of the universe never ceases to amaze me when I dig up clues and connections like these. At the moment

186 https://www.biblegateway.com/passage/?search=Psalms+84%3A11+&version=NKJV.
187 https://www.biblegateway.com/passage/?search=malachi%204:2&version=NKJV.
188 https://www.alaskacenters.gov/explore/attractions/midnight-sun.

the universe was created, the Creator must have figured that we would have some questions about who we are and what we're doing here. He has certainly left plenty of fascinating clues and patterns to be discovered by anyone who truly seeks to understand the divine mind and immerse themself in the wonder of exploring the mysteries of creation.[189]

Notice the sine wave that the sun's elevation traces in the sky during the period of twenty-four hours.

In 2018, the winter solstice occurred at 22:22 on 12/22 Greenwich mean time.[190] In ancient religions based on the sun as being God, this represented the sun's lowest point of descent during the northern hemisphere's year, followed by his rebirth and resurrection. Between the summer and winter solstices, the amount of daylight steadily decreases before reaching a minimum on December 22. After the winter solstice, the amount of daylight per 24-hour period steadily increases in a sinusoidal manner until reaching a peak at the summer solstice. There are some interesting parallels between these ancient (pre-Christian) beliefs and the story of Christ's birth, death, and resurrection. If you perform an image search on the internet for the terms "precession of the equinoxes," you'll see that the two solstice points, the two equinoxes, and the sun all form the shape of a cross with the sun at the center.

189 http://www.atlanteanconspiracy.com/2016/06/arctic-midnight-sun-proves-flat-earth.html.
190 https://greenwichmeantime.com/longest-day/equinox-solstice-2010-2019/.

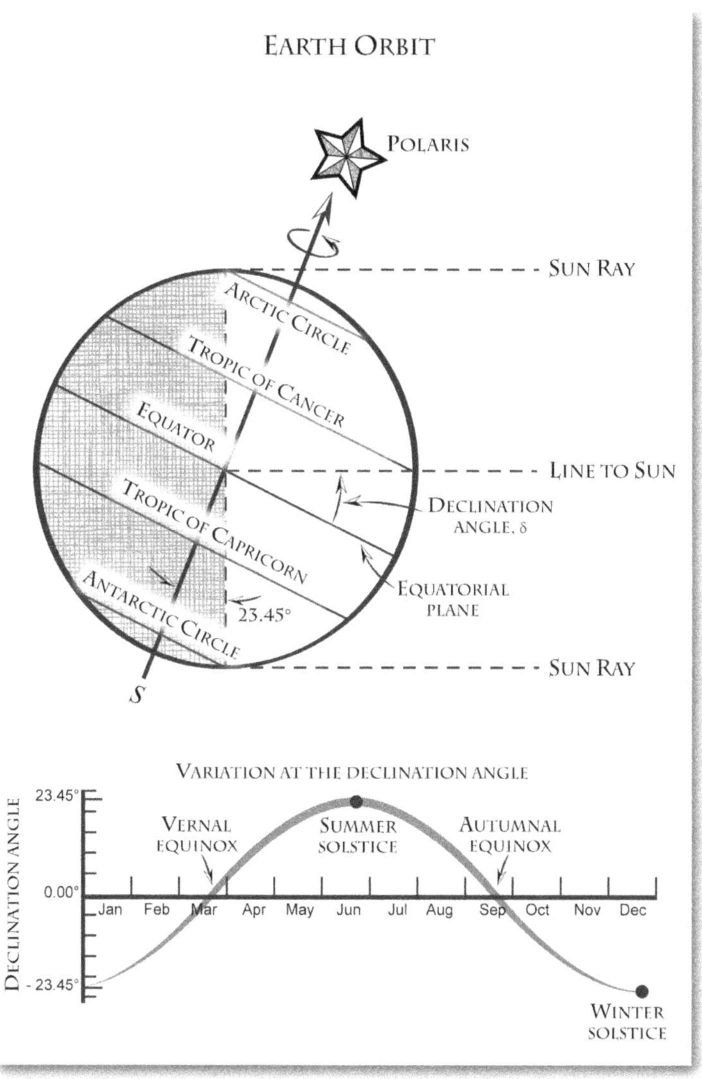

Furthermore, the tropical circles of Cancer and Capricorn are located 23.4 degrees north and south of the equator respectively. Geometrically, these are the north and south limits of what latitudes a person is able to experience the sun being exactly 90 degrees overhead during the year. At the peak of summer, a person standing at 23.4 degrees north of the equator will have the sun exactly overhead on the day of summer solstice, the longest day of the year in the northern hemisphere.[191] Add 23.4 plus its

191 http://www.powerfromthesun.net/Book/chapter03/chapter03.html.

mirror image (43.2) together, and you get 66.6. Add 23.4 degrees for the northern tropic sector to the 23.4 degrees for the southern tropic sector, and you get 46.8 degrees, which is very close to a metaphor for the fact that two parents contributing 23 chromosomes each produce a child with 46 chromosomes. A deeper allegory can be understood when we realize that when the northern hemisphere is in winter, the southern hemisphere is in summer and vice versa. Could this be a further extension of the 23 + 23 = 46 chromosome allegory, whereby male and female energies are opposites yet complementary?

It is also noteworthy to remark that the ~46 degree sector between the tropic circles is a zone where life never stops producing. There is no distinguishable winter season to speak of.

When we look at the sun's size, it has a diameter of 864,000 miles, which is twice the radius of 432,000 miles. If we take the 432 and add it to its mirror image, we again get 432 + 234 = 666. This is the number of the sun *again*. In order to try to paint a picture of just how large the sun really is, let's compare its 864,000-mile diameter to the average Earth-moon distance of 239,000 miles. Dividing the two, we see that the sun's diameter is about 3.6 times the Earth-moon separation distance. Stop for a moment and contemplate that.

The moon is nearly a quarter-million miles away, and its 2,159-mile diameter disk appears the size of a coin in the sky despite being as wide as the distance between Chicago and Phoenix. The moon is a large distance away, but if you placed the sun directly next to the Earth so that they touched each other, the body of the sun would continue out past the moon an additional 625,000 miles into space before you reached the other side. That's a remarkably massive object, but it's quite tiny when compared to some of the other massive stars in the universe, such as UY Scuti, the largest known star, with a diameter that is about 1,800 times that of our sun. For comparison, the orbit of the planet Saturn has a diameter of about 2,000 times the sun's diameter.[192]

Now try this. The Sun's diameter of 864,000 miles can be factored out to 6 x 6 x 6 x 6 x 666.666, which even I couldn't believe until I actually got the calculator and proved it to myself. As with all of the numerical facts

192 https://arxiv.org/abs/1305.6179.

presented in this book, I urge you not to take my word for it but try it on your own calculator.[193] That's ten sixes in a row.

Before we segue to the next topic, let me challenge you with one more thought on the sun. *You* are solar-powered. That's right. Start with the glucose and other nutrients that your body is operating on right now and trace their energy back to their original source. The hamburger or piece of pizza you ate for dinner is made up of components that derived their energy from the sun. The grain used to make the bread directly received sunlight and converted it into chemical energy that your body can use. As for the meat, the animal ate plant matter (or another animal), which simply added another step to the process. The point here is that all life energy can be traced back to the sun.

You and I are quite literally star-powered. In business and politics, the saying is "follow the money." In physics & engineering, we tend to follow the energy.

Tidal Influences

Tides are defined as "the alternate rising and falling of the surface of the ocean and of water bodies (such as gulfs and bays) connected with the ocean that occurs usually twice a day and is the result of differing gravitational forces exerted at different parts of the earth by another body (such as the moon or sun)."[194] Approximately twice a month, when the moon is at new phase and full phase (both positions being called syzygy) the gravitational attractions of the moon and sun act to reinforce each other. Since the resultant or combined tidal force is also increased, the observed high tides are higher and low tides are lower than average. The moon's gravity contributes the majority of the tidal forces, while the sun's influence is about half as strong because it is approximately 400 times farther from Earth in comparison to the moon's distance from Earth.[195]

Earth tides or terrestrial tides affect the entire Earth's mass, which acts similarly to a liquid gyroscope with a very thin crust. The Earth's crust shifts (in/out, east/west, north/south) in response to lunar and solar gravitation, ocean tides, and atmospheric loading. While negligible for most human activities, terrestrial tides' semidiurnal (12 hour) amplitude can

193 http://www.secretsinplainsight.com/sixes/.

194 https://www.merriam-webster.com/dictionary/tide.

195 https://tidesandcurrents.noaa.gov/restles4.html.

reach about 22 inches at the equator.[196], [197] Oh, and let's mention that the Atlantic Ocean covers 22 percent of the Earth's surface area.[198] Here we have found the number 22 at work in the tidal forces of our mother planet. In a graduate course on the physics of satellite sensors, I learned that water vapor is detected most effectively using electromagnetic radiation at the specific frequency of 22.2 gigahertz to take advantage of water's natural absorption peak. Twenty-two or 11+11 seems to be the number of water as well![199]

Numbers on the Moon

In honor of the 50-year anniversary of the first lunar landing, I'd like to explore some facts about the moon and see if there are any interesting numerical Easter eggs buried there as cosmic fingerprints of intelligent creation. For starters, the Apollo program didn't put a man on the moon until the 11th mission. A *Saturn V* rocket launched *Apollo 11* from Launch Pad 39A, part of the Launch Complex 39 site at the Kennedy Space Center, on July 16, 1969, at 13:32:00 GMT. The first human foot touched the surface of the Moon on July 20, 1969, at 20:18 GMT. The digits of 20:18 add to 11.[200] The *Saturn V* (pronounced "Saturn five") rocket was 111 meters tall (363 feet), and the first two stages were both 33 feet in diameter. A total of 13 Saturn V rockets were successfully launched.[201] The rocket launch gantry, which was used to load the Apollo astronauts into the *Saturn V* rockets to go to the moon, was 322 feet tall.[202]

During the launch, Armstrong's heart rate is reported to have peaked at a leisurely 110 beats per minute while being blasted into orbit by the most powerful piece of machinery ever devised by humankind. The final assignment for Armstrong in the Gemini program was as the backup command pilot for *Gemini 11*, announced two days after the landing of *Gemini 8*. Following his return from this mission, he went on an 11-country world tour to celebrate the successful completion.[203]

After one and a half orbits, *Apollo 11*'s third-stage engine rocketed the spacecraft onto its trajectory toward the moon with the translunar injec-

196 https://en.wikipedia.org/wiki/Tide.
197 https://www.nationalgeographic.org/encyclopedia/tide.
198 http://www.marbef.org/outreach/downloads/Atlantic%20ocean%20pullout.pdf.
199https://tmo.jpl.nasa.gov/progress_report/42-144/144E.pdf
200 https://airandspace.si.edu/explore-and-learn/topics/apollo/apollo-program/landing-missions/apollo11-facts.cfm.
201 https://www.space.com/18422-apollo-saturn-v-moon-rocket-nasa-infographic.html.
202 https://www.kennedyspacecenter.com/info/travel-information.
203 https://en.wikipedia.org/wiki/Neil_Armstrong.

tion (TLI) burn at 16:22:13 UTC. Notice 22 in the time stamp for the rocket burn that put *Apollo 11* past the point of no return.[204]

At least three new minerals were discovered in the rock sample brought back to Earth. The sample contained 47.5 pounds of lunar rocks, which works out to about 22 kilograms. The three novel minerals were called *armalcolite*, *tranquillityite*, and *pyroxferroite*. Arm-Al-Col-ite was named after the three *Apollo 11* astronauts—Armstrong, Aldrin, and Collins. I also noticed that the first two humans to touch the surface of the moon both had family names starting with letter A, the first letter of the alphabet, giving another occurrence of 11.[205], [206], [207]

At the 111-hour mark in the mission, the crew concluded their moon walk and reentered the lunar excursion module (LEM) to make preparations for the return trip to Earth.[208] Aldrin brought a US flag with him to the moon at the behest of the 33rd degree Scottish Rite.[209] Humorously, Aldrin filed an expense report for $33.31 upon his return from the moon to cover his travel and lodging costs from Houston to Florida and to the moon and back.[210] And I thought I was bad for expensing $1.25 in tolls after a return trip from Australia!

The lunar landing site for *Apollo 11* in selenographic (moon-based) coordinates were 0.6875 degrees N + 23.4 degrees E. Adding that number to its mirror image gets 23.4 + 43.2 = 66.6. Remarkably, the moon's diameter can be factored out to 6! + 6! + 6! = 2,160 miles. (Recall the definition of the factorial as 6! = 6 x 5 x 4 x 3 x 2 x 1 = 720).

Call me a lunatic, but I'm starting to see that nothing is random, especially when we delve deep into numbers associated with many of the most significant discoveries, disasters, or achievements in the human story.[211] It may interest the reader to learn that the crew of *Apollo 17*, the last manned mission to the moon, spent 22 hours exploring the lunar surface, beginning with the first EVA at 114 hours and 22 minutes into the mission. *Apollo 17* was the 11th manned mission of the Apollo lunar program.[212] Interestingly, this historic voyage took place a little more than a

204 https://www.hq.nasa.gov/alsj/a11/A11_MissionReport.pdf.
205 http://spiritualparadigm.org/numerology/word.
206 http://freetofindtruth.blogspot.com/2014/02/neil-armstrong-numerology-space-hoax.html?m=1.
207 http://www.abovetopsecret.com/forum/thread914326/pg1.
208 https://www.hq.nasa.gov/alsj/a11/A11_MissionReport.pdf.
209 http://www.secretsinplainsight.com/nazis-nasa-freemasons-and-33/.
210 https://www.theguardian.com/science/2015/aug/03/buzz-aldrin-travel-expenses-moon-apollo-11.
211 https://www.hq.nasa.gov/alsj/alsjcoords.html.
212 https://www.hq.nasa.gov/alsj/a17/A17_MissionReport.pdf.

century after Jules Verne published his novel *From the Earth to the Moon* in 1867. In the year 1903, Konstantin Tsiolkovsky refuted Verne's idea as technically infeasible, demonstrating that by the laws of physics, the gun used to launch the rocket would subject the spacecraft to an acceleration of 22,000 times the force of gravity, which is at least a thousand times greater than the force that would kill a human passenger.[213]

Buzz Aldrin flew on the *Gemini 12* mission prior to going to the moon. This mission launched from Cape Canaveral on 11/11/66, and the mission had a duration of 3 days and 22 hours (322). The year 1966 is equal to 3 x 22, and the 12 from the mission name factors to 3 x 2 x 2 and the digits sum to 1 + 9 + 6 + 6 = 22. Here's one last tidbit on this mission. At exactly 66 hours and 6 minutes, the astronauts opened the spacecraft hatch and performed an extravehicular activity (EVA or space walk) and then climbed back in after just under one hour in the vacuum of space.[214]

On January 4, 2019, China became the first country to successfully make a soft landing on the far side of the moon. The spacecraft *Chang'e 4* landed at 2:26 a.m. GMT on the dark side of the moon. At 2:22 p.m. GMT on the day of landing, the lunar lander released the *Jade Rabbit 2* robotic rover to explore the moon's backside.[215] The *Yutu-2* rover from the previous *Change'e 3* mission was able to take photos of the sister mission.[216] According to *The Daily Mail* news website:

> A post from the *Yutu-2* rover's social media account on Chinese micro-blogging website Weibo on January 11 at 11:22 Beijing time read: 'Would you like to take a 360-degree moon walk? Here is a high-resolution panoramic photo of the moon taken by my fourth sister.[217]

The point here is that I have seen the numbers 11 and 22 clustered heavily around many of the great first achievements of humankind.

The average distance between the Earth and moon is about 239,000 miles. The radius of the moon is 1,079 miles. Dividing the two numbers gives a ratio of about 222.

---

213 https://infogalactic.com/info/From_the_Earth_to_the_Moon.
214 http://www.ibiblio.org/apollo/Documents/Gemini12MissionReport.pdf.
215 https://www.dailymail.co.uk/sciencetech/article-6580779/Stunning-panoramic-image-far-moon-captured-Chinas-Jade-Rabbit-rover.html.
216 http://www.pulispace.com/en/media/news/231-change-3-revealed-and-its-massive.
217 https://www.dailymail.co.uk/sciencetech/article-6580779/Stunning-panoramic-image-far-moon-captured-Chinas-Jade-Rabbit-rover.html.

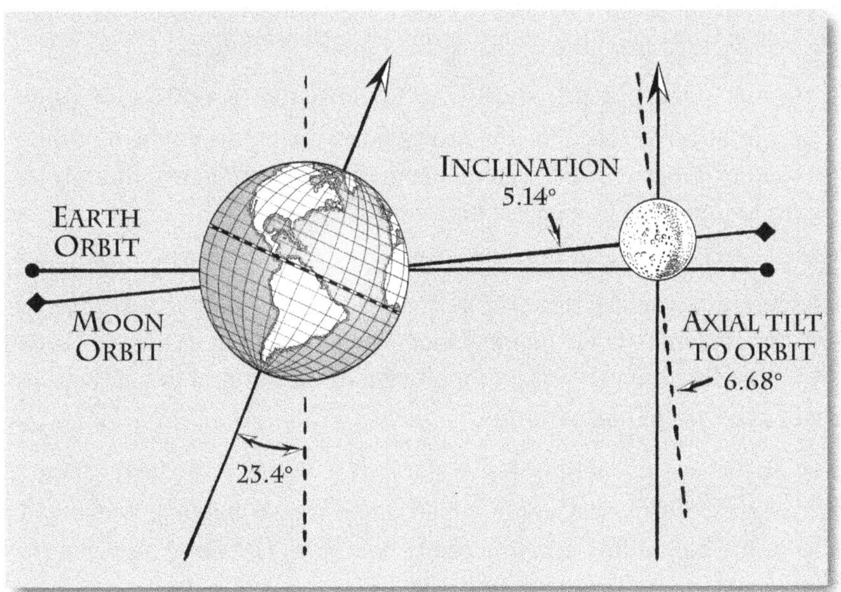

The moon's gravity causes an object to accelerate toward it at a rate of 1.62 m/s^2. We can see that this is extremely close to the conversion factor relating miles to kilometers, where 1 *mi* = 1.609 *km*, which are within 0.7 percent. Each of these numbers is shockingly close (within 0.6 percent) to the golden ratio, 1.618, which is a coincidence that I believe cannot be explained by pure chance. What are the odds? Perhaps *astronomical.*

While being the second man to place his feet on the moon (despite landing there at exactly the same time), Buzz Aldrin maintains the distinction of being the first man to urinate while standing on the moon as well as having held the first Christian Communion on a celestial body other than Earth.

Aldrin received the nickname *Buzz* from his older sister, who had a hard time pronouncing "my baby brother," which usually came out as "my baby buzzer." After that, the name Buzz stuck. I learned this fact after reading his doctoral thesis on line-of-sight orbital rendezvous techniques for lunar landing while I was in university for a research project after custom ordering a copy from MIT's document archives; where Aldrin earned his doctorate in astronautical engineering. This nickname went on to inspire the cartoon character *Buzz Lightyear*. Dr. Aldrin's thesis was *th*e most challenging document I had ever read at the time, but I had an incredible desire to understand the mathematics of how they were able to put men on the moon *and* get them back safely to Earth. One of my favorite phrases from the thesis was his prescient statement:

> In the hopes that this work may in some way contribute to their exploration of space, this is dedicated to the crew members of this country's present and future manned space programs. If only I could join them in their exciting endeavors![218]

Probably my favorite fact about my hero, Buzz Aldrin, is that his mother's maiden name was Marion Moon.[219] Imagine the odds of a woman born with the uncommon last name Moon one day watching her son become one of the first men to walk on the lunar surface! I find this to be a wonderful example of cosmic irony.

One of the most touching parts about Dr. Aldrin is to learn about the weaknesses of this seemingly superhuman moon-walking, rocket-riding hero in his biography, *Magnificent Desolation: The Long Journey Home from the Moon.*[220] The book very candidly details his deep-seated disappointment about always being known as the *second* man to step on the moon. At the time, he really wanted to have the honor and spotlight of being the first to set foot on the lunar surface, whereas his partner, Neil Armstrong, was ambivalent about it. Since Neil didn't care and Buzz would have relished the spotlight, he admits that it deeply bothered him that they couldn't have just swapped seats. It's a perfectly human emotion to feel! I don't honestly understand how Armstrong was able to contain his excitement through this incredible mission.

The thing I admire most about Buzz is to understand how alcohol almost ruined his life as he took to the bottle to cope with the shock of returning to Earth after such a superhuman trek to the moon. The struggles of reintegrating back into terrestrial reality were almost more than he could bear. As the alcohol abuse continued, he candidly tells how the second man on the moon was relegated to being a used car salesman to make ends meet. As a recovered alcoholic myself, I found a sense of solace in knowing that alcoholism affects all people, at all intellectual levels, and all levels of achievement, and that it doesn't pick favorites. Alcohol is an equal-opportunity destroyer of lives. Reading about how Dr. Aldrin was able to finally put the plug in the jug and embrace the life of sobriety was a great

218 Edwin Aldrin, *Line of Sight Guidance Techniques for Manned Orbital Rendezvous* (Boston: Massachusetts Institute of Technology Library Archives, 1963).

219 https://en.wikipedia.org/wiki/Buzz_Aldrin.

220 Edwin Aldrin, *Magnificent Desolation* (New York: Harmony Books, 2009).

inspiration to me as I eventually made my peace with the bottle. As of the time of writing, I am entering my fourth year of complete sobriety. Buzz Aldrin was one of the people who most inspired me to make alcohol a part of my past before it ruined my future. One of my dreams is to place a copy of this book in his hands and see my young son meet him. He was one of my life's greatest inspirations as he showed that through a deep understanding of mathematics and the hard work it takes to obtain it, you might just land yourself on the moon one day.

I want to remind the reader that in the autobiography *Last Man on the Moon*, Cernan writes that he inscribed his daughter's initials in the lunar surface, which will be undisturbed for all eternity as long as the surface doesn't get impacted by a meteor because of the absence of an atmosphere to blow it around. What a wonderful idea and eternal tribute to his daughter!

Apollo 17 was the last manned mission to the moon. Eugene Cernan was the commander, and geologist Jack Schmidt accompanied him to the lunar surface, where they had the pleasure of driving an electric-powered rover and covering 22 miles of alien territory during their three days of extravehicular activity. Cernan was the 11th person to step on the moon's surface and the last man to depart for a total of 12 humans who had walked on the moon. The importance of the number 12 has already been discussed and should not be missed here. Cernan was born on Pi Day, March 14, 1934.

They achieved a maximum speed of 11.2 miles per hour in the rover. (Did they round up from 11.11?) While in the navy, Cernan practiced his flying skills on a T-33 *Shooting Star* airplane. His first trip to space was aboard *Gemini 9A* in June 1966.[221] Cernan's mother pinned his "wings of gold" on his blue aviator outfit on 11/22/1957.[222]

I find it serendipitous that the *first* man (Armstrong) and the *last* man (Cernan) on the moon had both earned their engineering degrees from Purdue University.

Lastly, Israel's space agency launched a spacecraft to the moon on February 22, 2019 (2/22/19) in response to the Google Lunar X Prize challenge. Out of 32 original teams, only five remained active participants, and Israel's team was the 22nd to register. The challenge called for teams

221 https://en.wikipedia.org/wiki/Eugene_Cernan.
222 http://airportjournals.com/gene-cernan-always-shoot-for-the-moon-part-i/.

to produce an autonomous landing craft capable of traveling at least 500 meters and transmitting photographs back to Earth.[223] The mission, which was scheduled to reach the lunar surface on April 11, 2019, carried a time capsule loaded with digital files containing a Bible, children's drawings, Israeli songs, memories of a Holocaust survivor, and the blue-and-white Israeli flag. The spacecraft's name was *Beresheet,* or *Genesis* in English.[224]

LUNAR ECLIPSE OF JANUARY 2019

On January 21, 2019, there was a total lunar eclipse known as a "super blood wolf moon." A wolf moon refers to it being the first full moon of the year. The moon orbits the Earth in an elliptical path, with its closest approach at 221,681 miles and its farthest distance at 252,622, and during the eclipse it was approximately 222,274 miles away.[225] Notice that the moon's closest approach has a 22 in the most significant digits, while the farthest excursion has 22 in the two least significant digits, and has 2222 during an eclipse. That's a lot of 22s, wouldn't you agree? As if these numbers aren't interesting enough, consider that the eclipse reached totality at 12:12 a.m. (eastern time) on 1/21/19.

Acts 2:14 begins:

> Then Peter stood up with the *Eleven*, raised his voice and addressed the crowd: Fellow Jews and all of you who live in Jerusalem, let me explain this to you; listen carefully to what I say.

Verses 19–21 state:

> I will show wonders in the heavens above and signs on the earth below, blood and fire and billows of smoke. The sun will be turned to darkness and the moon to blood before the coming of the great and glorious day of the Lord. And everyone who calls on the name of the Lord will be saved.[226]

The last book of the Bible also speaks of the blood moon. Revelation 6:12–14 reads:

> And I beheld when he had opened the sixth seal, and, lo, there was

223 https://en.wikipedia.org/wiki/Google_Lunar_X_Prize.
224 https://news.yahoo.com/israels-first-lunar-mission-launch-week-163307004.html.
225 https://www.nbc26.com/news/national/a-super-blood-wolf-moon-eclipse-is-happening-this-weekend.
226 https://biblehub.com/niv/acts/2.htm.

> a great earthquake; and the sun became black as sackcloth of hair, and the moon became as blood.[227]

Adding to intrigue, current President Donald Trump was born on June 14, 1946, a day on which there was a total lunar eclipse.[228] Trump's birthdate 6/14 has digits which sum to 20, as well as his birth year 1946, whose digits also total 20, for a numerological signature of 20/20. Will Trump be reelected in 2020? Everything I have read seems to suggest this will happen. As the saying goes, "Hindsight is 20/20!" And so is perfect vision. 2020 will be a year of great illumination, hopefully in no small part due to the book in your hands right now. It's up to you to spread this message of hope!

> Behold, I shew you a mystery; We shall not all sleep, but we shall all be changed, In a moment, in the twinkling of an eye, at the last **trump**: for the **trumpet** shall sound, and the dead shall be raised incorruptible, and we shall be changed. For this corruptible must put on incorruption, and this mortal must put on immortality.
>
> –1 Corinthians 15:51-53 (KJV)[229]

While in the process of writing, I ordered another book titled *Fingerprints of the Gods* by Graham Hancock. It is more than 550 pages long, and I decided to quickly thumb through it after opening the package from the mail and landed on page 95, which talked about the ancient Mayan city in Mexico, Chichen Itza. Hancock goes on to explain that once a year at the spring equinox on March 21, a snakelike figure appears to dance down the north staircase of the Chichen Itza pyramid and persists for exactly 3 hours and 22 minutes.[230] Clearly, 3/21 is one day before 3/22, and compare that to the duration of the "snake," 3:22 hours. Remember this fact for when we get to the discussion about the planet Mars. As it turns out, my first overseas trip took place at age 7 while I lived at the address of 322 Hull Court, and I visited Chichen Itza during that trip. The number 322 will be revisited many more times in this book, so keep a mental note of this.

By itself, the discovery of this connection would have been interesting, but by itself, it would have been amazing for a few minutes before I got

227 https://www.express.co.uk/news/weird/1070303/Blood-moon-prophecy-eclipse-2019-super-blood-moon-bible-christianity/amp.
228 https://eclipse.gsfc.nasa.gov/LEplot/LEplot1901/LE1946Jun14T.pdf.
229 https://www.biblegateway.com/passage/?search=1+Corinthians+15%3A51-53&version=KJV.
230 Graham Hancock, *Fingerprints of the Gods* (New York: Three Rivers Press, 1995), 95.

over it, moved on, and just chalked it up to random coincidence. But these *coincidences*, or more appropriately, *synchronicities*, kept stacking up in my life's unfolding story, and each time I encountered the number 22, the impact grew progressively greater, to the point of being undeniable that a preordained, choreographed story was being shown to me, guided by an invisible hand in my life.

222 IN ROCKET SCIENCE

One of the more interesting courses I took during my undergraduate career was on orbital mechanics. While many of my peers were busily searching for the easiest blow-off elective courses they could find to round out their senior year, I chose to challenge myself with a course in rocket science. (One friend chose glass blowing, which I now regret not taking as a "blow"-off course.) I appealed to the University of Illinois Department of Aeronautical and Astronautical Engineering and was accepted into this class as well as a course on Satellite Dynamics in Space taught by a retired missile guidance expert from Lockheed-Martin. The teaching assistant, Bruce Powers, who I am good friends with to this day, told me that I was the first electrical engineering student in his twenty-five-plus years at the university to take these courses just for fun. As a bit of trivia, orbital mechanics falls at 522 under the category of "techniques in celestial mechanics" in the Dewey decimal system for categorizing books.[231]

In order for a satellite to maintain a geostationary orbit, whereby the orbital period of the satellite is exactly synchronized to the Earth's rotational period about its axis, a satellite must be parked at a radius of 22,236 miles above the Earth's equator at sea level. Any satellite that is at this magic distance from Earth will appear to remain parked over the same spot below. As the Earth rotates below, the satellite above also takes exactly 24 hours to make a complete revolution about the Earth's center of mass, causing the satellite to appear stationary overhead. This radius can be computed by equating the centripetal force equation to Newton's law of gravitation equation of the satellite with the same angular velocity as the Earth and then solving for the radius. I thought it was pretty cool to see the number 222 showing up in satellite orbit calculations.

As a humorous aside, I would like to remind the reader that Marvin the

231 http://bpeck.com/references/ddc/ddc_mine500.htm.

Martian from the *Looney Tunes* cartoon series that defined childhood for my generation was a character based on the Roman god of war, *Mars.*

That was the uniform that Mars wore—that helmet and skirt. We thought putting it on this ant-like creature might be funny. But since he had no mouth, we had to convey that he was speaking totally through his movements. It demanded a kind of expressive body mechanics.[232]

Marvin the Martian was probably my favorite of all the *Looney Tunes* characters.

Having seen the number 22 in popular culture, this is a perfect moment to transition into the actual history of the red planet. Mars in real life also has some interesting numbers that define its heavenly wanderings.

In ancient times, astronomers noted how certain lights moved across the sky as opposed to the *fixed stars,* which maintained a constant relative position in the sky. Ancient Greeks called these lights **πλάνητες ἀστέρες** (*planetes asteres*, meaning wandering stars) or simply **πλανῆται** (planetai, meaning wanderers), from which today's word *planet* was derived.[233], [234]

Mars made its closest approach to Earth (55,758,006 km) and maximum apparent brightness in nearly 60,000 years on August 27, 2003. This occurred when Mars was one day from opposition and about three days from its perihelion, making it particularly easy to see from Earth. The last Mars opposition occurred on May 22, 2016, at a distance of about 76 million kilometers. The last time it came so close is estimated to have been in the year 57,617 BC, and the next time will be in 2287. This record-close approach was only slightly closer than other recent close approaches. For instance, the minimum distance on August 22, 1924, was 0.37285 AU[235], and the minimum distance on August 24, 2208, will be 0.37279 AU.[236] For me, it is interesting to see all of the 22s associated with some of the major events in Mars' orbital history.

THE FIRST LANDING ON MARS: VIKING 1

The Mars Lander launched by NASA at 21:22 on August 20, 1975, known as *Viking 1,* made the first successful landing on the Martian surface on

232 https://en.m.wikipedia.org/wiki/Marvin_the_Martian.
233 http://www.perseus.tufts.edu/hopper/text?doc=Perseus%3Atext%3A1999.04.0058%3Aentry%3Dplanh%2Fths.
234 https://en.wikipedia.org/wiki/Planet.
235 1 AU or Astronomical Unit is defined as the Earth-sun distance or about 93 million miles
236 http://www.space.com/spacewatch/mars_10_closest_030822.html.

July 20, 1976, America's 200-year anniversary. At that time, it was quite possibly humanity's most spectacular achievement. The launch year, 1975, has digits that sum to 22. Let's investigate if there are any interesting numerical fingerprints at the landing site.

The *Viking 1* lander touched down in western Chryse Planitia (Golden Plain) at 22.3 degrees north, 48.0 degrees west. The lander's legs provided the craft with a 22-inch ground clearance. The Viking lander was programmed with enough instructions to operate for exactly 22 days without any contact with Earth. The lander operated for 2,245 sols until 11/11/1982, when a faulty command sent by ground control resulted in loss of contact.[237] (One sol equals one Martian day, and 2,245 sols is about 2,306 Earth days.) Approximately 22 kilograms of propellants were left at landing.[238]

It should come as no surprise by now to find out that the amount of time it takes to send a signal from Earth to Mars is between a minimum of 3 minutes, to a maximum of 22 minutes, depending on the relative distance between the two planets during their cosmic dance around the sun. Think of the two planets as two runners in a race around an elliptic racetrack with the sun in the middle. One racer, the Earth, goes faster because it is closer to the sun (under greater gravitational pull), and thus, it needs to resist a higher centripetal force. Its celestial dance partner, Mars, is farther from the sun and takes a more leisurely stride because the sun's gravitational field is significantly weaker out at Mars's orbital radius. At some point, the Earth catches up on Mars, and at this point when they pass, they are at their closest approach. Similarly, there will be a point when the two planets are farthest apart, when they are aligned in such a way that the two planets lie on a line with the sun in between them (or in *opposition*). The closest approach is when light takes 3 minutes, and at opposition, electromagnetic energy takes 22 minutes to go from one planet to the other. Electromagnetic energy means light, radio communications, and infrared energy all take between 3 and 22 minutes to span the distance between Earth and Mars.

I'd like to take this moment to remind the reader that my birthday is 3/22 and 3 represents March, the ancient Roman god, *Mars*.[239] It is quite fascinating to see the numbers 3 and 22 in the time it takes light to traverse

237 https://www.jpl.nasa.gov/news/fact_sheets/viking.pdf.
238 https://en.wikipedia.org/wiki/Viking_1.
239 https://www.mars-one.com/faq/mission-to-mars/what-will-the-astronauts-do-on-mars.

the Earth-Mars distance as well as in the GPS coordinates of the *Viking 1* lander at 22.3 degrees north latitude. While on the subject, it bears mentioning that March 21 typically heralds the spring equinox, when night and day are exactly divided into 12 hours each. Beginning on March 22, the amount of light during a 24-hour period begins to exceed the amount of dark in the northern hemisphere. This represents a transition out of the dark and into the light. The theme of light is a central theme in this book and will be expounded upon in exceptionally greater detail as we make progress toward the back cover. Now remember earlier in the book when I told you to remember the following sentence: "Hancock goes on to explain that once a year at the March equinox, a snakelike figure appears to dance down the north staircase of the Chichen Itza pyramid and persists for exactly 3 hours and 22 minutes."

Are you starting to pick up what I'm putting down here? My research into the number 22 has taken me down a rabbit hole of epic proportions. The topic seems virtually inexhaustible.

Let's get back to more facts on the dusty red planet. Mars's aphelion (maximum distance from sun) is 1.666 AU. Mars's diameter is roughly 4,222 miles.[240] Mars has no global magnetosphere as Earth does. Combined with a thin atmosphere, this permits a significant amount of ionizing radiation to reach the Martian surface. The *Mars Odyssey* spacecraft carries an instrument called the Mars Radiation Environment Experiment (MARIE), which measures the radiation. MARIE found that radiation levels in orbit above Mars are 2.5 times higher than at the International Space Station. The average daily radiation dose was about 220 Gy (22 mrad). A three-year exposure to such levels would be close to the safety limits currently adopted by NASA.[241] As a point of comparison, the Nuclear Regulatory Commission (NRC) limits nuclear power plant workers to a total dose of 5,000 millirems of radiation per year.[242] On Mars, at 22 mrem per day, you would reach the NRC limit after 227 days.

One of the most compact and lovely equations I've ever seen is $\pi^e = 22.459157$. It ties together two of nature's most beautiful numbers—the constants of Euler (e) and Archimedes (pi)—with one of the universe's other favorite numbers, 22.

You'll notice the spacecraft landed at 22.48 degrees north of the Martian

240 https://www.space.com/1582-earth-mars.html.
241 https://en.wikipedia.org/wiki/Colonization_of_Mars.
242 https://www.nrc.gov/about-nrc/radiation/health-effects/info.html.

equator, which is close to $\pi^e = 22.459157$. That's within eight parts in 10,000. We also notice that the duration of the lander's working life on the Martian surface was 2,248 sols, which is a most impressive $100\,\pi^e \approx 2{,}246$. Because it takes as long as 22 minutes for a radio signal to reach Mars, by the time of the landing, the last minutes of the descent into the alien atmosphere were made without real-time human involvement. We did our best to pick the zip code and neighborhood, but the invisible hand of God determined the precise landing spot, which locked all these GPS coordinates into the permanent record in the history of our galaxy.

Without the contributions of the classical mathematicians Archimedes and Euler, along with their respective famous numbers, phi and e, we would have never been able to design the equipment to get the spacecraft off the ground, much less to land it on Mars. Pi, e, and 22 have come together in a fascinating way. They are tributes to God, math, and the humans who figured out the natural laws of the universe and eternally memorialized them in mathematical form in such a way that allowed us to land earthly equipment on an alien planet millions of miles away.

MARS PATHFINDER

Just as I was planning to close out the section on Mars, I looked into the *Mars Pathfinder* mission to see if I could find any interesting clues, and once again, I was not disappointed. *Pathfinder* launched from Earth on December 4, 1996 (22 years before writing this!) and touched down on the red planet on July 4, 1997, at a place named Ares Vallis in a region called Chryse Planitia in the Oxia Palus quadrangle. The lander then opened, exposing the rover, which went on to conduct many experiments on the Martian surface.

The mission carried a series of scientific instruments designed to analyze the Martian atmosphere, climate, geology, and the composition of its rocks and soil. The spacecraft touched down at the GPS coordinates $19.13°N + 33.22°W$. Right away that was cause for excitement as once again, the numbers 22 and 33 showed up in an indisputable way.[243] The *Sojourner* rover took 16,500 pictures and transmitted them back to Earth.

Notice the uncanny collection of 11s, 22s, and 33s associated with this historic landing. This was the first time man-made equipment had touched the red planet in all human history! In my own life experiences, these three

243 https://tools.wmflabs.org/geohack/geohack.php?pagename=Mars_Pathfinder¶ms=19.13_N_33.22_W_globe:Mars.

numbers always seemed to show up in abundance around important times and events. The name of my birth month, March, comes from *Martius*, the first month of the earliest Roman calendar. It was named after Mars, the Roman god of war, and an ancestor of the Roman people through his sons, Romulus and Remus.[244] Perhaps my connection to the red planet through my birth month is what gave me the inspiration to dig for clues of God's handiwork in the Martian sand. The word *martial,* as in martial arts and martial law, owes its etymological origins to the god of war as well.

Mars has two very small moons, Deimos and Phobos, which mean *terror* and *fear* respectively in Greek. Phobos has an average diameter of 22 kilometers.[245] The second moon, Deimos, is 11 kilometers across at its smallest axis, and has a total volume of 999.8 cubic kilometers. Pretty darned close to a perfect 1,000.[246] Deimos was discovered on August 11, 1877, by Asaph Hall.[247]

It seems that I'm not the only one who has the numbers 11, 22, and 33 occurring at pivotal moments in the movie of life. NASA seems to have the same phenomena going on for them as well. It's almost as if our visit was anticipated. I think that time will bear out that we know much more about Mars than the government would have us know.

I'd like to close out the section on Mars with one last interesting fact. The largest mountain on Mars, Olympus Mons, is also the largest mountain in the *entire solar system*. It is also one of the physically biggest occurrences of the number 22, with an impressive height of 22 kilometers above the surrounding terrain, which is about 2.5 times the height of Mt. Everest. Mons is so massive that it would cover most of France or 100 percent of the surface area of Italy.

OTHER FAMOUS SPACE PROBES

The *Pioneer 11* spacecraft was shut down after 22 years of operation, after NASA determined that the intrepid explorer could no longer muster enough electric power to continue its functions. On September 29, 1995, NASA announced its decision to abandon the mission. *Pioneer 11* was the first spacecraft to encounter Saturn and the second of five artificial objects to achieve a high enough velocity to leave the solar system. The onboard

244 Mary Beard, John North, and Simon Price, *Religions of Rome* (Cambridge: Cambridge University Press, 1998), 47–48 and 53.
245 https://www.space.com/20413-phobos-deimos-mars-moons.html.
246 https://en.wikipedia.org/wiki/Deimos_(moon).
247 https://solarsystem.nasa.gov/moons/mars-moons/deimos/in-depth/.

computer was configured to accept 222 different commands from ground control, communicated over a radio frequency of 2292 Megahertz.[248]

NASA's *Voyager 1* probe is the most distant manmade object from Earth. As of July 19, 2019, the spacecraft had achieved a distance of 13.6 billion miles from the sun, or 22 billion kilometers. That's 11 + 11 billion. At this truly astronomical distance, it takes over 20 hours for radio signals traveling at the speed of light to reach Earth.[249] *Voyager 1* was originally planned to be called *Mariner 11* and its mission consisted of 11 scientific investigations.[250] Deep space exploration is a key component of the 11:11 Code of human awakening.

CELESTIAL HARMONIES

The planet Venus orbits the sun in a most elegant manner, which over a period of years exhibits the beautiful pattern as seen below. The "morning star" planet completes a circuit around the sun every 225 days.

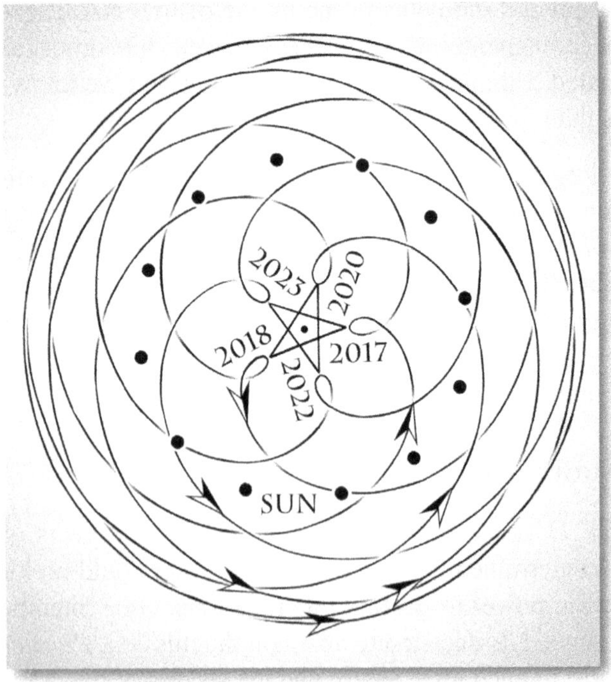

The five petals of Venus

248 https://en.wikipedia.org/wiki/Pioneer_11.
249 https://voyager.jpl.nasa.gov/mission/status/#where_are_they_now.
250 https://voyager.jpl.nasa.gov/mission/spacecraft/.

The pentagram of Venus is the path Venus makes as observed from Earth. Successive inferior conjunctions of Venus repeat very near a 13:8 orbital resonance, meaning Earth orbits 8 times for every 13 orbits of Venus.

While on the topic of Venus, there is a similar phenomenon to an eclipse in the Earth-moon-sun system: when a planet passes between the Earth and the sun, it is called a transit. These events do not block a high enough proportion of the solar flux to be seen without the aid of special telescopic equipment fitted for observing the sun. Venus transits the sun on a recurring pattern of 243 years (243 = 3 x 3 x 3 x 3 x 3 = 3^5), and the next transit will occur on 11/12/2117. Mathematics never ceases to profoundly fascinate those engaged in the scientific unraveling of nature's mysteries.

Pluto

Over the period of my lifetime, there has been considerable debate over whether or not Pluto should be considered a planet. The current agreed status is that of a dwarf planet. Does it have any impact on the price of a gallon of milk? Probably not. Let's roll with it for purposes of this discussion. The farthest known planet has a mass of 1.31 x 10^{22} kilograms or about one-sixth of Earth's moon. Pluto has five known moons—Charon, Styx, Nix, Kerberos, and Hydra—that orbit around the most solitary member of the solar system club.[251]

The innermost and largest moon, Charon, was discovered by James Christy on June 22, 1978, nearly half a century after Pluto was discovered. Charon's surface temperature is estimated to be -220 Celsius.[252] The Plutonian moons Styx, Nix, and Hydra are thought to be in a three-body orbital resonance with orbital periods in a ratio of 18:22:33. Here again, we see the numbers 22 and 33 showing up in the fundamental gears of the solar system's heavenly machinery.[253]

Comets

Comet 55P/Tempel-Tuttle is an interesting piece of ice whose orbit brings it near the sun once every 33.222 years.[254] Visits by the comet were noted in 1366, 1433, 1466, 1533, 1566, 1599, 1733, 1866, and 1933, and the

251 https://space-facts.com/pluto/.
252 https://space-facts.com/charon/.
253 http://www.historyoftheuniverse.com/index.php?p=pluto_2.htm.
254 https://en.wikipedia.org/wiki/55P/Tempel%E2%80%93Tuttle.

following cycles occurred in multiples of 33. Even more amazing is the fact that this comet is solely responsible for the Leonids meteor shower phenomenon. Adding further to the intrigue of this celestial show is the fact that these showers occur at a declination of 22 degrees above the plane of the ecliptic. With an estimated quarter-million shooting stars in a nine-hour period in one night alone, the shower of 1833 was so prolific that people were convinced the second coming of Christ was imminent.[255] Here we see the numbers 22, 33, and 222 showing up.

Comet Elenin 2010 X1, also dubbed the doomsday comet because of its relatively close approach to Earth at 22 million miles on October 16, 2011, sparked fears of an apocalypse if it veered off course and headed into Earth.[256] Elenin entered into opposition on Pi Day, 3/14/2011, while inbound toward the sun when the comet and the sun appeared to be on opposite sides of the celestial sphere as observed from an Earth-based frame of reference. Elenin achieved opposition again on its way back out into the solar system on 11/22/2011.[257]

If you thought that was a close shave, Comet P/2016 BA14 made the closest approach in 246 years at one-tenth of Elenin's distance at 2.2 million miles on March 22, 2016.[258]

The closest recorded comet encounter with Earth occurred on 7/1/1770 when Lexell's Comet came within 1.4 million miles or 2.2 million kilometers—a virtual scrape by astronomical standards![259] If there was just one more coat of paint on your house, it would have hit you.

Comet 46P/Wirtanen was affectionately dubbed the Christmas Comet because of its visibility up to December 22, 2018. Wirtanen also gave off a festively greenish color to match the holiday.[260]

I find it remarkable to observe these occurrences of 11 and 22 showing up in the orbital parameters of some of the most significant comet encounters in recorded history. Why hasn't someone else already put this together? Why did it take a kid with the life number 22 to tie it all together? I don't know, but I'm sure happy to have this opportunity do it.

255 https://en.wikipedia.org/wiki/Leonids.
256 https://www.space.com/13302-doomsday-comet-elenin-pieces-earth-flyby.html.
257 http://www.icq.eps.harvard.edu/C2010X1_ICQ_MSS-R2.pdf.
258 https://earthsky.org/space/twin-comets-approach-closely-in-march.
259 https://www.skyandtelescope.com/observing/p2016-ba14-closest-comet-in-almost-250-years03162016/.
260 https://www.npr.org/2018/12/17/677342378/green-christmas-comet-visible-in-night-sky.

MERCURY

Transits of Mercury with respect to Earth are much more frequent than transits of Venus, 13 or 14 happening per century, in part because Mercury is closer to the sun and orbits it more rapidly. Transits of Mercury occur in May or November. The last four transits occurred on November 15, 1999; May 7, 2003; November 8, 2006; and May 9, 2016. The next will occur on November 11, 2019. That's 11/11/19. Think *The 11:11 Code*.[261], [262]

The constant motion of planets around the sun means that the distance between Earth and Mercury is in constant flux. When both planets are on opposite sides of the sun, they can achieve their maximum distance of 137 million miles (222 million kilometers). When they are at their closest, they are only 48 million miles (77.3 million kilometers) apart.[263] In a few more pages, you will be introduced to the magical number 137, but for the moment, just make another mental note of this very important number for later. The reader should have a pretty good feel for the number 222, but I will continue to build your understanding as the book develops further. In the section on the golden ratio, you saw that the leaves of a plant instinctively place themselves at a spacing of 360 degrees divided by phi (1.618), so we get 222.5 degrees, or if we take the short way around the circle, we get 137.5 degrees. These two numbers add up to 360. This seems to be an odd coincidence, but it is easily explained because the conversion factor between miles and kilometers is 1.62, which is very close to the golden ratio. But it is fascinating to see it show up in the geometric properties of the planets of our solar system. It's utterly remarkable to me.

There are far more examples of geometric harmonies in the solar system, but in order to keep this book at a reasonable length, the curious reader should research *planetary orbital resonance* independently to see more examples. This noble subject deserves its own book.

PHI IN THE EARTH-MOON SYSTEM

The Earth-moon system has the golden ratio hidden within its design as well. The line connecting the center of the Earth to the center of the moon is 8,114.07 kilometers. This forms the adjacent side of the triangle below. The radius of the Earth is 6,378.10 kilometers. The hypotenuse connect-

261 https://in-the-sky.org/news.php?id=20191111_11_101.
262 https://en.m.wikipedia.org/wiki/Transit_of_Mercury.
263 https://amp.space.com/18646-mercury-distance.html.

ing the radius of the Earth to the center of the moon is gotten by using the Pythagorean theorem as 10,321 kilometers. Now divide the hypotenuse by the Earth's radius, and you get 10,321/6,378 = 1.618, which is almost *exactly* the golden ratio.[264] Unbelievable!

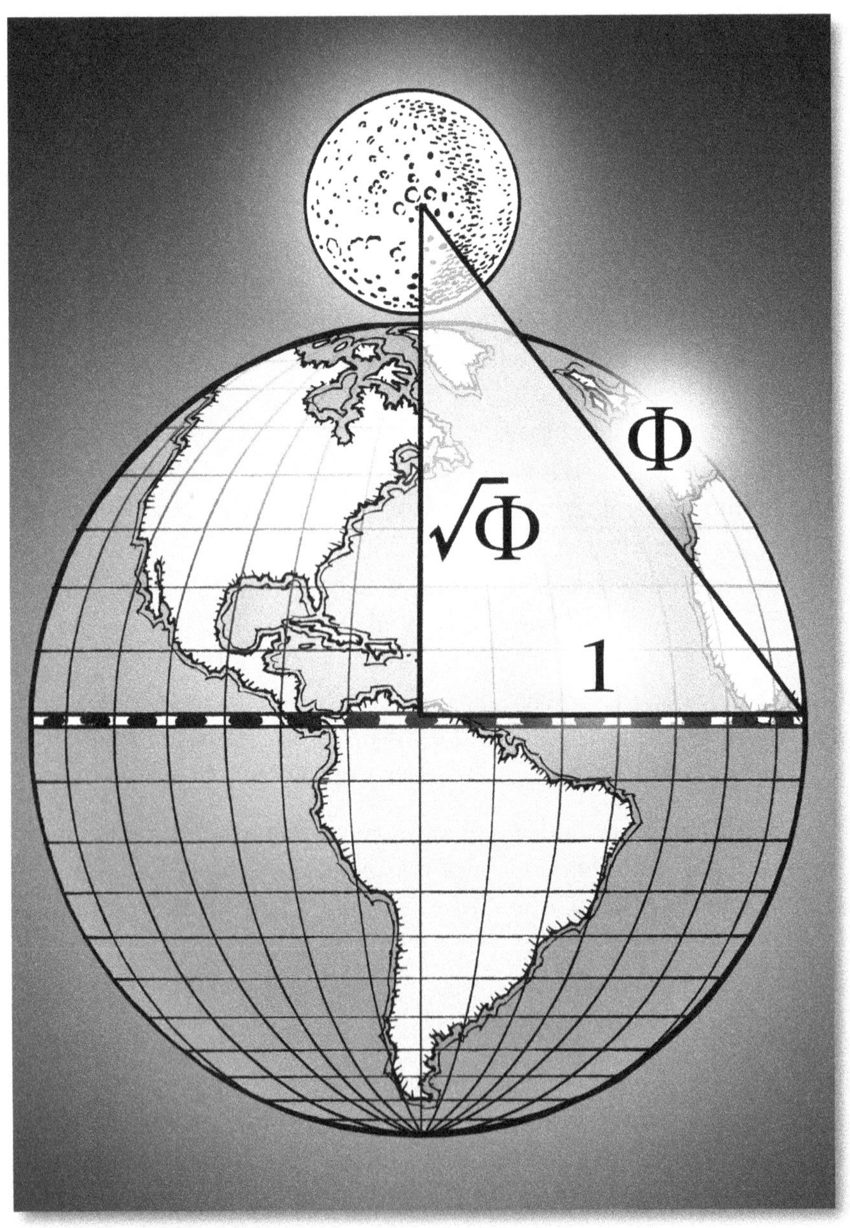

264 www.goldennumber.net.

But wait, it gets better. The moon's mass is 7.435 x 10^{22} kilograms, which is equivalent to 1.619 x 10^{23} pounds. The former has 22 zeroes following the number 7.35, while the pound equivalent has the golden ratio followed by 23 zeroes. Pick your pleasure. Does the golden ratio occur anywhere else in the solar system?

PHI THROUGHOUT THE SOLAR SYSTEM

Let's look into the "spacing of the spheres" in our solar system and look for harmonies. As with the relative dimensions of the Earth and moon containing the golden ratio, it turns out that all the planets in the solar system on average have a spacing that obeys the golden ratio. Based on data taken from NASA's website, I have compiled the following table:[265]

Planet	Dist/Sun	Ratio
Mercury	57.91	1
Venus	108.21	1.86859
Earth	149.6	1.3825
Mars	227.92	1.52353
Ceres	413.79	1.81552
Jupiter	778.57	1.88154
Saturn	1,433.53	1.84123
Uranus	2,872.46	2.00377
Neptune	4,495.06	1.56488
Pluto	5,869.66	1.3058
Average		1.618736

The "dist/sun" column is each planet's mean distance from the sun in kilometers. The right column is derived by first calling Mercury's distance "1 unit." Then we took Venus's distance divided by Mercury's and got 1.868. Next, I took Earth's distance and divided it by Venus's and so on out to Pluto. All ten of these ratios add up to 16.187, so dividing by 10 gives us the average spacing ratio of 1.618736, which is equal to phi within 0.04 percent or 4 parts in 10,000! This works whether you are using miles, kilometers, furlongs, cubits, or barleycorns. The units divide out when we take the ratio of the dimensions. On average, the ratio of the distance of one planet to the sun is equal to its inner neighbor's sun distance multi-

265 https://nssdc.gsfc.nasa.gov/planetary/factsheet/planet_table_ratio.html.

plied by the golden ratio. This should make the hair stand up on your arms and neck.

How could this *possibly* be coincidental and not be the product of some cosmic architect? Why should the Fibonacci sequence that we used to derive the golden ratio have anything whatsoever to do with the proportions of the Earth and moon?

But wait. There's one more zinger I'd like to throw at you before we jump to the next topic. During my research, I randomly decided to research significant events that occurred in the year 1618, which of course is the golden ratio (1.618) times a thousand, just to see what if anything remarkable may have happened during that year. Clearly, I wouldn't be writing about it here if this search turned up without something fascinating. After reading the foregoing section on the golden ratio occurring in the relative arrangement of the planets, would you be shocked to learn that Johannes Kepler discovered his famous third law of planetary motion in the year 1618?[266] Kepler's third law, which gives a relationship between the amount of time that a planet (or any celestial body or spacecraft) takes to complete a full revolution around the sun, based on the knowledge of how far the planet is from the sun.

Additionally, these facts were connected by this book almost exactly four hundred years after Kepler's great discoveries. How's that for timing?

While we're at it, it's worth mentioning that the next year, in 1619 (think about the golden ratio again), Galileo first coined the term *aurora borealis* to refer to the northern nights, borrowing from the Roman goddess of the dawn and the Greek name for the north wind.[267] It has been discovered that the peak aurora activity correlates very closely with the 11-year sunspot activity cycles.[268] In 1966, a spacecraft named *Explorer 33* was launched to study the sun's behavior, specifically as it pertains to the aurorae and the coronal mass ejections that cause them.[269] When we dig into the numerology of the Sun, you'll see that the choice of 33 for the *Explorer* spacecraft is quite fascinating, and lucky, as I will demonstrate shortly.

Before we transition from the astronomical scale to the quantum scale, let's recognize a unifying principle. The solar system is composed of eight

266 https://www.nasa.gov/kepler/education/johannes.

267 https://www.aurorahunter.com/photos/goddess-of-dawn.html.

268 https://deepblue.lib.umich.edu/bitstream/handle/2027.42/94796/grl13462.pdf;jsessionid=4CC113B55FCF8E727D8F2E239CEDFD23?sequence=1.

269 https://nssdc.gsfc.nasa.gov/nmc/experiment/display.action?id=1966-058A-05.

undisputed planets, and much of the rules of chemistry obey the octet rule, which states that atoms of main-group elements tend to combine in a manner such that each atom has eight electrons in its valence shell, giving it the same stable electron configuration as a noble gas.[270] So there you have it—eight planets orbiting a central star and eight electrons orbiting the central atom. Same cosmic intelligence behind both models of reality at two vastly different scales.

Golden Ratio at the Quantum Scale

In quantum physics, the smallest distance physically possible based on our current understanding is called the Planck length, which is equal to 1.616 x 10^{33} centimeters. The Planck length can be defined from three fundamental physical constants—the speed of light in a vacuum (c), the Planck constant (h), and the gravitational constant (G). This most basic unit of length in the universe as we know it is within 0.1 percent of being equal to the golden ratio (1.618) with the decimal point moved 33 places to the left. This is equivalent to a person who is 99.87 years of age simply rounding up to say he or she is a hundred. This is a remarkable finding.

As we observed a few pages ago, the divine fingerprint phi showed up in the proportions of the solar system and in the proportions of the spiral arms of the Milky Way galaxy at the grandest scale. Now we see Phidias's number (phi) showing up at the tiniest distance known to man—the Planck length. It seems as though the universal Creator may have left some signature clues to let us know that none of this is random but rather the result of a deliberate and extremely intelligent act of creation by someone with the ability to *simultaneously* view the universe at *all* scales of magnification—from the greatest cosmic scale to the most miniscule quantum scintilla.

The Sun and The 11:11 Code

Let's return to investigating the physical properties of our nearest star, the sun. The surface area of the sun is 12,000 times that of the Earth, and its volume is 1.3 million times that of the home planet.

The sun completes a sunspot activity cycle every 11 years on average, and the Babcock-Leighton cycle is completed every 22 years, which cor-

270 https://www.britannica.com/science/octet-rule.

responds to an oscillatory exchange of energy between toroidal (rings that encircle the sun around its polar axis) and poloidal (field lines that connect between the poles) solar magnetic fields. The sun's rotational rate varies depending on latitude, spinning at a faster rate near the poles as compared to the zones closer to the equator. Because of convective motion owing to heat transport as well as the Coriolis effect, the sun exhibits this phenomenon of differential rotation. When compared to the fixed background of the stars, the poles rotate at a rate of one rotation approximately every 33 (11 + 11 + 11) days.[271]

Russian archaeologist Aleksandr Chizhevsky authored a paper titled "Physical Factors of the Historical Process," which documented how he compared sunspot records to major historical events in 72 countries from 500 BC to 1922, and he found a high correlation around solar maxima. He divided the solar cycle into four periods and found correlations between human behavior and these periods. He discovered (1) a three-year period of minimum activity characterized by passivity and autocratic rule; (2) a two-year period during which masses begin to organize under new leaders and one theme; (3) a three-year period of maximum excitability, revolution, and war; and lastly (4) a three-year period of gradual decrease in excitability until the masses are apathetic. He considered these variations as mass human excitability.[272] According to David Wilcock, Chizhevsky found that 80 percent of the most significant events on Earth took place during solar maxima.[273]

According to the UCAR website,

> The 11-year sunspot cycle is actually half of a longer, 22-year cycle of solar activity. Each time the sunspot count rises and falls, the magnetic field of the Sun associated with sunspots reverses polarity; the orientation of magnetic fields in the Sun's northern and southern hemispheres switch. Thus, in terms of magnetic fields, the solar cycle is only complete (with the fields back the way they were at the start of the cycle) after two 11-year sunspot cycles. This solar cycle is, on average, about 22 years long—twice the duration of the sunspot cycle.[274]

271 https://en.wikipedia.org/wiki/Sun & https://www.aanda.org/articles/aa/pdf/2014/03/aa22635-13.pdf
272 http://www.marketoracle.co.uk/Article33586.html
273 David Wilcock, *The Synchronicity Key: The Hidden Intelligence Guiding the Universe and You* (New York: Dutton, 2013), 33
274 https://scied.ucar.edu/sunspot-cycle.

> On top of these two cycles, there is also an 88-year cycle known as the Gleissberg cycle. (Recall that 88 = 4 x 22.) If you take 11 + 22, you get 33, the age of Jesus Christ when he died two millennia ago. Side note: The Catholic rosary contains 33 beads, while its Islamic counterpart has 99 (3 x 33) as an aid to memorizing and reciting the 99 attributes of God.[275]

Swiss mathematician and astronomer Rudolf Wolf was a professor of astronomy at the University of Bern in 1844 and became director of the Bern Observatory in 1847. Inspired by the discovery of the sunspot cycle by German astronomer Heinrich Schwabe, he dug up all of the historical sunspot activity observation records he could get his hands on, going back all the way to the year 1610, and calculated a period of 11.1 years. Isn't that amazingly close to 11.11 years? The difference is only one hundredth of a percentage point from being exactly 11.11 years! The difference between 11.1 and 11.11 is a mere 3.7 days. In 1852, Wolf was one of four people who discovered the link between the cycle and geomagnetic activity on Earth. The Wolf number is now the standard unit used in modern astronomy to quantify the intensity of a sunspot.[276] That guy sure had a cool last name.

The sun's mass is approximately 333,000 times that of the Earth.[277] The sun is primarily composed of hydrogen, 73 percent to be exact, and let's note that 73 is a star number! Hydrogen will spontaneously combust in air if exposed to a temperature of 500 degrees Celsius (932 degrees Fahrenheit).[278] Another fact that I discovered while writing this book is that light takes 8 minutes and 20 seconds to travel from the sun to the Earth. That's not terribly interesting until you convert it to seconds, which reveals 8 x 60 + 20 = 500 seconds. The trip takes exactly 500 seconds for light to reach us from our nearest star! Now let's take the sun-Earth mass ratio of 333,000 and divide it by the spontaneous combustion temperature of hydrogen, 500 degrees Celsius. The following comes out: 333,000/500 = 666. The number 666 is clearly associated with the physical characteristics of the sun. The same result happens if we take the 333,000 size ratio and divide it by the 500 seconds that light takes to reach Earth.

From the foregoing investigation, we have the numbers 11, 22, and 33

275 https://www.theclassroom.com/difference-between-rosary-islamic-prayer-beads-5660.html.

276 https://en.m.wikipedia.org/wiki/Rudolf_Wolf.

277 http://solar-center.stanford.edu/vitalstats.html.

278 P. Patnaik, *A Comprehensive Guide to the Hazardous Properties of Chemical Substances* (Wiley-Interscience, 2007), 402.

embedded into the physical properties of the sun. Is this a veiled message that Christ, the *Son* of God, who lived to age 33, is associated with the *sun,* and he is the God of light? In the tradition of Christmas, the sun *dies* for three days at the winter solstice, 12/21, which is the point in the year when the sun is at its lowest peak (noon) elevation in the northern hemisphere sky for the year, and it is born again or resurrected on December 25. Note the 22 sandwiched in the middle of an 11 on the date 12/21. This also corresponds to the Mayan calendar prediction that a new great cycle of time would begin on 12/21/2012, with digits that add up to 11 as (1 + 2 + 2 + 1 + 2 + 0 + 1 + 2). At this point in time, the sun was aligned with the center of the Milky Way for the first time in about 26,000 years. This was a rare astronomical alignment. This means that whatever energy typically streams to Earth from the center of the Milky Way was disrupted on 12/21/12 at 11:11 p.m. Greenwich mean time.[279] Gregory Sams has written a fascinating book on the spiritual aspects of the sun.[280]

The sun converts 3.7 x 10^{38} protons into alpha particles (helium nuclei) every second. If we shift the decimal point one place to the right and reduce the exponent by one power, we are left with the same exact number but written in a slightly different way. The equivalent is 37 x 10^{37} protons being converted to alpha particles per second.[281] That's 37 followed by 37 zeroes. That's a *lot* of activity, and even more interestingly, we see the *star* number 37 show up twice in the activity of the star that is directly responsible for all life on Earth and that supplied the power to run my computer as I type this. Having seen the numbers 33, 37, and 333 showing up in the Sun's physical process, I thought it was fascinating to discover that if you take 3.333333 … and raise it to the 3rd power, you arrive at 37.037037037 …which is 37 + 37/1,000 +37/1,000,000 +…

Now you have seen 11, 22, 33, and 37 in the sun's physical processes. What an ingenious way for God to have left the sun with a method of literally *sending* us numerological clues encoded as electromagnetic (light) signals from 93,000,000 miles away. I'll remind the reader that 11 + 22 + 33 = 66, which gives us the number of books in the Bible.

Now let's get back to the number of man. In 1666, Isaac Newton first observed the sun's light using a prism, and he showed that it is made up of

279 http://www.dimension1111.com/the-number-11-celestial-events-and-calendars.html.

280Gregory Sams, *Sun of gOd: Discover the Self-Organizing Consciousness That Underlies Everything* (San Francisco: Weiser Books, 2009).

281 K. J. H. Phillips, *Guide to the Sun* (Cambridge: Cambridge University Press, 1995), 47–53.

light of many colors (actually 7 principal colors on the R-O-Y-G-B-I-V[282] rainbow scale accepted by science). Notice the number 666 is embedded in that year. The frequency boundary between the blue and violet spectra was arbitrarily chosen to be 668 terahertz, which is within 0.3 percent of 666 THz.[283]

Under the tropical zodiac, the sun transits the constellation Virgo (the virgin) sector of the heavens on average between August 23 and September 22. While this is only one story in one myth of the origin of Virgo, she is seen throughout all matter of myths. According to Egyptian myths, when the constellation Virgo was in the sun, that signaled the start of the wheat harvest season, thus connecting Virgo to the wheat. She also has various connections with the India goddess Kanya and even the Virgin Mary.[284] While some believe this may be the basis of the virgin birth story of Christ, I am not representing this to necessarily be true. Nor am I stating it as my opinion. I am offering this to help understand ancient beliefs that preceded Christianity. Christianity is an ancient religion, but it is not the oldest by any means. One need only consult the fossil record to understand that the Earth is a *lot* older than two thousand years. Much of the Bible is written allegorically to explain inexplicable concepts through abstract means. The Bible was never meant to be interpreted 100 percent literally.

It is important to remember that the word *myth* in the context of this book is not the same as the common cultural connotation of a naïve, childish story based on puerile fiction. According to *Merriam-Webster's* online dictionary, the word *myth* is defined as follows:

> "1 **a**: A usually traditional story of ostensibly historical events that serves to unfold part of the world view of a people or explain a practice, belief, or natural phenomenon. Creation *myths*
>
> **b**: PARABLE, ALLEGORY Moral responsibility is the motif of Plato's *myths*.
>
> "2 **a**: A popular belief or tradition that has grown up around something or someone; *especially*: one embodying the ideals and institutions of a society or segment of society."[285]

282 ROYGBIV stands for red, orange, yellow, green, blue, indigo, and violet, which is the spectrum of visible light in order of increasing frequency or decreasing wavelength.

283 Thomas J. Bruno and Paris D. N. Svoronos, *CRC Handbook of Fundamental Spectroscopic Correlation Charts* (CRC Press, 2005).

284 https://www.britannica.com/place/Virgo.

285 https://www.merriam-webster.com/dictionary/myth.

Merriam-Webster's offers a more dignified definition than society's idea that a myth is something generally taken to be false or purely fictional. This section of the book was written in the spirit of definition #2 for myth.

Here you see an amulet with the magic square of the sun that has all the numbers 1 through 36 listed once but in a clever way such that all the numbers in any row or column sum to 111.[286] As discussed in the previous section, summing all numbers from 1 through 36 gives us the following: 1 + 2 + … + 36 = 666. This is the same result if you stacked up logs in a triangular pile where the first layer had 36 logs (36 = 6 x 6), piled 35 logs on the next layer and then 34 and so on till the last single log completed the top of the pyramid. Finally, you would then have 666 logs in the pile. Also note that 36 is equal to 6 times 6. Lastly, I'll leave you with one more solar fact. The sun orbits the center of the Milky Way galaxy at an estimated velocity of 220 kilometers per second.

Escaping Earth's Embrace

In order to escape the Earth's gravitational pull, a spacecraft must achieve a speed of 11,100 meters per second (24,900 miles per hour). Going that speed, you won't fall back to Earth. The number 11,100 is equal to 100 x 111, and remember that 111 is composed of 3 x 37. This figure does not take into account the fact that Earth is rotating. Thus, that movement contributes to the tangential (west-to-east) launch velocity if the rocket is

286 http://cosmos2000.chez.com/Numbers/666_Origins.html.

launched eastward. If a rocket is launched tangentially from the Earth's equator toward the west, it requires an initial velocity of about 11.665 km/s relative to Earth in order to escape. This is extremely close to 11.666 km/sec.[287]

The Earth's circumference is 24,900 miles, so the speed to escape its gravitational pull (24,900 miles/hour) is the same speed to take a trip around the Earth's circumference of 24,900 miles in one hour. As if this wasn't interesting enough, the escape velocity is equal to 33 times the speed of sound. This number 33 keeps showing up in so many unexpected places.

Global Positioning System

Would it surprise you to know that the GPS navigation system was originally composed of 33 (11 + 11 + 11) satellites orbiting Earth? According to Geospatial World, 31 of the original 33 are still operational today.[288] Now would be an intriguing moment to connect the fact that these 33 satellites guide literally billions of people about their daily travels. Adding further to intrigue, the Geospatial World site explains that China's national GPS system, which is called *BeiDou*, has 22 operational satellites currently in orbit, and Europe's GPS system, Galileo, is also presently comprised of 22 satellites. What gives? Is it pure coincidence that these multiples of eleven keep showing up in the heavens, in man-made systems and endeavors as well as in celestial bodies?

Twinkle, Twinkle, Little Star

In his book *Cosmos*, physicist Carl Sagan wrote that there are approximately hundred billion galaxies (10^{11}). Sagan further estimates that on average, each galaxy contains about one hundred billion stars (10^{11}). Combining these two estimates, we get (10^{11}) x (10^{11}) = (10^{22}), ten billion trillion stars in total.[289]

It is exciting for me to see our little friends 11 and 22, showing up in the estimate of the number of stars and galaxies in the universe.

Discovering this occurrence of the 11:11 code in the vastness of space was

287 https://infogalactic.com/info/Escape_velocity.

288 https://www.geospatialworld.net/blogs/what-are-the-various-gnss-systems/.

289 Carl Sagan, *Cosmos* (New York: Ballantine Books, 2013).

one of my most significant *Aha!* moments while researching and writing this work.

Carl Sagan also pointed out that the total number of elementary particles in the universe is around 10^{80} (the Eddington number) and that if the whole universe were packed with neutrons so that there would be no empty space anywhere, there would be around 10^{128}. He also noted the similarity of the second calculation to that of Archimedes in *The Sand Reckoner*.[290]

Taking the concept of the googol to an insanely higher level, Kasner defined a mind-warping number termed the googolplex, which is defined as $10^{googol} = 10^{10^{100}}$. In the PBS science program *Cosmos: A Personal Voyage*, episode 9, titled "The Lives of the Stars," astronomer and television personality Carl Sagan estimated that writing a googolplex in full decimal form (i.e., "10,000,000,000 …") would be physically impossible since doing so would require more space than is available in the known universe.[291] Not too surprisingly, Google Inc.'s global headquarters is nicknamed the Googleplex, located in Mountainview, California.[292] Founded on September 4, 1998, Google will celebrate its (11 + 11)th year in business in 2020, the same year this work was published.

As if our brains aren't already hurting enough, there is still an unimaginably larger number than the googolplex, known as the googolplex*plex*, written as $10^{googolplex} = 10^{10^{googol}}$, which is far beyond anything we can compare to in the known universe. I imagine God could handle such numbers in his head quicker than Mary Poppins could say *supercalifragilisticexpialidocious*. For the rest of us mere mortals, the concept of infinity will probably continue to boggle the human mind for all eternity. Even more mind-boggling than all of that is the fact that mathematics gives us the power to express numbers that wouldn't fit in the volume of the universe but can be expressed in the space of less than a postage stamp here on this paper! Let that set in. Mathematics is quite literally the universal language.

I'll leave the reader another gem of inspiration: I wondered, on a chance thought while writing, "…how many atoms of carbon would there be in

290 Carl Sagan, *Cosmos* (New York: Ballantine Books, 2013).
291 https://curiosity.com/topics/how-big-is-a-googolplex/.
292 https://www.economist.com/briefing/2007/08/30/inside-the-googleplex.

a 1-carat diamond?" The answer was as brilliant as a well-cut, one-carat diamond.

One mole of diamond material (carbon) weighs 12.01 grams. From the definition of Avogadro's number, we know that one mole of *any* substance contains 6.022 x 10^{23} molecules. One carat is defined as 0.2 grams.[293] Putting all of this together, we can come up with the *actual number* (not just an estimate!) of carbon atoms contained in a flawless 1-carat diamond:

$$\left(6.022\times10^{23}\frac{atoms}{mole}\right)\times\left(\frac{1mole}{12.01gram}\right)\times\left(\frac{0.2gram}{1}\right)=1.003\times10^{22}\,atoms$$

Notice that the units of moles and grams cancel out through the factor label operations. This means that there are almost exactly 10 sextillion atoms, or you can think of this as ten billion groups of one trillion atoms in a single-carat diamond.[294] That's enough atoms for each of Earth's 7.53 billion people to have 1.328 trillion atoms apiece. Remember that 22 = 11 + 11. There you have *The 11:11 Code* in a diamond! I'd also like to remark that one pound of diamonds corresponds to 2264 carats.[295]

Let's explore this large number/small space phenomenon in the context of a physical object. The number of carbon atoms in a 1-carat diamond is approximately equal to the number of stars in the universe (remember Dr. Sagan's estimation of the number of stars in the known universe being 10^{22}?). Let that sink in.

When you look into a diamond, do you see millions of tiny, twinkling stars? When you look at the night sky, do you see millions of sparkling diamonds? Was there something deeper to the childhood rhyming song? Could this be some form of divine reciprocity/duality principle at work with some cosmic creative intellect that is as perfectly comfortable operating at the infinite scale as it is at the infinitesimal?

Here's one last fact on diamonds. If you shine a light perpendicularly into the surface of a diamond, the light will pass through. As you increasingly vary the angle, light will begin to internally reflect once the angle reaches the critical angle of 23.4 degrees as determined by Irish physicist John Tyndall.[296] Add 23.4 to its mirror image, 43.2, and you get 66.6, or ten percent of the so-called number of the beast, 666.

293 https://en.wikipedia.org/wiki/Carat_(mass)

294 https://socratic.org/questions/a-1-00-carat-pure-diamond-has-a-mass-of-0-2-grams-how-many-carbon-atoms-are-ther

295 https://sciencenotes.org/karat-vs-carat/

296 https://www.gutenberg.org/files/14000/14000-h/14000-h.htm.

We have seen and discussed the properties of the number 23.4 many times earlier in this book. I don't know what to make of this other than to say it is fascinating to see this number showing up in diamonds. It is this property of total internal reflection that allows the diamond to collect light from many different directions and emit it out in a few chosen directions so as to appear most brilliant to the observer. Let's recall that a diamond is made of pure carbon, which has 6 electrons, 6 protons, and 6 neutrons (6-6-6). Would you be surprised to find out that the most popular diamond cut, the brilliant cut, has 33 facets on the top side or *crown*? The marquise, oval, and pear cuts also have 33 facets on top and 22 facets on the pavilion (underside).[297]

Look for the mathematical harmonies, symmetries, and patterns in nature, and with enough persistence, you may just happen to find the creative spirit of the universe waiting to connect with you. Everything has purpose.

ANDROMEDA

Our nearest galactic neighbor is the Andromeda galaxy, also known as NGC 224, and it has about one *trillion* stars in it. That's enough for each and every one of Earth's 7.6 billion people to wish upon 132 unique stars.

This massive collection of stars is so wide that it takes light approximately 220,000 years to travel across its diameter at a speed of 300,000 kilometers per second. The Andromeda galaxy is so massive that it weighs an estimated 1.1×10^{11} (1.1 with 11 trailing zeroes) *times* the mass of our sun, which is already incomprehensibly huge, as it would take 1.3 million Earths to fill the volume of our sun. The size of Earth is already hard enough to comprehend when considering it takes about fifteen hours to fly from Chicago to Tokyo at 560 miles per hour or 75 percent of the speed of sound! The Andromeda galaxy has an apparent magnitude of approximately -22. Andromeda is estimated to be located at a distance of 1.625×10^{11} astronomical units (1 AU = 93,000,000 miles, the average Earth-sun distance). Notice that 1.625 is very close to the golden ratio, 1.618 and is probably in the same ballpark as the accuracy of the distance estimate.

In 1922, Ernst Öpik was the first astronomer to attempt to estimate the distance of Andromeda using the measured velocities of its stars. His result placed the Andromeda nebula far outside our galaxy at a distance of

297 https://www.info-diamond.com/polished/diamond-shape-cut.php.

about 450,000 parsecs (1,500,000 light-years), which is nearly within the same order of magnitude as the currently accepted estimates.[298]

Tycho's Supernova

Suggested listening: *Chilloutdeer* – "Peaceful Winter Chillout Mix"

On November 2, 1572, famous Danish astronomer Tycho Brahe noticed during observation of the heavens that a new star had appeared out of nowhere. The appearance of the Milky Way supernova of 1572 belongs among the more important observation events in the history of astronomy. Until this point in time, the Aristotlean school of thought held that the realm of the stars was not subject to change. It was the realm of eternal permanence. The prevailing viewpoint held that the heavens were essentially in their steady state condition and no new stars were forming since the original creation event. The appearance of the new star helped revise ancient models of the heavens and speed on a revolution in astronomy that began with the realization of the need to produce better astrometric star catalogues and, by extension, the need for more precise astronomical observing instruments.

The supernova of 1572 is often called Tycho's supernova because of Tycho Brahe's extensive work, *De nova et nullius aevi memoria prius visa stella* (which translates to "Concerning the Star, new and never before seen in the life or memory of anyone," published in 1573 with reprints overseen by Johannes Kepler in 1602 and 1610), a work containing both Tycho Brahe's own observations and the analysis of sightings from many other observers. Tycho was not the first to observe the 1572 supernova, although he was believed to have recorded the most accurate observations of the stellar explosion.

In Ming dynasty China, the star became an issue between Zhang Juzheng and the young Wanli emperor. In accordance with the cosmological tradition, the emperor was warned to consider his misbehavior since the new star was interpreted as an evil omen.[299]

More reliable contemporary reports state that the new star itself burst forth soon after November 2, and by November 11, was already brighter

298 https://www.cfa.harvard.edu/~dfabricant/huchra/ay202/opik.pdf.
299 https://en.wikipedia.org/wiki/SN_1572.

than Jupiter. Around November 16, 1572, it reached its peak brightness at about magnitude -4.0, some descriptions saying that it was equal to Venus when that planet was at its brightest. The supernova remained visible to the naked eye into early 1574, gradually fading until it disappeared from view.

There you have it. On 11/11/1572, the world witnessed the first death of a star in recorded history.[300]

While on the subject of famous astronomers, I want to talk about Edwin Hubble, after whom the Hubble Space Telescope was named. It is remarkable that his observations of distant nebulae (stellar clouds), which began in 1922, resulted in the discovery that proved conclusively that these nebulae were much too distant to be part of the Milky Way. Based on his revolutionary observations, he was able to prove that these were, in fact, entire galaxies outside our own. This discovery was one of the greatest contributions to humankind's understanding of the mind-shattering vastness of space.[301]

Take ten minutes and look up the video
"AmBeam—5th Dimension."

The Crab Nebula

On New Year's Eve of 2018, I was stargazing and for some unexplainable reason, my eyes were drawn to the constellation Taurus. There was an expanse of apparently empty space between Orion and Taurus where I tried to peer with my naked eyes to see if there was anything there to be seen. After about thirty seconds, I was able to make out a star so tiny that it was at the limits of my visual acuity. Keep in mind that I wasn't looking for anything in particular. I have been using the *SkyView* app on my smart phone and wanted to test the limits of how small an object the app could detect, so I trained it on the infinitesimal speck of light. I wasn't expecting anything to come up but was absolutely gobsmacked to find out that I had accidentally happened to stumble upon the Crab Nebula. Out of all the millions of stars in the sky, why was my attention drawn to this imperceptibly tiny mote of light? This sent chills down my spine.

The neutron star at the center of the Crab Nebula emits a burst of electro-

300 http://www.astronomy.com/magazine/ask-astro/2018/03/supernova-of-1572.
301 http://www.sciography.com/edwi-hubble.htm.

magnetic energy every 33.11 milliseconds, which spans frequencies from radio waves to X-rays.[302] These energetic bursts are the result of the central star rotating at an astonishing rate of 30.2 times per second. The Crab Nebula is so far away as to be virtually invisible to the naked eye, but in fact, it is so massive that it takes 11,000 years for light to travel from one side to the other. What a paradox it is that one of the most massive objects in the sky appears as one of the smallest. During moments like this, I begin to grasp the greatness of the divine mind. Finally, if you want to locate the Crab Nebula, you'll have to look for it at a position of 22 degrees declination relative to the celestial equator.[303] This is yet another example of one of the crown jewels of the heavens exhibiting the numbers 11, 22, and 33 in their physical properties.

Kepler 22b

Kepler 22b is a planet outside of our solar system that is similar to Earth, and astronomers believe it may be capable of supporting life. It's situated 638 light-years away in the Cygnus constellation. That's about 41 million times the Earth-sun distance, which is an already a staggering 93 million miles. Discovered on December 5, 2011, by NASA's Kepler Space Telescope, the planet was designated as Kepler-22b. Kepler-22b orbits the star Kepler 22. Scientists theorize that if the greenhouse effect operates there similarly to how it does on Earth, the average surface temperature on Kepler-22b would be 22 degrees Celsius (72 degrees Fahrenheit), which is about room temperature, placing it in the habitable zone.[304] These estimates are based on how much energy the star Kepler 22 emits and how much of that light flux impinges on the planet.

The Most Earthlike Planet

The extrasolar planet Gliese 667Cc (or simply GJ667Cc) has been declared the most Earthlike object known outside of our solar system. Exoplanet GJ667Cc is even more similar to our Earth than Kepler-22b, which was confirmed as a potentially habitable planet. GJ667Cc, the new prime candidate for a habitable world, is *only* 22 light-years (or 200 million *million* kilometers) away, which is still considered to be in our cosmological backyard. Gravity on GJ667Cc is estimated to be 1.6 times Earth's at-

302 W. J. Kaufmann, *Universe* (fourth edition). (London: W. H. Freeman, 1996), 428.
303 https://www.constellation-guide.com/constellation-list/taurus-constellation/.
304 https://www.space.com/13821-nasa-kepler-alien-planets-habitable-zone.html.

tractive force, which is very close to the golden ratio.[305] Gliese 667Cc was discovered by astronomers combing through data from the European Southern Observatory's 3.6-meter telescope in Chile in November of 2011.

Did you catch that? Yep, it was discovered during 11/11.[306]

THE 11:11 CODE IN THE CLOSEST STAR

In the process of writing this book, I discovered that our nearest star, Proxima Centauri, is approximately 4.22 light-years from Earth and is the closest star other than the sun. It has an apparent magnitude of 11 and a density of 33 times that of our sun. Our nearest stellar neighbor has an orbital period of approximately 11 Earth days and a radial velocity toward the sun of 22.2 km/s or 13.7 miles per second. A Harvard University photometry observation for a period of 212 days found the magnitude of our second closest star to be 11.11 to 11.22.[307] Note that 13.7 is also the estimated age of the universe in billions of years.[308] Out of ~250 billion stars in our galaxy, the closest one has two instances of 22 in it as well as 11 twice and 33 once. The interested reader may want to place a bookmark here and search "33 stars from heaven in DNA" or visit the Gnostic warrior site.[309]

German mathematician Friedrich Bessel was born on July 22, 1784 and is perhaps best known for his work in the area of differential equations. The Bessel function was named in his honor. Bessel functions are solutions to complex physical phenomena involving cylindrical coordinates, such as modeling the behavior of the surface of a musical drum as a function of time and position, as well as wide-ranging applications in electromagnetics. YouTube has some fascinating videos on this class of functions, which rank among some of the toughest math I've ever used. I've provided a link in the footnotes for anyone wanting to see how difficult this function is to understand.[310] Bessel is also famous for his work in astronomy and worked on James Bradley's stellar observations to produce precise positions for some 3,222 stars. He was also famous for being the first astrono-

305 https://www.mn.uio.no/astro/english/research/news-and-events/news/astronews-2012-02-17.html.
306 https://www.jpl.nasa.gov/news/news.php?feature=4666.
307 http://adsabs.harvard.edu/full/1993PASP..105..487B.
308 https://www.space.com/18090-alpha-centauri-nearest-star-system.html.
309 https://gnosticwarrior.com/33-stars-dna.html.
310 https://www.youtube.com/watch?v=uLORiAWe63A

mer to utilize the concept of parallax to estimate the distance of remote stars.[311] Bessel was the first to calculate the orbit of Halley's Comet.[312]

THE 11:11 CODE IN THE MOST DISTANT OBJECT FROM EARTH

Out of pure curiosity, I decided to research the most distant star ever observed. What I found did not disappoint. The star colloquially known as Icarus has a technical designation officially named MACS J1149+2223 Lensed Star 1.[313] The technical name is loaded with details for where to locate it. The number 1149 is the right ascension coordinate of 11 hours 49 minutes, and the number 2223 corresponds to 22 degrees and 23 minutes north of the celestial equator. Here we have the numbers 11 and 22 showing up in the universe's most distant object ever detected by humans. Icarus is so far that it takes light nine billion years to reach us. In other words, what we are observing today is what the star looked like 9,000,000,000 years ago!

On November 11, 2014 (11/11/14), astronomers were scanning the heavens with the Hubble Space Telescope and investigating a strongly lensed supernova, which led to the discovery of Icarus.[314]

Prior to Icarus stealing the number-one position, a blue supergiant star whimsically named SDSS J1229+1122 held the title for most distant known object. Intriguingly, this star is located at 12 degrees and 29 minutes with a right ascension of 11 hours and 22 minutes and has an apparent magnitude of just more than 22.[315], [316]

11.11 LIGHT-YEARS FROM HOME

Now that we have investigated our closest and most distant stellar neighbors, let's see if there's something interesting in between. As with 90 percent of the topics covered in this book, I decided to Google "11.11 light-years" and see if any stars are known to be located at such a radial distance from Earth. If you're reading this far, I must have found something, eh? You betcha. To my astonishment, I found a triple-star system

311 http://todayinastronomy.blogspot.com/2009/07/july-22-friedrich-bessel.html.
312 D.G. Zill, *Differential Equations and Boundary-Value Problems*. (Boston: PWS Publishing, 1993), 306.
313 https://www.smithsonianmag.com/smart-news/meet-icarus-most-distant-star-ever-detected-180968667/.
314 http://science.sciencemag.org/content/347/6226/1123.
315 http://ned.ipac.caltech.edu/cgi-bin/objsearch?search_type=Obj_id&objid=47435649&objname=9&img_stamp=YES&hconst=73.0&omegam=0.27&omegav=0.73&corr_z=1.
316 https://iopscience.iop.org/article/10.1088/2041-8205/767/2/L29/meta.

named EZ Aquarii located (unsurprisingly) in the Aquarius constellation. It gets better. In terms of locating the star cluster in the heavens, its right ascension is 22 hours, 38 minutes, and 33 seconds. The mass is 11 percent of our own sun's mass.[317] Just when I think I've gotten to the bottom of the rabbit hole, it gets even weirder than I could have imagined. What's going on here? I've mentioned Aquarius before in this book, and it will be mentioned again later. Trust.

But 11.11 light-years doesn't seem all that long ago, does it? Careful! Many people forget that a light-year is a measure of distance—the distance that light travels in one year. Bearing in mind that the sun's light takes a mere 8 minutes and 20 seconds to cover the immense distance of 92.9 million miles (defined as one astronomical unit or AU), it takes some clever mathematical games to put into perspective just how insanely far 11.11 light-years (ly) is. In short, 11.11 ly works out to 703,608 AU or nearly three-quarters of a million times greater than the distance to our sun. To put this into scale, a simple proportion is helpful.

Using an "A is to B, as X is to Y" proportionality, the Earth-sun distance compares to the distance to EZ Aquarii just as 250 feet compares to the distance between New York City and Los Angeles. The distance to the sun is nearly 400 times the distance to the moon, and the distance to the moon is equivalent to circumnavigating the planet ten times. These are truly astronomical distances! As far as EZ Aquarii is from us, it's still considered in our cosmic backyard—actually quite close compared to the vast majority of known stars. It's just a snowball's throw away.

"I must study politics and war that my sons may have
the liberty to study mathematics and philosophy."

—John Adams[318]

317 https://www.universeguide.com/star/ezaquarii.
318 https://www.pinterest.com/pin/720927852824801665/.

CHAPTER 6
NUMBERS IN THE PAST AND FUTURE

Ferdinand Magellan

In 1505, at just twenty-five years of age, this prolific Portuguese explorer enlisted himself into the flotilla of 22 ships sent to host Francisco de Almeida as the first viceroy of Portuguese India. Magellan's quest to realize Christopher Columbus's dream of establishing a spice route via a western route began on March 22, 1518, when King Charles I named Magellan as captain of a ship that would pursue this revolutionary undertaking.[319] And so Magellan set about organizing the first circumnavigation of the planet in recorded history. His ships began their journey in 1519 and concluded in 1522—though Magellan wouldn't see the journey to completion.

I had the honor of visiting Magellan's final resting spot in 2007 when I traveled to Lapu Lapu City, Philippines. Magellan suffered a gory death at the hands of a local ruler named Lapu Lapu, who is a national hero in the Philippines to this day. The city where Magellan died was named in the warrior's honor because of his successful effort to repel the Spanish attempt to force Christianity upon them during his visit. Magellan was first wounded by being impaled by Lapu Lapu's bamboo spear and then finished off with mortal strikes from swords and other weapons. After Magellan's death on April 27, 1521, the round-the-world trip was completed by Juan Sebastian Elcano.

319 https://www.britannica.com/biography/Ferdinand-Magellan.

On May 6, 1522, the ship *Victoria* made a key milestone in the circumnavigation voyage as the vessel rounded the Cape of Good Hope at the southern tip of Africa. Another key milestone was on September 6, 1522, when the remaining crew of Magellan's voyage, led by Juan Sebastian Elcano, returned to Spain, completing the landmark quest.[320]

Here, once again, we have the number 22 showing up with numerous occurrences at one of humankind's first great achievements.

AVIATION FIRSTS

The Wright Brothers were the first humans to ever achieve powered flight, which took place at Kill Devil Hills, four miles south of Kitty Hawk, North Carolina, on December 17, 1903. This is interesting for two reasons. First, Apollo 11 was the first time humankind set foot on the moon, almost 66 (3 x 22) years after the first flight on Earth. Secondly, the name Kill Devil is extremely pertinent when we go back a few pages and recall how we looked into the mysteries of the numbers 66 and 666 and their occurrences in the physical parameters of the Earth, moon, and sun. Between the first time an aircraft *landed* on Earth (December 17, 1903) and the first time a spacecraft landed on the moon (July 20, 1969), there were 3,422 weeks or nearly 66 years. Coincidence?

I don't believe in coincidences—only divinely planned events with a cosmic mathematical order that will be discovered at the appropriate time in the future (such as *now*, in this book).[321]

But wait. Maybe you're still skeptical about this numerology stuff. Would you believe me if I told you that the Wright Brothers were awarded US patent #821,393, which was granted on May 22, 1906, for "new and useful improvement in Flying Machines"?[322] The number 22 is a key signature of the 11 + 11 code, which has been cleverly flying beneath the radar all these years. Until now. But you want more proof that the 11:11 code has something to do with the spirit of adventure? Okay, let's go!

AMELIA EARHART

Continuing on the theme of first flights, no discussion would be complete

320 https://www.history.com/news/was-magellan-the-first-person-to-circumnavigate-the-globe.
321 https://www.airspacemag.com/history-of-flight/wright-brothers-first-flight-photo-annotated-180949489/.
322 https://airandspace.si.edu/exhibitions/wright-brothers/online/fly/1903/patenting.cfm.

without mentioning two legendary aviation pioneers, Earhart and Lindbergh. Amelia Earhart was the first person, let alone the first female, to fly across the Atlantic Ocean. On October 22, 1922, Earhart flew her single-engine Kinner Canary plane to an altitude of 14,000 feet at Rogers Field in Los Angeles shortly after receiving her pilot's license that same month from the Federation Aeronautique Internationale. Achieving this altitude set a record for the highest flight by a woman pilot.[323]

Upon her return from California, she bought a 1922 Kissel Goldbug car, which she promptly nicknamed Yellow Peril.[324]

Earhart made two unsuccessful attempts to be the first person to circumnavigate the Earth in an airplane. The first attempt failed because of technical and logistical problems. The second attempt brought her 22,000 miles around the world, but she disappeared during the final 7,000-mile leg.[325] Keep the numbers 22 and 7 in mind and recall that 22/7 is a very good approximation for pi. Also bear in mind that in this circumstance, the topic pertains to someone navigating the circumference of the Earth.

Are light bulbs starting to turn on? We will be talking about light bulbs later on as well. I love saving the best for last.

CHARLES LINDBERGH

Another iconic aviator, Charles Lindbergh, became world famous for his feat of being the first person to fly an aircraft nonstop from New York City to Paris. His aviation career jump started in February of 1922 (2/22) after he left the University of Wisconsin to pursue the study of aeronautics, and he got his pilot's license with the Nebraska Aircraft Corporation in March of 1922 (3/22).[326] By April 9, 1922, Lindbergh had performed his first solo flight.[327] After a successful demonstration flight from San Diego to New York, he was ready to take on the transatlantic challenge in his custom aircraft, the iconic *Spirit of St. Louis*. After a voyage of 33 hours and 30 minutes (333), he touched down in Paris on May 21, 1927. The plane was powered by a 223-horsepower Wright Whirlwind J-5C radial engine.[328]

Upon his return to the United States, Lindbergh used his newfound fame

323 https://worldhistoryproject.org/1922/10/22/amelia-earhart-sets-altitude-record-for-female-pilots.
324 https://www.ameliaearhartmuseum.org/AmeliaEarhart/AEFunFacts.htm.
325 https://www.ameliaearhartmuseum.org/AmeliaEarhart/AEAccomplishments.htm.
326 https://airandspace.si.edu/collection-objects/ryan-nyp-spirit-st-louis-charles-lindbergh.
327 http://www.charleslindbergh.com/timeline/.
328 http://www.charleslindbergh.com/plane/mahoney.asp.

to promote the development of aviation. At the request of the Guggenheim Fund for the Promotion of Aeronautics, Lindbergh toured the United States in the *Spirit of St. Louis* during the summer and fall of 1927. Traveling a total of 22,350 miles, he visited seventy-five cities and dropped messages over towns where he couldn't stop.[329]

Why are so many of humanity's firsts clustered with such obvious instances of the numbers 11, 22, and 33?

During my own world travels, I have noticed that a very large portion of airports in the United States charge an 11.11 percent special tax to rental car companies that operate on airport premises. Why 11.11 percent, of all numbers? An interesting forum online has several travelers discussing this bizarre finding.[330]

Hertz
RR 113218431
CHARLES WOLFE
CC
INITIAL CHARGES
SUBTOTAL
CHARGES ADDED DURING RENTAL
LDW DECLINED
LIS DECLINED
PAI, PEC DECLINED
PREM RD SVC DECLINED
SERVICE CHARGES/TAXES
CONCESSION FEE RECOVERY 11.11% T $ 9.67
CUSTOMER FAC T $ 6.00
TAX 20.000% ON TAXABLE TTL OF $ 102.67 $ 20.53
TOTAL AMOUNT DUE $ 123.20
CHARGED ON AMX
FOR EXPLANATION OF THE
PLEASE ASK A REPRESENT
WWW.HERTZ.COM/CHARGE
VEHICLE: 01798
LICENSE: MA 9ZL923

Albany, New York, airport concession fee, 11.11%

THE SOVIET UNION

The former Soviet Union, also known by its full name, the Union of Soviet Socialist Republics (USSR), was the world's largest country during its existence from 1922 to 1991. It wasn't until 11 years after its formation that the United States officially recognized the USSR as a legitimate country in 1933. The USSR covered an area of 22,402,200 square kilometers and spanned 11 time zones. In 1933, the famine known as the *Holodomor* in the Ukraine SSR killed somewhere between 3 and 7 million people. Josef

329 https://www.ncpedia.org/aviation/Lindbergh.

330 https://www.flyertalk.com/forum/national-emerald-club/1784650-exhaustive-national-airport-fees-list.html.

Stalin was sworn in as general secretary of the Communist Party of the Soviet Union on April 3, 1933. During that year, as many as 11 million people were exterminated by mass executions under Stalin's iron-fisted rule. Germany invaded the Soviet Union on June 22, 1941, officially dragging the country into World War II.

Speaking of war, the second concept for the title of this book was originally going to be *XXXIII* or 33 (a multiple of 11) in Roman numerals, the letter X preferred over the letter that precedes it in the alphabet, W. The title of this book might have been *WWIII* (had I survived to write it and had you survived to read it) had it not been for the infinite wisdom and divine grace of God, who foiled man's elaborate and misguided plans bent toward imminent self-destruction. Through the deep, all-encompassing divine intelligence of numbers, as history will eventually bear out, World War III was fought almost exclusively through covert electronic means, punctuated by surgically targeted military operations, thus saving humankind from destroying itself and ushering in a new era of peace.

One of the scariest times in US history was the Cuban Missile Crisis, when the Soviets were stationing nuclear missiles in Cuba and had them pointed at the major American population centers. On October 22, 1962, after rejecting a surgical air strike against the missile sites, President John F. Kennedy announced the enforcement of a naval blockade against all future military ships from Russia making their way to Cuba and a demand that the bases be dismantled and missiles removed. Six days later, the crisis was defused when Soviet president Nikita Khrushchev announced his government's intent to dismantle and remove all offensive Soviet weapons in Cuba.[331] Here we see the number 22 coming to the rescue, saving the world from nuclear oblivion. And it just occurred to me that JOHN KENNEDY is composed of 11 letters.

Here we have multiple occurrences of the numbers 11, 22, and 33 showing up in key data from the history of the largest country that ever existed.[332] While not directly related to the Soviet Union, I'll add an interesting fact here anyway. After the fall of the Berlin Wall, the Brandenburg Gate was first opened for unfettered border crossings between East and West Germany on December 22, 1989.[333]

---

331 https://www.history.com/this-day-in-history/cuban-missile-crisis.

332 https://www.bbc.com/news/world-europe-17858981.

333 http://www.chronik-der-mauer.de/en/chronicle/_year1989/_month12/.

One of the toughest places I have ever worked was the oil boom town of Atyrau, Kazakhstan, which is also home to the world's lowest commercial airport at an elevation of 22 meters (72 feet) below sea level in the basin of the Caspian Sea.[334] Atyrau is divided into two parts by the Ural River. One portion of the city is technically on the European continent, and the east side is situated in Asia. I walked across a bridge connecting the two continents. Upon landing at Atyrau's tiny airport, it was getting late and I was hungry and wanted to get a sandwich and a beer, so I went to a little café/bar just outside the airport entrance and ordered what I wanted and presented a 1,000-tenge banknote, the equivalent of roughly $10 US. The Russian-speaking woman behind the counter asked me if I had change, and I said, "Sorry." I had just landed, and this was literally my first time spending money in Kazakhstan. Without flinching, she calmly walked over to a slot machine and played it several times using coins from the cash register until she hit the jackpot, and then she proceeded to give me my change from her winnings. She did this all with a completely straight face, as if this were how they normally did business. During my nearly half year in Kazakhstan, I came to realize that most businesses expect the buyer to come with exact change and often act very irritated if they are expected to provide change. Little stories like this are the essence of why I find foreign travel so rewarding and enjoyable.

Inside the poorly lit café/bar/ casino at Atyrau airport

The author in front of a sign just outside of Atyrau airport, touting the USSR victory and freedom sixty years after World War II. The top-left section shows the Kazakh language written in modified Cyrillic orthography, and the bottom-right portion is written in Russian. It was very strange to see a Turkic language written in Cyrillic.

334 https://www.air-port-codes.com/airport-info/GUW/.

I bet you didn't know that apples originally came from Kazakhstan! The old capital and current largest city in Kazakhstan is Alma-ata (also known as Almaty), which translates to "father of the apple."[335] Alexander the Great is credited with having first discovered the apple in Kazakhstan in 328 BC.[336] There is even a book written by Christopher Robbins titled *Apples Are from Kazakhstan: The Land that Disappeared.*

Korean DMZ

On October 15, 2018, an agreement had been reached between North and South Korea toward demilitarizing the demilitarized zone (DMZ), a no-man's-land that had separated the two Koreas since 1948. One of the first steps was to decommission the 22 guard posts (11 on each side) from which the soldiers from both sides stared one another down with loaded weapons.[337] The 11:11 code showed up in one of the greatest thaws in international relations history.

While working at a power station in Yeosu, South Korea, the plant manager approached me one day and asked if I was a Christian. I replied, "Yes, of course I am!" A long conversation ensued, and we spoke every day after that. On the day I left, we prayed together for peace between the two Koreas. That was in 2016. Today we are on the brink of complete disarmament and peace on the Korean peninsula. The power of prayer should never be underestimated. As a bonus, I noticed that my Korean customer's address and phone number contained "222" and "22," respectively, as can be seen below.

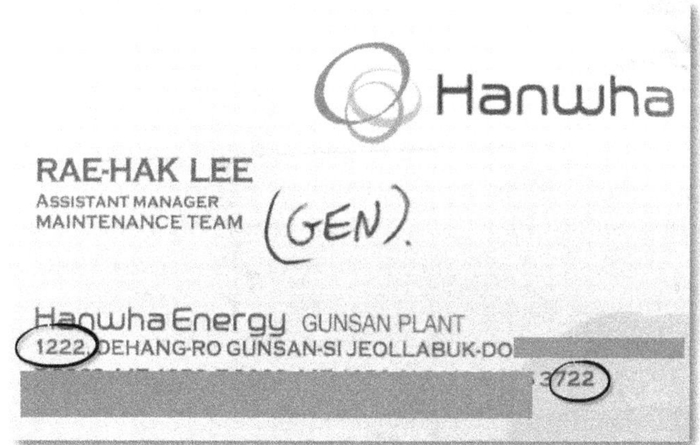

335 https://www.atlasobscura.com/places/the-last-wild-apple-forests-almaty-kazakhstan.
336 https://www.washingtonsgreengrocer.com/blog/b/apple-mythology-fruit-launched-thousand-ships.
337 http://www.kait8.com/2018/10/15/koreas-hold-high-level-peace-talks/.

> Take a moment and look up the Japanese music video "Closer to You" by Kaisaku. It sounds amazing in the car. At least it does in mine!

THE DEATH OF A COMPANY

On the morning of October 15, 2018, as I was drinking my morning coffee and reading the news, I saw the sad report that Sears had filed for chapter 11 bankruptcy after 132 years of being in business. The number 132 is an interesting number with a prime factorization of 3 x 2 x 2 x 11. As a kid raised in the Chicago metropolitan area under the long shadow cast by the Sears Tower, I grew up with tremendous admiration for the once world-class company that pioneered the concept of catalog shopping. I remembered the joy of flipping through the pages of the toy section in their catalogs and fantasizing about my next Christmas presents. I remember with much joy my first tour of the Sears Tower Sky Deck Observatory on the 103rd floor of Chicago's tallest building. I remembered the pride of having the world's tallest building in my home city throughout my entire childhood. Growing up in the Chicago area taught me to dream big and always reach for the sky. I also remember my disappointment in 2009 when Sears relinquished the naming rights for the iconic structure to the British insurance company, Willis Group. Whatchoo' talkin' 'bout, Willis?! To me and probably most of the people in Chicagoland, it will always remain the Sears Tower in our hearts and memories. I've taught my son that the iconic structure is *still* the Sears Tower. I make no apologies to the Willis Company. I'm sorry, but you didn't build that. Sears *did*. That's the end of discussion. Fiat bought the Jeep brand, but new Jeeps still proudly bear the Jeep logo.

Setting nostalgia aside, this news story earned mention in the book because I wanted to give you a prime example of how this work has taken on a mind of its own. As I sat this morning sipping my coffee, I saw "chapter 11," and just out of curiosity, I decided to do some research on bankruptcy law. As it turns out, chapter 11 is just one of nine different types of bankruptcy filings (and there used to be more) that are provided for under what is known as title 11 of the US Code. Did you catch that? The death of a company is handled under chapter 11 of title 11 of the US Code—*the 11:11 code*![338] I didn't expect this discovery at all. This is a prime example

338 https://www.justice.gov/ust/bankruptcy-fact-sheets/overview-bankruptcy-chapters.

of how the material of this book revealed itself to me based on simply looking up something innocuous.

But it goes even further. After filing for bankruptcy, a company can regain the ability to continue doing business under title 11, chapter 11, subchapter 1, section 1108. That's 11:11-1-1108.[339] Wow. As it turns out, every major US airline company has filed for chapter 11 bankruptcy since 2002. In 2008, there were 1,117,771 bankruptcy filings in US courts.[340]

Between my 127th and 128th attempts to finish writing this book (that's sarcasm), I discovered that on January 22, 2002, Kmart filed for chapter 11 bankruptcy under title 11 of the US Code. The S. S. Kresge Corporation was formed in 1899 and changed its name to the ubiquitous Kmart in 1977. On November 17, 2004, Kmart Corporation bought Sears for $11 billion. Kmart filed chapter 11 bankruptcy a second time (11 twice, which is 11:11) on October 15, 2018.[341] The most interesting aspect of the Sears and Kmart stories is that they are linked because of Kmart buying Sears for $11 billion.

THE 11:11 CODE IN GOVERNMENT

I discovered that the US national debt was at $21,974,000,000,000 as of December 31, 2018, according to the US Treasury website. This is exactly 0.11 percent short of being $22 trillion.[342] According to the RT website, the US debt has climbed by $11.2 trillion over the last 11 years.[343] There you have it—11 and 22 in the national debt.

Why are the numbers 11 and 22 showing up in one of the largest financial total calculations in human history? What, or more appropriately *who* may be trying to get our attention?

Speaking of the national debt, the reader will recall that on December 22, 2018, President Trump shut down the US government at a cost of $11 billion.[344] A joint study by Yale University and MIT concluded that there are approximately 22 million illegal immigrants in the United States. This result refutes the data provided by the US Census Bureau's annual American Community Survey (ACS), which placed the undocumented population at around 11 million people. Here we have 11 and 22 in the

339 https://www.law.cornell.edu/uscode/text/11/1108.
340 http://www.abajournal.com/news/article/bankruptcy_filings_up_31_in_2008_mortgage_foreclosures_hit_new_high.
341 http://www.fundinguniverse.com/company-histories/kmart-corporation-history/.
342 https://www.treasurydirect.gov/govt/reports/pd/mspd/2018/opds122018.pdf.
343 https://www.rt.com/business/446355-us-debt-financial-crisis/amp/
344 https://marketbusinessnews.com/us-shutdown-cost-cbo/195317/

illegal immigration debate.[345] US Coast Guard cutter *William Trump* operates out of its home port of Key West, Florida, and is designated with a hull number of 1111. The *William Trump* was the 11th vessel of its class when it was delivered in the 11th month of 2014.[346] Have you noticed the number 88022 at Trump rallies, campaign ads, and in other pictures? This is the short code for his re-election campaign.[347] Maybe President Trump likes the number 22? Donald and Melania's February 2020 visit to India took them on a 22-kilometer (11+11 km) road trip dubbed #theBiggestRoadShowEver?

WALL STREET AND THE NEW YORK STOCK EXCHANGE

No discussion of the death of iconic corporate giants would be complete

345 https://thehill.com/latino/407848-yale-mit-study-22-million-not-11-million-undocumented-immigrants-in-us?amp
346 https://en.m.wikipedia.org/wiki/USCGC_William_Trump
347 https://usshortcodedirectory.com/directory/short-code-88022/

without a quick look into Wall Street itself and the world's largest financial trading center, the New York Stock Exchange (NYSE). The following is a collection of facts about the NYSE with some of my favorite numbers 11, 22, and 33 showing up at some of the most important moments in the history of the stock exchange.

- On December 13, 1711, the New York City Common Council made Wall Street the city's first official slave market for the sale and rental of enslaved Africans and Indians.
- In 1884, Charles H. Dow began tracking stocks, starting out with an initial 11 stocks, mostly railroads, and monitored the average prices for these eleven companies. When the average peaks and troughs went up consistently, he deemed it a bull market condition. If averages dropped, it was a bear market. He added up prices and divided by the number of stocks to get his Dow Jones average.[348]
- The NYSE is located at 11 Wall Street.
- On September 16, 1920, a bomb exploded on Wall Street outside the NYSE building, killing 33 people.
- On October 19, 1987, the Dow Jones Industrial Average (DJIA) dropped 508 points, a 22 percent loss in a single day, the second biggest one-day drop the exchange had experienced.

THE GREAT CHICAGO FIRE

During October 8–11, 1870, the city of Chicago experienced one of the most devastating urban fires in human history. The commonly accepted story is that the fire was sparked off by Mrs. O'Leary's cow tipping over a lantern in a barn adjacent to the address 137 DeKoven Street. According to Wikipedia, 2,112 acres of land were charred at a cost of $222,000,000 in damages. That is equivalent to about $4.56 billion in 2018 figures, adjusting for the compounded effect of inflation.[349] The House Hotel burned to the ground in the fire 13 days after its grand opening.[350], [351] Refer to the

348 https://www.loc.gov/rr/business/businesshistory/May/djia.html
349 http://www.in2013dollars.com/1871-dollars-in-2018?amount=222000000.
350 https://en.wikipedia.org/wiki/Great_Chicago_Fire.
351 https://palisadespete.wordpress.com/2012/12/04/10-facts-about-the-great-chicago-fire/.

section on the number 13. By the World's Columbian Exposition 22 years later, Chicago hosted more than 21 million visitors.

CHERNOBYL

On April 26, 1986, at 01:23 GMT, reactor four suffered a catastrophic power increase, leading to explosions in its core. As the reactor had not been encased by any kind of hard containment vessel, this dispersed large quantities of radioactive isotopes into the atmosphere and caused an open-air fire that increased the emission of radioactive particles carried by the smoke. At 1:23:40 (1-2-3-4), as recorded by the SKALA centralized control system, a SCRAM (emergency shutdown) of the reactor was initiated.[352]

Chernobyl (Чернобыль) means wormwood in Russian. Wormwood (ἀψίνθιον *apsinthion* or ἄψινθος *apsinthos* in Greek) is a star or angel.[353] The word *wormwood* appears several times in the Old Testament, translated from the Hebrew term הנעל (la'anah, which means *curse* in Hebrew). The term wormwood is used a total of seven times in the Bible, in Deuteronomy 29:18, Proverbs 5:4, Jeremiah 9:15 and 23:15, Lamentations 3:15 and 3:19, and Amos 5:7. All seven cases clearly are painting a picture of bitterness.[354] A strong alcoholic liquor made from wormwood called absinthe is illegal in most places, including the United States, but it can be purchased in many countries throughout Europe. While on a business trip in Spain, I tried it and brought a bottle of 100-proof absinthe home with me, foolishly thinking I'd eventually come to enjoy it. It tasted a lot like black licorice but more bitter and left a very strong burn in my pipes on the way down. It wasn't much fun to drink, in my opinion. Being completely straight with you, it was absolutely disgusting and gave me a mind-altering headache and hangover the next day. Steer clear of it unless you're a glutton for punishment.

Revelation 8:10–11 says, "The third angel sounded his trumpet, and a great star, blazing like a torch, fell from the sky on a third of the rivers and on the springs of water—the name of the star is Wormwood. A third of the waters turned bitter, and many people died from the waters that had become bitter."[355]

---

352 https://www.nrc.gov/docs/ML0716/ML071690245.pdf.
353 https://rdmr.eu/2018/chernobyl-2/.
354 https://www.bibletools.org/index.cfm/fuseaction/Lexicon.show/ID/H3939/la%60anah.htm.
355 https://www.biblegateway.com/passage/?search=Revelation+8%3A10-11&version=NIV.

Many people view the Chernobyl accident as fulfillment of the Revelation 8:10–11 prophecy. I would tend to agree, particularly if you consider that the Bible was written nearly 2,000 years prior to the discovery of atomic energy. They didn't have a very good word for radioactive contamination, so they used the term *bitter*, and who knows what other layers of nuance may have been lost in many centuries of translations. Furthermore, the verse refers to wormwood as the name of a star that fell to Earth. Science has proven that stars produce their power via nuclear reactions, and I personally believe the nuclear materials on Earth that we use in nuclear power are leftover active, *raw, unbaked* cosmic cookie dough particles from the time that our planet condensed from star material during the creation event/big bang or whatever you want to call it. Many of the concepts in the Bible are difficult or impossible to prove, but there is enough linguistic and contextual information for me to feel confident in my belief that Chernobyl probably corresponds to the wormwood referred to in Revelation 8.

Fukushima Disaster

The 9.0-magnitude earthquake that precipitated the Fukushima nuclear disaster struck at 14:46 on Friday on 3/11/11. The ensuing 43-foot high tsunami wave effortlessly overtook the plant's 33-foot high sea wall and inundated the plant with a flood of truly biblical proportions. As an interesting fact, the word tsunami comes from the Japanese phrase 津波, meaning "harbor wave."[356], [357] The Fukushima nuclear disaster was by far the most severe atomic energy accident in human history, and the plant has still not been cleaned up and restored to a safe condition as of the time of this writing.

Lituya Bay Tsunami

My good friend Wesley, who lives in Alaska, sent me an article about the number 22 occurring in the largest tsunami ever recorded. On July 9, 1958, at 22:15 in Lituya Bay, Alaska, when a magnitude-7.8 earthquake caused approximately 40 million cubic yards of rock to slough off into the water causing a mega-tsunami with a peak height of 1,722 feet.[358] This measurement was verified by climbing successively higher until they

356 https://web.archive.org/web/20110225143835/http://nthmp-history.pmel.noaa.gov/terms.html.
357 http://jagadees.wordpress.com/2012/02/13/tepco-did-not-act-on-tsunami-risk-projected-for-nuclear-plant/.
358 https://www.weather.gov/media/ajk/brochures/Alaska_Tsunamis.pdf.

stopped seeing broken trees and erosion. The epicenter of the quake was 22 miles below the surface. Lituya Bay has a maximum depth of 722 feet, or 220 meters.[359] That's an awful lot of 22s attached to the greatest wave ever measured in recorded history.

Why do we keep seeing all of these instances of 11 + 11 clustered around major historical events—both good and bad?

ADOLF HITLER

Hitler came to power in the year 1933. He applied to join the Nazi party, and within a week was accepted as party member number 555. Hitler's first DAP (Deutsche Arbeiterpartei or German Workers Party) speech was held in the Hofbräukeller on October 16, 1919. He was the second speaker of the evening and spoke to 111 people. In a 1922 speech, Hitler called Jesus "the true God" but also called him "our greatest Aryan leader."[360] On March 23, 1933, parliament passed the Enabling Act of 1933, which gave the cabinet the right to enact laws without the consent of parliament, effectively giving Hitler dictatorial powers.[361], [362]

During the summer of 1933, all competing parties were either outlawed or dissolved themselves, and subsequently, the law against the founding of new parties as of July 14, 1933, legally established the Nazi Party's monopoly. When it came to power in 1933, the Nazi Party had more than two million members. In the first round of the 1932 presidential election, Hitler garnered 11,339,446 votes.[363]

A recurring theme in this book is to observe that during some of the greatest and worst moments in human history, there is often a profusion of repeated digits. As a side note while speaking of Germany, Angela Merkel became chancellor on 11/22/2005.[364]

BENITO MUSSOLINI

In October 1922, an organized mass demonstration known as the March on Rome took place, resulting in Mussolini's National Fascist Party

359 https://en.wikipedia.org/wiki/1958_Lituya_Bay,_Alaska_earthquake_and_megatsunami.
360 https://www.equip.org/article/was-hitler-a-christian/.
361 https://www.dw.com/en/the-law-that-enabled-hitlers-dictatorship/a-16689839.
362 https://en.wikipedia.org/wiki/Nazi_Party.
363 http://www.historyplace.com/worldwar2/riseofhitler/runs.htm.
364 http://news.bbc.co.uk/onthisday/hi/dates/stories/november/22/newsid_4968000/4968864.stm.

(Partito Nazionale Fascista or PNF) coming to power over the kingdom of Italy. Later that same month, the fascist party leaders planned a coup, which occurred on October 28. When fascist troops entered Rome, then Prime Minister Luigi Facta wished to declare a state of siege, but this was overruled by King Emmanuel III. The next day, October 29, 1922, the king appointed Benito Mussolini as prime minister, thereby transferring political power to the fascists without armed conflict.[365] As a side note, Emmanuel III was born on 11/11/1869 in Naples.[366]

Here's some bonus trivia. As long as we're talking about Italian history, let's step even further back in time to when Elagabalus (a.k.a. Marcus Aurelius Antoninus Augustus) was Roman emperor for four years until his assassination on March 11 in the year AD 222. His tender and loving grandmother, Julia Maesa, arranged for his assassination, which was carried out by disgruntled members of the Praetorian Guard. He would be remembered as one of the worst Roman rulers of all time. [367]

The Manhattan Project

In 1933, Hungarian-German-American physicist Leo Szilard first conceived the idea of a nuclear chain reaction. The following year, he and Italian physicist Enrico Fermi jointly patented the nuclear reactor.[368] Late in 1939, Szilard wrote the letter for Einstein's signature that would end up creating the Manhattan Project, which produced the atomic bomb. Szilard lived to 66 years of age.[369]

The Manhattan Project was initiated in 1939 in a top-secret effort to create a new class of weapons the likes of which the planet had never seen before, one that would change earthly war strategies forever—nuclear weapons. The project ended up costing more than $2 billion in 1939 dollars, which is equivalent to $22 billion in 2016 dollars when the source article was written.

While reading the article about the Manhattan Project, I noticed in the section on how the original nuclear weapons were designed and was shocked to see that the impactor segments were shaped as a truncated icosahedron with 12 pentagonal faces and 20 hexagonal faces similar to a soccer ball.

365 https://www.history.com/this-day-in-history/mussolini-founds-the-fascist-party.
366 https://www.encyclopedia.com/people/history/italian-history-biographies/victor-emmanuel-iii.
367 https://www.historychannel.com.au/this-day-in-history/teenage-emperor-assassinated/.
368 https://www.famousscientists.org/leo-szilard/.
369 https://en.m.wikipedia.org/wiki/Leo_Szilard.

Have a gander at the paper polyhedron model on the first page of the book. At a molecular level, we are composed of chemical structures all composed of pentagons and hexagons for the creation of life. Here with atomic weapons, we see these polygons combining to form the ultimate symbol of destruction.

Furthermore, the critical mass for a nuclear reaction requires a minimum of 10 kilograms of plutonium or 22 pounds, or else an explosion is not physically possible.[370] The words *nuclear bomb* are composed of 11 letters. For obvious reasons, I purposely limited the depth and breadth of my research into this topic and confined myself to what can be openly found on Wikipedia. I don't need the FBI knocking at my door. Relax, guys.

Did you know that the very first nuclear weapon tested at Trinity Site, NM, had an explosive yield of 22 kilotons of TNT and was detonated at just north of the 33rd parallel in New Mexico? Seven men completed the preparation and setup of the device nicknamed "The Gadget" at about 11 hours after 11:00 a.m., or 22:00 the day before the test that would take place on July 16, 1946.[371]

JFK ASSASSINATION

According to archive.org, on June 4, 1963, a virtually unknown presidential decree, Executive Order 11110, was signed with the authority to basically strip the Rothschild-owned Federal Reserve Bank of its power to loan money to the US federal government at interest. With the stroke of a pen, President Kennedy declared that the privately owned Federal Reserve Bank would soon be out of business. This instance of 1111 would spell the beginning of the end for JFK, which would culminate in his assassination later that same year.[372] Notably, the New York Federal Reserve Bank has an address of 33 Liberty Street (11 + 11 + 11).[373] The irony of the foreign bank responsible for our financial enslavement taking up headquarters on Liberty Street...

President John F. Kennedy was assassinated on the 22nd day of the 11th month, and it occurred at the 33rd parallel (11-22-33).

370 https://en.m.wikipedia.org/wiki/Critical_mass.

371 https://en.wikipedia.org/wiki/Trinity_(nuclear_test).

372 https://archive.org/stream/pdfy-FwFDQIaEzDngblj0/John%20F.%20Kennedy%20vs%20The%20Federal%20Reserve_djvu.txt.

373 https://www.newyorkfed.org/contacts.

Other high-profile deaths that occurred on November 11 include Martin Luther King, Sr. (father of the civil rights activist)[374] who died on 11/11/1984, and Palestinian Liberation Organization Chairman Yasser Arafat, who died on 11/11/2005.[375]

Parkland School Massacre

On February 14, 2018, one of the nation's worst mass shootings took place at Marjory Stoneman Douglas High School in Parkland, Florida, where 17 students were shot to death between 2:21 and 2:27 p.m. Police radios were heard stating that shots were fired at 2:23 p.m. On 2/22/18, President Trump met with students and others at the White House for a listening session, where he suggested arming up to 20 percent of the teachers to stop *maniacs* from attacking students.[376]

Marjory Stoneman Douglas was famous for her efforts to prevent draining the Everglades swamp for civil and business purposes. Many people, including myself, find it interesting that (a) the choice of Parkland for the shooting may be a coded message to President Trump to abandon his campaign promise to "drain the swamp," and (b) the choice of a school named Parkland may have been a veiled threat from the deep state, who could be giving President Trump a reminder that John F. Kennedy died in a hospital named Parkland. Draw your own conclusions.

Norway Massacre of 2011

On July 22, 2011, two attacks occurred in Oslo, Norway, that together constituted the deadliest attack since WWII. At 3:25:22, a van loaded with explosives detonated in downtown Oslo adjacent to Prime Minister Jens Stoltenberg's office. Eight people lost their lives and 209 were injured. Approximately two hours later at a youth camp in Utoya, the first shot rang out at 5:22 p.m. during what would become a 1.5-hour shooting massacre of young children. Assailant Anders Brevik proceeded to methodically stalk and kill 69 people using his .223 Ruger Mini-14 rifle, injuring 110 and bringing the total count for the day to 77 dead and 309 injured. In two rare cases of mercy, he allowed one 11-year-old boy and one 22-year-old

374 https://blackthen.com/%E2%80%8Bnovember-11-1984-martin-luther-king-sr-died/.

375 https://mybirthday.ninja/?m=November&d=11&y=2005&go=Go.

376 http://www.fdle.state.fl.us/MSDHS/Meetings/2018/December-Meeting-Documents/Marjory-Stoneman-Douglas-High-School-Public-Draft1.aspx.

man to live after both pleaded for their lives. Brevik's trial was completed on April 22, 2016.

This is one of the most disturbing and utterly bizarre instances of repeated sightings of the numbers 11 and 22 that I have found in my research. The 11:11 code doesn't always follow necessarily *good* or *bad* events, but it does seem to have a penchant for clinging to infamous events that loom large in history.[377]

LAS VEGAS MASSACRE

On October 1, 2017, a horrific shooting took place at a concert in Las Vegas when lone shooter Stephen Paddock opened fire upon the crowd of approximately 22,000 revelers from his perch on the 32nd floor of the Mandalay Bay Hotel. Paddock fired a total of 1,100 rounds using at least 14 AR-15 rifles with 0.223-caliber ammunition. A total of 851 people were injured, 422 due to gunshot wounds. Among the 58 deaths, 36 were women, and 22 were men.[378]

INDONESIAN EARTHQUAKE AND TSUNAMI

On 12/26/2004, Indonesia was rocked by an earthquake of magnitude 9.3 on the Richter scale, and a massive tsunami followed. The earthquake released approximately 1.1×10^{22} joules of energy. (Think about 11 and 22 and remember that 22 = 11 + 11.) That's the equivalent of 26 megatons of TNT. This energy is equivalent to more than 1,500 times that of the Hiroshima atomic bomb. The earliest shockwave signal is that of the compressional (P) wave, which takes about 22 minutes to reach the other side of the planet (the antipode, which was in this case near Ecuador). The tsunami had a wave amplitude of 2.2 meters (about 7 feet) when it hit the Maldives.

According to the US Geological Survey, a total of 227,898 people died. Measured in lives lost, this is one of the ten worst earthquakes in recorded history, as well as the single worst tsunami in history. Indonesia was the area worst affected, with most death toll estimates at around 170,000. However, another report by Siti Fadilah Supari, the Indonesian minister

377 https://en.m.wikipedia.org/wiki/2011_Norway_attacks.
378 https://en.m.wikipedia.org/wiki/2017_Las_Vegas_shooting.

of health at the time, estimated the death total to be as high as 220,000 in Indonesia alone.[379]

The earthquake was so severe that the fault moved on average 33 feet, going as far as 50 feet in some instances.[380]

On 12/22/2018, tragedy struck Indonesia once again in the form of an earthquake-triggered tsunami because of activity inside the active volcano Anak Krakatau (or Son of Krakatau). The death toll was estimated at around 437.[381]

I think the message here is that a higher power is in control and these events are all an important part of the overall human experiment. Pain creates texture and meaning in life and showcases our temporal and fragile nature, lest we become too arrogant to need to look to the heavens for guidance, healing, and protection.

9/11

September 11, 2001 is etched into the mind of every living adult on the planet as the day when the World Trace Center was destroyed. A great deal of numerological clues surround this event. Beginning with September 11, 1609, Henry Hudson first discovered Manhattan as he sailed south down the river that now bears his name.[382] HENRY HUDSON is composed of 11 letters.

On September 11, 1941, construction of the Pentagon officially began, and exactly 60 years later to the day, the forces of evil would attempt to destroy it.[383]

On September 11, 1990, which occurred exactly 11 years to the day before the towers came down, President George H. W. Bush gave a speech about the new world order.[384]

Hebrew scriptures consider September 11, 1999, as the 6,000th anniver-

379 https://en.wikipedia.org/wiki/2004_Indian_Ocean_earthquake_and_tsunami.
380 https://www.nsf.gov/news/news_summ.jsp?cntn_id=104179.
381 https://news.detik.com/berita/d-4355640/pvmbg-gunung-krakatau-meletus-423-kali?_ga=2.252556046.681891274.1547203043-1347269580.1527499678.
382 https://www.landofthebrave.info/henry-hudson-facts.htm
383 https://www.history.com/topics/us-government/pentagon
384 https://history.house.gov/Historical-Highlights/1951-2000/President-George-H-W--Bush-s-Joint-Session-on-the-Iraqi-invasion-of-Kuwait/

sary of Adam's creation and mark the year 4000 BC as year one on the Hebrew calendar.[385]

The twin towers were each 110 stories in height, and together they formed a huge 11 in the sky—in fact, the largest example of the number eleven the world has ever seen. One of the towers was struck by American Airlines Flight 11. Between the two aircraft that hit the two towers, a total of 11 crew members perished. If you add up the digits of the date 9/11 you get 9 + 1 + 1 = 11. Construction began in 1966, and 66 = 6 x 11. In 2001, September 11 was the 254th day of the year. This means that there were 111 days left to the end of the year. NEW YORK CITY is composed of 11 letters.

Ground was broken for construction of the Pentagon building on September 11, 1941,[386] and American Airlines Flight 77 (7 x 11) was hijacked and flown into the western side of the building, killing 189 people exactly 60 years after construction began. The building is approximately 22 meters (71 feet) tall, and each of the five sides of the building is 921 feet long. Prior to construction, an additional 1.1 square kilometers of land was purchased at a cost of $2.2 million.[387] Furthermore, the reader is now familiar with how the interior angles of a pentagon relate to the golden ratio, quite possibly invoking divine power through geometry and number. As the greatest symbol of military power on Earth, the Pentagon measures 1,414 feet when measured from the center of one side to the diametrically opposing vertex.[388] This corresponds to **$1000\sqrt{2}$** feet or equivalently, the square root of 2 million within 99.9 percent accuracy! Note that it takes 11 letters to spell *the Pentagon*. The Pentagon building has five concentric pentagonal rings, each with five floors and five sides. While I do not have research to back up my claim, I'd venture a guess that the choice of five rings, floors, and sides for the building may have some connection to the five branches of the military at the time of construction. This seems logical as most symbolic military concepts are.

September 11 isn't the only date when a major tragedy struck New York City. During the reverse of that date (11/9) in 1965, the entire northeast region experienced a massive power blackout. The northeast blackout of 1965 was a significant disruption in the supply of electricity, affecting

385 http://www.september11news.com/

386 https://web.archive.org/web/20140819162620/https://pentagontours.osd.mil/facts-construction.jsp

387 https://web.archive.org/web/20081015022535/, http://www.greatbuildings.com/buildings/The_Pentagon.html and https://www.arlingtontours.com/pentagon

388 https://en.wikipedia.org/wiki/The_Pentagon

parts of Ontario, Canada, and Connecticut, Massachusetts, New Hampshire, New Jersey, New York, Rhode Island, Pennsylvania, and Vermont in the United States. More than 30 million people and 80,000 square miles (207,000 square kilometers) were left without electricity for up to 13 hours.[389]

The Hindenburg Disaster

On May 3, 1937, the largest aircraft in history, the *Hindenburg*, exploded over Lakehurst, New Jersey, because of a hydrogen gas explosion that engulfed the Nazi swastika symbol on the rear flank of the zeppelin.[390] While I didn't want to devote a lot of space to this topic, I did want to mention the fact that the vessel was operated by a crew of 22 people and had 13 "unlucky" passengers who all lost their lives. The significance of the numbers 13 and 22 have already been made clear earlier in this book, so I won't repeat it here.

US Highways

One of the oldest and best-known highways in the United States is, without a doubt, Route 66. For starters, the number 66 is interesting for reasons already laid out in detail, not least of which being that the Bible has 66 books. Route 66 was established on November 11, 1926 (11/11/26). After the highway was decommissioned, the section connecting Oklahoma City to St. Louis was paved and renamed Interstate 44, whereas the St. Louis to Chicago portion became Interstate 55, both being multiples of 11.[391]

The petroleum company Phillips 66 got its name in a very interesting way. In 1927, the company's gasoline was being tested on US Highway 66 in Oklahoma. When it turned out that the car reached the then breakneck speed of 66 miles per hour, the company decided to name the new fuel Phillips 66.[392] The first Phillips 66 service station opened November 19, 1927, at 805 E. Central in Wichita, Kansas. This station has been preserved by the local historical society.[393]

While on the subject of US highways, Interstate 22 connects Byhalia, Mississippi, south of Memphis, Tennessee, with Birmingham, Alabama,

389 http://www.newenglandhistoricalsociety.com/great-northeastern-blackout-1965/.
390 https://www.u-s-history.com/pages/h1648.html.
391 https://www.legendsofamerica.com/66-timeline/.
392 https://www.phillips66fleet.com/about-us/.
393 https://en.wikipedia.org/wiki/Phillips_66.

along a roughly northwest-to-southeast pathway. The first major completed section of the route between the Mississippi state line and Jasper was opened to traffic on November 22, 2007 (11/22/07). The highway runs a total distance of 202.22 miles.[394]

In 1922, the Bureau of Public Roads commissioned Gen. John J. Pershing, who had been a son-in-law of Wyoming's US Sen. Francis E. Warren, to draw a map that could be used for the construction of roads and also for the purpose of clarifying which roads would be most important for defense if the nation became involved in a war. The Pershing Map became the first official topographical map of the United States. Pershing had commanded the American Expeditionary Force (AEF) on the Western Front during World War I. He also became a mentor to a number of other illustrious US generals, including Dwight D. Eisenhower.[395] This important map laid the groundwork for what was to become the US interstate highway system, one of the greatest achievements in civil engineering in the planet's history.

Numerology in the Bible

The Bible has 31,102 verses in total. This works out to two equal halves, each with 15,551 verses (a prime number). If you take the total number of verses and divide it by the golden ratio, you get an interesting result as in $\frac{31{,}102}{\phi}=\frac{31{,}102}{1.618}=19{,}222$. Taking this to the next level, I wanted to see if perhaps the golden section of the Bible may have a verse of some consequence or import. I was able to find a resource online that lists all verses by multiples of a thousand. I found the verse #19,000, which is Jeremiah 2:34, and then counted up 222 verses, which landed me at Jeremiah 10:22. Much to my surprise, it landed me right in the midst of a prophetic story about the impending battle of Moab! This section was written in the last week of April 2018, and at *that very moment*, the United States was involved in covert military strikes in the Middle East intended to eradicate Iran's nuclear stockpiles buried in Syria and Jordan.

Isaiah 46:11 states,

> From the east I summon a bird of prey; from a far-off land, a man to

394 https://en.wikipedia.org/wiki/Interstate_22.
395 https://www.wyohistory.org/encyclopedia/eisenhowers-1919-road-trip-and-interstate-highway-system.

> fulfill my purpose. What I have said, that I will bring about; what I have planned, that I will do.[396]

If we take *birds of prey* to be a futuristic reference to warplanes and take *from the east* to possibly mean the United States when we consider that the author was probably in the Middle East when writing, it seems reasonable that the United States could be referenced here.

Jeremiah 48 tells a tale of fire and brimstone, foretelling the absolute destruction to come in the ancient territory of Moab, located in southern present-day Jordan. Having done a lot of work in the Middle East, this is particularly interesting to me.

Revelation 20:1–3 states:

> Then I saw an angel coming down from heaven, holding the key of the abyss and a great chain in his hand. And he laid hold of the dragon, the serpent of old, who is the devil and Satan, and bound him for a thousand years; and he threw him into the abyss, and shut it and sealed it over him, so that he would not deceive the nations any longer, until the thousand years were completed; after these things he must be released for a short time.[397]

George Washington

The first president of the United States was born on 2/22/1732. Uncommon for his times, Washington exhibited religious toleration while he attended services of different denominations and suppressed anti-Catholic celebrations in the army. Washington permitted Jews, Muslims, Christians of any denomination, and atheists to work at Mount Vernon. While president, he saluted 22 major religious sects and gave speeches on religious tolerance and acceptance. Washington was a Freemason, and in 1777 (add 1111+666), a convention of Virginia lodges asked him to be the grand master of the newly established Grand Lodge of Virginia. However, he declined because of his commitment to leading the Continental Army. In 1788, he was named master in the Virginia charter of Alexandria Masonic Lodge No. 22.[398]

The George Washington Masonic National Memorial is a Masonic build-

396 https://www.biblegateway.com/passage/?search=Isaiah+46%3A11&version=NIV.
397 https://www.biblegateway.com/passage/?search=Revelation+20%3A1-3&version=NIV.
398 https://en.m.wikipedia.org/wiki/George_Washington.

ing and memorial located in Alexandria, Virginia, outside Washington, DC. The tower is fashioned after the ancient Lighthouse of Alexandria in Egypt, which was one of the original seven wonders of the world. The 333-foot-tall memorial sits atop Shooter's Hill at 101 Callahan Drive. Construction began in 1922, and the building was dedicated in 1932. In July 2015, it was designated a national historic landmark for its architecture and is one of the largest private memorials meant to honor Washington.[399]

WASHINGTON MONUMENT

The Washington Monument is an obelisk on the National Mall in Washington, DC, built to commemorate George Washington for his roles as commander-in-chief of the Continental Army and first president of the United States. Located almost due east of the Reflecting Pool and the Lincoln Memorial, the monument, which is made of marble, granite, and bluestone gneiss, is both the world's tallest predominately stone structure and the world's tallest obelisk.[400]

The monument stands 555.5 feet tall, and when multiplied by 12 to get the height in inches, we find it is 6,666 inches or 6 x 1111! Its foundation is 37 feet thick. (Recall the discussion on star numbers.) The monument is composed of a 500-foot-tall tower capped by a 55-foot tall pyramidion on top, making a 10-to-1 ratio between tower and pyramidion, a tradition that goes back to the original ancient Egyptian obelisks. The monument was officially opened on 10/9/1888. The obelisk is located at the center of a vesica piscis, the lens-shaped area within the intersection of two overlapping rings. 1888 = 1111 + 777.

I'll leave George Washington alone in a moment, but I'd like to mention that Washington state received congressional approval to pursue statehood along with Montana and North- and South-Dakota on 2/22/1889. The territory officially attained statehood on 11/11/1889 after receiving President Benjamin Harrison's signature, becoming the 42nd state.[401]

11:11 AND THE SYMBOLISM OF LIBERTY

As the reader will recall, Hong Kong was a British territory up until 1997,

399 https://en.m.wikipedia.org/wiki/George_Washington_Masonic_National_Memorial.
400 https://en.m.wikipedia.org/wiki/Washington_Monument.
401 https://historylink.org/File/5210

when the 99-year lease was up and control was returned to mainland China. As of September 3, 2019, Hong Kong was experiencing unprecedented levels of violence as the people fight for their freedom. All of this kicked off exactly 22 years (11 + 11) after the July 1997 handover to China.[402] In October of 2019, the Hong Kong government bowed to pressure from mainland China to invoke a 1922 law preventing the protestors from wearing face masks to shroud their identity.[403]As with other symbols of liberty, such as the Statue of Liberty (standing at 111 feet and 1 inch tall from her heel to the top of her head)[404], the 11:11 code is a symbol of light and liberty. The base of the statue is an 11-point star as well!

Can you see the 1111 hiding there in plain sight? Perhaps the 11:11 code is a harbinger of freedom as the light of her torch welcomes foreign immigrants to her shores to pursue a better life. I cannot imagine the delight in my ancestors' hearts to see that beacon of freedom as they landed in New York City from their exhausting journeys.

Just wait till I start explaining the physics of electromagnetism behind the 11:11 code and *prove* that it is a cosmic code of light! This is about the halfway point in the book, and I have saved the very best material for last.

Prohibition

On December 18, 1917, the 18th Amendment prohibiting the "manufacture, sale, or transportation of intoxicating liquors for beverage purposes" was enacted by Congress and then passed to the individual states to be ratified. On January 29, 1919, the measure achieved the three-fourths majority vote needed to enact it into law. The law, known as the Volstead Act, officially went into effect exactly one year later on January 29, 1920. The 18th Amendment to the US Constitution took effect, banning the consumption of alcoholic beverages throughout the country. The controversial and highly unpopular law remained in full effect until it was abolished in 1933 with the enactment of the 21st Amendment. Mississippi was the last *dry* state to end prohibition in 1966.[405] Here we have the numbers 33 and 66 showing up at key moments in the timeline of the legislative and constitutional history of the United States.

402 https://www.nytimes.com/2019/07/01/world/asia/hong-kong-china-handover.html.
403 https://www.dailymail.co.uk/news/article-7536757/Protests-expected-ban-face-masks-Hong-Kong.html.
404 https://www.nps.gov/stli/learn/historyculture/statue-statistics.htm.
405 https://www.history.com/this-day-in-history/prohibition-ends.

Growing Up with Modern Prohibition

I spent my middle and high school years in the city of Zion, Illinois, which was originally founded by eccentric evangelical faith healer John Alexander Dowie with the Christian Catholic Church (CCC) at the geometric center of the city. The city was all about the CCC, with banks, bakeries, and entire industries centered around the church. Zion was to religion what Amana, Iowa, is to appliances. It was a city built around a church that had a litany of bizarre laws such as no spitting, no smoking, no eating pork, no swearing, and alcohol was strictly forbidden.

The city posted a sign at one of the main entry points that said:

> NO GENTLEMAN—KNOWING THAT THE USE OF TOBACCO HAS BEEN STRICTLY PROHIBITED IN THIS CITY FROM THE VERY BEGINNING OF ITS EXISTENCE—WILL USE TOBACCO WITHIN ITS BORDER. THIS IS THE HEADQUARTERS AND THE PRIVATE HOME OF THE CHRISTIAN CATHOLIC CHURCH OF ZION. WE ESTABLISHED IT, AND WE WILL FIGHT FOR IT, IN THE NAME OF THE LORD OF HOSTS, THE GOD OF THE ARMIES OF ZION. WICKED MEN, OUTSIDERS AND BUTTINSKYS HAVE NO BUSINESS, NOR ANY RIGHTS IN THE CITY OF ZION, AND THEY WILL NOT BE PERMITTED. NOTICE TO ALL VISITORS. WHENEVER AND WHEREVER YOU SEE A MAN USING TOBACCO, EITHER SMOKING OR CHEWING, YOU ARE HEREBY INFORMED THAT, THAT MAN IS AN ENEMY OF ZION AND VOLIVA. MARK HIM! [406]

My great-grandfather, Henry Albrecht, was the electrical engineer at the city/church's first radio station. Dowie's successor, Wilbur Glenn Voliva, was equally eccentric and headed up the world's main center of the Flat Earth Society. Voliva famously quipped:

> Books tell you the sun is ninety-three million miles away. That's nonsense. The sun is only three thousand miles away, and is only thirty-two miles in diameter. It circles above the flat earth, spirally, and makes one circuit every twenty-four hours, always at the same

406 http://www.forensicgenealogy.info/contest_121_results.html.

> height. All that talk about the rising and setting sun is an optical illusion.[407]

Voliva even went so far as to offer a $5,000 reward for a challenge to anyone who could disprove his flat Earth theory using mathematics and published it in the October 1931 edition of *Modern Mechanics* magazine.[408]

The history of the city is complex enough to deserve the space of its own book. For starters, the city had its own version of prohibition that lasted until 2017. The closure of the Zion nuclear plant in 1998 and subsequent loss of about $18.5 million in annual tax revenue forced the city to reconsider its stance on granting liquor licenses.[409] Before moving to the next topic, the reader would certainly be shocked and disappointed if there weren't a numerological signature from the 11:11 code. How about the fact that the Zion church was formally organized on February 22, 1896, in Chicago?[410] Yep, that's 2/22.

One last thought on my other hometown: television star Gary Coleman was born and raised in beautiful downtown Zion, Illinois, and I would often ask my mother to drive me past his home on Paxton Drive in the hopes that I might catch Gary out riding his bike and say hello to him. It never happened, and Mom would explain that he was probably busy filming. I've never been starstruck, but I was always so proud to see someone famous on one of my favorite television shows and know he shopped at the same Kmart and ate at the same McDonalds as I did.

AL CAPONE

Having grown up in the Chicago metropolitan area, Al Capone was the stuff of legends. When I traveled out of state and told people I was from the Chicago area, nine times out of ten, they would say, "Ah, yes…Al Capone!"

Al Capone (a.k.a. Scarface) first showed up in the Chicago papers in 1922 for driving his car into a cab, flashing a gun, and showing the cops a bogus police badge. Capone is synonymous with the dark underside of Chicago—a metropolis nicknamed *The Second City* for being smaller than

407 Irving Wallace, *The Square Pegs: Some Americans Who Dared to be Different* (New York: Borzoi Books, 1957).
408 http://blog.modernmechanix.com/5000-for-proving-the-earth-is-a-globe/.
409 https://www.chicagotribune.com/suburbs/lake-county-news-sun/news/ct-lns-zion-nuclear-plant-demolition-st-0916-20170915-story.html.
410 https://wiki.tfes.org/Christian_Catholic_Apostolic_Church.

New York City. Al, a ruthless mobster heavily involved in liquor bootlegging during the prohibition era, flew under the wing of his mentor, Johnny Torrio, the notorious Chicago gangster. Together, they ran Chicago's underground crime syndicate from the club Four Deuces located at 2222 South Wabash Avenue, that's 1111+1111.[411] The Four Deuces operated as a speakeasy as well as a brothel, of which Capone would later become the owner.[412] At age 33, he was convicted of tax fraud after 7 years as crime boss and sentenced to 11 years in prison, becoming one of the earliest prisoners at the famed Alcatraz prison in San Francisco.[413] Alcatraz Island occupies an area of 22 acres.[414]

Al Capone's story is marked with the key numbers 11, 22, and 33, as with many other topics of historical importance that I have investigated in this work. The Bible talks a great deal about good and evil and is composed of 11 + 22 + 33 = 66 books. It doesn't seem terribly odd that we see these numbers glomming on to so many key events in human history—the best and the worst of everything! Pretty schweet, huh?

THE TITANIC

On April 15, 1912, the Titanic had between 2,222 and 2,224 passengers on board, depending on which source you research. While still cloaked in conspiracy, there is ample evidence that a large contingent of high-powered American bankers were invited to ride on the maiden voyage of the Titanic.[415] This took place during the same period of time when the global cabal was trying to force the United States to adopt a Rothschild-owned Federal Reserve Bank to control the country's finances. The bankers who died on the Titanic were the primary opponents of the Fed. It is an awfully odd coincidence that the very next year, in 1913, on December 22, Congress approved the establishment of the Federal Reserve Bank, which became the official center of control of American fiscal policy and the issuing of money.[416] It was at this time that the economy was removed from the gold standard in favor of the cabal's fiat currency. Draw your own conclusions if you think the Titanic really hit an iceberg or if it was an act of sabotage. In May of 1922, Thomas Edison authored a fifteen-point

411 Deuces is slang for the number two, deriving from French *deux*.
412 https://www.chicagotribune.com/news/ct-xpm-1997-01-25-9701250098-story.html.
413 https://www.thevintagenews.com/2017/05/19/al-capone-started-one-of-the-first-soup-kitchens-during-the-great-depression/.
414 https://www.britannica.com/place/Alcatraz-Island.
415 https://www.livescience.com/38102-titanic-facts.html.
416 https://en.wikipedia.org/wiki/Federal_Reserve_Act.

proposal to break the United States out of the Federal Reserve Bank fiat currency in favor of a commodity-backed dollar.[417]

It is also an interesting coincidence that April 15, the anniversary of the Titanic sinking, coincides with the annual deadline for submitting personal income tax returns. It is an annual reminder of who we are *submitting to* and who really controls us. To my intellectually open-minded reader, please visit www.qmap.pub and go to posting #142, which was issued one day after 11/11/2017 and hints that the Titanic sinking was a deliberate act. I'm not here to convince anyone to believe me just because you read it here; I simply show the reader where to obtain facts, and it's up to him or her to do his or her own due diligence and research prior to forming an opinion. Horses and watering troughs come to mind.

I'd like to mention that a replica of the Titanic called *Titanic II* is currently being built and is planned to make her maiden voyage in the year 2022, the 110-year anniversary of the original ship's fateful voyage.[418] Notice how the Roman numeral II looks like an eleven, and the ship sails in 2022. Is this purely coincidental, or is something deeper going on?

Lastly, the 1997 film *Titanic* earned 14 Oscar nominations, resulting in 11 wins, including best picture.[419]

1776: Much More than Just Independence

Something that I discovered recently and have not found pointed out anywhere else on the internet is the fact that the time between 1776, the year of US independence, and the year 2018, when the first half of this book was penned, spans a period of 242 years. At first, 242 seems like a boring enough number, but on a not-so-random whim, I decided to see what was lurking inside this number, if anything, and was stunned. Watch this. The number 242 breaks down to 2 x 11 x 11, so we have two elevens inside of 242's prime factorization. It is also true that 242 = 11 x 22, which can be equivalently expressed as 11 x (11 + 11), and the sum of these two factors is 11 + 22 = 33, whose significance has already been discussed. Going still further, the year 1776 factors out to 2 x 2 x 2 x 23 x 37, or compactly as 2^4 x 3 x 37, or yet another way as 16 x 111. By now you're already (hopefully) convinced of the mystical power of repeated 2s and

417 https://www.pmgnotes.com/news/article/6704/Thomas-Edison-Patents-and-Paper-Money/.

418 https://www.logisticsmiddleeast.com/transport/maritime/31491-titanic-ii-replica-ships-cruise-from-dubai-delayed-until-2022.

419 https://www.oscars.org/collection-highlights/titanic.

the numbers 3, 37, and 111. While this topic deserves the space of its own book, I will briefly mention here that on May 1, 1776, Adam Weishaupt founded the Illuminati secret society in Bavaria, Germany.[420]

Going even deeper, 242 is interesting under Gaussian factoring in the complex plane.

(11 +11i) x (11 - 11i) = 242, where *i* is the imaginary (but extremely useful) number, the square root of negative one. This is particularly interesting in that it has the number 11 featured four separate times.

If you set up a cipher where A = 6, B = 12, C = 18, D = 18, E = 24, etc. … (multiples of 6) out to Z = 156, the letters in "MAY" equate to 234, and the letters of "FIRST" add up to 432, which is the mirror image of 234. The sum of value of MAY + FIRST = 234 + 432 = 666. If you add 234 days to the date of September 9, 2009 (9/9/9 or 666 upside down), you arrive at May 1, 2010, which is the 234th anniversary of the founding of the Illuminati. Again, when 234 is added to its mirror image, you have 666.[421] Is this just a rarefied coincidence, or are these people a LOT more clever than we would like to give them credit for?

Continuing on the path of analyzing the secrets hidden within the number 1776, looking at the base of the unfinished pyramid on the back of a US $1 bill, the date in Roman numerals is "MDCCLXXVI," which adds up as <u>1000</u> + **500** + **100** + <u>100</u> + **50** + **10** + <u>10</u> + 5 + **1** = 1776. If we omit the underlined terms, we get the bold terms to add up to 500 + 100 + 50 + 10 +5 + 1 = 666. The underlined terms add to 1000 + 100 + 10 = 1110. Clearly, we can also write 1110 + 666 = 1776. I find it interesting that these numbers can be rewritten in terms of descending powers of ten, as in $10^3 + 10^2 + 10^1 = 1110$. Just as the pyramid is unfinished, the partial sum just listed is just 1 short of being 1111, again showing incompletion but in numerical form! This reminds me of how the Bible's last verse is Revelation 22:21, just one verse short of being Revelation 22:22 or 2 x (11:11). So, too, 1776 is just one number short of being 1777. It's almost as if we are just one *BenBen stone* away from a complete pyramid, isn't it?

Lastly, it is interesting to remark that 1776 = 888 + 888. The book of Revelation reportedly has exactly 888 Greek words.[422] In Chinese culture,

420 https://www.nationalgeographic.com/archaeology-and-history/magazine/2016/07-08/profile-adam-weishaupt-illuminati-secret-society/.

421 https://www.themystica.com/666-dna-pi/.

422 http://www.astrovera.com/bible-religion/189-bible-number-8.html.

888 is widely regarded as the luckiest of all numbers. You may notice that many Chinese restaurants will have phone numbers with 888 in them. I doubt that any human or group of humans had the foresight or knowledge to plan the independence of the United States to occur during 1776 just to make a numerological statement such as this. In my view, these are huge fingerprints of a universal cosmic plan and that the numerical codes interwoven into scripture serve as mathematical watermarks of authenticity to prevent tampering or alteration over the two millennia since its original writing and beyond. I believe that these numerological watermarks were purposely put in place when the Bible was first written as the authors were probably fully aware that human nature would eventually yield and some kings or dictators in the future would alter the book in some fashion or another to serve their own purposes.

The Great Disappointment

The Great Disappointment in the Millerite movement was the reaction that followed Baptist preacher William Miller's proclamations that Jesus Christ would return to the Earth on 10/22/1844, what he called the Advent. His study of the Daniel 8 prophecy during the second great awakening led him to the conclusion that Daniel's "cleansing of the sanctuary" was the cleansing of the world from sin when Christ would come, and he and many others prepared. However, when October 22, 1844, came, they were all disappointed.[423]

The Battle of Brandywine

During the American Revolutionary War, the Battle of Brandywine Creek was fought on September 11, 1777, between the American Continental Army under General George Washington and the British Army under General Sir William Howe. The British redcoats defeated the American rebels and forced them to withdraw northeast toward the American capital and largest city of Philadelphia, where the Second Continental Congress had been meeting since 1775. The engagement occurred near Chadds Ford, Pennsylvania, during Howe's campaign to take Philadelphia. More troops fought at Brandywine than any other battle of the American Revolution. It was also the longest single-day battle of the war, with continuous fighting for 11 hours.[424] Notice that the battle started on 9/11/1777 and the first day

423 https://www.adventistreview.org/church-news/great-disappointment-remembered-170-years-on.
424 https://en.m.wikipedia.org/wiki/Battle_of_Brandywine.

lasted 11 hours. There are two occurrences of 11 along with the number 777. Intriguingly, 224 years later, to the day—the twin towers would fall in NYC. 1111+666=1777.

Too interesting to omit, but too short to warrant its own section or chapter, so I'll drop it here: the last shot of the US Civil War was fired on June 22, 1865.[425]

According to the Veterans Administration website, their data found that among cases where history of US military service was reported, veterans comprised approximately 22.2 percent of all suicides reported during the project period. If this prevalence estimate is assumed to be constant across all US states, an estimated 22 veterans will have died from suicide each day in the calendar year 2010.[426]

One of the servers (Hi, Katie!) at my favorite organic restaurants in Sturgeon Bay, WI, "Get Real Café" had a bracelet supporting this noble cause, as seen below:

The reader may be starting to ask the same question I've been pondering. "Is there a deeper meaning, a common thread that binds these diverse occurrences of the same special numbers spanning all time, space, and virtually every area of human knowledge?" This is the core question that sparked the creation of this treatise you're hopefully enjoying right now

THE MAYFLOWER COMPACT

On November 11 of 1620, the Mayflower Compact was signed onboard the *Mayflower*. The colonists used the Julian calendar, also known as Old

425 https://www.defensemedianetwork.com/stories/how-the-rebels-saved-the-whales/.
426 https://www.va.gov/opa/docs/suicide-data-report-2012-final.pdf.

Style dates, which was ten days behind the Gregorian calendar we use today. Signing the covenant were 41 of the ship's 102 passengers while the *Mayflower* was anchored in Provincetown Harbor within the hook at the northern tip of Cape Cod. Here is another historical event taking place on 11/11. Five of those passengers were ancestors of my friend and explorer, Donald M. Parrish, Jr.

The original plan was to make a stop in Massachusetts after crossing the Atlantic from England, eventually coming to rest in Virginia. Running low on supplies, the crew decided to abandon the original mission, defying orders from home, and set up a system of government based on the Mayflower Compact.[427] The *Mayflower's* historic voyage across the Atlantic took 3x22 = 66 days to complete.[428]

11/22: Something to Be Thankful For

While writing, I noticed that a calendar on the wall at work with the month of November (2018) had two dates highlighted. The 11th was Veteran's Day, and the 22nd happened to be Thanksgiving that year. This is remarkable enough to mention here because November is the 11th month and the digits of 2018, the year I decided to write this book, add to 11. Thanksgiving always falls on the last Thursday of the month of November and has occurred as early as the 20th and as late as the 30th. A review of all dates from 1900 to 1999 showed there were eight occurrences of it taking place on the 22nd, or about 8 percent of the time.[429] By itself, this fact is interesting, but it takes on added significance in light of all the other facts considered in this book.

11:11 in a Ball of Twine

The world's largest ball of twine is located in Darwin, Minnesota, and was made by Francis A. Johnson. After the conclusion of a work project in nearby Benson, Minnesota, I succumbed to my curiosity and pulled off the highway to go experience this eighth wonder of the world for myself. The ball weighs approximately 11 tons and has a height of 11 feet, according to the news article posted at the ball display (shown below). There you have it. The 11:11 code in another human achievement. The 11:11

427 https://en.m.wikipedia.org/wiki/Mayflower_Compact.
428 http://mayflowerhistory.com/voyage.
429 https://www.timeanddate.com/holidays/us/thanksgiving-day.

code often shows up around humankind's innovations, small or large, significant or trivial.

THE 11:11 CODE MEMORIAL TO FREEDOM

Get ready to have your mind blown. Now we are getting into the really good stuff. In Anthem, Arizona, there is a unique veterans memorial park. This memorial has a vitally important place in the book because of how it interacts with the sun and eternally memorializes the men and women who gave everything to make our world a safer, freer place to live. The centerpiece of the memorial is a sculpture composed of five vertical marble pillars—one to represent each of the five branches of the military and their fallen soldiers. Each pillar is progressively taller than the one next to it and has an elliptical hole through the top of each column. The magic happens every Veterans Day (11/11) at exactly 11:11 a.m. when the rays of the sun align in such a way that they pass through the geometric central axis of the five perfectly aligned holes and project circular beams onto a precisely located target image where the great seal of the United States is affixed.[430] Within this great seal is a star composed of 13 smaller five-pointed stars, 13 leaves of an olive branch, 13 arrows, and 13 stripes of the US flag.[431] Furthermore, the memorial is located at the 33rd parallel (11 + 11 + 11). The memorial sculpture was conceived by local artist Renee Palmer-Stevens, and the deeply involved mathematical design was undertaken by James Martin, P.E. with the help of Rear Adm. Ron Tucker and Steve Rusch. The monument was commissioned on 11/11/11 to top it all off! I plan to attend the 2020 Veteran's Day ceremony with my wife and son in honor of both of my grandfathers who served in WWII, as well

430 https://www.onlineatanthem.com/visitors/veterans_memorial/index.php.
431 https://diplomacy.state.gov/exhibits-programs/the-great-seal.

as all of the warriors who fought for our freedoms—some gave all, and all gave some. My paternal grandfather, Rush Wolfe, served in the army in the Battle of the Bulge while my maternal grandfather was a Navy Frogman (precursor of the Navy SEALs) as an underwater demolition expert at Pearl Harbor.

What greater symbol of the 11:11 code could I have possibly stumbled upon? In case after case, the common denominator in my research of the 11:11 code comes down to *light and liberty*. To all my readers who had a hunch that 11:11 was some sort of enlightenment code, here is your validation—we had it right all along. We just weren't asking the right questions, and humanity had never looked at numbers in such a peculiar manner as I've outlined here.[432]

A number of countries outside the United States that were members of the British Commonwealth also celebrate Remembrance Day on November 11 each year to commemorate the end of WWI hostilities. Following a tradition inaugurated by King George V in 1919, the day is also marked by war remembrances in many non-Commonwealth countries. Hostilities formally ended "at the 11th hour of the 11th day of the 11th month" in accordance with the armistice signed by representatives of Germany and the Entente (the Allies) between 5:12 and 5:20 that morning.[433] Think about one of the most catastrophic and barbaric events in all human history coming to a close in the 11th hour of 11/11.

The US Pledge of Allegiance received official recognition by Congress on June 22, 1942, when the pledge was formally included in the US Flag Code.[434]

432 https://www.codaworx.com/project/anthem-veterans-memorial-anthem-community-council.
433 https://en.m.wikipedia.org/wiki/Remembrance_Day.
434 https://www.legion.org/flag/pledge.

Photos used with written permission of the Anthem Council

THE MUELLER INVESTIGATION

Robert Mueller's ostensible investigation into Russian interference in the 2016 presidential election and alleged collusion by now-President Trump was one of the biggest investigations in all of human history. The investigation took place over a 22-month period and ended on my birthday on 3/22/19. What a wonderful present! There you have it, two instances of 22 or 11+11 imbedded in the biggest witch-hunt of all time!

Mueller's report was delivered on the 46 year anniversary of the recording of a conversation between former President Richard Nixon and his former attorney general, John Mitchell— a conversation that was later used to indict Mitchell on charges of conspiracy, obstruction of justice, and perjury for his role in the attempted cover-up of the Watergate scandal of 1972. In this recording, Nixon can be heard instructing Mitchell to "stonewall" the ongoing Watergate trial and "save the plan."[435] Rounding out the brief section on the Mueller report, the mainstream television media had devoted a total of 2284 hours of coverage time to this wild goose chase![436] The Russia-did-it hoax fell apart when it was determined that the DNC data rate was 22.7 megabytes per second and would not have been technically

435 https://theweek.com/speedreads-amp/830898/mueller-delivered-report-anniversary-nixon-tapes

436 https://www.newsbusters.org/blogs/nb/rich-noyes/2019/03/24/fizzle-nets-gave-whopping-2284-minutes-russia-probe

feasible to achieve such a high data rate at that time if the leak happened via internet.[437]

 [438]

Chicago Tribune

NATION & WORLD

Robert Mueller has turned in his Russia report. What happens now?

…OCIATED PRESS

Now what?

Special counsel Robert Mueller has concluded his Trump-Russia investigation and on Friday delivered his final report to Attorney General William Barr.

But what the report looks like isn't clear. Justice Department regulations required only that Mueller give the attorney general a confidential report that explains the decisions to pursue or decline prosecutions. It could have been as simple as a bullet point list, but the Justice Department has described it as "comprehensive."

Whatever is in the report, we may not get all the juicy details that were uncovered over the past 22 months — at least not right away. But this story is far from over.

The Q Phenomenon

Someone very close to President Trump who has a Q-level security clearance has been posting high-level global intelligence hints on the 8chan board on the so-called dark web since October 2017. In a very successful attempt to circumvent a crooked, compromised mainstream media and to evade widespread censorship by the major social media platforms, Q has been able to give people around the world access to an unredacted, unspun source of direct information about current and upcoming world events, including political scandals and corruption in business, exposing evil worldwide crime rings that included human trafficking, pedophilia,

437 https://www.thenation.com/article/a-new-report-raises-big-questions-about-last-years-dnc-hack/

438 https://www.chicagotribune.com/nation-world/ct-mueller-report-russia-release-20190323-story.html

and human sacrifice (and worse). If information of this magnitude and gravity were delivered through mainstream media (MSM), it would have been branded as a conspiracy and covered up.

I started out following Q's postings in the first week of the movement on Twitter by following the #QANON hashtag, and in March 2018, one of the anons created a phone app called Qdrops that lets the user know when Q has posted new information. The Q phenomenon has shifted power away from MSM and put control of information into the hands of *we the people*. The site **www.qmap.pub** has been one of the richest sources of information I have ever had access to in my lifetime and was one of the key motivating factors for me to begin this herculean writing project. In the third week of April 2018, a series of postings by Q contained an uncanny amount of material with the numbers 11, 22, and 33 in them. Q has reminded his followers several times that "time stamps are very important." Pay attention to them. On August 14, 2018, Q posted drop #1871, which explained how the worldwide media is controlled at the highest levels by the Mossad, the Israeli equivalent of the CIA. In this posting, Q wrote "1:1:1:1," quite similar to the old familiar 11:11. Whenever I'm trying to login to WiFi and having difficulty connecting to the server, I found that typing in the IP address 1.1.1.1 works 90% of the time to get to the sign in screen.

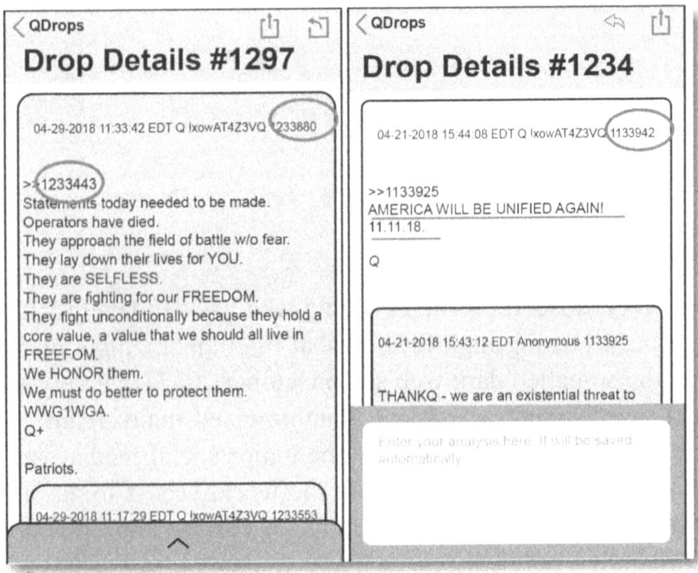

The date 11/11/2018 of posting #1234 as outlined previously, not to mention the fact that the digits of 2018 sum to 11 (2 + 0 + 1 + 8 = 11), this is numerologically equivalent to 11-11-11, which sums to 33 and symbolizes *mastery* and *perfection* in numerology. It was the posting on April 21 that caused me to have a deep, visionary dream that night, which I felt led me to immediately start writing this book. When I woke up the next morning, I looked at my iPhone and saw that it was April 22, and then it all clicked! I immediately set forth writing this book and *voila*! Here we are reading it. These are the images I saw the next day after my dream that I discussed in the first chapter of the book.

I would have to say that posting #2222 was the most profoundly interesting one of all, where an anon posted a question to Q, asking if we are alone in the universe, and Q replied by saying no.

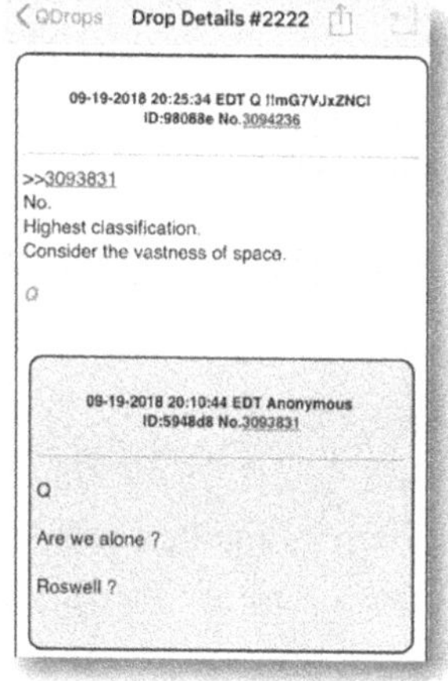

May I remind you of Isaiah 22:22, which says:

> I will place on his shoulder the key to the house of David; what he opens no one can shut, and what he shuts no one can open.

Posting #2222 seems to be foretelling the revelation of some amazing secrets!

In *The Synchronicity Key*, David Wilcock talks about the second coming of Christ:

> Part of our transitional process into becoming "double-bodied", with fourth-density activation while still in a human form, does involve disclosure, when we fully realize we are not alone. Although there have been many efforts to make the public feel afraid of extraterrestrial life, once we realize these people are human—and that they have been helping us all along—this could be a powerful influence

> to enable a much greater awakening to take place. Once we find out that the world we were taught to believe in by the media was fake, it will be an unprecedented transformation. Until we defeat financial tyranny—or at the very least strike a truce where the Cabal allows the truth to be exposed—this information will probably never be able to reach a widespread level. The patriotic elements of the U.S. military cannot step forward and reveal that they have had ongoing diplomatic relationships with a wide variety of extraterrestrials, as well as star gates and antigravity spacecraft.[439]

Owing to its origins on the 4Chan and 8Chan dark internet, the Q movement de facto mascot has come to be *Pepe the Frog*. Various verses in the Bible tell about an impending plague of frogs that no one can escape. With literally millions of people following Pepe around the world, the following verse may be very apropos. Psalm 105:30 says:

> Their land swarmed with frogs, even in the chambers of their kings.

To those familiar with the Q movement, and its mascot, Pepe, we know that the word "KEK" is equivalent to "LOL" in this underground world. The key takeaway is that an ancient Egyptian deity named Kek had the form of a frog and was known as the bringer of light. A statuette that was for sale on Amazon had hieroglyphic inscriptions that appeared to depict a person looking at a computer, along with two twisted snake-like rods intertwined that may represent electromagnetic waves that could correspond to an internet signal, as will be discussed later in the section on physics. I don't have enough proof to take a position on the veracity of these claims, but I present it here for the interested reader to pursue if he or she pleases. A truly fascinating article is linked below[440] and the reader is encouraged to go through this excellent write-up.

The letter Q has long stood as a placeholder or a code name for a mysterious figure. For example, in 1922, the generic name John Q. Public was coined by editorial cartoonist Vaughn Shoemaker of the *Chicago Daily News* to satirize how "taxes and stupid officials" made life hard on the average American. In the '50s, he started showing up in the pages of the *Oklahoman*, where another cartoonist named Jim Lange envisioned him

439 David Wilcock, *The Synchronicity Key: The Hidden Intelligence Guiding the Universe and You* (New York: Dutton, 2013), 452–53.

440 https://pepethefrogfaith.wordpress.com/.

mustachioed, fedoraed, bespectacled—a "common citizen trying to understand the political maneuvers of the powerful."[441]

Many biblical scholars believe that a source of the gospel books existed prior to Matthew and Luke being written. In this context, Q is an abbreviation for the German word *quelle,* meaning source.[442]

In *Star Trek*, a mysterious character identified only as Q was described as being the Federation designation for an impudent, self-superior, and sometimes malevolent being from the otherwise mysterious Q Continuum. Beginning in 2364, the alien literally began to pop up in Federation space to tease, torment, and try Starfleet officers, especially Captain Jean-Luc Picard of the *USS Enterprise*.[443]

In 1963, in the James Bond thriller *From Russia with Love*, the Quartermaster (also known as simply Q) made his first foray into 007's world (initially played in the films by Desmond Llewellyn). An endlessly inventive scientific genius, he runs a department within British Intelligence that stands at the forefront of technological innovation and often lifesaving ingenuity. His creativity and craftsmanship have rescued Bond in tight situations on many occasions.[444]

- For those among us who have been following Q since inception, let's recall that "Epstein Island" was mentioned for the very first time on 11/11/2017 in Q posting #133. One of the recurring themes in the Q operation is the phrase "dark to light." Epstein and his associates' dirty deeds have been found out, but it didn't happen until summer of 2019, nearly a year and a half after Q started dropping dirt on Epstein. Curiously, Q posting 907 simply says "11:11." I felt as if this was one more way the universe was nudging me to research and write in depth about this most unusual subject. Finally, I'd like to mention it was reported that Epstein bought 22 tubes of toothpaste during his imprisonment, which began on June 30, 2008, and ended on July 22, 2009.[445] Jeffery

441 https://slate.com/human-interest/2015/03/john-q-public-or-joe-blow-the-history-and-use-of-words-for-the-common-man.amp.

442 https://www.bibleodyssey.org/en/tools/ask-a-scholar/q-source.

443 http://www.startrek.com/database_article/q.

444 http://www.007.com/focus-week-q-desmond-llewelyn/.

445 https://www.dailymail.co.uk/news/article-7368157/Jeffrey-Epstein-bought-two-pairs-size-small-womens-panties-incarcerated-Florida-jail.html.

> Epstein's apartment in Paris had an address of 22.[446] The 11:11 code may very well be a code of humanity's mass awakening.

After 112 days of silence from August 1, 2019, on 11/11/19, Q posted twelve times on that date, and most remarkably, posting 3585 provided a link to a Twitter user who had researched and discovered that the US Department of Defense had reserved an entire block of IP addresses from 11.11.18.01 through 11.11.18.255—a total of 256 IP addresses all beginning with 11.11.18.xxx dedicated to furthering the Qanon military intelligence operation on the newly established 8kun deep web forum after having been removed forcefully from the familiar 8chan board. This revelation raised the hair on my neck, as it was a confirmation of posting 1234 which stated that "AMERICA WILL BE UNIFIED AGAIN! 11.11.18. Q." It is noteworthy to observe that there are decimals between the numbers, versus the usual dashes or slashes, in the common notation for dates.

Q posting #3585 was the biggest confirmation of my 11:11 studies. When it was explained that the statement "AMERICA WILL BE UNIFIED AGAIN. 11.11.18" in posting #1234 they were referring to these 256 I.P. addresses locked down for the Q movement. Goodness gracious, great balls of fire, this was a hair-raising thing for me to read!

This was a massive confirmation to me that I have been on the right path all along during the process of researching and writing. Posting #3773 makes a reference to posting #436, which posted on 12/22/17 and said

446 Jeffery Epstein's apartment in Paris has an address of 22.

"ONE OF 22." I'm still not certain what to make of this posting, but the numbers are fascinating. 3773 factors out to: 7x7x7x11, and it's nice that both 37 and 73 are star numbers sitting side by side, narcissistically admiring what they see in the mirror: 37|73. Who ever told you that math had to be hard and boring? I think of recreational math as taking my mind to the gym for a good iron-pumping session. It just feels great!

The topic of Qanon would require a multi-volume series of books to even begin to cover it. The interested reader is directed to British computer scientist, Martin Geddes's website link below for an excellent writeup.[447] Literally hundreds of books will be written on this subject over the years to come. Watch for it. I've enjoyed the last 2.5 years of being on the inside track of this, the greatest movement in human history, before the general public became fully aware of it. This book is a direct result of my involvement in the Qanon movement as one of the original digital soldiers who helped propagate the flow of the truth via Twitter. Follow the #qanon hashtag to see what the rest of the world is buzzing about!

I'll conclude my remarks about the Q movement with the following reader exercise:

> Search the internet for a website that calculates the difference between two dates. Use 10/28/2017, when Q made his first posting, as the start date, and Veteran's Day, 11/11/2020 as the end date. You should get 1111 days! A special thank you to Scott McElroy for alerting me to this fascinating discovery!

THE PARADIGM

In his 2017 *New York Times* bestseller, *The Paradigm: The Ancient Blueprint That Holds the Mystery of Our Times,*[448] *author Jonathan Cahn writes about a pattern of several world leaders who held positions of government authority for 22 years from beginning to end. Bill Clinton entered the political arena in January 1979 when he was inaugurated as governor of the state of Arkansas. He would remain in politics until January 2001, when he completed his final term as the US president. This is a span of 22 or 11 + 11 years. Cahn draws a direct correspondence to his ancient archetype, King Ahab, whose controversial rulership ended after a period of 22 years. Similarly, Cahn found a correspondence between his wife*

447 https://mailchi.mp/martingeddes/wwg1wga-thestorm-and-qanon-red-pill-websites-now-available

448 Jonathan Cahn, *The Paradigm* (Lake Mary, FL: Charisma House Book Group, 2017).

Hillary Rodham Clinton's time in politics, and that of Queen Jezebel. Jezebel enjoyed the reins of power throughout her husband's, King Ahab's, rule over Israel. As it turns out, both Hillary and Jezebel were effectively queens, while their husbands were kings, for a period of 22 years. Why 11 + 11 years? Get Cahn's The Paradigm, it's amazing. But please finish this book first! But wait, in the back matter of Cahn's book, he lists his contact address as:

Hope of the World
P.O. Box 1111
Lodi, NJ 07644

Osama Bin Laden, who is believed to be responsible for the 9/11 attacks on New York City, was assassinated ten years after the catastrophe, in the year 2011. This is a clear case of something bad that started with an 11 and ended with an 11 signature.

PRESIDENTIAL NUMBERS

February 2, 2018 (2/2/2018) was the day the vaunted FISA Memo was delivered by the Republicans, headed by Devin Nunes who leads California's 22nd congressional district. This clearly infuriated the deep state players, and very interestingly, the DOW Jones average closed down 666 points that very same day.[449] President Obama was 55.5 years of age during his last month in office, and when you multiply that age by 12, you arrive at 666 months of age at the end of his term. Barack Hussein Obama received 333 (half of 666) electoral votes, securing him the presidency in 2008.[450]

Even more interestingly, President Donald J. Trump was exactly 70 years, 7 months, and 7 days of age (777) on January 20, 2017, the exact date of his inauguration. While writing, I personally verified the math to arrive at this result. In order to impeach a sitting president, the legislature requires a supermajority vote of two-thirds or 66.6 percent. The year 2017 equates to the year 5,777 in the Hebrew calendar. It is also somewhat remarkable that the sun's surface temperature is estimated to be about 5,777 degrees Kelvin (5,504 C).[451] The year 2017 was also the year during which Israel celebrated 70 years of nationhood. Almost immediately upon entering office, President Trump recognized Jerusalem as the legitimate capital city

449 https://www.marketwatch.com/story/dow-futures-tumble-more-than-250-points-on-jobs-day-2018-02-02
450 https://amp.economist.com/united-states/2008/11/04/obamas-historic-victory.
451 http://stars.astro.illinois.edu/sow/sun.html.

of Israel and subsequently moved the US embassy to Jerusalem in a move that many people believe is fulfillment of biblical prophecy. The interested reader is referred to the footnoted story.[452] Isaiah Chapter 45 talks about King Cyrus, which curiously matches Trump's president number, 45, as well as many of his actions in the Middle East.

Adding still further to intrigue, Donald Trump's paternal grandmother was born Elisabeth Christ in Kallstadt, Germany. When she was 22 years old, she received a marriage proposal from Frederick Trump in 1901, who was 33 years of age at the time. Frederick Trump would go on to marry Mary Anne McLeod, who would give birth to Donald Trump. Elizabeth Christ Trump died on June 6, 1966 (6/6/66) at the age of 85.[453]

I find it fascinating to see that he is the grandson of someone named Christ, connecting the 777 numerology of his inauguration date and the biblical prophecy that he fulfilled by moving the US embassy in Israel to Jerusalem. Why is the number 777 often associated with Jesus? The best Bible passage I can find is Matthew 18:21–22, which says,

> Then Peter came to Jesus and asked, "Lord, how many times shall I forgive my brother or sister who sins against me? Up to seven times?" Jesus answered, "I tell you, not **seven** times, but **seventy-seven** times."

But maybe physics could offer some deeper answers? Stand by for more on that later on.

452 https://www.thetrumpet.com/21036-a-prophesied-resurgence-in-israel
453 https://en.wikipedia.org/wiki/Elizabeth_Christ_Trump

Let your speech always be with grace, as though seasoned with salt, so that you will know how you should respond to each person.

—Colossians 4:6[454]

Salt is born of the purest parents: the sun and the sea.

—Pythagoras[455]

You are the salt of the earth; but if the salt has become tasteless, how can it be made salty again? It is no longer good for anything, except to be thrown out and trampled underfoot by men.

—Matthew 5:13[456]

Salt is good; but if the salt becomes unsalty, with what will you make it salty again? Have salt in yourselves, and be at peace with one another.

—Mark 9:50[457]

454 https://biblehub.com/colossians/4-6.htm.
455 https://quotefancy.com/quote/1374576/Pythagoras-Salt-is-born-of-the-purest-parents-the-sun-and-the-sea.
456 https://www.bible.com/bible/compare/MAT.5.13-16,43.
457 https://biblehub.com/mark/9-50.htm.

CHAPTER 7
PLANET EARTH

MOUNT EVEREST

Up until now, we have been mostly focused on human achievements. Now we turn our attention to Earth itself. The 1922 British Mount Everest expedition was the first mountaineering expedition with the express aim of making the first ascent of Mount Everest. This was also the first expedition that attempted to climb Everest using bottled oxygen.[458]

The expedition was conducted by General Charles Granville Bruce, with Lt. Col. Edward Lisle Struttacting as the expedition leader. George Mallory, who had previously attempted the summit unsuccessfully, was back again, this time with the intention of reaching the peak. On the 22nd of May, 1922, the expedition managed to reach a very impressive 8,170 meters (26,804 feet) of the north ridge before deciding to retreat. The very next day, George Finch and Geoffrey Bruce attempted the same challenge and reached 8,320 meters (27,000 feet). A very short while after that, on the 7th of June, the infamous George Mallory was caught in a dramatic avalanche that claimed the lives of 7 Sherpas. These were to be the first reported fatalities on Everest but certainly not the last. Despite the fact that this particular expedition claimed the lives of those highly experienced Sherpas, they did manage to set a new world record by reaching 27,000 feet up the mountain.[459]

It wasn't until May 29, 1953, that Edmund Hillary and Tenzing Norgay

458 https://en.m.wikipedia.org/wiki/1922_British_Mount_Everest_expedition.
459 http://www.everest1953.co.uk/1921-1953.

became the first people in human history to ascend the top of the world's highest mountain, but the 22 markers outlined previously are important because these were the first serious attempts at achieving this nearly superhuman feat.[460]

It is worth noting that 5 out of the 7 tallest mountains on each continent bear either a 22 signature or a number very close to the golden ratio in their peak heights. These are tabulated in the following table, along with deviation from the golden ratio times 10,000 (16,180):[461]

Peak	Height	Deviation from 10,000 x Phi	Continent
Aconcagua	**22**,838 feet	N/A	South America
Denali	20,**322** feet	N/A	North America
Mt. Kosciuszko	**2,222** meters	N/A	Australia
Mt. Vinson	16,050 feet	-0.8%	Antarctica
Puncak Jaya	16,024 feet	-0.9%	Australasia

PERU'S INTIHUATANA STONE

Recommended listening: Frente Bolivarista Vol 4 - Nômades 2016

In Peru's ancient city of Macchu Picchu, they have a very curious ritual stone artifact known as the Intihuatana stone that is one of many ritual stones in South America. These stones are arranged to point directly at the sun during the winter solstice. The name of the stone comes from the Quechua language. *Inti* means sun, and *wata* means "to tie, hitch up." The suffix *-na* comes from nouns for tools or places. Hence, Intihuatana is literally an instrument or place to "tie up the sun," often expressed in English as "the hitching post of the sun." The Inca believed the stone held the sun in its place along its annual path in the sky. The stone is situated at 13° 9′ 48″ S latitude. At midday on 11/11 and again on 1/30, the sun stands almost exactly above the pillar, casting no shadow. On June 21, the stone casts the longest shadow on its southern side, and on December 21, it casts a much shorter shadow on its northern side. Adding further to the intrigue of this enigmatic monument to the sun is the fact that the Intihuatana of Machu Picchu was found intact by Bingham in 1911, indicating

460 https://www.britannica.com/on-this-day/May-29.
461 https://en.m.wikipedia.org/wiki/Seven_Summits.

that the Spanish conquerors had not found it. Here we have 11 turning up once again.[462]

Did the ancients have a numerological fascination with 11-11 too? If so, why? Will the answer to the 11-11 mystery be revealed later in this book? What is a rhetorical question? No jumping ahead now!

Using the Sun to Measure the Earth

The ancient Greek mathematician Eratosthenes was able to not only prove that Earth is a sphere but also measure its diameter and calculate its circumference without the aid of any modern instruments. But *how*???

Around the year 240 BC, or about 2,260 years ago, he observed that during the summer solstice in Syene, Egypt (modern Aswan), at noon local time, the sun was 90 degrees directly overhead. Syene is located at 24 degrees north of the equator, which is 0.6 degrees north of the Tropic of Cancer. He noticed that when looking down the bore of a deep, perfectly vertical water well in the ground, the reflection of the sun could be observed shining directly back. He traveled 5,000 stadia (575 miles) north to the city of Alexandria (where I worked in 2006) and used a vertical rod called a gnomon to measure the sun's angle of elevation at noon as well as the length of the shadow projected on the ground. Utilizing basic properties of triangle geometry and knowing that the sun's rays are essentially parallel, he was able to determine that they deviated 7 degrees from vertical, which is approximately one-fiftieth of the circumference of a circle. Knowing that the arc length traveled from Syene to Alexandria was 575 miles and this was approximately one-fiftieth of the Earth's circumference, he was able to estimate the planet's circumference to be about 50 x 575 = 28,750 miles. The modern accepted value of the Earth's circumference is about 24,901 miles, which puts his measurement at an error margin of about 14 percent. That isn't bad considering (a) it was more than 2,200 years ago, (b) there was no widely agreed-upon value of what the true measure of a stadion should be, (c) he assumed Earth was perfectly spherical, which fails to account for the Earth's oblateness or equatorial bulge, and (d) Alexandria was exactly due north of Syene. All in all, his experiment achieved its purpose to demonstrate for the first time that the Earth is a sphere and to give an estimate of how big it is. I would have to give this man a solid A+ for his work.

462 https://en.m.wikipedia.org/wiki/Machu_Picchu.

EARTH DAY

In 1969 at a UNESCO conference in San Francisco, peace activist John McConnell proposed that a day be set aside to honor our planet and the concept of peace originally aligned to the spring equinox, March 21—the first day of spring in the northern hemisphere. Earth Day was born. A separate Earth Day was later sanctioned to occur on April 22 in a proclamation penned by McConnell and endorsed by US Senator Gaylord Nelson in 1970. The original concept of Earth Day was confined to the United States, but the event's original coordinator, Denis Hayes, launched the event internationally in 1990. The event is recognized by 141 nations.

During my exhaustive research, I discovered that the Paris Agreement on climate (Paris Accord) was put in place on December 12, 2015, in an effort to combat global warming by means of engaging the agreement of more than 196 countries to pledge to reduce their production of greenhouse gases. The agreement was signed on April 22, 2016.[463] As part of the agreement, France pledged to completely wean itself from the use of coal for the production of electricity by the year 2022.[464]

It's quite a coincidence to see the number 22 showing up in these two high-visibility events dedicated to saving our planet. Recall that I began writing this book on 4/22/2018, long before making these discoveries and connections to that same date, which I uncovered in late September of that year.

EARTH NUMBERS

The Earth rotates on its axis at an inclination of 23.4 degrees from the plane of the ecliptic (the orbital plane occupied by Earth's elliptic orbit around the sun), giving us distinct seasons. Without this tilt angle, it would be the same season all year round. Now take the number 23.4 and add the mirror image of the digits. You get 43.2 + 23.4 = 66.6, which is clearly one-tenth of 666 degrees. The arctic and Antarctic pole circles are located at 66.6 degrees north and south of the equator, respectively.

Here's a fun fact. When standing at the north pole, *every* direction you look is south. Similarly, every direction is north when standing at the south pole. The ideas of east and west are abstract concepts at these geometric

463 https://unfccc.int/news/over-150-countries-to-sign-the-paris-agreement-on-friday-22-april-2016.
464 https://www.thelocal.fr/20181127/france-to-close-14-nuclear-reactors-by-2035.

singularities. Did you know that there are no time zones at the poles? All the lines of longitude converge to a point, and the geocentric concept of time vanishes. In speaking with the world's greatest explorer Donald M. Parrish, Jr., I learned that the concept of timekeeping while at the poles is to keep the same time as the support country. In the case of a Norwegian researcher, he or she would keep the same schedule as their home base in Norway, GMT + 1. The concept of east-*ness* and west-*ness* vanishes at the singularity of the poles. It's sort of like the zero vector—"the vector that *refuses* to point," as my vector calculus professor Carol Ash explained at the University of Illinois during my undergraduate work. Similarly, the concepts of northness and southness die at the poles, whereas you can go infinitely far in the east or west directions and never reach the end.

The northernmost piece of land on Earth is located at 83.666 N - 29.833 E and is named Kaffeklubben Island, which in Danish translates to Coffee Club Island! Note the 666 and 33 in the GPS coordinates.[465] The term arctic derives from the Greek word αρκτικος (arktikos), meaning "near the bear, northern." The name refers either to the constellation Ursa Major, the "Great Bear," which is prominent in the northern portion of the celestial sphere, or to the constellation Ursa Minor, the "Little Bear," which contains Polaris, the pole star, also known as the North Star.[466] Earth's equatorial circumference is 21,600 nautical miles, which factors out to (6 x 6 x 6) x 1000.[467]

According to John Knauss in *Introduction to Physical Oceanography*:

> A second variation is related to the precession in the elliptical path of the earth around the sun. The earth's orbit about the sun is an ellipse, which means that the distance of sun to earth is not constant. At present, the earth is closer to the sun in early January, during the Southern Hemisphere summer, than in June, during the Northern Hemisphere summer. The ellipse precesses with a period of about 22,000 years; thus 11,000 years from now the earth will be closer to the sun during the Northern Hemisphere summer and farther away during the Southern Hemisphere summer.[468]

Continuing the discussion of Earth's axial tilt or obliquity, the reader might be surprised to know that while this 23.4 degree axial tilt is es-

465 https://en.wikipedia.org/wiki/Kaffeklubben_Island.
466 https://en.m.wikipedia.org/wiki/Arctic.
467 https://www.thehour.com/norwalk/article/The-origins-of-the-nautical-mile-8255497.php.
468 John Knauss, *Introduction to Physical Oceanography* (Long Grove, IL: 2017).

sentially a constant during our mere mortal life span of a hundred years or so, like most systems in our universe, it is also operating on a cycle of change. As it turns out, Earth's angle of obliquity varies from a minimum of 22.1 degrees up to a maximum of 24.5 degrees over a cyclical period of approximately 41,000 years. At our present inclination of 23.4 degrees, we are almost exactly at the midpoint between the two extremes. We are currently headed back down toward 22.1 degrees tilt, but don't hold your breath till we get there.[469] I learned this in a graduate level Physical Oceanography course by Dr. David Porter that I took toward my Master of Physics degree with Johns Hopkins University last year. Exciting stuff!

While we are talking about degrees of arc on Earth's surface, it is interesting to notice that at the equator, one degree of movement takes a traveler 111.33 kilometers. Remember that Earth is not a perfect sphere but rather an oblate (smooshed) spheroid where the radius of the planet is 22 kilometers greater at the equator than it is at the poles. This means that slightly less arc (surface distance) will be traversed at the poles—and anywhere in between, for that matter.

One minute of arc equals 1/60 of a degree. Earth orbits around the sun at an average speed of 106,000 kilometers per hour. To convert this to miles per hour, we divide by 1.62 and get 106,000/1.62 = 66,666 miles per hour.

Taking these facts in isolation, one might conclude that 666 is the number of the Earth. With its molten mantle and core that occasionally blasts through the surface in the form of lava, it's not too far an abstraction to connect the hellish conditions that exist within the planet to the religious concept of hell.

When we normally think about a spherical ball rotating, most of us only think of the rotational speed and orientation. The rotation of heavenly bodies is actually much more complicated. Referring to a child's spinning a toy top or a gyroscope, you notice that the axis of rotation precesses in such a way that the axis of the toy scribes out a cone shape in space, while the north pole traces out an imaginary circle in the air above it. This is called precession. If the motion is sufficiently perturbed, the axis may actually nod as it precesses around, bouncing up and down in the vertical plane as the axis precesses around in the tangential direction. Additionally, large spheres such as the moon also have a wobble rate in the

469 https://www.sciencedirect.com/topics/earth-and-planetary-sciences/earth-axis.

rotational period called libration, whereby the rotational speed alternately increases and decreases cyclically. All these effects must be considered when attempting to land a spacecraft on the surface of a celestial body. The Earth's polar axis precesses in such a way that the north pole inscribes a cone or circle in the north sky every 25,920 years as it gently and slowly wobbles like a toy top.

Below is a link to an excellent YouTube video that shows how the Earth's precession causes the stars appear to change position over the long term. Take three minutes and check it out. I think you'll be glad you did.

Recommended video: "Precession of the Earth" by Steven Sanders

In *The Secret History of the World*, Booth states that "over a period of some 2,160 years, the sun rises in the same constellation. We are currently coming out of the age of Pisces, and are entering into the Age of Aquarius."[470] The firmament of the heavens has long been considered divisible into the twelve zodiac sectors. In order for Earth's north pole to sweep through all twelve zodiacs, this takes approximately 12 x 2,160 = 6 x 6 x 6! = 25,920 years. Aquarius is the 11th astrological sign in the zodiac, originating from the constellation Aquarius.[471] The age of Aquarius is widely acclaimed in the astrology community to be the age of the awakening of humankind.

Have they been right all along? We will see! The fact that the entire Earth and all its residents are entering into the 11th house is particularly remarkable in light of this book's title and the timing of my inspiration to write it.

In *The Synchronicity Key*, David Wilcock also looked into the concept of the *great year* (or one period of Earth's precession) and noted that in 25,872 years (though no one knows the exact precessional period), you can divide that period of time into 48 units of time, each 539 years long (48 x 539 = 25,872), which is equal to 7 x 77 = 539. As mentioned earlier, in Matthew 18:22, Jesus tells Peter to forgive his brother "seven times seventy-seven times" or 539 times.[472] Recalling that Earth takes approximately 2,160 years to pass through one house of the zodiac, this period can be divided into 4 periods of 539 years. Wilcock refers to the Great Year

470 Mark Booth, *The Secret History of the World* (New York: The Overlook Press, 2008), 107.

471 https://www.gaia.com/series/eleventh-house.

472 David Wilcock, *The Synchronicity Key: The Hidden Intelligence Guiding the Universe and You* (New York: Dutton, 2013), 257.

as being the mainspring of the cosmic clock and calls it the synchronicity key.[473] Anyone wishing to go deeper with this discussion should pick up a copy of Wilcock's book.

The number 2,160 can be factored to 10 x (6 x 6 x 6). Here we see 666 embedded in yet another way into the motions of Earth over great scales of time. The prime factorization of 25,920 comes out to (2 x 2 x 2 x 2 x 2 x 2) x (3 x 3 x 3 x 3) x 5 or just: 2^6 x 3^4 x 5, which is a lot of 2s and 3s. Written more compactly, this is 2^6 x 3^4 x 5, or if we want to be cute and include all numbers from 1 through 6, we could write 25,920 = 2^6 x 3^4 x 5^1. It can also be written as 25,920 = 6 x 6 x 6! (6! = 6 x 5 x 4 x 3 x 2 x 1 = 720). This analysis of the precessional period of Earth seems to add to a growing body of evidence of intelligent design of the solar system. The number 2,160 is also an important number to the moon, as it enumerates the lunar diameter in miles and can be written as 6! + 6! + 6!. Here again, we see the number 666 deeply rooted in the basic geometric properties of the heavenly bodies of the solar system. Earth's mean diameter is 7,920 miles, which works out to 11 x 6!. Because of the Earth's spin, the centrifugal forces at the equator cause the planet to bulge slightly, causing the equatorial radius to be 22 kilometers greater than the polar radius.[474]

Anyone who has spun a child's top also has experienced nutation, which is Latin for nodding. Like a spinning top, the Earth's axis doesn't sweep out a perfect ring in space, but rather, it nods as it precesses. To see this graphically, please check out YouTube for videos under the search terms "gyroscope nutation." The video by CGS is quite fascinating, trust me! A link is in the footnotes.[475] Fact: The Earth makes a full nutation cycle every 223 months.[476] A year on Earth lasts exactly 365.2422 days according to NASA.[477]

The last thing I'd like to illuminate in this section is the curious fact that light takes 11 + 11 or 22 minutes to cross the entire elliptical disk of Earth's orbital path around the sun. Danish scientist Ole Christensen Rømer used an astronomical measurement to make the first quantitative estimate of the speed of light. When measured from Earth, the periods of moons orbiting a distant planet are shorter when Earth is approaching the

473 Ibid., 380.
474 https://www.space.com/17638-how-big-is-earth.html.
475 https://www.youtube.com/watch?v=5Sn2J1Vn4zU.
476 https://solarsystem.nasa.gov/basics/chapter2-1/.
477 https://pumas.jpl.nasa.gov/files/04_21_97_1.pdf

planet than when Earth is receding from it. The distance traveled by light from the planet (or its moon) to Earth is shorter when Earth is at the point in its orbit that is closest to its planet than when Earth is at the farthest point in its orbit, the difference in distance being the diameter of Earth's orbit around the sun. The observed change in the moon's orbital period is caused by the difference in the time it takes light to traverse the shorter or longer distance.[478] Rømer observed this effect for Jupiter's innermost moon Io and deduced that light takes 22 minutes to cross the diameter of the Earth's orbit. Romer submitted his findings to the *Academie Royale des Sciences* on 11/22/1676.[479] Here we have the numbers 11 and 22 showing up in a major scientific discovery about the physical properties of light. When we start talking about the physics of light, I'll explain the secret of why 11:11 and 22 conceal the secret of light.

The Easter Island Enigma

One of Earth's greatest mysteries is the ancient history of Easter Island, and the enigmatic Moai human-shaped statues made of stone. The island is sometimes affectionately referred to as *the navel of the world* or by its name in the local language, *Rapa Nui.* The island was believed to have been first inhabited in the 1,100-AD time frame. (Possibly the year 1111??) Replete with its own ancient hieroglyphics and Polynesian language, it is an island of untold stories. This chapter looks into some of the numerological mysteries of this world wonder.

Easter Island's first European visitors arrived in 1722, when the Dutch mariner Jacob Roggeveen made landfall. In 1770, two Spanish ships arrived at the island, under the command of Felipe Gonzalez de Ahedo. In 1774, the famous British captain James Cook made a pit stop on his global voyage. The next visitors were the French, in 1776, piloted by Admiral Laperouse. Notice that all four of these key dates contained repeated digits.

Here are a few interesting facts about Easter Island: The all-time low population was 111 in the year 1877. As of the 2017 census, the head count was up to 7,750. The island's largest park, Rapa Nui National Park, has an area of 6,666 hectares (16,472 acres). Chile annexed Easter Island on 9/9/1888. The native Rapa Nui people were granted Chilean citizen-

478 https://www.space.com/17638-how-big-is-earth.html.
479 http://adsabs.harvard.edu/full/1983JHA....14..137V.

ship in 1966. The island averages 44 inches of rain per year. The nearest civilization of 500 people or more is located 1,619 miles away, which is almost exactly 1000 times the golden ratio (1.618) within a precision of 0.06 percent.[480]

For such a small island, it sure has a fascinating history, and from the facts listed above, there seem to be some very interesting coded messages within the repeated digits. Perhaps they are a stepping stone toward cracking some of the ancient mysteries of *Rapa Nui*. What if this island is one of the last remnants of ancient Lemuria?

SALT OF THE EARTH

Sodium chloride, commonly known as table salt (NaCl), has some interesting properties. When salt is added to water to the point of saturation, the water freezing point reaches a lower limit at -21.12 Celsius. The same solution will have an elevated boiling point as well, specifically 227.7 degrees Fahrenheit.[481]

Salt has been used by humans for thousands of years for things ranging from food preservation to seasoning. Its ability to preserve food was a foundational contribution to the development of civilization. It helped eliminate dependence on seasonal availability of food and made it possible to transport food over large distances, making it possible to make longer voyages. However, salt was often difficult to obtain, so it was a highly valued trade item and considered a form of currency by certain peoples. Many salt roads, such as the Via Salaria in Italy, had been established by the Bronze Age.

All through history, availability of salt has been pivotal to civilization. The word *salary* is derived from the Latin word for salt. *Sal* is the word for salt in many languages, including Spanish. In Britain, the suffix *-wich* in a place name means it was once a source of salt, as in Sandwich and Norwich. The Natron Valley was a key region that supported the Egyptian Empire to its north because it supplied it with a kind of salt that came to be called by its name, natron. This is where the element sodium got its counterintuitive chemical symbol [Na]. Today salt is almost universally accessible, relatively cheap, and often iodized. There have been reports

480 https://whc.unesco.org/en/list/715.
481 https://gcaptain.com/salt-earth/.

as to the value of salt in historical times, though it has never been more valuable than gold.[482]

I once worked at a PVC (polyvinyl chloride) plant in the charming and quaint Messaieed Industrial City in Qatar where they pulled raw seawater into a series of salt pans, which are shallow, rectangular pools where the water is allowed to evaporate off. As the water gets more and more concentrated with salt, it gets pumped to the next stage until it is eventually a thick brine. This brine is run through electrolysis units where tens of millions of watts of high-voltage power electrically strip the sodium and chlorine atoms apart, and the chlorine ions are used to provide the "C" in PVC.

Working late at night in the Messaieed Industrial City, Qatar

In *Biocentrism*, Lanza gives an interesting perspective about one of the most ubiquitous food additives:

> No chemist who has studied the properties of chlorine, a poison, and sodium, an element that reacts explosively when it meets water, could have possibly guessed the properties that would be exhibited when the two combine as sodium chloride—table salt. Here suddenly we have a compound that is not only non-poisonous, but is in fact indispensable to life. Moreover, sodium chloride does not react violently when it meets water, it meekly dissolves in it! This larger

482 https://en.wikipedia.org/wiki/History_of_salt.

> reality could not have been inferred from a mere study of the nature of its components.[483]

So here, in simple table salt, we see an essential component of life with an interesting story—and a fascinating connection to our significant numbers 11, 22, and 77.

EARTH'S HYDROLOGICAL CYCLE

It always used to irk and perplex me as some sort of cosmic prank that the vast majority of Earth's water contains salt and thus cannot be used to support land-based life. It seemed cruel to have the world's land masses surrounded by a virtually infinite amount of life's most important resource, and yet we cannot use it to sustain life. But in recent years, it started to make sense. If all the oceans were pure, drinkable water, the resource would no longer be precious, and we wouldn't need the hydrological cycle of evaporation and rain in order to sustain land-based life. If you think about it, it's pretty remarkable to note that all Earth's fresh water via precipitation is the direct result of an evaporation and condensation cycle powered by sunlight. The hydrological cycle is quite remarkable when you consider that all fresh water is purified and transported by means of light energy produced in a star 93,000,000 miles away by means of nuclear fusion taking place inside the sun.

Each year, an average of 121,000 cubic miles of liquid water falls as precipitation on Earth, which is of course 11 x 11 x 1,000. That's another occurrence of 11:11.[484]

In the ancient near east, Hebrew scholars observed that even though the rivers ran into the sea, the sea never became full. Some scholars conclude that the water cycle was described completely during this time in the following passage:

> The wind goeth toward the south, and turneth about unto the north; it whirleth about continually, and the wind returneth again according to its circuits. All the rivers run into the sea, yet the sea is not full; unto the place from whence the rivers come, thither they return again.[485]

483 Robert Lanza, *Biocentrism* (Dallas: Benbella Books, 2009).
484 https://scied.ucar.edu/learning-zone/water-cycle
485 https://en.wikipedia.org/wiki/Water_cycle.

In the *Adityahridayam*, a devotional hymn to the sun god of Ramayana, a Hindu epic dated to the fourth century BC, it is mentioned in the 22nd verse that the sun heats up water and sends it down as rain.[486]

Please make a mental note of these two connections between the number 22, the sun, light, and life. This is a key fact that will contribute greatly to the conclusions that can be drawn from this book.

486 https://www.rhymezone.com/r/rhyme.cgi?typeofrhyme=wke&loc=thesql&Word=Ramayana.

CHAPTER 8
WEATHER PHENOMENA

SUN DOGS

A *sun dog* is an optical phenomenon technically referred to as a *parhelion* in meteorology, in which a halo appears around the sun at an angle of 22 degrees to either side of the line between the sun and observer. There are often two bright spots ("dogs") on the halo at the three- and nine-o'clock positions relative to the sun. Since the 1510 timeframe, the English word *dog* has meant "to hunt, track, or follow." The origin of the term *dog* to describe this optical phenomenon is not completely certain, but the strongest lead points to the Swedish language, in which the term *solvärg*, which means "sun wolf," describes two wolves hunting or following the sun with one on each side.[487] Interestingly, my last name is *Wolfe*, and I have Swedish roots.

Sun dogs occur because of sunlight refracting through the hexagonal structure of ice crystals in the atmosphere. The crystals cause the sunlight to bend at a minimum angle of 22 degrees. All the crystals are refracting the sun's rays, but we only see the ones that are bent toward our eyes. Because this is the minimum, the light looks more concentrated starting at 22 degrees away from the sun—about forty times the size of the sun in the sky. At this 22 degree point, you can get arcs, a halo, or just bright spots in the sky.[488]

487 https://en.wikipedia.org/wiki/Sun_dog.
488 https://www.universetoday.com/47609/sun-dog/.

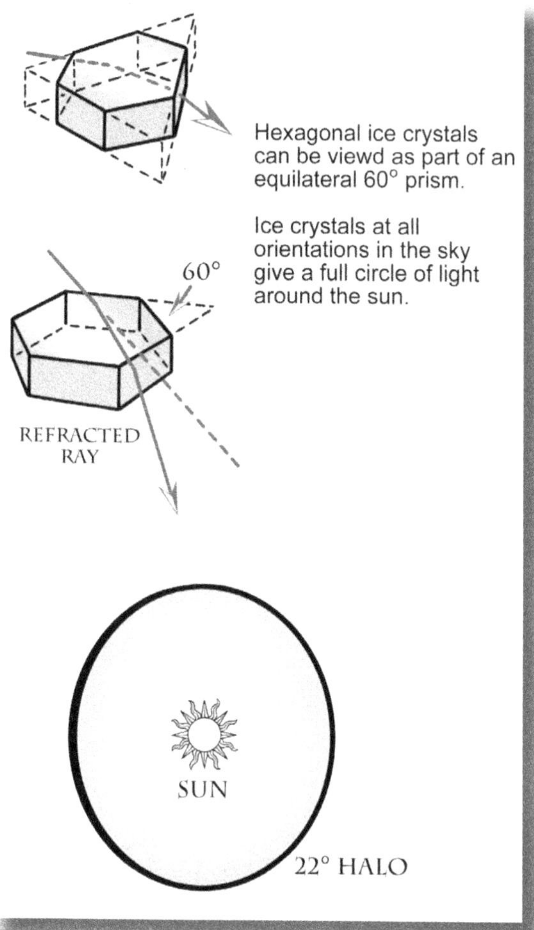

Once again, we have the number 22 (11 + 11) showing up in the context of light, which lays a concrete foundation upon which the core claims of *The 11:11 Code* now stand, and we will continue to build upon this. Countless numerology websites speak about the numbers 11, 22, and 33 as being enlightenment codes, but no one has yet figured out why. Skeptical? Just try an internet search of "11:11 enlightenment" and see what comes up! The word *light* is used 264 times in the Bible.[489] This works out to 12 times 22. The same website stated that *light* is used 22 times in the gospel of John. The 22nd time John uses the word, he quotes Jesus as saying:

> I have come into the world as a light, so that no one who believes in me should stay in darkness.[490] (John 12:46)

489 http://www.biblestudy.org/bibleref/meaning-of-numbers-in-bible/22.html.

490 https://www.biblegateway.com/passage/?search=John+12%3A46&version=NIV.

Sun Dog Art ***Sun Dog Impression***

VERT
ANTHELY
LOWITZ ARC
46°
HALO
PARENTHELY
SUN
PARTHELY
CIRCLE
PARTHELY
OBS
22°
HALO
LOWITZ ARC

Sun Dog Dome

Moon Halo

On the evening of March 16, 2019, just six days before submitting this work for final editorial review, my wife rushed into my office and exclaimed, "Charlie, get out here quick! You gotta check out the moon!" I got outside, and she pointed to the moon, which was encircled by a perfect 360-degree circular halo. I excitedly googled "moon halo" and was once again pleased to see that the halo makes a 22-degree cone with the moon at the center. The optical geometry and physics are the same as previously described for the sun dog phenomenon, only the moon is swapped for the sun as the light source.

Mark 4:22 states:

> For everything that is hidden will eventually be brought into the open, and every secret will be brought to light.

Here again, we have a connection between the number 22 (11 + 11) and light.

The Great Blue Norther of 1911

On November 11, 1911 (11/11/11), a storm that came to be known as the *Great Blue Norther* struck the central United States as a result of a huge arctic air mass colliding with a warm air mass. During this weather event, record high temperatures were registered as well as many all-time records for cold temperatures, all within the same day. This is the only day in many Midwest cities' weather bureau jurisdictions where the record highs and lows were broken for the same day. The states of Illinois, Iowa, Missouri, Indiana, Wisconsin, and Michigan were the states registering both record highs and record lows on this historic date. As an example case, Springfield, Missouri, registered a record 80 degrees Fahrenheit before the cold front arrived, and once it came, the city experienced a record low of -11 degrees Celsius (13 degrees Fahrenheit). Here we have the 11:11 code in a record-setting weather system.[491]

491 https://en.wikipedia.org/wiki/Great_Blue_Norther_of_November_11,_1911.

There is geometry in the humming of the strings,
there is music in the spacing of the spheres.

—Pythagoras[492]

The highest goal of music is to connect one's soul
to their Divine Nature, not entertainment.

—Pythagoras (569-475 BC)[493]

The light of the body is the eye: if therefore thine eye
be single, thy whole body shall be full of light.

—Matthew 6:22 KJV[494]

You, Lord, are my *lamp*;
the Lord turns my darkness into *light*.

—2 Samuel 22:29[495]

This is the message we have heard from him and declare to
you: GOD IS LIGHT; in him there is no darkness at all.

—1 John 1:5[496]

In the beginning was the Word, and the Word was with God, and the Word was God. He was with God in the beginning. Through him all things were made; without him nothing was made that has been made. In him was life, and that life was the *light* of all humankind. The *light* shines in the darkness, and the darkness has not overcome it. There was a man sent from God whose

492 http://humanityhealing.net/2010/09/music-spheres-pythagoras/.
493 https://www.quotemaster.org/qc2efb98d6fa056e4b56ed46f4083ca67.
494 https://biblehub.com/matthew/6-22.htm.
495 https://www.biblegateway.com/passage/?search=2+Samuel+22%3A29&version=NIV.
496 https://www.biblegateway.com/passage/?search=1+John+1%3A5&version=NIV.

name was John. He came as a witness to testify concerning that *light*, so that through him all might believe. He himself was not the *light*; he came only as a witness to the *light*. The true *light* that gives light to everyone was coming into the world.

—John 1:1–9[497]

He reveals deep and hidden things; he knows what lies in darkness, and light dwells with him.

—Daniel 2:22[498]

When Edison … snatched up the spark of Prometheus in his little pear-shaped glass bulb, it meant that fire had been discovered for the second time, that mankind had been delivered again from the curse of night."

—German historian Emil Ludwig[499]

You are the *light* of the world. A city set on a *hill* cannot be hidden; nor does anyone *light* a lamp and put it under a basket, but on the lampstand, and it gives *light* to all who are in the house. Let your *light* shine before men in such a way that they may see your good works, and glorify your Father who is in heaven.

—Matthew 5:14–16[500]

---

497 https://www.biblegateway.com/passage/?search=John+1%3A1-9&version=NIV.
498 https://www.biblegateway.com/passage/?search=Daniel+2%3A22&version=NIV.
499 https://www.instituteforenergyresearch.org/history-electricity/.
500 https://bible.knowing-jesus.com/readings/The-Sermon-On-The-Mount:-Salt-And-Light.

CHAPTER 9

PHYSICS

Room Temperature

According to the *American Heritage Dictionary*, the concept of room temperature is accepted to be a value between 20 and 22 degrees Celsius (68–71.8 degrees Fahrenheit).[501] While it would be impossible to determine an exact value for the most desirable room temperature because of the subjective nature of how we experience temperature, a study undertaken by Helsinki University and Lawrence Berkeley Laboratory concluded that "performance increases with temperature up to 21-22 Celsius (69.8 to 71.6 degrees Fahrenheit). The highest productivity is at a temperature of around 22 Celsius (71.6 degrees Fahrenheit)."[502]

Somehow, our bodies naturally feel the most comfortable at a temperature right around 22 Celsius, or 11 + 11. Why?

The Number of Sound

It is interesting to observe that the speed of sound at 20 degrees Celsius (68 degrees Fahrenheit) is 767 miles per hour, which corresponds to almost exactly 666 knots (1 mile per hour = 0.868976 knots). Recalling that the escape velocity of a spacecraft trying to leave Earth's gravitational pull needs to be traveling at least 33 times the speed of sound, this corresponds to 33 x 666 knots = 21,978 knots, or 22 x 3^3 x 37. All three factors

501 https://ahdictionary.com/word/search.html?q=room+temperature.

502 https://www.pgi.com/blog/2016/05/the-optimal-office-temperature-for-workplace-productivity/.

have tremendous significance in the context of this book, which the reader now is familiar with.[503]

It is interesting to see that 666 is showing up in the fundamental physics of our planet. Is it the number of the beast or perhaps the number of sound? Could this be related to the concept of the number of man as it relates to how we perceive auditory inputs?

As a side note, the unit of the knot is used in meteorology, aircraft, and marine navigation. It is defined as one nautical mile per hour, and it works out such that a vessel traveling at this speed will traverse one minute (one-sixtieth of a degree) of arc on one of the Earth's meridian lines.[504] A ship traversing one degree of arc at the equator will travel 111 kilometers. Do you see here that we have 111 in the fundamental geometry of the Earth? [505]

NUMBERS IN MUSIC

One of the most unexpected discoveries I made during the process of writing this book was that the standard musical scale is composed of multiples of 110 hertz (cycles per second). Late at night on May 27, 2018, I decided to randomly perform an internet search of the terms "music mathematics," and I hit upon this discovery. The following table summarizes the key harmonic frequencies in the musical scale:

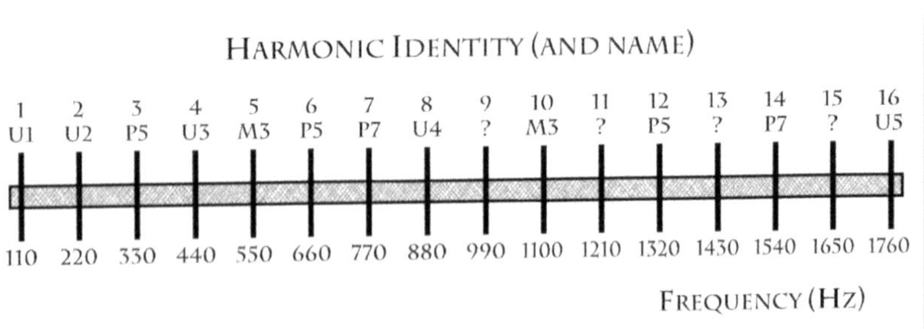

Octave	A3 – 220 Hz
Perfect Fifth	E4 – 330 Hz
Octave	A4 – 440 Hz
Major Third	C#5 –550 Hz
Perfect Fifth	E5 – 660 Hz
Harmonic Seventh	G5 – 770 Hz
Octave	A5 – 880 Hz

503 https://www.universetoday.com/77077/how-fast-is-mach-1/.
504 https://www.marineinsight.com/guidelines/nautical-mile-knot-units-used-sea/.
505 https://www.britannica.com/science/latitude_and_mathematics.

Notice that 220 = 2 x 11 x 10, and 330 = 3 x 11 x 10, and so on up to 1760 = 16 x 11 x 10. Discovering that the repeated double digits central to this book are embedded into the structure of the musical scale that has literally been in use for centuries was quite astounding. This discovery illuminated that multiples of 11 are not only beautiful to the eye but also to the ear!

Going back to the discussion on star numbers, it is interesting to observe that the star numbers 37 and 73 add to 37 + 73 = 110. There are no other star numbers between 37 and 73. Basically, the fundamental tones of the musical scale also embody these key star numbers and their 6-pointed star symmetry and beauty. On the musical scale, the note A_3 – 220 Hz comes out to 2 x (37 + 73). Similarly, A_5 – 880 Hz works out as 8 x (37 + 73)! This is essentially 8 copies of the 6-pointed star plus 8 copies of the 37-dot hexagon! It's also worthy of mention that the standard piano has 88 keys (8 x 11 or 4 x 22).

This makes a stunningly beautiful connection between geometry, the phenomenon of the 11-base repeated digit numbers (11, 22 … 88), and musical harmonies that are naturally most pleasing to the human ear. As with many concepts in this book, these tie together in many different ways. To put book ends on this music section, it was tantalizing to discover that in traditional music of India, the octave is divided into 22 *shrutis*, which are believed to be the smallest audible differences in tone. These 22 frequencies come from the basic 7 shrutis known as *shuddha* (the Sanskrit word for *pure*) in Hindustani classical music.[506]

The human ear can hear tones between approximately 20 and 20,000 cycles per second (hertz), and many hearing exams will test the subject's sensitivity to tones ranging from as low as 8 Hz to as high as 22,000 Hz. Anyone who owned a CD player in the 1990s or thereafter may remember seeing the term *oversampling* on the CD player. The minimum oversampling rate is called the Nyquist rate and corresponds to twice the maximum audio frequency to be reconstructed. Sony and Phillips, the two market leaders in compact disc technology, set the standard at 44,100 Hz, which is twice 22,050 Hz or 10 percent above the average maximum frequency limit of human hearing, for the purpose of improving resolution and signal-to-noise ratio. The frequency 44,100 Hz is the product of the squares of the first four prime numbers 2, 3, 5, and 7 as in 2^2 x 3^3 x 5^2 x 7^2 = 44,100. It is also interesting that the subharmonics 22,050 and

506 http://22shruti.in/?page_id=611.

11,025 Hz (think 11 and 22) are utilized for *.*WAV* files, which are lower bandwidth formats. Higher multiples such as 88.2 kHz and 176.4 kHz are utilized in certain higher fidelity applications such as DVD and higher-quality audio.[507] German Physicist Heinrich Hertz was born on 2/22/1857.

The Nyquist rate was a concept developed by Swedish-American electrical engineer Harry Nyquist, who immigrated to the United States in 1907 just a few years after my ancestors.[508] As it turns out, when I was visiting my ancestral homeland in Sweden, I toured the still-functioning grade school that some of my ancestors attended and unexpectedly noticed that Harry Nyquist in fact went to that same school in the town of Stora Kil. The school had some of Nyquist's old report cards on display. I took photographs of them because I recognized his pioneering work in electrical signal processing, which underpinned the key signal processing mathematics that helped lead the digital revolution. The Nyquist sampling theorem is a key development that led to the creation of digital music and compact disc players, as well as DVD and BluRay technologies. Nyquist was also instrumental in the development of AT&T's first facsimile ("fax") machine that was made public in 1924.[509]

As an interesting cultural sidebar, the traditional naming convention in Sweden was for children to append -son to their father's first name. For example, a boy named Erik whose father's name was Jon would take on the last name of Jonsson, and his son would have Eriksson for his last name. In the Varmland region where my ancestors with last name Soderquist lived, it was a common practice to use the *-quist* (meaning *branch*) ending in lieu of the father's first name because of an overwhelming number of people with the same last name. *Soder* means south, and *Ny* means new, so my ancestors were "south branch," and Nyquist was "new branch." This must have represented a fresh start on a new family branch.

Atmospheric Physics and Weather Prediction

Did you know that in 1922 the science of weather prediction was born? It was 1922 when Lewis Fry Richardson published his watershed paper titled "Weather Prediction by Numerical Process." "It was Richardson who was the first to apply mathematics, in particular the method of finite differences, to predicting the weather in 'Weather Prediction by Numeri-

507 https://en.wikipedia.org/wiki/44,100_Hz.
508 https://www.electronicdesign.com/digital-ics/harry-nyquist-founding-father-digital-communications.
509 https://en.wikipedia.org/wiki/Harry_Nyquist

cal Process' (1922). He first developed his method of finite differences in order to solve differential equations which arose in his work for the National Peat Industries concerning the flow of water in peat. Having developed these methods by which he was able to obtain highly accurate solutions, it was a natural step to apply the same methods to solve the problems of the dynamics of the atmosphere which he encountered in his work for the Meteorological Office."[510]

The Number of Nuclear Fission

Radium is an interesting element. It was first isolated in its metallic state by Marie Curie and André-Louis Debierne through the electrolysis of radium chloride in 1911. If we segue briefly into nuclear physics, the unit of the Becquerel (Bq) is defined as one particle of matter disintegrating per second. The unit of the Curie (Ci) is defined as 37 x 10^9 Bq or 37 billion disintegrated nuclear particles per second. The Curie was originally defined as "the quantity or mass of radium emanation in equilibrium with one gram of radium." The number 37 is therefore a fundamental number to the nuclear properties of matter and how it decays as mass is converted into energy.[511] The number 37 is also noteworthy as it is a star number, and our sun is a star powered by nuclear fusion. Also remember that 37 and 666 are related through the number 18 as follows: $37 = \frac{666}{18} = \frac{666}{6+6+6}$. It is also worthwhile to remark that radium is element number 88 (4 x 22) and has an atomic mass of 226. Radon has 33 known isotopes, and the most commonly known isotope is Radon-222, which is the typical culprit in radon intrusion issues in the basements of all-too-many homes because of this naturally occurring radioactive substance.[512] The number 37 is considered prime, but there was also a time when the atom was thought to be the smallest indivisible unit of matter, that is until we started to smash them! If we hit the number 37 with a bigger hammer, it splits into two complex numbers, each composed of a real and imaginary part! Watch this: multiply (6+i) times (6-i). These two numbers are complex conjugates with the imaginary parts being mirror images of each other across the real axis, and the number I times itself comes out to -1. You should get (6+i) x (6-i) = 37. So, 37 factors to two complex conjugates, 6+i. This is

510 http://mathshistory.st-andrews.ac.uk/HistTopics/Weather_forecasts.html
511 https://en.wikipedia.org/wiki/Curie.
512 https://www.chemicool.com/elements/radon.html.

called a Gaussian prime. Wikipedia has an excellent article on this for the interested reader. Not every number does this!

Julius and Ethel Rosenberg were US citizens who spied for the Soviet Union and were tried, convicted, and executed by the federal government of the United States. They provided top-secret information about radar, sonar, and jet propulsion engines to the USSR and were accused of transmitting nuclear weapon designs to the Soviet Union. At that time, the United States was the only country in the world with nuclear weapons. The pair was indicted on August 11, 1950, for 11 alleged counts of espionage. They were executed at the Sing Sing Correctional Facility at 11:00 p.m. on June 19, 1953. That's another occurrence of 11-11-11.[513]

Here we have an element producing many of the universe's favorite numbers, including 11, 22, 33, 37, 88, and 222, and we understand their connection to the number of man, or quite possibly the number of the universe.

LUCIFER: THE BRINGER OF LIGHT

Phosphorus means "bringer of light" in Greek, and Lucifer means the same in Latin. One of the most crucial components of DNA, RNA, and adenosine triphosphate (ATP), all of which underpin life, is phosphorus. Phosphorus burns with a bluish-green flame when lit and does not occur in pure form in nature because of its high reactivity. A pure sample will emit a cool, soft glow when exposed to oxygen. Hence, the name "light bearer." The luminescent chemical that allows fireflies to emit light is called luciferin, which contains phosphorus. The ancients attributed the morning star Venus to Lucifer, the bringer of light.

Many scientists and philosophers believe that phosphorus is the God spark in our DNA that is at least partially responsible for consciousness.

Speaking of light, optical energy oscillating at 666 terahertz (666 trillion alternations per second) falls right at the boundary between the blue and violet light frequency bands.[514] What scientific discovery has the capacity to do the most damage to our planet? Nuclear reactions would have my vote. When the speed of a charged particle such as an electron exceeds the speed of light in that medium (given that light travels 25 percent slower

513 https://en.m.wikipedia.org/wiki/Julius_and_Ethel_Rosenberg.
514 https://infogalactic.com/info/Violet_(color).

through water as opposed to air), it gives off a characteristic blue glow that most people are familiar with in the context of nuclear fuel assemblies, as seen in the photo below, similar to what I observed during my employment at Commonwealth Edison's Byron Nuclear Plant in Illinois where my career was born. The electron is exceeding the speed of light in water, and there is an energetic price to be paid, which takes place through the emission of the pale blue light (i.e., Cherenkov emission).

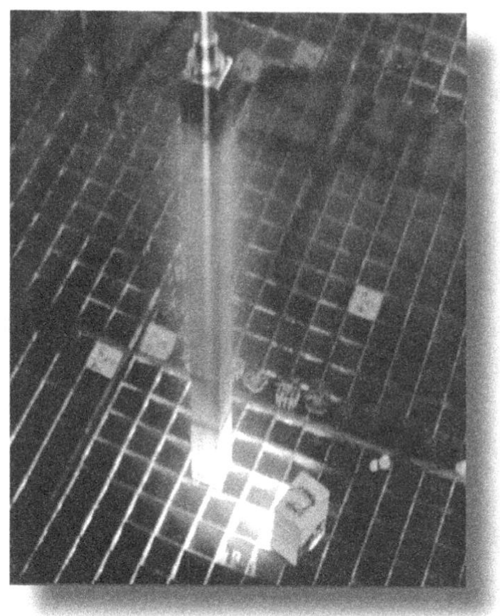

Cherenkov radiation around a radioactively** hot **nuclear fuel assembly

Thinking about how much trouble that nuclear energy has gotten us into already, could the blue glow be a reminder of the fact that 666 terahertz is in the blue spectrum? Is the beast hiding within the atom?

The Universe's Favorite Numbers

Newton's law of gravitation states that the gravitational attraction force between any two bodies in space is given by the equation $F=GM_eM_s/r^2$, where M_e represents the Earth's mass, M_s represents the mass of a satellite orbiting the Earth, and r is the separation distance between the two. The universal gravitational constant, $G = 6.67 \times 10^{-11}$ [$N*m^2/kg^2$] is and applies everywhere in the universe as we currently understand it. You'll notice that the mantissa (the number to the left of the exponent) for this constant is 6.67, extremely close to 666 divided by 100, differing only by 0.15 percent.

The Number of Everything

Now that we understand how 666 is imbedded in the universal law of gravitation, let's take that still one step deeper. What is gravity? Is it a power of attraction that only planets and stars wield upon smaller objects under their influence? Obviously, big objects like the Earth, moon, and sun have gravitational forces, but what about a mountain, a car, or a person? What about a small rock or a grain of sand?

Everything has a gravitational force proportional to its mass. While the force would be so small as to be immeasurable, any two grains of sand exert a gravitational attractive force between them. This fact can be abstracted further to say that the gravitational constant applies to absolutely every particle of matter in the entire universe. The number 666 governs the attractive force between all particles everywhere. Could 666 be the number of literally *everything*?

COSMIC CALENDAR

The concept of the *cosmic calendar* was devised by physicist Carl Sagan to give humans an intuitive feeling about the immensity of the time scales of the universe from creation to the present by scaling the history of the universe to play out proportionally over the course of a normal year. Bear with me, this will make sense by the end of this paragraph. Sagan defined January 1 to coincide with the original big bang creation event and set midnight on December 31 as the present moment and then scaled the rest of the history of the universe to that *year*. The first galaxies began to form on January 22 of the cosmic year. The solar system formed on September 2. Photosynthesis began September 30. Fish didn't show up until December 7. Primates made their arrival on December 30, the second to last day of the year. Primitive humans and stone tools arrived on December 31 at 22 hours and 24 minutes. Jesus came 25 minutes later. In 1492, Christopher Columbus sailed the ocean blue at 23:59:58. One second later, here you are reading this page.[515]

Based on researching numerous scientific and academic sources, the consensus seems to be that the universe is about 13.8 billion years old. If true, then that would be awesome. If you take 13.8 apart and divide 13 by 8, you get a number extremely close to the golden ratio. The result 1.625 is only 0.4 percent higher than phi. For curiosity's sake, I took the product of the three coolest universal constants—pi, phi, and Euler's constant—and got the following: $\pi \times \phi \times e = 3.141 \times 1.618 \times 2.718 = 13.818$. In 2015, using data collected by the Planck spacecraft, scientists estimated

515 https://www.ccsf.edu/Departments/History_of_Time_and_Life/content/CosmicCalendar.htm.

the age of the universe to be 13.82 billion years.[516] Multiplying the three universal constants π, ϕ, and e times one another gives 13.818, which is a number within 0.03 percent or 3 parts in 10,000 of being accurate to the estimated age of the universe. Other estimates pin the universe at 13.7 billion years. That's 137 divided by 10, and by now you have a much deeper understanding of why the fine structure constant (alpha) of 137 is such a universally important number. Furthermore, it wasn't until 1922 when Russian cosmologist Alexander Friedmann produced the first solutions to Einstein's equations, which contained matter but also predicted that the universe might expand. Unfortunately for Friedmann, he died in 1925, and his work went largely unnoticed at the time, probably because he only published in Russian. A few years later in 1927, Belgian cosmologist and Catholic priest Georges Lemaître independently came up with the same idea as Friedmann. Today it is universally accepted that the universe is expanding.[517]

The special numbers discussed here are *truly universal*. Is this just a fascinating coincidence or something deeper? I'll simply call it fascinating and leave it for the reader to draw their own conclusions. Need more proof of an intelligent cosmic mind and the idea of purposeful creation?

> Take a moment and pull up the following video: "Odyssey" by Olie Bassweight.

516 https://www.space.com/24054-how-old-is-the-universe.html.
517 https://thecuriousastronomer.wordpress.com/tag/alexander-friedmann/.

CHAPTER 10

ENGINEERING

Kitchen Inventions

As a young boy, I always enjoyed flying with my grandfather in his Beechcraft Bonanza airplane. Usually, he would pick me up at home on a Friday afternoon after getting off from work, and we would go to Andy's Restaurant in Kenosha, Wisconsin, for a perch dinner with French fries and a malted milkshake. These are some of my fondest childhood memories.

As luck would have it, I happened to find an 11+11 connection to the malted milkshake recipe as well as the mixer to blend it. In 1922 in Chicago, Walgreens employee Ivar "Pop" Coulson invented the malted milkshake by adding two scoops of vanilla ice cream to the standard-issue pharmacy beverage comprised of milk, chocolate syrup, and Horlick's malted milk powder. An instant classic was born.[518] To mix the concoction, they used Steven Poplawski's invention, the beverage mixer, for which a US patent was filed on February 18, 1922.[519] One of my favorite treats was conceived in 1922, and the machine to mix it together was constructed that same year. Poplawski hailed from the next town north of Kenosha—Racine, Wisconsin.

518 http://www.walgreens.com/about/history/hist4.jsp.

519 https://patents.google.com/patent/US1480914A/en?oq=US1480914.

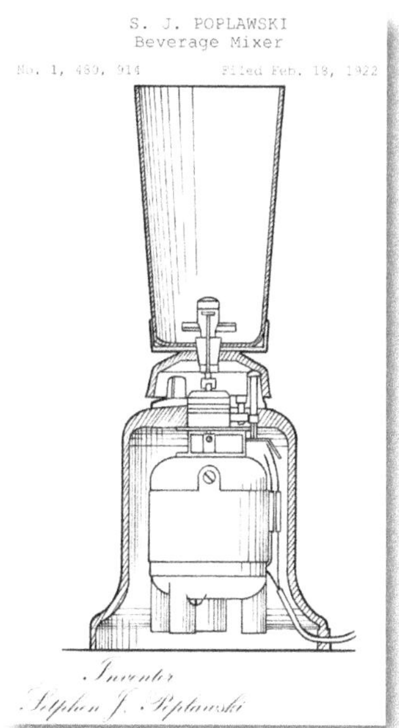

Beverage mixer patent[520] filed on February 18, 1922

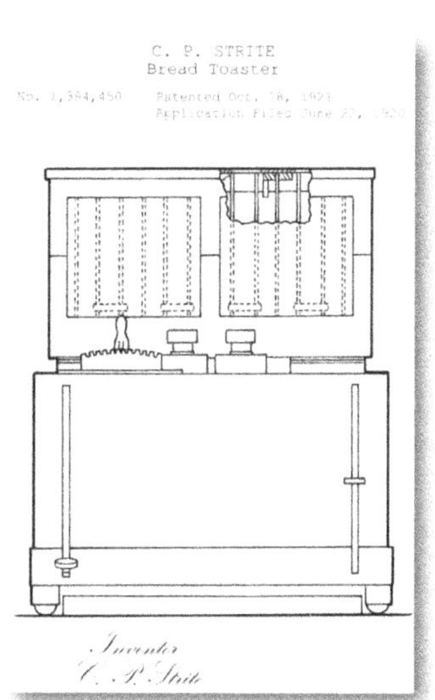

The automatic electric toaster was invented by Charles P. Strite, and he filed for a patent on June 22, 1920. After that, he was granted a patent. Strite worked at a factory in Stillwater, Minnesota, during World War I, where he became frustrated with the burned toast served in the cafeteria. Determined to find a way of toasting bread that did not depend on human attention, Strite invented the pop-up toaster with a variable timer. In 1925, using a redesigned version of Strite's toaster, the Toastmaster Company began to market the first household toaster that could brown bread on both sides simultaneously, set the heating element on a timer, and eject the toast when finished. By 1926, Charles Strite's Toastmaster was available to the public and a huge success. The number 22 showing up again in a key innovation in human history.[521]

520 https://patents.google.com/patent/US1480914A/en?oq=US1480914.

521 https://www.uspto.gov/about-us/news-updates/patent-bread-toaster-issued-october-18-1921.

Another device that has brought so much convenience to the modern kitchen is the garbage disposal. John W. Hammes of Racine, Wisconsin, filed his patent application for the garbage disposal device, which would spawn the birth of the InSinkErator Company and give way to an entire new class of kitchen convenience appliances.[522] With his patent application filed on 5/22/1933, Hammes was awarded his patent a bit more than two years later.[523] Here we have both 22 and 33 showing up in the birth of another key advance in kitchen technology and in a town just twenty miles north from where I grew up.

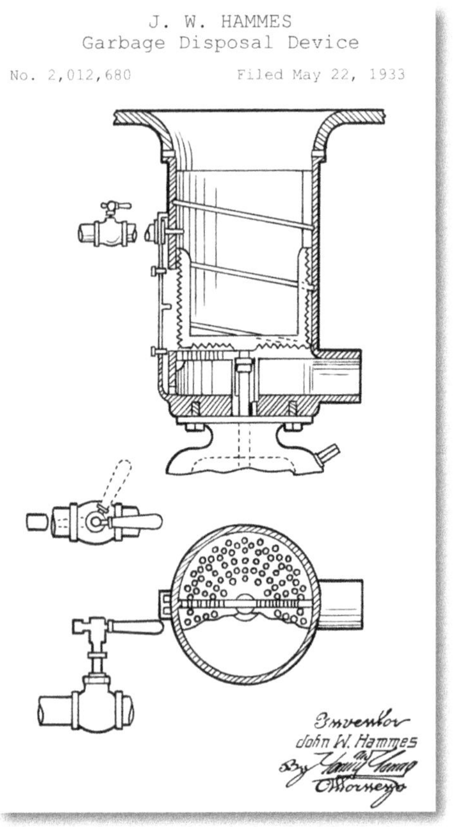

In 1933 at the World's Fair in Chicago, George Westinghouse demonstrated the first instance of using microwave electromagnetic energy to heat a food product.[524] With the advent of the cavity magnetron during World War II for usage in military radar, production and usage of microwave energy soon spread outside the military domain.

On May 22, 1952, inventors Judd Blass and Louis Schall applied for a patent for the microwave oven. On March 22, 1955, patent #2,704,802 was awarded.[525]

Here we have seen how the numbers 22 (11 + 11) and 33 (11 + 11 + 11) played into several of the most revolutionary and useful kitchen inventions of all time.

522 https://insinkerator.emerson.com/en-us/about-us.
523 https://patents.google.com/patent/US2012680A/en.
524 https://www.americanradiohistory.com/Archive-Short-Wave-Television/30s/SW-TV-1933-11.pdf.
525 https://patentimages.storage.googleapis.com/68/25/57/e64f01e0bc793b/US2704802.pdf.

TELEVISION

The television was pioneered by American inventor Charles Francis Jenkins. He published an article on "Motion Pictures by Wireless" in 1913, but it was not until December 1923 that he transmitted moving silhouette images for witnesses. On June 13, 1925, he publicly demonstrated synchronized transmission of silhouette pictures by transmitting the silhouette image of a toy windmill in motion over a distance of five miles from a naval radio station in Maryland to his laboratory in Washington, DC, using a lensed disk scanner with a 48-line resolution. He was granted a US patent under the title of *Transmitting Pictures over Wireless* on June 30, 1925, which he had filed March 13, 1922. Here is the number 22 showing up again in another of the most transformational inventions in human history.[526]

By March 22, 1935, 180-line black-and-white television programs were being broadcast from the Paul Nipkow TV station in Berlin. In 1936, under the guidance of the Nazi minister of public enlightenment and propaganda Joseph Goebbels, direct transmissions from fifteen mobile units at the Olympic Games in Berlin were transmitted to selected small television houses (Fernsehstuben) in Berlin and Hamburg.[527]

The first television station to ever operate west of the Mississippi River was KTLA, broadcasting to a total of just 322 TV sets in the Los Angeles area on January 22, 1947.[528]

While on the topic of wireless broadcasting, it's a good time to mention that the FM (frequency modulation) radio scheme was invented by electrical engineer Edwin Armstrong and received multiple patents on December 26, 1933.[529]

The number 22 and other numbers that are multiples of 11 tend to show up around humanity's greatest achievements without regard to whether it is something inherently good or bad—it just has to be something important and impactful.

Here's a fun fact. The first operational computer was a purely mechanical device called a "difference engine" by its inventor, Charles Babbage, who

526 https://en.m.wikipedia.org/wiki/Television.
527 https://en.m.wikipedia.org/wiki/Color_television.
528 http://thisdayintechhistory.com/01/22/first-tv-station-west-of-mississippi/.
529 http://www.fathom.com/seminars/10701020/session2.html.

started working on it in 1822. On January 21, 1888, Babbage's analytical engine operated for the first time.[530] The date 1/21/1888 is an interesting collection of numbers. Let's break down 1/21. Remove the forward slash, and you have 121. The astute reader will immediately see 11 x 11 = 121 again in the birth of the age of computers. (Think *The 11:11 Code*.)

WELL, I'LL BE DAMMED!

The Sir Adam Beck hydroelectric power station at Niagara Falls, Ontario, held the world record for largest power plant electrical output from the year 1922, when it was commissioned, until 1939, when it was usurped by the Hoover Dam.[531]

The current largest power station on Earth both in terms of physical size and electrical output is the Three Gorges hydroelectric plant. This behemoth puts out an unfathomable 22.5 gigawatts of power (*giga* denotes billions). The plant was constructed at an estimated $22.5 billion US. A large dam across the Yangtze River was originally envisioned by Sun Yat-sen in the International Development of China in 1919. He stated that a dam capable of generating 30 million horsepower (22 gigawatts) was possible downstream of the Three Gorges. In 1932, the Nationalist government, led by Chiang Kai-shek, began preliminary work on plans in the Three Gorges. In 1939, forces occupied Yichang and surveyed the area. A design called the Otani plan was completed for the dam in anticipation of a Japanese victory over China. The reservoir's flood storage capacity is 22 cubic kilometers. Imagine a cube of water that is a thousand meters on a side, and then imagine 22 of them together. That is a tremendous amount of water![532], [533]

The first generator of the second phase of the project to become fully operational was unit #22, which began producing power on June 11, 2007. Here we have the numbers 11 and 22 showing up at a historic moment at the world's largest source of electrical energy.[534]

The second largest power plant on the planet is the Itaipu Dam on the border of Brazil and Paraguay with a generating capacity of 14.0 gigawatts. The concept behind the Itaipu Power Plant was the result of serious ne-

530 http://www.computinghistory.org.uk/det/1819/Charles-Babbage/.
531 https://www.opg.com/generating-power/hydro/southwest-ontario/Pages/sir-adam-beck-i.aspx.
532 http://large.stanford.edu/courses/2010/ph240/ma2/.
533 https://www.yangtzeriver.org/threegorges_dam/history-of-three-gorges-dam.htm.
534 https://www.power-technology.com/projects/gorges/.

gotiations between the two countries during the 1960s. The Ata do Iguaçu (Iguaçu Act) was signed on July 22, 1966.[535], [536]

It is exceptionally fortuitous to see the result after we divide the capacity of the largest power station (Three Gorges at 22,500 MW) by the capacity of the second largest (Itaipu at 14,000 MW) as 22,600 ÷ 14,000 = 1.607, which by now the reader should readily recognize as being none other than the golden ratio (~1.618), at least within 0.7 percent accuracy! I would put the probability that this was intentional at exactly 0 percent. What a cool co-inky-dink, huh?

To anyone who may call foul on this connection because it isn't exact, this is no greater a stretch of the truth than a parent telling someone their daughter is one year old when the truth is that she is one year and two-and-a-half days of age! Both scenarios have the same margin of error—0.68 percent. Unless you're designing a spacecraft to land on a distant planet, 99 percent of important engineering considerations would place a 0.68 percent error within acceptable limits of accuracy. In our quest for exactness, I wonder how many valid connections such as this have been overlooked throughout history because of a rigid quest for perfection. In the vast majority of science and engineering applications, 99.3% accuracy is most definitely good enough!

These connections were truly remarkable, and I did not expect to find them when I started writing this section. These discoveries are at the heart of what this book is all about. In my initial inquiry, I simply wanted to see how much bigger the largest dam was compared to its closest competitor, never imagining that I would find phi showing its pretty face! It is an exceptional coincidence or perhaps some cosmic message that the Three Gorges plant produces 22.5 billion watts of power at an initially estimated cost of $22.5 billion, and I noticed the number 322 here again—the 3 from the name Three Gorges and 22 appearing twice in the plant's price *and* in its power output capacity. These two dams certainly represent two of humanity's greatest civil engineering achievements in our rich planetary history. To see the numbers 3, 22, and the golden ratio show up here could very well be evidence of a higher intelligence having had a hand in these historical milestones.

I'd like to round off this section by mentioning that Brazil's Belo Monte

535 https://www.sec.gov/Archives/edgar/data/1439124/000119312508153744/dex41.htm.
536 http://www.engineersjournal.ie/2016/11/01/itaipu-dam-water-renewable-energy/.

Dam is expected to be the world's third largest power station with an anticipated capacity of 11,233 megawatts at completion.[537]

Why do so many of humankind's biggest endeavors—whether good or bad—bear the signature numbers 11, 22, and 33 with such frequency?

GREAT WALL OF CHINA

The section on China would not be complete without a discussion of the country's Great Wall. Several sections of the wall were constructed in the seventh century BC, but the most famous sections of the wall were built in 220–206 BC by Qin Shi Huang, the first emperor of China. It is noteworthy to remark that the wall was under construction during the year 222 BC and would become one of the 7 wonders of the world. The wall is comprised of 6,259 kilometers (3,889 miles) of actual wall, 359 kilometers (223 miles) of trenches, and 2,232 kilometers (1,387 miles) of natural defensive barriers, such as hills and rivers.[538] One of the most famous and well-preserved watchtowers is called *Wangjinglou* and is one of Jinshanling's 67 watchtowers at an impressive altitude of 3,220 feet above sea level. Some segments of the Great Wall have been demolished because the wall was in the way of imminent construction plans. A 2012 report by the State Administration of Cultural Heritage estimates that 22 percent of the Ming Great Wall has disappeared.[539]

As the reader is probably aware, Hong Kong underwent massive anti-China protests during the summer of 2019, which was 22 years after Britain's 99-year lease of the territory expired and it was handed over to China on July 7, 1997. That's 11 + 11 years apart. Today, Hong Kong's people are rising up and demanding freedom.

537 https://www.hydroworld.com/hydro-projects/belo-monte-hydropower-project.html.

538 http://news.bbc.co.uk/2/hi/asia-pacific/8008108.stm.

539 William Lindesay, *The Great Wall Revisited: From the Jade Gate to Old Dragon's Head* (Cambridge, MA: Harvard University Press, 2008).

The mysteries of the human experience are revealed through explanation of the numbers 11, 22, and 33 and the transcendentals.

—Charles J. Wolfe, BSEE, M.Eng

God is that kind of artist whose greatness is seen just as much in his minor works as in the great masterpiece.

—Augustine of Hippo (AD 354–430)[540]

I believe in the brotherhood of man and the uniqueness of the individual. But if you ask me to prove what I believe, I can't. You know them to be true but you could spend a whole lifetime without being able to prove them. The mind can proceed only so far upon what it knows and can prove. There comes a point where the mind takes a higher plane of knowledge, but can never prove how it got there. All great discoveries have involved such a leap.

—Albert Einstein[541]

A man is the whole encyclopedia of facts. The creation of a thousand forests is in one acorn, and Egypt, Greece, Rome, Gaul, Britain, America, lie folded already in the first man.

—Ralph Waldo Emerson[542]

Call to me and I will answer you and tell you great and unsearchable things you do not know.

—Jeremiah 33:3[543]

---

540 http://www.godindna.nz/introduction.html.
541 https://www.mat.univie.ac.at/~neum/contrib/lesikar.html.
542 https://www.gutenberg.org/files/2944/2944-h/2944-h.htm.
543 https://www.biblegateway.com/passage/?search=Jeremiah+33%3A3&version=NIV.

Then God said, "I give you every seed-bearing plant on the face of the whole earth and every tree that has fruit with seed in it. They will be yours for food."

—Genesis 1:29[544]

In the beginning was the Word, and the Word was with God, and the Word *was God*.

—John 1:1[545]

544 https://biblehub.com/genesis/1-29.htm.
545 https://www.biblegateway.com/passage/?search=John+1%3A1&version=NIV.

CHAPTER 11
THE HUMAN EXPERIMENT

Life's Screenplay

Human life is a long, flowing movie that has a script, a director, and actors. *You* are the lead actor in *your* play. In his book *DNA: The Secret of Life,* the co-discoverer of DNA, James Watson, states:

> If the genome is ultimately understood in its more dynamic reality, not as a mere set of instructions for life's assembly but as the screenplay for life's movie—all the drama described in the precise order it is meant to occur—then proteomics and transcriptomics provide the keys to glimpsing the live action. The more we learn, the more we see *Life, the Movie.*[546]

Proteomics is the study of proteins encoded by genes. Transcriptomics is devoted to determining where and when genes are expressed—that is, when genes are transcriptionally active in a given cell.[547]

Time is in place so that your entire life doesn't begin, happen, and *end* in the same instant. Be thankful for time. Time has the wondrous property of prolonging the human experience and allowing us the opportunity to get the absolute maximum amount of energy and experiences out of life as we allow ourselves. Time (or at least the concept thereof) gives us a sense of linearity and a framework by which to reference the passage of the key moments and stages of our lives and a sense of relativity about those

546 James Watson, *DNA: The Secret of Life* (London: Arrow Books, 2004).
547 Ibid.

who have preceded us as well as those who will follow us. Time gives us the opportunity to experience and develop love, memories, talents, gifts, skills, and build our own tree—our *family tree* and our *legacy*. In general, we are here to experience and interact with a world that has already been created. The miracle of reproduction is a wondrous opportunity to directly participate in the creation process—to create new life. Bringing a new child into the world is a daunting task, but it is a sacred process whereby we add the next link to an otherwise unbroken chain of life that stretches back to the original creation event, perhaps 4.54 billion years ago.

HEIGHT

According to a study by economist John Komlos and Francesco Cinnirella, in the first half of the eighteenth century, the average height of an English male was 165 cm (5 ft 5 in), and the average height of an Irish male was 168 cm (5 ft 6 in). The estimated mean height of English, German, and Scottish soldiers was 163.6 to 165.9 cm (5 ft 4.4 in to 5 ft 5.3 in) for the period as a whole, while that of Irish soldiers was 167.9 cm (5 ft 6.1 in). The average height of male slaves and convicts in North America was 171 cm (5 ft 7 in).[548]

It would be virtually impossible to get an exact figure on the average height of men and women worldwide taken in aggregate, but based on the data listed previously, it seems reasonable that the average human height is very close to 5 feet and 6 inches tall, or 66 inches.

My own height is 5 feet 6.5 inches, but the eternal optimist within me usually invokes the mathematical privilege to round up to 5 feet 7 inches. I smiled and winked at the sky when I was driving the other day and realized that my height is extremely close to 66.6 inches, which is the number of a man divided by the number of fingers on my two hands.

The shortest human height to ever be verified was that of a Nepalese man named Chandra Bahadur Dangi, who reached a peak height of 21.5 inches. (Can we just round up to 22, a 2.3 percent cheat?)[549]

According to the *Guinness Book of World Records*, the tallest human in history was Robert Wadlow of Alton, Illinois. Born of normal-sized par-

548 https://en.wikipedia.org/wiki/Human_height.

549 http://www.guinnessworldrecords.com/news/2012/2/shortest-man-world-record-its-official!-chandra-bahadur-dangi-is-smallest-adult-of-all-time/.

ents, he reached a colossal height of 8 feet, 11.1 inches.[550] He was born on 2/22/1918 and died at age 22 on 7/15/1940. (Note that 7 + 15 = 22.) Did you catch the 111 and 222? Unsurprisingly, he had the world's largest feet, commanding a record-setting size 37A! Recalling earlier material, 37 is a prominent star number.[551] While on the subject of human extremes, the world's oldest person in modern history was Jeanne Louise Calment, who lived an astonishing 122 years and 164 days and was born on 2/21/1875, according to the Guinness Book of World Records. Calment passed away on 1/11/1988, and note the consecutive digits: 1-1-1-1. [552]

What are these numbers trying to tell us? To me, these occurrences of 11s and 22s are the subtle fingerprints of a higher intelligence, putting the master stroke on his creations. I'm not looking for 11s and 22s on the back of cereal boxes. I've focused on the most exceptional achievements of man and God alike and always found these numerological stamps of authenticity associated with the extremes of greatness and wickedness alike.

Looking at the title page, you see a globe constructed of vertices (junctions of dimension zero), edges occupying one dimension, two-dimensional faces bounded by the edges, which altogether form a three-dimensional sphere. Think of each of the individual facts as dots, and the explanations connect the dots, leading to a multidimensional understanding of how all events in our universe are interconnected.

Temperature

Now that we know star number 37 is a factor of 666, let's dig deeply into 37. It is universally known that the normal human body temperature is 37 degrees Celsius (98.6 degrees Fahrenheit). The human body is a miraculous machine. Whether we are in an arctic snowstorm or in a hot desert of Saudi Arabia, our bodies work diligently to maintain a steady temperature of 37 centigrade.

Remember that 0 degrees is the freezing point of water and 100 degrees is the boiling point on the Celsius scale—two facts of nature. It is interesting to observe that the temperature of the human body is exactly 37 percent

550 https://en.wikipedia.org/wiki/Brobdingnag.

551 http://www.guinnessworldrecords.com/news/2017/6/on-this-day-in-1940-the-tallest-man-ever-is-measured-478854.

552https://www.guinnessworldrecords.com/world-records/oldest-person-(female)?fb_comment_id=534519726650546_648614835241034

of the span between the freezing and boiling point of water! Taking it still one more step, noting that water freezes at 32 degrees Fahrenheit and boils at 212 Fahrenheit, this is a span of 180 degrees (212 – 32 = 180). Taking 37 percent of this 180 span gives us 66.6 or 37 percent of the temperature span between freezing and boiling on the Fahrenheit scale, which is eerily similar to 666, the number of man, differing only by a factor of 10, the number of fingers on our hands.[553]

While on the topic of the number 37, an internet search of the question "How many cells are in the human body?" universally comes back with the answer of 37.2 trillion cells in the average human body. I find it utterly remarkable to see the number 37, a star number and the number of the human body's temperature in centigrade, showing up in this extraordinarily large collection of cells.[554] I've often heard it said that we are made of star dust. Maybe we really are after all.

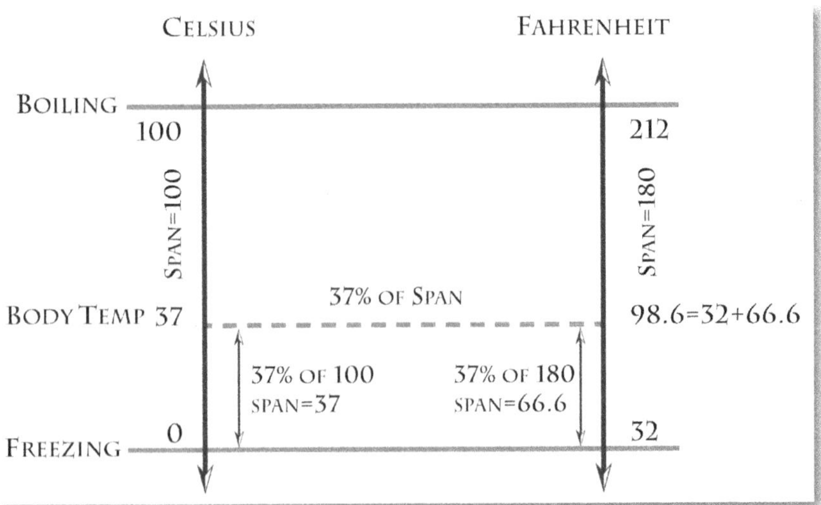

Adding to the intrigue, if we divide 666 by the number of degrees between freezing and boiling on the Fahrenheit scale, we get $\frac{666}{180}=\frac{37}{10}=3.7$, which is one-tenth of 37, our body temperature in Celsius. The digits of 37 also sum to 3 + 7 = 10. Lastly, I discovered while playing with the calculator that if you divide 666 by pi, you get the boiling point of water in Fahrenheit exactly as in $\frac{666}{\pi}=211.9$. Playing with 777 and the golden ratio, 1.618, we get $\frac{7\times7\times7}{\phi}=\frac{7^3}{\phi}=211.9$. These are both almost exactly 212, and they are certainly well within the measurement accuracy of even the most precise

553 http://daniel11truth.com/number-of-the-beast-666-antichrist.htm.

554 https://www.smithsonianmag.com/smart-news/there-are-372-trillion-cells-in-your-body-4941473/.

human body temperature measurement. I discovered these two gems and have yet to see anyone else reference these two interesting relations. Combining the last two equations into one, we get the interesting connection between pi and the golden ratio as follows:

$\pi = 666\ \varphi/(7 \times 7 \times 7) = 3.1416$ or π within one ten-thousandth accuracy.

While on the topic of physical chemistry, it's worth mentioning that a triple point is a specific set of conditions in which temperature and pressure are such that a material could simultaneously exist as a gas, a liquid, or a solid. Water has one such triple point, which occurs at -22 degrees Celsius and a massive pressure of 2,070 atmospheres (30,429 PSI).[555] This is a fascinating occurrence of the number 22.

The Tree of Life

I was in a Barnes and Noble bookstore with my wife and son in Ocala, Florida, casually browsing books to see if I could find anything interesting to back up my research for this book. *Genome—The Autobiography*

555 https://en.wikipedia.org/wiki/Triple_point.

of a Species in 23 Chapters by Matt Ridley grabbed my eye. Given what you already know about my interest in the number 22, you can probably guess which chapter I flipped to immediately. Yep, I instinctively went straight to the chapter on chromosome 22. And what I discovered left me absolutely gobsmacked.

In the final months of the final year of the second millennium, 1999, geneticists unlocked the secret code of the first of 23 chromosomes and started with the smallest of all the chromosomes—chromosome 22. The number of man, 666, is lurking upside down in the year 1999. The devil's in the details—but so is God! Here's the nuts and bolts of it. DNA software was written by the master architect of the universe using atoms and molecules as the alphabet, and electrical forces as the glue. The human DNA alphabet is made up of four chemical letters—A, C, G, and T. Amino acids are formed in blocks of three base pairs of these letters. Amino acids are the three-letter words of DNA language. The decoding of the 22nd chapter of the software of life contains just over 33 million letters, which when divided by three, gives us 11 million words. That's 11 million words that write the 22nd chromosome software module, composed of 33 million letters. This code has been waiting for us to discover it through the use of the artificial intelligence of computers that God gifted us the insight to create from melted silica sand. Think 11-22-33. Think 11 + 22 + 33 = 66, the number of books in the Bible, the Book of Life.

As if that wasn't amazing enough, each of the 23 chromosomes has a specific function. Some code for gender, race, height, eye color, etc., but chromosome 22 has been identified as the part of our genetic code that gives us *free will*.[556]

During the process of writing this book, I learned that the 23 chromosomes are grouped into autosomes and allosomes. The first 22 chromosomes form the group of autosomes, which determine the physical characteristics, and the 23rd chromosome is the lone allosome, which determines gender and nothing else. So in essence, the 22nd chromosome is the last of the regular chromosomes and the first of the human chromosomes to be completely decoded.

As I was explaining the 11-22-33 bombshell in chromosome 22 on the phone to my mother, I was pacing around the parking lot, talking on the phone during my work lunch break, and just after I had verbally added up

556 Matt Ridley, *Genome: The Autobiography of a Species in 23 Chapters* (New York: Harper Perennial, 1999).

11 + 22 + 33 = 66 and compared it to the Word of God, the Bible with its 66 books, I glanced up and noticed that the three vehicles right in front of me had parking permits on the rearview mirrors with tag numbers 133, 922, and 110 in consecutive order as seen in this section. This is a prime example of divine confirmation through numbers. The probability of those three numbers showing up in consecutive order at the spot in a parking lot with more than 300 vehicles at the precise moment as I was talking about the subject of 11-22-33 is absolutely uncanny. Pictures—or else it didn't happen, right? Here you go.

As if that wasn't miraculous enough, to have the equivalent of a million encyclopedia pages worth of information coded into an atomic string of molecules within our DNA, the data also revealed that a huge plethora of some of the most horrible diseases that have plagued humankind have instructions for a cure written within this sacred chapter of the human genetic code.[557] I cannot stress strongly enough what an amazing book *The Cosmic Serpent* is!

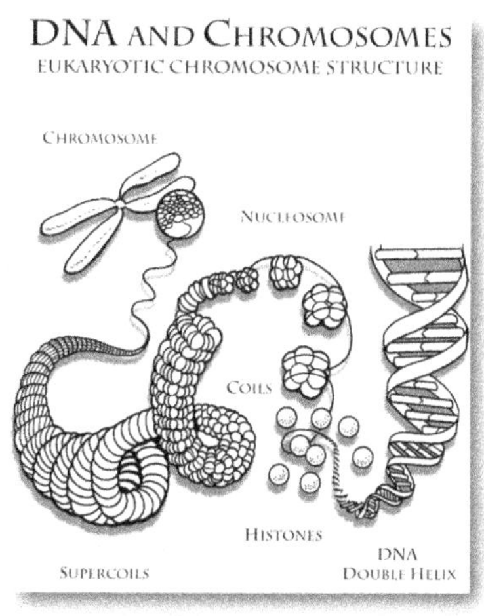

The anatomy of DNA[558]

557 Jeremy Narby, *The Cosmic Serpent: DNA and the Origins of Knowledge* (New York: Jeremy P. Tarcher/Putnam, 1998).

558 https://qph.fs.quoracdn.net/main-qimg-d09101de79ff095c41a8b280ce0b2c94-c.

I have pondered my entire life why the number 11 keeps showing itself to me in uncanny ways. When I looked at a scanning electron microscope photo of the 23 chromosomes, you can see in the photo here that they all resemble the number 11 to some degree in their physical forms.

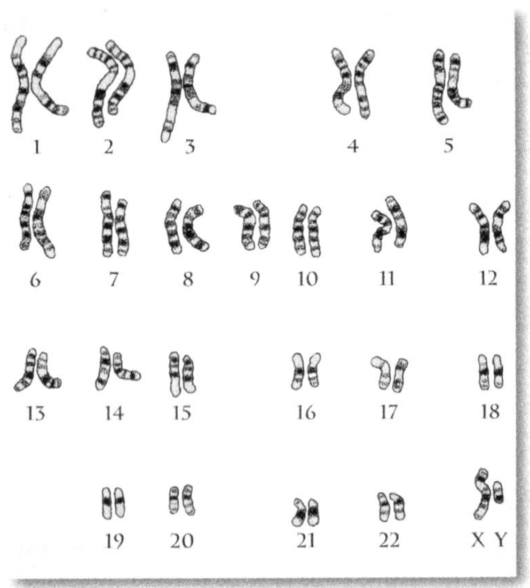

Family portrait of all 23 human chromosomes[559]

The point here is to share a wonderful secret about something very special that every single human on the planet has in common—we *all* have this 22nd chromosome with its 11 million words and 33 million letters, with its message of free will and hope for a cure to all our earthly medical troubles. This is something that is common to everyone regardless of race, creed, religion, geography, language, age, height, gender, and orientations of all sorts.

The reader may find it interesting to know that Charles Darwin's iconic book *On the Origin of Species* went on sale on 11/22/1859 in an attempt to fulfill the 1,500 copies that had been ordered. Only 1,192 copies were actually delivered, and they sold out that same day.[560] Darwin proposed to Emma Wedgewood on 11/11/1838. They went on to marry in January 1839. Curiously enough, she was his first cousin.[561]

559 https://blog.23andme.com/wp-content/uploads/2016/12/1_karyotype-640x338.png.
560 https://www.earthmagazine.org/article/benchmarks-november-22-1859-origin-species-published.
561 http://darwin-online.org.uk/timeline.html.

Science has proven that DNA is the software that determines all our physical traits as well as the timing of major body changes, such as growth spurts, teething, puberty onset, when it's time to start growing gray hair, menopause, onset of male pattern baldness, and many other time-based events in the human life. If these big events are predetermined by DNA, it begs the question if smaller, less significant events may also be predetermined? What if our entire lives have been predetermined and coded into our DNA, and we just get the illusion that we are causing events to take place?

DNA AND DMT CONNECTION

The basic building blocks of life are the DNA bases of tyrosine, guanine, adenine, and cytosine. These four basic chemicals are formed by polygons composed of pentagons and hexagons, similar to the tiles that are used to create polyhedra. This is truly remarkable, as all life exhibits this sacred geometry of 5- and 6-sided figures at our most fundamental level. DNA is well known to have a double helix spiral structure. As we have covered previously, DNA is essentially composed of two serpent-like ribs twisting together in a virtually endless dance, forming a twisted-ladder structure. Many scholars of archaic Christianity believe that the biblical story of Jacob's ladder represents the ladder structure of DNA.

Genesis 28:12 states:

> He had a dream in which he saw a stairway resting on the earth, with its top reaching to heaven, and the angels of God were ascending and descending on it.[562]

Our DNA contains about 3.5 gigabytes of software instructions for how to build a human—slightly less than the capacity of a standard DVD. That's 3.5 *billion* bits of information. This sheer amount of data is sufficient to fill more than a thousand encyclopedia volumes at a thousand pages each coupled with the twisted-ladder structure of the microscopic DNA molecule. It's not hard to imagine that we may be tapping into the hidden information coded into our DNA when we dream. Only recently has our high technology even come close to achieving similar information storage density on microchips compared to DNA's ancient technology that has been around for perhaps billions of years!

562 https://www.biblegateway.com/passage/?search=Genesis+28%3A12&version=NIV

After reading this entire book, you will have consumed 3.95 megabytes worth of 1s and 0s (text only, no pictures or illustrations). Congratulations! This is equivalent to having read 0.11% of your DNA information. You've only got to read another 886 books of this size to understand how much information is stored in your DNA.

Given that the neurotransmitter DMT is believed to be responsible for dreams and out-of-body experiences and visions, it is very likely that DNA acts as a storehouse of information on the human operating system, and DMT provides the means for us to consciously access that information.

Colossians 1:27 says:

> To them God has chosen to make known among the Gentiles the glorious riches of this mystery, which is Christ in you, the hope of glory.[563]

This is an extremely important verse, the key words being *mystery* and *within.* This ancient book of collected wisdom is telling us that the glory of Christ is a mystery *and* that this mystery is embedded within each of us. An untrue book would not have lasted 2,000 years and would not have retained the title of best-selling book ever written. A quick internet search of the terms "Jacob's ladder DNA" will turn up a plethora of interesting articles, but I don't want to take up space here. We have many other topics to cover.

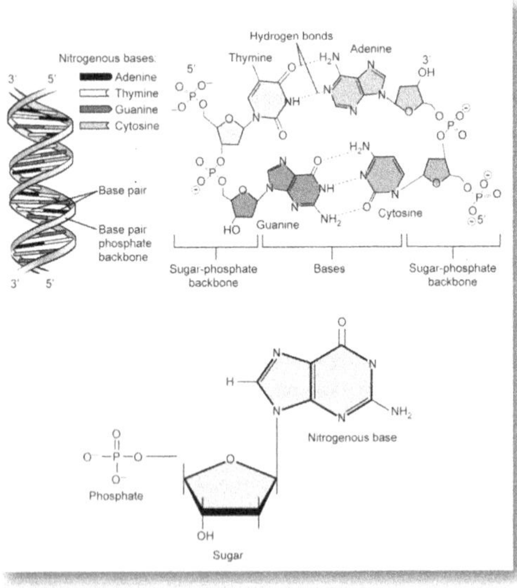

The graphic following depicts the geometry of the DNA molecule as well as the geometry of the nucleotide molecules.[564] We see examples of pentagons and hexagons showing up in the other two kingdoms of life—the plant and fungus kingdoms (more on this in later text)—and now we are seeing it in the third, the animal kingdom, to which we humans belong.

563 https://www.biblegateway.com/passage/?search=Colossians+1%3A27&version=NIV
564 https://en.wikipedia.org/wiki/Nucleotide.

I've included an extremely interesting website in the footnotes for the interested reader.[565]

In genetics, the alphabet is composed of the four bases A, G, C, and T, and a *word* is composed of combinations of three bases. A group of three bases makes an amino acid. Following the laws of combinatorics, a very closely-related mathematical cousin of probability and statistics, there are $4^3 = 4 \times 4 \times 4 = 64$ total possible unique 3-letter *words* called amino acids that can result from the combinations of bases. Only twenty of the possible words are used uniquely, with the other 44 combinations acting as chemical synonyms for the same expression. With the twenty words, there are two more—a *start* and a *stop* command. Altogether, there are 22 commands in the genetic lexicon.[566] Now 11+11 is showing up at the DNA-molecular level in the human story! Furthermore, tying the fact that each of the 22 amino acids is composed of 3 *letters*, I am once again reminded of my birth date, 3/22, and the address of my first home, 322 Hull Court. I don't believe in coincidences anymore. These number clues have been my guideposts through life, which would eventually bring me to the point of compiling all of these discoveries and writing this book.

The geometric properties of DNA are such that its two unequally spaced spiral grooves are 12 and 22 ångströms[567] wide for the minor and major grooves respectively.[568] An ångström is equivalent to one ten-billionth of a meter. James Watson and Francis Crick were the co-discoverers of the helical structure of DNA utilizing X-ray crystallography. Crick was one of 22 Nobel laureates who signed the second edition of the 1933 *Humanist Manifesto*.[569] 11+11.

Fun fact: On December 22, 1895, Wilhem Roentgen took the first X-ray photograph. The subject was his wife's hand, and her wedding ring is clearly visible in this, the first radiograph. A new technology was born, which would have massive implications in medicine, industry, astronomy, and many other areas of human endeavor.[570]

Does the number 22 show up anywhere else in our DNA? You bet it does! Keep reading, and find out how! I try to save the more exciting points for later in the book. It is also illuminating to return to the topic of 11:11

565 http://www.mostholyplace.com/book-01_chapter-02.html.

566 Jeremy Narby, *The Cosmic Serpent: DNA and the Origins of Knowledge* (New York: Jeremy P. Tarcher/Putnam, 1998).

567 Pronounced "ong-strum". In Swedish, ång = steam, and ström = stream, so it means "a narrow jet of steam"

568 http://sciencewise.info/resource/DNA/DNA_by_Wikipedia.

569 https://en.wikipedia.org/wiki/Francis_Crick.

570 https://www.the-scientist.com/foundations/the-first-x-ray-1895-42279/amp.

showing up as an awakening code for certain people. Think of the number 11 as two parallel DNA strands showing up twice—once for each of our parents. Fun fact: The nucleotide cytosine has a molecular weight of 111.1 g/mol.

As the book title is *The 11:11 Code*, let's pause for a moment to look at the polyhedron model on the first page of the book and remark that all life's chemical building blocks (T, G, A, and C) and many of our neurotransmitters are composed of 5- and 6-sided polygon molecules. Adding 5 and 6 together, we arrive at 11. The number 11 is fundamental to all life-forms as every living organism has the same DNA software written in the same 4 *letters* and composed of the same 22 *words* or amino acids composed of 3 letters each. Whether we are talking about a snail, a mosquito, zebra, mushroom, a tree, an octopus, a coral reef, a bacterium, a human being, the mold on a rotten strawberry, or the strawberry itself, we are all made of the *exact same stuff*. Gregory Sams said the following:

> Virtually every food we consume, with the exception of salt and some food additives, is a form of stored sunlight. This is originally laid down as energy through the photosynthesis of plants, and subsequently released as energy to sustain the life of those things eating the plants, and those eating those eating the plants, and so on up the food chain. A carrot takes light, air, water, and earth, converting them into a crunchy, pointy, orange vegetable, and you turn this carrot into a moving, intelligent, seeing, human being. What an amazing world![571]

Plants essentially take the fundamental chemical elements of the Earth and assemble them into the basic building blocks of life, which are amino acids and proteins. Humans and the rest of the animal kingdom dwellers use these to build flesh. When you burn a log, all the carbon, oxygen, nitrogen, and hydrogen atoms are released as gases, and the ashes that are left are simply the raw soil elements that went into the physical structure of the tree that produced it. It's really remarkable when you think about it. Life truly is a miracle.

After having unraveled the mysteries and number codes in my own life, I am left with an overwhelming body of evidence that my entire life up to this moment has been preplanned by my higher power. This caused me to logically reason that my future must also be predetermined. Knowing

571 Gregory Sams, *Sun of gOd: Discover the Self-Organizing Consciousness That Underlies Everything* (San Francisco: Weiser Books, 2009).

what I know about my magic numbers showing up in every major event in my past, I now take comfort in sitting back, relaxing, and enjoying my life as it comes, knowing that God has a plan for my life and for everyone else in the world. As I look back on the most important lessons in my life, I see that the majority involved some sort of pain, loss, or trauma. Rumi once said, "The wound is the place where the light enters you."[572] I have learned to embrace the good and the bad in every situation. All the bad people I have had contact with in the past were put into my life to show me what kind of person *not* to be, so in retrospect, I am thankful for them. In the same vein, all the good people were put into my life to help me achieve my highest purpose in life through their good example. The universe has a strange ability to give you exactly what you need, exactly when you need it, when you have faith that it actually works that way.

Caveat: As my research continued well after writing this section, I discovered that many sources list the number of base pairs in the 22nd chromosome to be 51 million in contrast to the 33 million that I wrote about earlier in this section. I decided to leave this section unaltered because of how deeply this event impacted me. I'll leave it to the reader to decide if it was worth keeping. Sometimes the spirit of a message is more important than the actual words of the message.

The Missing Link

On March 12, 2019, I saw a news article on FoxNews announcing that scientists had discovered the fossilized remains of a primate species they believe to be the missing link in the human evolution from apes to Homo sapiens. Identified by its fossilized teeth, the new species, known as *Alophia metios*, was found in the badlands of northwest Kenya. The teeth may give clues on how their diets helped shape the course of evolution. Radiocarbon dating of the jawbone determined its age to be 22 million years old.[573] Last time I checked, 11 + 11 = 22, making this yet another fascinating contribution to *The 11:11 Code*.

From DNA to DMT

During one of my work trips to Egypt, I took the opportunity to tour the Great Pyramid of Giza. This was one of the most remarkable experiences of my life. As an engineer who works in heavy industry, I marveled at the massive stones cut to near perfection and placed hundreds of feet into

572 https://www.goodreads.com/quotes/103315-the-wound-is-the-place-where-the-light-enters-you

573 https://www.foxnews.com/science/missing-link-found-22-million-year-old-monkey-species-found-in-africa.

the air with nearly laser-like perfection, presumably without the aid of cranes. The three pyramids appear to have been placed in the exact same layout as the stars in the belt of the constellation Orion. The three stars of Orion's belt do not form a perfectly straight line, the dimmest of the three stars, Mintaka being slightly out of line with the other two brighter ones, Alnitak and Alnilam. The smallest of the three pyramids is also out of line with the two larger pyramids by *exactly* the same angle. The smallest pyramid is also smaller, corresponding to the third star, which is also smaller and less bright than its two companions.

I wondered how they achieved the mystical states of mind that would have probably been necessary to conceive these tremendous feats of art and architecture that continue to baffle humanity into the modern era. Graham Hancock's book *The Message of the Sphinx* is an excellent read for anyone wanting to learn about ancient Egypt and get some deep insights into the secrets contained in the ancient structures.

The Egyptians believed in the "as above, so below" correspondence principle. In the next sketches, two concepts appear clear to me.

1. The sphinx has its gaze cast upon the constellations Leo (the lion) and Orion (the hunter). Note similarities between the DMT molecule and the Orion constellation.

2. The star shafts are pointed toward Draco, the Dragon (the 13th constellation) as a symbol of the dragon or serpent.

Egyptian-born construction engineer-turned-Egyptologist Robert Bauval has written several books on the mysteries of ancient Egypt and linking the pyramid texts with astronomy. In *The Egypt Code*, through painstaking geographic surveys followed by computerized geometric modeling, Bauval essentially proves that the relative arrangement of the three pyramids bears a one-to-one correspondence to the arrangement of the three prominent stars in Orion's belt. Bauval states:

> It was while working in Saudi Arabia that I made a startling and unexpected connection between Orion and the Giza pyramids that was to change the course of my life. One night, while looking at the three stars of Orion's belt in the clear desert night sky, it struck me that these stars had exactly the same layout of the three pyramids of Giza and their positioning relative to the Nile.[574]

574 Robert Bauval, *The Egypt Code* (San Francisco: Disinformation Books, 2008).

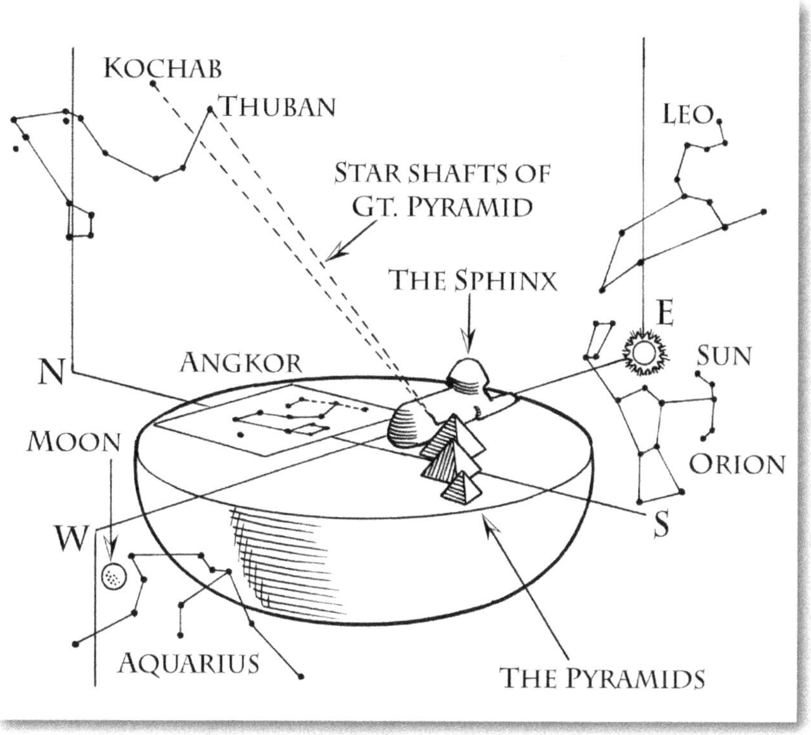

KOCHAB
THUBAN
LEO
STAR SHAFTS OF
GT. PYRAMID
THE SPHINX
E
N
ANGKOR
SUN
MOON
ORION
S
W
AQUARIUS
THE PYRAMIDS

Author's impression of Giza complex alignment with Orion[575]

ORION
DMT
NH
THYMINE
CYTOSINE
ADENINE
URACIL
GUANINE
DIMETHYLTYRPTAMINE
(DMT)

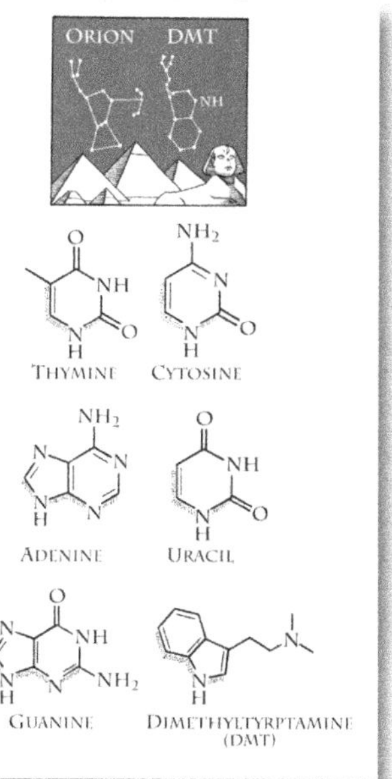

Inspiration for Orion-DMT equivalence given in footnotes[576]

575 http://www.helulf.se/Rongorongo/Stories/Draco.htm.
576 www.naturalbornalchemist.com.

It is also thought-provoking to think about what the sphinx is. It is a chimera, a mythical being that is half human and half lion in this case. Now look at the two constellations (Leo and Orion) and what they represent (a hunter and a lion). Boom! Look what I did there. Again, the principle of "as above, so below" seems perfectly apropos here. The ability to interpret the ancient Egyptian hieroglyphic writings was an utter enigma until the Rosetta Stone was discovered in 1799, inscribed with three versions of a decree issued at Memphis, Egypt, in 196 BC during the Ptolemaic dynasty on behalf of King Ptolemy V. The top and middle texts are in Ancient Egyptian using hieroglyphic script and demotic script respectively, while the bottom is in ancient Greek. The famous stone was being analyzed for more than twenty years, but it wasn't until transliteration of the Egyptian scripts was announced by Jean-François Champollion in Paris in 1822 that people opened the door to translating Egyptian hieroglyphs elsewhere, outside the scope of the Rosetta stone.[577] Here we go again, the number 22, the 11 + 11 code opening another big door of human understanding. We are really getting into the yummy stuff now, aren't we? Still more than 100 pages to go, and I have saved the most interesting stuff for last!

As above, so below.

—Hermes Trismegistus[578]

577 https://en.m.wikipedia.org/wiki/Rosetta_Stone.
578 http://www.xfacts.com/2012.php.

Remember that ancient Egyptians revered the acacia tree as the vessel in which the god of the underworld and afterlife, Osiris, resided. They probably didn't have the benefit of knowing that the tree's roots contained the human neurotransmitter DMT in high enough concentrations to cause the visions that we've discussed previously. It is very illuminating to compare the molecular structure of DMT, a human neurotransmitter, to the constellation of Orion. Are the stars and pyramids trying to tell us something? Could this be a hint that DMT is our direct link to the spirit realms?

In Freemasonry, the oldest fraternity in the planet's history, a sprig of acacia is one of the most important symbols of a Master Mason and is a key component of a Masonic funeral. Does the oldest remaining fraternity on Earth conceal secret knowledge that has otherwise been lost to humankind? Has the secret society itself forgotten the deeper meaning of one of its key symbols?

The book *The Masonic Magician* by Philippa Faulks is recommended to anyone seeking to research this topic any deeper.

In the Bible, Matthew 6:22 says, "The light of the body is the eye: if therefore thine eye be single, thy whole body shall be full of light." While all religious texts are open to interpretation, the verse is clearly talking about a singular eye, which may very likely refer to the pineal gland. In Dr. Rick Strassman's *DMT: The Spirit Molecule*, he states than the pineal gland "possesses a lens, cornea, and retina. It is light-sensitive and helps regulate body temperature and skin coloration—two basic survival functions intimately related to environmental light."[579] Many ancient Eastern religions, including Buddhism and Hinduism, as well as French mathematician Rene Descartes, have believed for centuries that the pineal gland is seat of the soul and a direct causal agent in the experience of spiritual awakening.

Going back to the topic of 666 and the number of man, I think it is fascinating to notice that the four bases of DNA (T, G, A, and C), the RNA nucleotide uracil, and the spirit molecule, DMT, all have a 6-sided molecular structure. It is baffling to me that DMT, a molecule that virtually every living being produces, is listed as a Schedule I illegal drug on the U.S. Federal Drug Enforcement Agency's list of drugs as "*...dangerous and lacking any potential for medical benefit.*" Schedule one is reserved

579 Rick Strassman, *DMT: The Spirit Molecule* (Rochester: Park Street Press, 2001).

for the highest classification of illegal substances, including heroin and methamphetamine. And yet the human body produces it. According to the US Department of Justice Title 21 CFR,[580] a drug must meet the following three criteria to be placed on the schedule-one list:

1. The substance or drug has a high potential for abuse.
2. The substance or drug has no currently accepted medical use or treatment in the United States.
3. There is a lack of accepted safety for use of the drug or other substance under medical supervision.

From what I have read about this mysterious compound, I feel it may be deserving of more research in the future. This might be one of humanity's greatest blind spots. Scientists and researchers mostly agree that understanding consciousness is one of the hardest, most impenetrable problems in human history. Could DMT hold the key to this mystery of all mysteries? To me it seems logical to say that if we are to fully understand consciousness, we need to first understand the purpose and function of each and every neurotransmitter compound produced by the body. Maybe some of my readers have experienced it? I'd be fascinated to hear from you.

The helical rails that compose DNA are formed of phosphate groups with phosphorous atoms at the center of each group. Recall the discussion on phosphorous earlier in this book and its role as the bringer of light. In the year 2016, researchers at Northwestern University discovered that when human sperm fertilizes an egg, it emits a small flash of light.[581] I have often heard it said that "we are beings of light." This research seems to confirm this old adage.

Recommended video: "How Earth Moves" by vsauce

If you watched the video above, did you notice how Earth's flight through space closely mirrors the spiral structure of DNA?

MAGIC DUST

> God wanted to hide his secrets in a secure place. 'Would I put them on the moon?' He reflected. 'But then, one day human beings could

580 https://www.deadiversion.usdoj.gov/21cfr/cfr/1308/1308_11.htm.

581 https://news.northwestern.edu/stories/2016/04/radiant-zinc-fireworks-reveal-quality-of-human-egg.

get there, and it could be that those who would arrive there would not be worthy of the secret knowledge. Or perhaps I should hide them in the depths of the ocean,' God entertained another possibility. But again, for the same reasons, he dismissed it. Then the solution occurred to Him—'I shall put my secrets in the inner sanctum of man's own mind. Then only those who really deserve it will be able to get it.'

A tale by an ice cream vendor in the Peruvian Amazon [582]

Suggested background music: Phelian & Ambyion's "Grey Unknown"

DNA is software. All software has a programmer. DNA must logically have a programmer. Who was the programmer for DNA? Is DNA *the* Word? At a mere 3.5 billion letters, I can imagine God uttering the entire human genome in one breath. Since the beginning of the human experiment, we have been studying all aspects of life and recording our discoveries as information in its many forms from clay cuneiform tablets millennia ago to quantum qubit data storage today. The theme over the ages is that we went from heavy, sparse systems of storage toward extremely lightweight, ultra-high-density data storage. The trend continues unabated. We are at the point now where our data storage density is approaching that of DNA. Could we one day reach the point where all the information in the universe as we know it will be condensed down to the space of an atom on the same scale as it was just prior to the initial big bang creation event? It's almost as if we are about to come full circle on information density. It only took us 13.8 billion years to get there.

According to SingularityHub, a gram of DNA could store all of the world's information on a four-gram storage device made of DNA, which would fit in a teaspoon.[583] Think about that—all the world's information, including all of the genetic instruction sequences to create every single plant, animal, and fungus uniquely on the planet. DNA has an incredibly high storage density!

Ecclesiastes 3:20 states, "All go to one place: All come from dust, and return to dust."[584] Genesis 3:19 says the same thing another way, "By

582 Benny Shanon, *Antipodes of the Mind: Charting the Phenomenology of the Ayahuasca Experience* (Oxford: Oxford University Press, 2002).

583 https://singularityhub.com/2015/02/20/worlds-data-could-fit-on-a-teaspoon-sized-dna-hard-drive-and-survive-thousands-of-years/.

584 https://www.biblegateway.com/passage/?search=Ecclesiastes+3%3A20&version=NIV.

the sweat of your brow you will eat your food, until you return to the ground, since from it you were taken; for dust you are, and to dust you will return."[585]

So what is this life all about? Why are we here? Why all the trouble and effort? Why not just let dust be dust?

Without life, the universe would be inert and boring, alone in its magnificence with no one present to observe the master architect's handiwork, and no one to praise him for it. It would be like a major league baseball game with no spectators. Humans and all other life-forms are here as a way for the atoms of the universe to discover what they are made of and what they are doing here too. We live in a universe that is universally intelligent and inherently curious about itself. We are simply matter discovering its own purpose as well as its context in space and time. I believe that the event of creation was ultimately the result of the great cosmic mind becoming bored for all of past eternity. Realizing his infinite, unrealized potential, he dreamed the universe into being, spoke the Word, and it became so. Whether you subscribe to the Christian creation story or the big bang story or a hybrid of the two, my point remains undiminished. Having pets is great practice for learning to speak to our own master. Just as dogs have limited ability to comprehend the mysterious nature of humans, our complex language, and our superior intelligence, they are able to communicate with us through making repeated conscientious efforts to communicate. For humans to communicate and interact with God, there is a similar jump in intelligence, and a protracted and purposeful effort must be made to learn the master's language.

Einstein's famous equation $e = mc^2$ is brilliant in insight, elegance, and simplicity. It equates energy to mass multiplied by a speed times speed again—the speed of light squared. In order to imagine the number of joules of energy in one kilogram of mass, you could visually represent this energy as a 3-sided box with the speed of light (300,000,000 meters per second) on two sides and the mass as the length of the third side. A joule is defined as the amount of energy you get if you use one watt of power for one second. The box would be 300 million units deep, 300 million units wide, and one unit thick. Basically, it's a huge, thin slab of little cubic boxes. It would be three million columns of little boxes arranged into three million rows. That's a lot of little boxes—nine trillion, to be exact. One kilogram, if converted from mass into energy via nuclear

585 https://www.biblegateway.com/passage/?search=Genesis+3%3A19&version=NIV.

fission, would result in 9 trillion units of energy. That's enough energy to run all the needs of the typical American home for 52 days, all coming from just 2.2 pounds of fuel. This gets to the heart of why nuclear energy is so immensely powerful. As I typed the previous sentence, I realized that our old friend 22 is imbedded into the conversion factor where 1 kilogram equals 2.2 pounds. The conversion between miles and kilometers is also interesting as 1 mile equals 1.62 kilometers, which is the golden ratio within 0.9 percent accuracy. That is close enough for most engineering calculations. I doubt this was intentional. Otherwise, wouldn't it have been set to *exactly* 1.618 (the golden ratio)? Are all of these curious occurrences pure coincidence, or is the entire show of life being put on by an intelligent creator?

The entire experience of life consists of converting energy from one form to another. Energy started out as mass. Then nuclear reactions in the stars turned it to electromagnetic energy. Then plants turned light into chemical energy. Our bodies convert chemical energy into thermal, mechanical, and electrical (nervous system) energy, which we then enjoy as this wonderful experience of consciousness. Every emotion, sound, sight, smell, taste, and feeling you have every experienced was the direct result of electrical impulses taking place inside your miraculous brain. We are here to marvel in the glory of participating as energetic beings and observing all the ways that the universe transports and converts energy—a statement that covers all forms of activity in the universe.

When you break down the human body, you are reduced to the raw nuts and bolts of the universe. Every single piece of us is made from the 118 elements on the periodic chart from chemistry. How these basic building blocks of the universe managed to arrange themselves in such a way as to create a self-aware, self-healing, intelligent, beautiful, and emotional machine capable of reproducing and establishing contact with its Creator is a feat that will never be beaten. So 13.8 billion years ago, God uttered *the Word*, and life began. His fingerprints are in your DNA, your world, the moon, Mars, and the stars.

Speaking of 118 elements, in 1911, Danish physicist Neils Bohr began his pioneering research into the atomic structure of matter. He received his doctorate in physics that same year. He was awarded the Nobel Prize in physics 11 years later in 1922 "for his services in the investigation of the structure of atoms and of the radiation emanating from them."[586] Eighty

586 https://www.thoughtco.com/niels-bohr-biographical-profile-2699055.

years before the knowledge or technology existed to synthesize unknown chemical elements, Bohr predicted in 1922 that an element with atomic weight 118 was theoretically possible and proposed that such an element would be situated in the periodic table just below radon as the seventh noble gas if anyone was ever able to synthesize it. In the year 2002, Russian physicist Yuri Oganessian was the first to demonstrate the nuclear decay of atoms of element #118, which was named in his honor as Oganesson.[587]

Recall Avogadro's number, 6.022×10^{23}, from earlier in the book? It's the most fundamental number in all chemistry as it tells the chemist how many atoms or molecules are in one mole of any of the natural elements and provides a relationship between moles and mass. In 1811, Italian physicist Amedeo Avogadro first proposed that the volume of a gas (at a given pressure and temperature) is proportional to the number of atoms or molecules regardless of the nature of the gas. I have to stop for a moment and gloat over the irony that one of the most fundamental numbers in all chemistry was discovered by a physicist (i.e., someone who was not a chemist). I mention this number in this book because it has the two numbers 22 and 23 in it, whose significance has already been made clear in earlier chapters.

Next time you walk through the grocery store, look at all the diverse types of food. With the exception of salt, virtually all other food items derive their existence from DNA—whether it's fruits, vegetables, grains, dairy, or meat. Cinnamon, cardamom, cayenne pepper, cloves, saffron, curry, mint, licorice, tea, coffee, chocolate, and thousands more flavors owe their existence to DNA instructions in the software of the plant that produced them. The DNA in food isn't just made of *similar* stuff but *exactly* the same stuff as we humans are. All life-forms have different DNA sequences, but they are all written from the same T, C, A, and G alphabet. These form the same exact 22 amino acids that make up all life in the plant, fungus, and animal kingdoms. All of this came into existence at the same moment—whether you believe in divine creation, the big bang, or both. I'm a proponent of evolutionary creationism whereby a divine intellect created life and then gave it the ability to improve itself through natural selection.

This book has been brought to you in part by the acacia tree of Genesis 3:22, whose metaphor helped me understand how 22 was my life number and led me to connect that with the codes in the Bible as well as the words

587 https://en.wikipedia.org/wiki/Oganesson.

that were written in our DNA, a message of hope and of the Christ, who has always been within us all.

I think this is the most important message in the entire Bible. What a miracle that God has hidden a piece of himself inside each of us to be discovered. I'll ask the orthodox religious reader to withhold fire against me for stating that God has programmed himself into each of us, at least for the moment. Suppose we make the analogy to radio wave transmission. I have made the claim that each of us has a spiritual radio receiver within us by which we are capable of communicating with the Creator. This is the God within. But what good is a radio without a broadcast station emitting a signal? I also believe that God has a presence outside of the human body and that his spirit is embodied within every single atom of the universe. All matter is made up of energy. The Creator is the source of all energy and all matter. Our internal spiritual radio has a tendency to get changed to the wrong stations during life, and it is easy to lose contact with the divine broadcast. The process of awakening involves tuning out the high-powered signals of the world that compete for our attention, time, and spirit. The inner signal is much quieter and subtler than the signals of the world and requires much discipline and effort to get our inner radio tuned to the sublime channel of the Spirit.

Following this paragraph there is a picture of *the Word,* DNA. Looking down the axis of a DNA molecule[588], you can admire the magnitude of genius that it took to author the tenfold symmetry of this most exquisite chemical structure in the universe—ten fingers, ten toes, tenfold symmetry copied 3.5 billion times, carrying a million pages of printed information on the atomic scale.

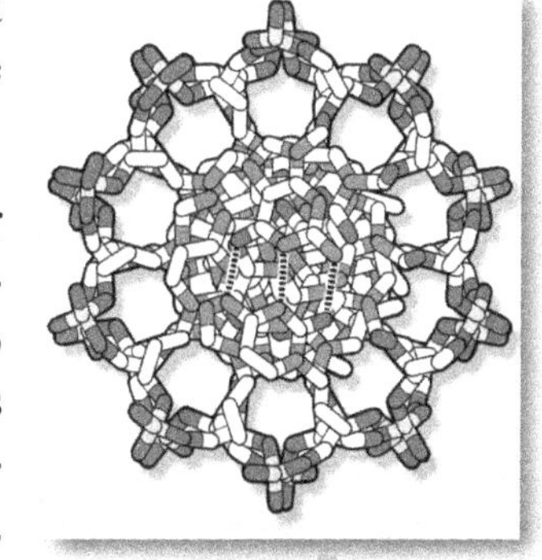

Axial view of the DNA molecule

God imbedded himself chemically into our DNA software, which included further instructions for our pineal gland and lungs to produce DMT and unlock its secrets. It is widely believed that the soul enters the human body 7 x 7 or 49 days after conception, which is the point at which the pineal gland takes form.[589] Never in my wildest imagination

588https://ww2.chemistry.gatech.edu/~lw26/structure/nucleic_acid/A_B_Z/b_dna_b.gif.

589 http://www.mysterious-times.com/2018/05/13/the-soul-enters-the-fetus-at-49-days-by-the-pineal-gland-according-to-a-scientist/.

did I think that during the process of writing this book, I would find God's universal signature 11-22-33 at the atomic level all the way to the moon, Mars, and the stars at the cosmic scale. Perhaps this is the missing key that so many of the world's numerologists have been grasping for to explain why 11, 22, and 33 are considered master numbers, angel numbers, and enlightenment codes. Whether through the microscope, telescope, or the naked eye, God's signatures are there to be seen at any scale you observe in nature. The Creator's handiwork can be admired equally at all powers of magnification.

THE NUMBER OF CARBON

It is a well-established fact that carbon forms the basis for all life as we presently understand it. A carbon atom has 6 electrons, 6 protons, and 6 neutrons. Does this suggest that all life is inherently a construct of the beast? Or should we stick to the alternate definition that 666 is the number of a man?

I would tend toward the *number of man*, especially when you consider Isaiah 6:6, which says, "Then one of the seraphim flew to me with a live coal in his hand, which he had taken with tongs from the altar." First off, let's observe the fact that this verse has 6:6 (66) as its address in the book of Isaiah and that coal is made of pure carbon! The indication that the Bible is referring to carbon couldn't possibly be any clearer.

How many wars have been fought and innocent lives lost or destroyed over the pursuit of carbon-based fuels? How much fear and panic has been perpetrated on the public about the woes of burning fossil-fuels and their purported impact on global warming and climate change? If you want to know the full picture of climate change, it is necessary to understand the Milankovitch Cycle, which I'll mention again later.

A SWEET DISCOVERY

Virtually all consciousness depends on hexagons in the form of glucose, the primary fuel of the brain. The molecular structure of the sugar molecule glucose has a hexagonal structure and is composed of 6 carbon, 12 hydrogen, and 6 oxygen molecules. In 1922, German biochemist Otto Fritz Meyerhof received the Nobel Prize in physiology and medicine for his pioneering research into how the body metabolizes glucose. He later emigrated to the United States and became a professor at the University of Pennsylvania.[590]

For those whose body cannot process glucose effectively, diabetes is the result of a defect in chromosome #11. It wasn't until 1922 when 2 Canadians, scientist Charles Best and biochemist James Collip, became the first to successfully demonstrate bovine-derived insulin as an effective treatment. This first treatment was injected into fourteen-year-old Leonard Thompson in Toronto on **1/11/1**922.[591] Here we go again—one of humanity's greatest problems finding a solution with multiple occurrences of the numbers 11 and 22.

Other Significant Medical Finds

Some other medical historical firsts with interesting numerological signatures include the following: In 1967, the first human heart transplant was performed by South African surgeon Christiaan Neethling Barnard, who was born in the 11th month of 1922.[592] In 1933, Ukrainian surgeon Yurii Voronoy attempted the first kidney transplant.[593] 11 + 11 + 11 = 33.

As long as we are on the topic of significant breakthroughs in the life sciences, I'd like to mention that Louis Pasteur was born on December 27, 1822, and later went on to invent the process we know today as pasteurization to which the world owes a great debt of gratitude for extending the life of various foods, particularly in the dairy section. His eponymous process involves heating a liquid to just high enough temperature where the bad bacteria are killed off but low enough that the fluid is not boiled or otherwise modified in any way.[594] French chemist Louis Pasteur was the first *zymologist* when he connected yeast to fermentation in 1857. Pasteur originally defined fermentation as respiration without air.[595] There you go. Now I can officially say we have covered topics from astronomy to zymurgy by the time you reach the back cover. Life is full of mysteries; let's keeping digging. See, I told you this book would cover everything from astronomy to zymology.

590 https://www.nobelprize.org/prizes/medicine/1922/meyerhof/biographical/.
591 https://www.diabetes.co.uk/pioneers/leonard-thompson.html.
592 https://www.jtcvs.org/article/S0022-5223(02)19201-4/fulltext.
593 https://onlinelibrary.wiley.com/doi/full/10.1111/j.1432-2277.2009.00986.x.
594 https://www.britannica.com/biography/Louis-Pasteur.
595 http://www.newworldencyclopedia.org/entry/Fermentation.

THE CHEMISTRY OF HAPPINESS AND SPIRITUALITY

In the composite graphic that follows, there are 6 chemical structures, and 3 of them are naturally occurring chemicals in the human body. Two are currently classified as illegal psychedelic drugs, and one is a legal drug. Can you spot the *one* drug that is a *depressant*? Can you tell which one is which? Is there one that doesn't seem to fit? Remember the vignette on Sesame Street in the 1980s "one of these things is not like the others"? Let's play that game now:

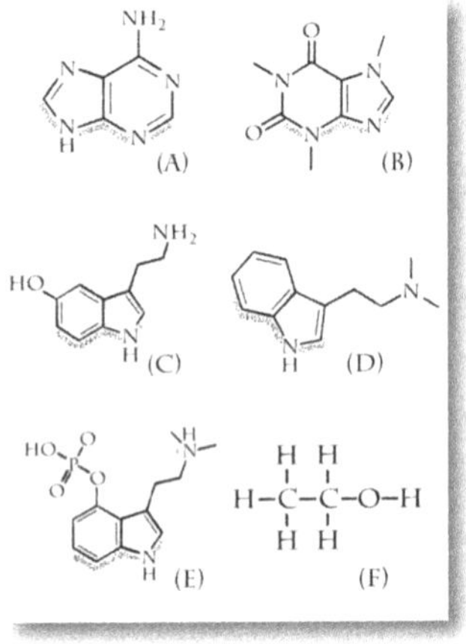

Here are answers: (a) adenine from DNA, (b) caffeine, (c) serotonin, (d) dimethyltryptamine, (e) psilocybin from magic mushrooms, and (f) ethanol (drinkable alcohol).

There is an almost indistinguishable difference between serotonin, one of the key chemicals that control mood, and dimethyltryptamine (DMT), which is believed to be responsible for spiritual connection. Our body produces DMT in both the lungs and the pineal gland. Remember, it is also a DEA schedule-one illegal drug in the same class as heroin and methamphetamine, and yet every single human has some trace amount of this compound in their body at all times. In order to complete our development as a species, I think humanity needs to rethink our relationship with entheogenic compounds that occur naturally throughout the natural world and also within our bodies.

Alcohol stands out as the oddball in the composite picture within this section. Just from looking at the structure of the natural chemicals that the body produces, alcohol bears no resemblance to the body's own chemicals and stands out as the intruder and impostor. It clearly is a foreign substance and bears no structural similarity to any of the chemicals the body produces to be *happy*. It is no secret that alcohol is classified as a depressant. Although I claim no expertise in biochemistry, I believe alcohol and other widely abused drugs can prevent the good endogenous neurotransmitters such as DMT from doing their job properly in the brain. A great deal of research has been performed in the recent couple of decades demonstrating the effectiveness of certain psychedelic substances in treating cases of addiction that defied all other forms of treatment. Highly respected universities such as Johns Hopkins are performing academic trials where entheogenic substances such as psilocybin are administered to depressed people, and the results have been overwhelmingly favorable.

By this point, the reader may be asking, "Why are we talking about the molecular chemistry of emotion in a book titled *The 11:11 Code*?" The answer is simple and clear. What do you get when you add up the number of sides in a pentagon and a hexagon? You get 6 + 5 = 11. Within the structure of DNA, we have two spiral strands of chemically encoded genetic information embraced in a microscopic spiral dance 3.5 billion base pairs in length, and each rung of the ladder has the pentagon and hexagon (11) structures on *both sides*. In short, 11 + 11 is the basis of life. We are truly beings of light, and I'll get into the reasons why in great depth a bit later.

SPACE-BASED AMINO ACIDS

Scientists found 19 different types of amino acids in samples of Comet Wild 2 and in various carbon-rich meteorites. Finding amino acids in these objects supports the theory that the origin of life may have gotten a boost from space. After all, the Bible says creation took six days but it doesn't really spell out how God did it, what he used, what aspects of the universe were in his toolbox or part of the materials used.

Amino acids are the fundamental building blocks of life, molecules used to make the proteins that are essential to life. "Finding them in this type of meteorite suggests that there is more than one way to make amino acids in space, which increases the chance for finding life elsewhere in the universe," Daniel Glavin of NASAs Goddard Space Flight Center said in a statement.[596]

596 https://www.abc.net.au/science/articles/2010/12/17/3095213.htm

The proteins created from amino acids are used in everything from structures like hair to enzymes, the catalysts that speed up or regulate chemical reactions. Just as the 26 letters of the alphabet are arranged in limitless combinations to make words, life uses 20 different amino acids in a huge variety of arrangements to build millions of different proteins.[597]

If we include the *start* and *stop* codons, there are a total of 22 amino acids used to write the entire Tree of Life's DNA structure. The interested reader should search "22 amino acids Hebrew."[598]

This is the stuff that has inspired countless books and movies in the science-fiction genre. But sometimes truth is stranger than fiction. Who knows? Is this all some sort of divine, cosmic coincidence, or is there a deeper secret message from our nearest galactic neighborhood? Not all mysteries are meant to be solved. Some are meant to be admired by all generations.

Returning to the Bible, Colossians 1:27 says:

> To them God has chosen to make known among the Gentiles the glorious riches of this mystery, which is Christ in you, the hope of glory.[599]

Could "chapter" 22 of the DNA story with its 33 million letters and 11 million words be the option to choose the Christ consciousness programmed directly inside of each of us at the atomic level, inside each of the 37 trillion cells that make up our bodies? Why 37? Because it is a primitive prime number and a star number and part of the prime factorization of the number of a man? Does the fact that this 22nd chromosome codes our free will and spirit have something to do with accepting Christ? Does the phrase "hope and glory" refer to the genetic treasure containing the recipes for genetically curing diseases? There is no shortage of wonderful mysteries to ponder and enjoy in this magical, perfect universe we call home. We are not simply humans having a spiritual experience. We are spirits having a human experience as well.

---

597 https://www.space.com/10498-life-building-blocks-surprising-meteorite.html.
598 http://www.abovetopsecret.com/forum/thread1086981/pg1.
599 https://www.biblegateway.com/passage/?search=Colossians+1%3A27&version=NIV.

If you want to find the secrets of the universe, think
in terms of energy, frequency, and vibration.

—Nikola Tesla[600]

All life is biology.
All biology is physiology.
All physiology is chemistry.
All chemistry is physics.
All physics is math.

—Dr. Stephen Marquardt[601]

600 https://www.goodreads.com/quotes/361785-if-you-want-to-find-the-secrets-of-the-universe.
601 https://www.goldennumber.net/life-design/

CHAPTER 12

PLANTS, FUNGI, BUGS, AND BONES

The Key to Life

Chlorophyll is the engine of all life on Earth. It is the substance that gives leaves their typical green color, and it is the chemical compound that allows plants to convert sunlight into carbohydrates through the process of photosynthesis. Virtually all known life-forms owe their existence to chlorophyll's ability to convert solar energy into chemical energy. All earthly life-forms belong to one of three taxonomic kingdoms—plant, animal, or fungus. The animal kingdom relies upon fresh vegetation (as well as other animals) to sustain itself, and similarly, the fungal kingdom derives its food source from dead matter from both the plant and animal kingdoms. The key-like shape of the chlorophyll molecule that follows is an uncanny metaphor for its *key* role in sustaining all forms of life on Earth.

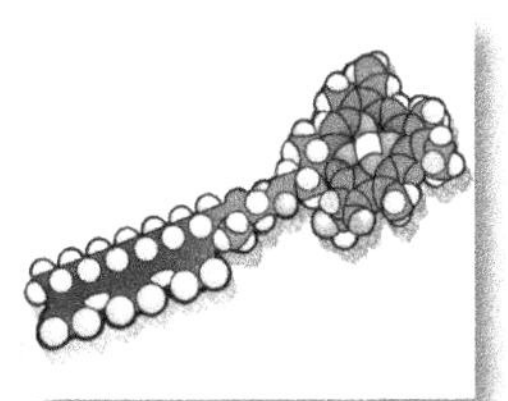

An artist's rendering of a chlorophyll molecule[602]

I believe this is a metaphorical symbol of chlorophyll as being fundamentally the key to life. Another tantalizing fact is that chlorophyll is most

602 https://commons.wikimedia.org/w/index.php?curid=1061563.

efficient at absorbing light in the blue light spectrum, which includes 666 terahertz (trillion cycles per second) *frequency*. In science and engineering, frequency is typically denoted by the Greek lowercase letter omega, ω.

Color	Wavelength	Frequency (Tera Hertz)
Violet	380–450 nm	668–789 THz
Blue	450–495 nm	606–668 THz
Green	495–570 nm	526–606 THz
Yellow	570–590 nm	508–526 THz
Orange	590–620 nm	484–508 THz
Red	620–750 nm	400–484 THz

Referring to the table in this section, you can see that this particular frequency is right on the border between blue and violet.[603] It's also interesting to note that the seven colors of the visible spectrum are abbreviated ROYGBIV: red, orange, yellow, green, blue, indigo, and violet.

POLYHEDRA IN THE PLANT KINGDOM

Nature intrinsically loves geometry. Geometric perfection is one of the highest forms of perfection. I did some research into the geometric structure of pollen and discovered that nature also seems to find polyhedra to be optimal structures. Nature is a master of optimizing limited natural resources in such a way that creates beautiful symmetries and visually pleasing shapes with minimal weight and maximum strength.

The photos here depict several examples of pollen particles that have polyhedral form.[604]

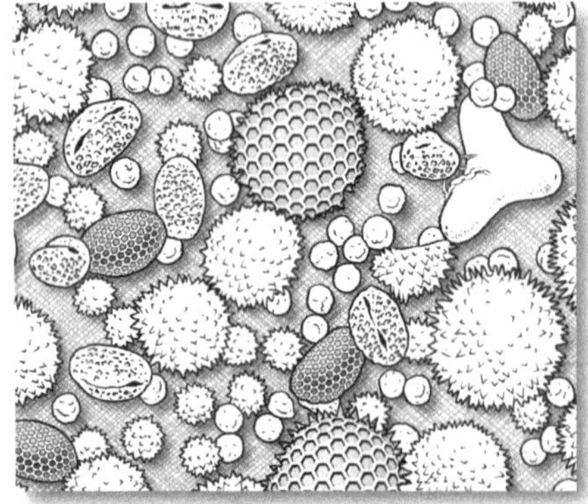

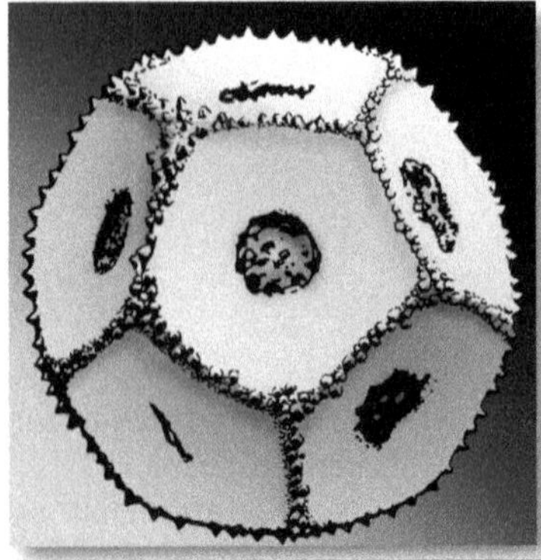

603 https://www.thoughtco.com/the-visible-light-spectrum-2699036.

604 https://www.pixcove.com/pollen-optical-microscope-electron-microscope-microscope-scan-image-plants-florae/.

A study by George Vasanthy and others[605] into the geometric structure of various pollen species found that many pollen types have a polyhedral form, and all the types they studied were composed of 5 pentagon faces and a varying number of hexagons similar to a soccer ball. Here we see again the molecular-level pentagon and hexagon motifs seem to be fundamental to all life-forms—not just in the DNA molecule but at a larger scale in the plant kingdom.[606]

POLYHEDRA IN THE FUNGUS KINGDOM

Polyhedra also occur in the fungus kingdom. The red cage fungus, whose official taxonomic name is *Clathrus ruber*, forms a beautiful polyhedron shape often composed of pentagons and hexagons.[607]

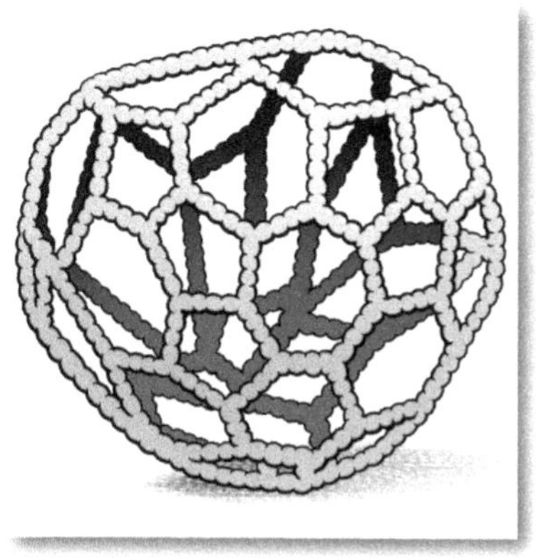

Clathrus ruber fungus

POLYHEDRA IN THE VIRUSES

In my research into the geometry of microscopic life-forms, I felt I should look into the shapes of viruses after I was pleasantly surprised by the diversity and beauty of pollen structures. I definitely wasn't disappointed. It was almost like looking at an alien life-form. There were so many degrees of symmetry and artful beauty. I'm sure some of these viruses could make me extremely sick or possibly dead, but I can still marvel at the beauty the Creator put into even the least of his creations.

The following is an artist's impression of what I found online.[608]

605 https://www.tandfonline.com/doi/pdf/10.1080/00173139309428977.

606 https://www.tandfonline.com/doi/pdf/10.1080/00173139309428977.

607 https://mushroomobserver.org/name/show_name/15220.

608 http://pubs.rsc.org/services/images/RSCpubs.ePlatform.Service.FreeContent.ImageService.svc/ImageService/Articleimage/2008/JM/b805874c/b805874c-f2.gif.

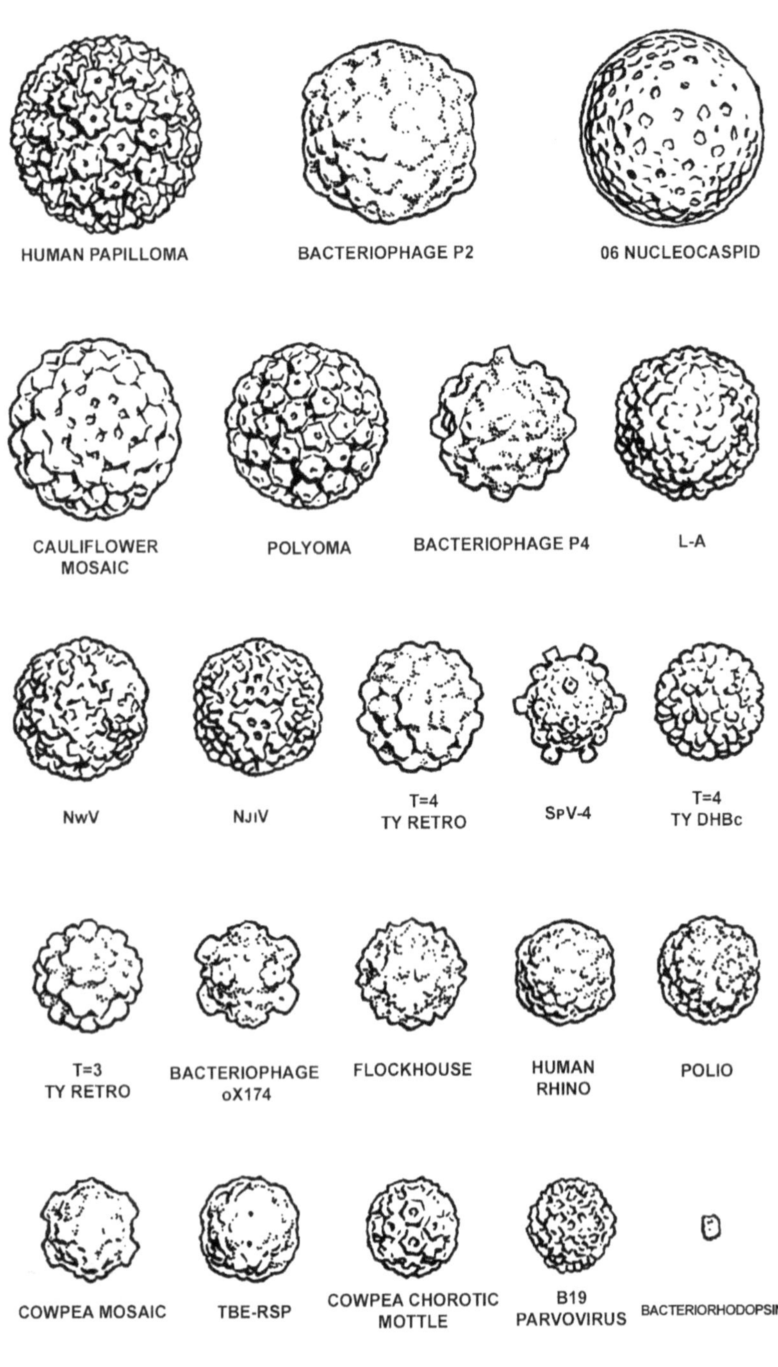
HUMAN PAPILLOMA
BACTERIOPHAGE P2
06 NUCLEOCASPID
CAULIFLOWER MOSAIC
POLYOMA
BACTERIOPHAGE P4
L-A
NwV
NJIV
T=4 TY RETRO
SPV-4
T=4 TY DHBc
T=3 TY RETRO
BACTERIOPHAGE oX174
FLOCKHOUSE
HUMAN RHINO
POLIO
COWPEA MOSAIC
TBE-RSP
COWPEA CHOROTIC MOTTLE
B19 PARVOVIRUS
BACTERIORHODOPSIN

Polyhedra in Fossils

While writing this book, I took numerous walks on the beaches of Lake Michigan and enjoyed my childhood hobby of being a beachcomber and rockhound. Among my favorite fossils to find are specimens of honeycomb coral, as seen in this section. You can readily identify both hexagons and pentagons in the cell structure.

Why do pentagons and hexagons keep showing up in various life-forms across all three kingdoms of life (animal, plant, and fungus)?

I find it intriguing to note that the number of sides on a pentagon (5) added to the number of edges on a hexagon (6) sums to 11, which plays the starring role in this book. Let's continue to dig deeper and see if we can get to the root of all this geometric beauty.

The following is a specimen of honeycomb coral fossil found on a beach five miles from my home. Have another peek at the title page, where I have a polyhedron composed of pentagons and hexagons.

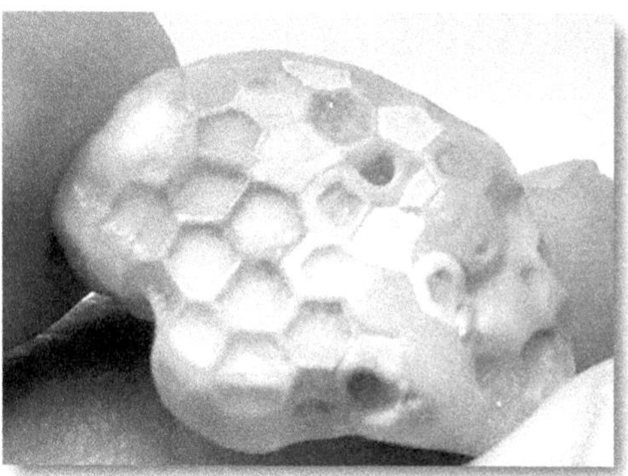

As a parting thought on this chapter on pentagons and hexagons in nature, let me leave you with the fact that every snowflake is a 6-pointed star and, just like all of nature's designs, each and every one is perfectly unique.

This calls for wisdom. Let the person who has insight calculate the number of the beast, for it is the number of a man.[a] That number is 666.

—Revelation 13:18[609]

Daniel, I now command you to keep the message of this book secret until the end of time, even though many people will go everywhere, searching for the knowledge to be found in it.

—Daniel 12:4[610]

---

609 https://www.biblegateway.com/passage/?search=Revelation+13%3A18&version=NIV
610 https://www.biblegateway.com/passage/?search=Daniel+12%3A4+&version=KJV.

CHAPTER 13

RELIGION

EASTER AND THE 11:11 CODE

During my childhood and into my adult years, I always found it perplexing and odd that the timing of the Easter observance moved to a different date every year. Without going into all the complicated details, suffice it to say that Easter always falls on a Sunday after the March 21 equinox and the first ecclesiastical full moon. As a numbers guy, I was interested in finding out the upper and lower bounds on the range of possible dates for Easter to occur, and once again, our old friend 22 showed up.[611] The earliest possible date for Easter occurs on March 22, as it is the first day that follows the March 21 equinox. The last time Easter fell on 3/22 was in the year 1818, and that date won't occur again until the year 2285, which is a span of 467 years between dates. It is intriguing to see 22 showing up in one of the most important religious observances celebrated on the planet.[612] Again, why 11 + 11? For my mathematically oriented readers, google "computus easter" and you'll be blown away by how complicated the calculation is to determine the date of Easter for each year![613] The intensive study of mathematics uncovers an inexhaustible supply of rabbit holes to research.

As a side note, the legend of the Easter Bunny has absolutely zilch to do with Christianity and is in fact a remnant of ancient Babylonian beliefs.

611 https://www.oikoumene.org/en/resources/documents/commissions/faith-and-order/i-unity-the-church-and-its-mission/frequently-asked-questions-about-the-date-of-easter

612 https://www.census.gov/srd/www/genhol/easter500.html.

613 https://en.wikipedia.org/wiki/Computus

Easter may derive its name from *Ishtar*, the ancient Babylonian name for the Mesopotamian goddess of fertility. The rabbit is known for its prolific reproductive capabilities.[614] Spring is a time of birth since the plant kingdom is awakening, flowering, and bearing fruit and seeds to create the next generation. The spring equinox also represents the time when light vanquishes darkness as the number of minutes of light in a twenty-four-hour period exceeds twelve hours for the first time since the day before the vernal (autumn) equinox.

While on the subject of calendars, it is noteworthy to observe that every month has on average 21.75 working days, which of course rounds nicely to 22 days. The average month has a total of about 30.5 days, comprised of 8.5 weekend days, leaving 22 working days.

THE NUMBER OF A MAN: 666

Revelation 13:18[615] refers to 666, and I'm not aware of another mathematical riddle being called out anywhere else in the Bible, but certainly, the writer is calling on any willing mathematician to give it a shot. Note that this is the 18th verse, in the 66th book of the Bible, and verse 18 = 6 + 6 + 6. Few numbers in the history of man have captured the imagination, intrigue, and fear as the number of man has. As with any good mystery, the focus should not necessarily be on solving the mystery but rather learning from the process of comprehending what meaning may be encoded within the puzzle. This section is added to show the complexity and richness of what meaning can be derived from dissecting this number. I attempted to pull together ideas from history, religion, geometry, and number theory to give a comprehensive overview of what the number means in the overall human story. I don't dwell on the darker connotations. I attempt to analyze it with the same scientific objectivity that I would reserve for any other number, despite its sinister reputation.

First Kings 10:14 (KJV) says, "Now the weight of gold that came to Solomon in one year was six hundred threescore and six talents of gold."[616] The term "score" represents a multiple of twenty.[617] So, the ancient math works out to: 600 + (3x20) + 6 = 666 talents of gold, where one talent is

614 https://en.m.wikipedia.org/wiki/Inanna.

615 https://www.biblegateway.com/passage/?search=Revelation+13%3A18&version=NIV

616 https://www.biblegateway.com/passage/?search=1+Kings+10%3A14&version=KJV

617 https://www.merriam-webster.com/dictionary/threescore

said to be equivalent to 60 pounds.[618] If there is any doubt in the foregoing calculation, we find confirmation in 2 Chronicles 9:13, which says, "The weight of the gold that Solomon received yearly was 666 talents."[619]

What is the significance of Solomon receiving 666 talents of gold every year?

Sixty talents works out to 39,960 pounds, and based on January 2019 gold prices when this section was written, totals $41,817 per kilogram or $19,007 per pound, which works out to a salary of $45,571,183,200 per year. He received this every year for forty years of his reign. Multiplying his annual salary by forty years, he should have been worth about $1.822 *trillion*!

In 2 Chronicles 7:5, we see the magic number 22 again. "And King Solomon offered a sacrifice of 22,000 head of cattle and 120,000 sheep and goats. So the king and all the people dedicated the temple of God."[620]

Interestingly, Thomas Edison is quoted as saying, "Gold is a relic of Julius Caesar, and interest is an invention of Satan."[621]

In modern culture we are taught that mysteries are meant to be solved. The Discovery Channel, Science Channel, and many other cable television programs are dedicated to cracking codes and unveiling ancient mysteries. I think this misses the main point of a divine mystery. If you kill the bird, you've got nothing but an empty cage. My analysis doesn't pretend to seek to put a mystery to rest but rather to bask in the wonder of trying to research and appreciate what can be learned through the process of inquiry. Humankind's quest to solve mysteries is an ego-based desire to claim triumph over the divine mystery as opposed to allowing the mystery to continue to shine on as a testament to the cosmic intellect that created it. I would like to again refer to a great quote by Seneca, who has greatly influenced my sentiments on the topic of mysteries.

"Our Universe is a sorry little affair unless it has in
it something for every age to investigate."[622]

618 http://www.secretsinplainsight.com/666/
619 https://biblehub.com/2_chronicles/9-13.htm
620 https://biblehub.com/2_chronicles/7-5.htm
621 https://timesmachine.nytimes.com/timesmachine/1921/12/06/98768710.pdf
622 https://www.goodreads.com/quotes/7675751-our-universe-is-a-sorry-little-affair-unless-it-has

THE APPLE

The second chapter of Genesis commanded us not to eat the fruit of the Tree of Knowledge of Good and Evil. What constitutes a *tree*? What does it mean to *eat* from it? Could partaking knowledge from an electronic tree (the internet) be a metaphorical equivalent of eating from the Tree of Knowledge of Good and Evil? Could it be something that is made of wires with the trunk circuit operating at 120 volts and branches breaking down to hundreds of circuits at 5–24 volts on the circuit boards and then breaking down to thousandths of a volt deep inside the extremely complex tree of circuits on the central processing unit and other integrated circuits? Would that electronic tree be capable of teaching us about good and evil? What can the internet teach us about those subjects? Why is the Apple logo a stylized apple with a bite taken out of it? Were they sending a deeper message, or was it all a huge coincidence? Think about Adam and Eve taking a bite from the Tree of Knowledge of Good and Evil? Could the garden of Eden metaphorically represent the process of how we become stripped of our childhood innocence by being exposed to learning—good and evil knowledge? Could this electronic tree be abstracted to include all forms of electronic media, including television and cell phones?

On April 11, 1976, Steve Jobs, the founder of the Apple computer company, launched the sale of the *Apple I* computer, and its initial price was set at $666.66, allegedly because his business partner, Dave Wozniak, was a big fan of repeating digits and simply put a 33 percent markup on the base price of $500. He claimed there was no religious or dark-occult intent in their choice of that price point, but I'm skeptical that anyone of their prominence could have been completely unaware of the darker connotations associated with this number. Apple's initial public offering of stock occurred on 12/12/1980, with an initial offering price of $22.00 (11 + 11) per share.[623]

Leading up to 11/11/19, one of Verizon's advertising campaigns displayed 11:11 over an invitation to "Make a wish and you could win iPhone 11 Pro."

Deepening the mystery still further, Isaac Newton is said to have been hit on the head by a falling apple in the year 1666, which led to his discovery of the universal law of gravitation, a key development without which

623 https://investor.apple.com/investor-relations/faq/

humankind would have never been able to develop rocketry to explore space.[624] Remember the gravitational constant is 6.67 x 10^{-11} [$m^3/kg*s^2$], which can be rewritten as 667 x 10^{-13}, which is within 0.18 percent of being exactly 666 x 10^{-13}, and it even has the unlucky number 13 in the exponent! The universal gravitational constant is used for all calculations pertaining to the force of gravity, whether we are launching a communications satellite or calculating the gravitational pull of a distant galaxy.

Revelation 13:15 states, "The second beast was given power to *give* **breath** *to the* **image** of the first beast, so that the *image could* **speak** and cause all who refused to worship the image to be killed."[625]

Sounds like a 2,000-year old description of present-day video technology, or perhaps artificial intelligence, don't you think? As a thought experiment in the context of the modern world, the beast might be thought of as the totality of all that is evil and available via the internet or through smart phone apps. I interpret the statement "to give breath to the image" to mean sending a picture through the air as in sending photos or video electronically via cell phones. Think spam, viruses, malware, pornography, bad news, and misinformation. Remember, they didn't have words to describe modern technology two millennia ago when the Bible was written. But certainly our creator would have written so cleverly as to guide his people through *all* ages. *Breath* implies air or wind, which suggests the image would be *blown* from one place to another. Sounds a lot like social media such as Instagram and YouTube were predicted to send images via electromagnetic waves (radio waves, cable TV signals, internet, Wi-Fi, cell phones, fiber optics, etc.) more than 2,000 years before it happened.

Today's smart phones have the capability to monitor every step we take and every beat of our hearts via technology such as the FitBit, spy on us through the camera and microphone, track our movements down to the nearest centimeter via GPS, and also monitor all calls, texts, and websites visited. Some phones have the ability to be unlocked by scanning our iris or fingerprints.

In Sweden, a company called Biohax leads the market for people who want to implant an RF device under the skin that can serve as a mode of touchless electronic payment and identification, while the national rail-

624 https://www.york.ac.uk/physics/about/newtonsappletree/

625https://www.biblegateway.com/passage/?search=Revelation+13%3A15-18&version=NIV

way company Sveriges Järnväg (SJ) even accepts it in lieu of a printed ticket.[626]

Going back to Revelation 13:15, what if the verse about giving breath to the image represents all forms of electronic information—phones, laptops, tablets, and televisions? Does ownership of a smart phone constitute acceptance of the mark of the beast? I hope not. If so, we're all doomed. Could the Apple iPhone be the modern day equivalent of the fruit of the tree of knowledge of good and evil? Why is there a bite missing from the Apple logo? I really like my iPhone and have decided to use it exclusively for good! This is a choice we all have to make. God gives us the free will to choose light or dark, but we have to pick a side!

ALL ROADS LEAD TO ROME

One of the most intriguing facts I discovered during my research on this subject comes from an understanding of the Roman numeral system. Take the first six Roman numerals (D = 500, C = 100, L = 50, X = 10, V = 5, and I = 1). Add these up, and you'll certainly arrive at 666, an exercise I invite the reader to try. I find this quite fascinating. While in the vein of ancient interpretations, using the technique of Gematria (assigning a numerical value to each letter of the alphabet and then summing the values of the letters in a word), the Hebrew name for Nero Caesar (רסקןורנ or Nero Kassar) has a numeric value of 666.[627] With Nero as one of the arch enemies of Israel in biblical times, this may be a very direct reference to him being the root of all that was considered evil at that time.

Here's one last fact on Israel. On May 22, 2017, President Trump became the first sitting US president to visit one of Israel's holy sites with a stop at the Western Wall in Jerusalem.[628]

THE NUMBER 112

Around the same time the FISA memo was dropped, there was a covert raid on the Rothschild family's estate in Austria, which was an estate the size of Manhattan with a massive mansion. Shortly after the raid, the property was sold for $112 million. Most interestingly of all, 112 is the

626 https://www.npr.org/2018/10/22/658808705/thousands-of-swedes-are-inserting-microchips-under-their-skin
627 https://israelstudycenter.com/666-or-616
628 https://www.nbcnews.com/storyline/trumps-first-foreign-trip/trump-becomes-first-sitting-u-s-president-visit-western-wall-n762891

European equivalent of the 9-1-1 emergency phone number! Keep the number 112 in mind.

Stop and take 10 seconds to perform an internet search for an image of the coat of arms of the Rothschild family. Notice the colors and the specific animals called out, then compare what you see against the verse below.

Revelation 9:17 reads:

> The horses and riders I saw in my vision looked like this: Their breastplates were fiery red, dark blue, and yellow as sulfur. The heads of the horses resembled the heads of lions, and out of their mouths came fire, smoke and sulfur.[629]

This was a vision of the forces of evil in the end times. As this is a black-and-white book, the reader is urged to look up the family coat of arms on the internet and compare the descriptions of the colors, animals, and other symbology. I'll let the readers draw their own conclusions.

Revelation 13:2 states:

> And the beast which I saw was like unto a leopard, and his feet were as the feet of a bear, and his mouth as the mouth of a lion: and the dragon gave him his power, and his seat, and great authority.[630]

Again, the prophetic imagery bears a striking resemblance to that seen in the Rothschild family crest, doesn't it? If you didn't look it up, I strongly encourage you to do it before continuing reading.

Let's shift gears slightly while continuing into the 112 topic. Each of the Vatican popes has had a motto associated with their papacy. Pope Francis is the 112th pope. After a review of Prophecy of the Popes, I learned it was foretold that pope #112 would be the *last* pope. Pope Francis chose the following as his motto:

> Peter the Roman, who will pasture his sheep in many tribulations, and when these things are finished, the city of seven hills [i.e. Rome] will be destroyed, and the dreadful judge will judge his people. The End.[631]

This seems to very clearly suggest that the Vatican has been planning for some sort of apocalypse to occur during the reign of the 112th pope. Did

629 https:// https://www.biblegateway.com/passage/?search=Revelation+9%3A17&version=NIV

630 https://www.biblegateway.com/passage/?search=Revelation+13%3A2+&version=KJV

631 http://www.catholic-pages.com/grabbag/malachy.asp

the Rothschilds and their global financial cabal signal the end of their world by throwing up the numbers 112 and 666?

It is interesting to note that the prime factorization of 112 is (2 x 2 x 2 x 2) x 7. The number 112 is also a heptagonal number, meaning that it can be drawn as a 7-sided polygon with 16 dots on each edge. An interesting property of the regular 7-pointed star is that the included angles within each point work out to about 77 degrees. This is particularly interesting when we reflect upon the fact that 7 is buried within the prime factorization of the number 112. I'm of the opinion that 112 may be an archaic, secret distress code within the global elite cabal.

Interestingly, at the time of publishing, a movie titled *Two Popes* was nominated for 2 Oscar awards for a movie that addresses the challenges of the controversy that currently surrounds the church.[632]

Delving Deeper into the 666 Code

It is also interesting to notice that the Chicago zip code 60606 breaks down as 7 x 13 x 666, and by now the reader is acquainted with the significance of all three of those factors. I'm not drawing any conclusions about the city of Chicago. I love Chicago and have always considered it an extension of my home city. Rather, I'm just putting it here for mathematical curiosity. Furthermore, 60606 = 6 x 10101, and the number 10101 has some truly fascinating and unexpected properties that I happened to discover during the process of writing this book, many of which will be explained a bit later.

I'd like to mention that the lowest assigned zip code is 00501, belonging to the Internal Revenue Service in Holtsville, New York.[633] A recurring theme in this book will be one of cosmic irony. Think about how the absolute lowest of all zip codes was reserved for the tax collector! To round out this brief foray into interesting zip codes, I'd hate to segue into the next topic without first mentioning that zip code 22222 is in Arlington, Virginia; the Department of Defense headquarters, the Pentagon, is in 22202; and many of our nation's greatest heroes are buried at Arlington National Cemetery, in postal code 22211. In keeping with the book's title, it may also interest the reader to know that the IRS headquarters is located

632 https://mol.im/a/7976207
633 https://facts.usps.com/size-and-scope/.

at 1111 Constitution Avenue in Washington, DC.[634] It's interesting how an agency of financial oppression has cloaked itself in the white robe of the word *constitution* along with the 1111 awakening code.

I like prime factorizations because they tell us what's silently lurking *inside* of a number, sort of like getting into its genetic code and understanding its numerical heritage. It is further interesting to note that 37 is a star number. As a prime number, it has no multiplicative ancestors, so it can be thought of as being in a class of high nobility, a pure breed among numbers. Star numbers are generated by the function $S = 6n^2 - 6n + 1$ for any whole number n and gives the outputs S = 1, 13, 37, 73, 121 .... It can be readily seen that all these numbers result in a 6-pointed star.

The word *beast* was mentioned 37 times in the apocalypse story. Mark 14:30 is the story of Judas betraying Jesus. "And Jesus said to him, Truly I say to you, that this very night, before a rooster crows twice, you yourself will deny Me three times."[635]

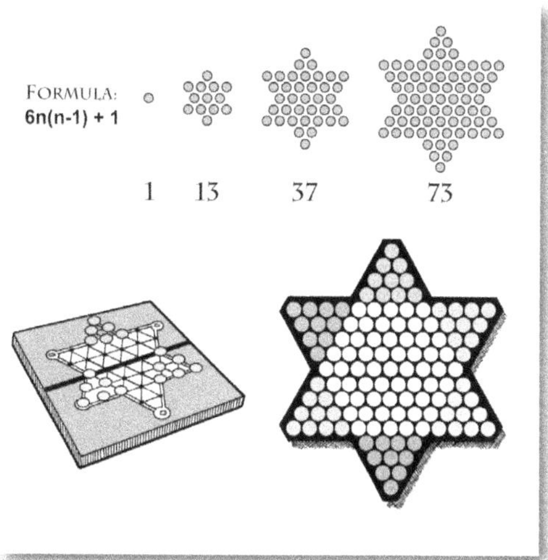

First four star numbers. Chinese checkerboard with 37 spots. Chinese checkerboard with 121 spots. Note that the array of 13 stars above the eagle on the right side of the back of a US one-dollar bill also forms a star that follows this pattern. Note the star number 1 is the degenerate case of the formula. It really isn't a star, but mathematicians like to show all possibilities, even the ones that aren't particularly useful.

634 https://www.irs.gov/about-irs/the-agency-its-mission-and-statutory-authority.
635 https://www.biblegateway.com/passage/?search=Mark14%3A30+&version=NIV.

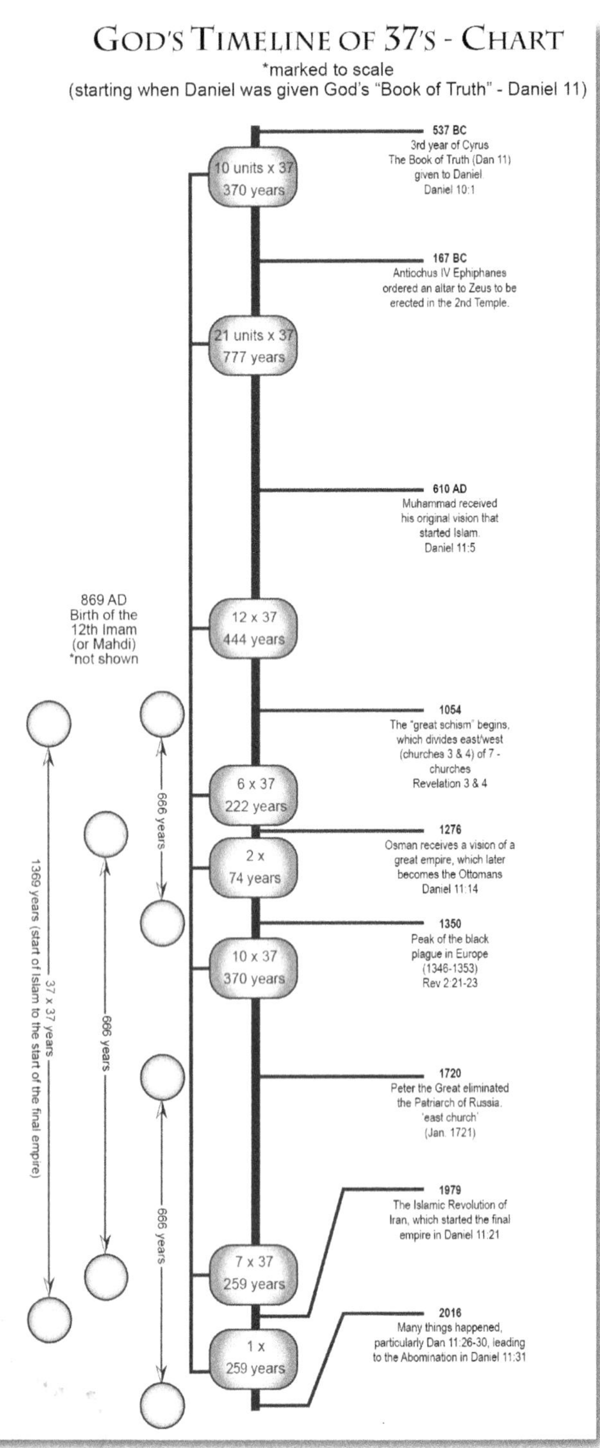
GOD'S TIMELINE OF 37'S - CHART
*marked to scale
(starting when Daniel was given God's "Book of Truth" - Daniel 11)
537 BC
3rd year of Cyrus
The Book of Truth (Dan 11) given to Daniel
Daniel 10:1
10 units x 37
370 years
167 BC
Antiochus IV Ephiphanes ordered an altar to Zeus to be erected in the 2nd Temple.
21 units x 37
777 years
610 AD
Muhammad received his original vision that started Islam.
Daniel 11:5
869 AD
Birth of the 12th Imam (or Mahdi)
*not shown
12 x 37
444 years
1054
The "great schism" begins, which divides east/west (churches 3 & 4) of 7 - churches
Revelation 3 & 4
6 x 37
222 years
666 years
1276
Osman receives a vision of a great empire, which later becomes the Ottomans
Daniel 11:14
2 x
74 years
1350
Peak of the black plague in Europe (1346-1353)
Rev 2:21-23
10 x 37
370 years
1369 years (start of Islam to the start of the final empire) 37 x 37 years
666 years
1720
Peter the Great eliminated the Patriarch of Russia. 'east church' (Jan. 1721)
1979
The Islamic Revolution of Iran, which started the final empire in Daniel 11:21
666 years
7 x 37
259 years
2016
Many things happened, particularly Dan 11:26-30, leading to the Abomination in Daniel 11:31
1 x
259 years

While we are at it, here are some more fun facts on the number 37. Any 6-digit number that has the form ABCZYX, where A, B, and C are increasing consecutive numbers and Z, Y, and X are decreasing consecutive numbers, the number ABCZYX will be divisible by 37. For example, the number 123987 divides by 37 to give an answer of 3,351.[636]

As a bit of fun trivia on the number 37, US Interstate highway 37 runs from Corpus Christi (Latin for *body of Christ*) to San Antonio, Texas (Spanish for *Saint Anthony*).

The number 37 is very richly embedded into many centuries of recorded human history. In the graphic that follows, the timeline shows numerous historical events that were spaced apart in time by multiples of 37 years.

It is notable that there are 37 miracles in the Bible. The curious reader is urged to dig deeper at the daniel11truth.com website.[637]

The Beast in the Library

According to Martin Gardner's "Dr. Matrix" columns, the Dewey Decimal System classification number for numerology is 133.335. If you reverse this and add, you get 133.335 + 533.331 = 666.666.[638] When I first read this fact, I was skeptical about such a coincidence, so I verified it independently and found it is indeed true! This can be verified at the US Library of Congress website.[639]

To leave things on a happier note, the reader should be pleased to know that the range of 220 – 229 in the Dewey system is reserved for the Bible.[640] A table below summarizes how the range is subdivided:

Dewey Code	Description
220	Bible
221	Old Testament
222	Historical books of Old Testament
223	Poetic books of Old Testament
224	Prophetic books of Old Testament
225	New Testament
226	Gospels & Acts
227	Epistles
228	Revelation (apocalypse)
229	Apocrypha & pseudepigrapha

636 http://thirty-seven.org/.
637 http://daniel11truth.com.
638 http://www.cadaeic.net/666.htm.
639 https://catalog.loc.gov.
640 https://library.moody.edu/crowell-library-chicago/begin-your-search/dewey-decimal-guides/200-299-religion-dewey-decimal-guide/.

Is it a pure coincidence that all of the Dewey decimal designations for the Bible occur in the 220s, or is this just another example of many diverse, seemingly unrelated concepts being tied together at a very high level through numbers?

EXODUS 25 AND THE NUMBER 37

> Make a lampstand of pure gold. Hammer out its base and shaft, and make its flowerlike cups, buds and blossoms of one piece with them. Six branches are to extend from the sides of the lampstand—three on one side and three on the other. Three cups shaped like almond flowers with buds and blossoms are to be on one branch, three on the next branch, and the same for all six branches extending from the lampstand. And on the lampstand there are to be four cups shaped like almond flowers with buds and blossoms. One bud shall be under the first pair of branches extending from the lampstand, a second bud under the second pair, and a third bud under the third pair—six branches in all. The buds and branches shall all be of one piece with the lampstand, hammered out of pure gold.
>
> —Exodus 25:31–36[641]

Add up the features, and you'll have 6 branches each with 3 appendages for 18. After placing 4 cups on top, you have 18 + 4 = 22 features in the arrangement being described.

Exodus 25:37 continues, "Then make its seven lamps and set them up on it so that they light the space in front of it."[642] This is a very esoteric, coded passage of scripture, with an arrangement including the numbers 22 and 7 in the instructions, so I must ask what the deeper message is here? Could it be a metaphor in which 22 stands for the various branches of science illumined by the 7 fundamental units of scientific measurement? Dividing 7 into 22 gives 3.14 or pi. *Hmmmph…*

Further deepening the mysterious description in Exodus 25, the Bible's description of the 22 parts of the golden lampstand is repeated almost verbatim once again in Exodus 37:17–24. Recalling that 37 is a star number, we are being reminded that whatever obscure message is being commu-

641 https://www.biblegateway.com/passage/?search=Exodus+25%3A31-36%2CExodus+37%3A17-22&version=NIV
642 https://www.biblegateway.com/passage/?search=Exodus+25%3A37&version=NIV

nicated in chapter 25 was important enough to repeat! Most mysteries are not meant to be solved but rather pondered and admired.

Take a moment and pull up the song "Grandyzer" by Lifeblood. It's such a beautiful song.

CHURCH OF ELEVEN22

While living in Florida in 2018, I found that there was a church in Jacksonville named the Church of Eleven22. Who would have ever thought? After looking into it, I was surprised to learn that it is a church with nearly 6,000 members spanning five campuses across the Jacksonville area. I was expecting some eccentric, fledgling cult operating in the back of a strip mall somewhere on the backside of town. Unable to fight off my curiosity, I took the family on a three-hour drive one Sunday to attend the church and experience it firsthand. What we found was an immaculate, contemporary church with a rock concert music system that rattled your rib cage and a powerful, well-delivered sermon. The energy in the room was palpable, and the majority of congregants appeared to be between the ages of fifteen and forty-five. Church services begin at 7:22 a.m. for early service and 11:22 a.m. for the late session. When I spoke with the pastor and asked for the motivation behind the name and also explained a bit about this book, he told me that I might be a little bit disappointed if I was looking for a deeply mystical reason. He simply stated that Mark 11:22 says, "Have faith in God, Jesus said to them."[643]

But why the 22-minute starting times for the services? The church website offers the following simple albeit incomplete answer:

> Under the leadership of Pastor Jerry Sweat, Beach Church started a weekly worship gathering to reach ages 18–35, the 'lost' generation—the un-churched, the de-churched. Pastor Jerry asked Pastor Joby Martin to lead this new service held Sundays at 11:22 AM.[644]

In any case, it was an interesting and enjoyable visit and certainly added a nice new dimension to the overall story that I am trying to tell here. It reaffirmed to me that I am not alone in my curiosity with the numbers 11 and 22. There are at least 6,000 more people in addition to the millions of people who searched for answers about these numbers on Google.

643 https://www.biblegateway.com/passage/?search=Mark+11%3A22-24&version=NIV
644 https://www.coe22.com/ourstory/

Visiting the San Pablo campus of the Church of Eleven22 in Jacksonville, Florida

A Cross Underwater

On March 11, 2019, I was casually reading on the FoxNews website and came upon a headline about a 1,850-pound crucifix statue made of marble in Italy in the waters of Lake Michigan, the lake I lived most of my life on the shores of. Curious, I opened the story and was shocked to see my favorite numbers showing up once again. The statue of Jesus on the cross is 11 feet tall and is sitting in 22 feet of water.[645] In summation, 11 + 22 = 33, the age of Christ at death. What's the deeper message here?

The 11-foot-tall crucifix with a 5-foot, 5-inch figure of Jesus Christ was placed in the Bay near the Petoskey breakwall at Bayfront Park by the Wyandotte-based Superior Marine Divers Club in 1962. Its original intent was to honor Charles Raymond, a Southgate diver who drowned in Torch Lake. Later, the club expanded the focus of the monument to memorialize all those who have perished at sea.[646]

The Golden Ratio in Ancient Religion

There are theories that many of the ancient classical structures, such as the Egyptian pyramids, the Parthenon, and ancient Roman ruins, may

645 https://www.foxnews.com/faith-values/hundreds-line-up-on-frozen-lake-michigan-to-view-giant-underwater-crucifix

646 https://www.emmetcounty.org/underwater-crucifix-petoskey/

have been constructed with the golden proportion in mind. In my research I was not able to find enough agreement between experts in order to suggest here that it is truly the case. But I do want to offer it for your consideration. Then you can draw your own conclusions or do your own research.

Well-known research has shown that paintings and other works of art with the proportions of 1:1.6 are the most pleasing to the eye.

Television screen height-to-width aspect ratios were set to the golden proportion.

In the Bible, 1 Kings 7:6 describes the proportions of King Solomon's temple as being 50 cubits long by 30 cubits wide. Dividing the length by the width gives 5/3 = 1.60, which is within 1.1 percent of the exact value of the golden ratio, phi (≈ 1.618).

The ratio of the ark of the covenant is close to the golden ratio within the same amount of error as if you fibbed about the age of your one-year-old child's age by rounding up by just four days. Why should we be any pickier about rounding by the same 1.1 percent? If you lost 1.1 percent of your body mass, would you notice it? I think it's not too much of a stretch to conclude that the ark of the covenant was essentially commanded to have the physical proportions of the golden ratio. They may not have developed the concept of a decimal point to make such an accurate calculation at the time. Anyway, let's not miss the forest for the trees here!

Exodus 25:10 says, "Have them make a chest of acacia wood, two and a half cubits long, a cubit and a half wide, and a cubit and a half high."[647]

This verse calls for the ark of the covenant (to hold the tablets of the Ten Commandments) to be made of acacia wood (refer to the section on the number 322 for the significance of acacia) with the proportions of $^{2.5}/_{1.5} = 1.667$, which is within 3.0 percent of the golden ratio.

Regarding the proportions of Noah's ark, Genesis 6:15 states, "And this is the fashion which thou shalt make it of: The length of the ark shall be three hundred cubits, the breadth of it fifty cubits, and the height of it thirty cubits." The ratio of breadth to width is again .5/3 = 1.60. The fact that the ark of the covenant was commanded to be made of acacia wood

647 https://www.biblegateway.com/passage/?search=Exodus+25%3A10-22&version=NIV

cannot be emphasized enough. Remember, the acacia inner root bark contains some of the highest concentrations of DMT in all of nature.

Revelation 22

The last chapter of the Bible, Revelation 22, seems to give the impression that the authors wanted to leave the best for last. (Think 11 + 11) In my viewpoint, this, the concluding chapter of the Book of Life, describes what happens at the moment of death when the human story reaches the end of its last chapter.

Revelation is among the most mysterious, abstract, and misunderstood books of the Bible. I consider it one of the more fascinating books. The purpose of this section is to peel back the layers of the onion and offer a deeper interpretation of what this highly complex and symbolic book may be trying to communicate to the reader.

Revelation 22:1 says, "Then he showed me a pure river of the water of life, clear as crystal, flowing from the throne of God and of the Lamb in the middle of its street."

The *pure river of the water of life* refers to the cerebrospinal fluid (CSF) that surrounds and bathes the brain and spinal cord. I credit the deceased author George Washington Carey for teaching me through his book *God-Man: The Word Made Flesh* about the symbolic correspondences between biblical concepts and the human body.[648] CSF protects the brain and central nervous system (CNS), nourishing the spinal cord and brain with nutrients and removing waste products from those systems. CSF also acts as a transport medium for various brain hormones and neurotransmitters. The *throne of God* possibly refers to the pineal gland, which produces dimethyltryptamine (DMT), the molecule many believe to be responsible for human consciousness and near-death experiences. Thus, it could hold the key to the door to the heavenly realms of existence. *The lamb* possibly refers to the gatekeeper of the pineal gland—the thalamus—when our egos control our thoughts and actions. For example, our addiction to things of this world, such as money, power, alcohol, drugs, sex, food, and others, act to build up our egos. The ego is the brick wall between a person and full realization of knowing God. Destruction of the ego renders the person to the status of the lamb—pure, innocent, vulnerable,

648 George Carey and Ines Eudora Perry, *God-Man: The Word Made Flesh* (Mansfield Centre, CT: Martino Publishing, 2013).

and peaceful. When we reach the lamb state, the pineal gland performs its function and freely produces increasing levels of DMT, increasing our sense of spirituality and connectedness, and it can even go so far as to give us a sense of being born again. *The lamb* may also be a reference to the lamblike, grayish, nebulous appearance of our brains as an alternate interpretation, or perhaps this is a dual reference. Lastly, *the middle of its street* refers to the chasm between the two hemispheres of the brain where the CSF flows freely, and it is also worthy of note that all the glands in the human endocrine system come in pairs (adrenals, testes, ovaries, thyroid, etc.) with the noble exception of the solitary pineal gland, which is situated deep in the center of the brain by itself, with no binary companion.

In the story of Christ's crucifixion, it is interesting to note that he died on Calvary or Golgotha. In Latin, *calvary* means skull, and similarly, *golgotha* means skull in Aramaic. In Greek, *christos* means oil. The story tells that Jesus was crucified between two thieves. Think about the physical location of the pineal gland. It is located in the center of the brain between the eyes. Could Christ (Greek for oil) also double as a metaphor for the CSF flowing through our central nervous system? Could the thieves represent the two eyes that allow us to perceive things in the physical world that give rise to greed, gluttony, and lust, distracting or *stealing our focus* from the purely spiritual realm? Certainly it was originally written to retell what actually happened, but could what happened and how that was written down have been divinely designed to also speak figuratively to mankind over time? I would offer that it is probably a combination of an actual event that happened millennia ago and giving a sublime message that the same process happens to all of us at some point in our life.

Let's get back to comparing human anatomy to the description in Revelation 22.

Revelation 22:2 says, "On each side of the river was the tree of life, which bore twelve kinds of fruit, yielding its fruit each month. The leaves of the tree were for the healing of the nations."[649]

One possible interpretation is that the Tree of Life is the nervous system, which could be seen as an upside-down tree with the brain as the ball of roots, the brainstem and spinal cord as the trunk, and the nerves that branch off the spinal cord as the limbs and twigs. This makes further sense

649 https://www.biblegateway.com/passage/?search=Revelation+22%3A2&version=NIV

when we consider that the human brain has twelve pairs of cranial nerves, each with its specific purpose. There is a single, solitary 13th cranial nerve referred to as the terminal nerve. It is largely considered to be vestigial, with some scientists claiming that it is a holdover from archaic stages of human evolution and may have been involved with the olfactory sensing of pheromones.[650] This follows along a similar blueprint as Jesus and his twelve disciples and twelve jurors serving under a judge.

The *fruits* of the tree could be thought of as the senses connected to the cranial nerve pairs (twelve fruits on each side of the river of life, perhaps referring to each hemisphere of the brain). The cranial nerves are the very essence of what makes us human. They control all our senses as well as the functions of our vital organs.

A wonderful book called *God-Man: The Word Made Flesh* by medical doctor George Washington Carey and Ines Eudora Perry, published in the year 1920, comes highly recommended to anyone wanting to take this symbolism further into interpreting the mysteries of the Bible as they pertain to the human body.[651]

650 https://en.wikipedia.org/wiki/Terminal_nerve
651 George Carey and Ines Eudora Perry, *God-Man: The Word Made Flesh* (Mansfield Centre, CT: Martino Publishing, 2013).

I form the light, and create darkness: I make peace,
and create evil: I the LORD do all these things.

—Isaiah 45:7[652]

There exists, if I am not mistaken, an entire world which is the totality of mathematical truths, to which we have access only with our mind, just as a world of physical reality exists, the one like the other independent of ourselves, both of divine creation.

—Charles Hermite (Paris, 1912)[653]

652 https://biblehub.com/isaiah/45-7.htm
653 https://www.maa.org/press/periodicals/convergence/quotations/hermite-charles-1822-1901-1

CHAPTER 14

SPIRITUALITY

Modern Pyramids of Power and Idolatry

The pyramid is a shape that has come to signify power and authority as far back as human history goes. Is it any surprise that it still is used symbolically by the powerful elite to remind us of their positions of power and control? Why is a pyramid and the all-seeing eye on the back of the US dollar bill? Is it any wonder that a Google search of the terms "Oscar award pyramid" turns up a plethora of images of statuettes being worshipped in front of pyramids? Remember the television game show from the 1980s, *The $25,000 Pyramid?* An entire game show dedicated to the worship of money and pyramids.

Stop now for a moment and Google search "$25,000 Pyramid" and select "images." What do you see? It is our overlords indoctrinating us to worship the almighty dollar! Think about it. We have all been brainwashed all our lives. No wonder God is such a difficult topic for us to comprehend.

Inside the Great Pyramid

The Bible has a lot to say about idol worship. Leviticus 19:4 says, "Do not turn to idols or make metal gods for yourselves. I am the Lord your

God."[654] In Second Chronicles 13:8 it talks about worshipping golden calves. "So now you intend to resist the kingdom of the LORD through the sons of David, being a great multitude and having with you the golden calves which Jeroboam made for gods for you."[655] What statue is built into the sidewalk outside of the New York Stock Exchange on Wall Street? A bronze bull. In my opinion it is a symbol of our greed and money worship, as a society.

Obsessive watching of television may constitute idol worship too, in my opinion. For example, take professional hockey draws on fans' attention for an entire season with each team's aspiration of earning the coveted Stanley Cup. Football has the Heisman and Lombardi trophies depicting the victory of man in a metal statue. The entire football season builds up to the all-encompassing Super Bowl event, and the winners get massive rings. All of our professional sports have similar rituals and ceremonies. In my view, this is all part of what Roman poet Decimus Iunius Iuvenalis, better known as Juvenal, referred to as "bread and circuses" or *panem et circenses* as a means of keeping the populace fat, dumb, and happy and thus distracted from the wiles of the ruling class.

The entertainment industry has a similar way of maintaining our focus and attention throughout the year. Award shows that represent the movie industry, music industry, and acting also have awards that beckon our worship. The Emmy Award is composed of a gilded angel on a pedestal. The Academy Award is a bronze statuette of a man similar to the Egyptian god Ptah. Perform an internet search for the terms "Egypt Ptah Oscars," and see what I'm talking about. The Tony Award is a silver coin trophy. MTV Music Award trophy is a silver statue of a man on the moon holding up the MTV flag staff.

According to Gregory Sams,

> The shift away from the directed worship of organized religion is perhaps being offset by a substantial increase in those who worship a growing array of celebrity figures. The media, sports, and entertainment industries constantly create celebrities to satisfy humanity's seemingly insatiable urge to adulate. Film stars who are adored

654 https://biblehub.com/leviticus/19-4.htm.

655 https://bible.knowing-jesus.com/topics/Golden-Calves.

> throughout the world achieve almost godlike status by pretending to be other people.[656]

By filling our minds with Hollywood's images of what they think we should be worshipping, they distract us from looking and listening within ourselves and within nature to find the true God's subtle voice. As the axiom goes, "Name the color, blind the eye." By filling our spiritual stomachs up with junk food, we are often left with no cravings for true spiritual knowledge and connection, and thus, we become complacent in looking for the truth.

THE 11:11 CODE IN EGYPT

Now that we have given some modern context to ancient Egypt, let's dig into Egypt! Of all the countries I have been to, no place on Earth holds greater mystery. Even the world's most traveled explorer, Donald M. Parrish, Jr., has stated similar impressions.

On 11/11 of 2008, a 118th pyramid was discovered in Saqqara, Egypt, which is estimated to date back to the year 2291 during the sixth dynasty under the rulership of Queen Sesheshet. The newly discovered pyramid measured 5 meters tall by 22 meters wide on each side.[657]

As mentioned already, there are a total of 118 fundamental chemical elements that comprise the material building blocks of the universe as we currently understand it. According to Egyptian archaeologist Dr. Abdel Hakim Awyan, there is an ancient hospital structure at Saqqara known as the House of Spirit, which has 22 investigation tables, 11 on each side of the hallway, each where a physician would visit his patients.[658]

656 Gregory Sams, *Sun of gOd: Discover the Self-Organizing Consciousness That Underlies Everything* (San Francisco: Weiser Books, 2009).

657 https://latimesblogs.latimes.com/babylonbeyond/2008/11/egypt-make-that.html.

658 https://egyptexperience.wordpress.com/2011/06/09/abdul-hakim-aywan-mystical-wisdom-keeper/.

In *The Secret in the Bible*, Tony Bushby wrote about the significance of the number 22 in ancient Egyptian spiritual awakening rituals. Citing the Egyptian *Book of the Dead*, he lays out the 22 locations within the Great Pyramid of Giza as well as beneath the great Sphinx. The initiates are directed through a series of 22 trials as they course through dark, hidden passages riddled with false doors, invisible drop-offs in the floor, mazes, and sensory deprivation. Here is a quick sampling of some of the 22 locations within the pyramid complex:

1. Chamber of the ordeal
2. The hall of truth in light
3. The gate of death
4. The false door
5. …and so on…

Bushby resides in Alexandria, Egypt, where he studies ancient literary works. He claims that the 22 trials correspond to the 22 symbols in the book of Thoth, which also correspond to the 22 divine letters. In turn, these correspond to 22 different shadows of a serpent viewed from many different angles. He further asserts that the secret in the Bible is encoded in Psalm 119 (discussed earlier) with each 8-verse section corresponding to one letter of the Hebrew alphabet.[659] It is utterly fascinating to me to know that James Clerk Maxwell, one of the three greatest scientists of all time along with Einstein and Newton, had committed Psalm 119 to memory by age 8 and later in life would be given the mathematical insights to comprehend the deep mysteries of light and electromagnetism. Just wait until you see what I have to say about Maxwell, one of the founding fathers of electricity and magnetism, the foundation upon which my entire career was built. I'm saving the very best for last, and we are almost there. Few things excite me more than a study of Maxwell's achievements and the struggles he overcame.

Bushby states that in the tomb of Miraroka at Saqqara, there are 22 female dancers inscribed on a stone wall with their arms and legs in various positions that depict (in outline) each of the sacred symbols of Thoth, the author of the Egyptian *Book of the Dead*.[660]

659 Tony Bushby, *The Secret in the Bible* (Queensland, Australia: Joshua Books, 2003), 265, 314.
660 Ibid., 318.

Consider the following red herring: While not directly related to Egypt, as long as we are on the topic of antiquities, I'd like to mention that in *The Mystery of Numbers*, Schimmel states that *Avesta*, the scripture of the ancient religion of Zoroastrianism, which predates the Abrahamic religions, contains 22 prayers.[661]

> For an excellent video on this subject, please look up the following on YouTube: "This Truth May Scare You See This Before it is Deleted 2018-2019 EVENTS WORLD EARTH UNIVERSE" by Anonymous Official.[662]

I'll conclude this section with one more tantalizing bit of trivia. In the 11th month of 1922, Howard Carter discovered King Tutankhamun's (King Tut's) tomb.[663]

THE KABBALAH CONNECTION

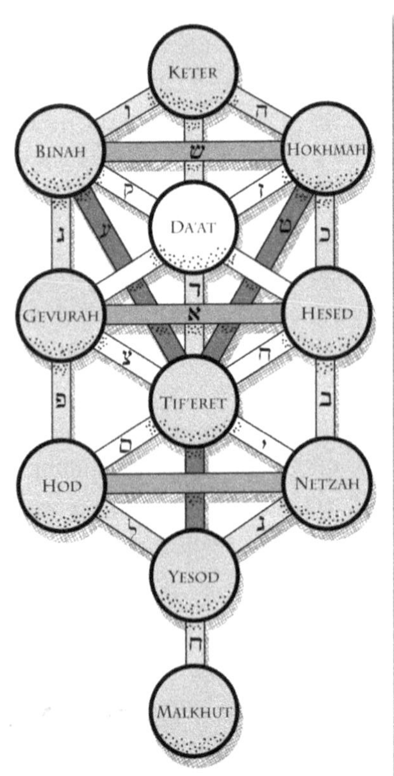

The Kabbalistic Tree of Life (also known as the *Yosher*) is illustrated here. The ten spheres or sephirot (the *-ot* ending indicates the plural in Hebrew) are the ten emanations or illuminations of God's infinite light as it manifests in creation. As revelations of the Creator's will, the sephirot should not be understood as ten different gods but as ten different channels through which the one God reveals his will. All three of the Abrahamic religions of Christianity, Judaism, and Islam each have their mystical or arcane counterpart—Gnosticism, Kabbalah, and Sufism respectively.

According to the Sacred Texts website, the Sephirothic Tree consists of ten globes of luminous splendor

661 Annemarie Schimmel, The *Mystery of Numbers* (Oxford: Oxford University Press, 1993), 234.
662 https://www.youtube.com/watch?v=tk7A-oOtjWM.
663 https://www.nationalgeographic.com/archaeology-and-history/magazine/2018/03-04/findingkingtutstomb/.

arranged in 3 vertical columns and connected by 22 channels or paths. (Think: 3/22) The ten globes are called the sephiroth and to them are assigned the numbers 1 to 10. The three columns are called *mercy* (on the right), *severity* (on the left), and between them, *mildness* as the reconciling power. The columns may also be said to represent wisdom, strength, and beauty, which form the triune support of the universe, for it is written that the foundation of all things is the *three*. The 22 channels are the letters of the Hebrew alphabet, and to them are assigned the major trumps of the tarot deck of symbolic cards.[664] The Yosher (straightness, uprightness) provides a framework and procedure for achieving enlightenment.

Let's pause for a moment and make a few key observations. The Yosher has 10 spheres and 22 paths between them and represents a road map to human enlightenment.

As mentioned earlier, Thomas Edison demonstrated the first viable light bulb on 10/22. Furthermore, I mentioned in the section on the planet Mars a deep connection between the speed of light and the time it takes for light to travel between their closest and farthest approaches—3 and 22 minutes respectively. The Yosher is composed of 22 paths and is arranged into 3 distinct columns. My birthday is 3/22. The Yosher bears an odd resemblance to that of a large light bulb, doesn't it?

Suggested video: Yuri Kane - Right Back (Official Video)

Understanding Universal Duality

One of the keys to making the most sense out of your experiences with spiritual awakening is understanding universal duality. Virtually everything in the world exhibits duality. In life, we have the male and female gender. You cannot create life without the union of the two.

In magnetism, there are north and south poles to every magnet. It is not possible to create a monopole magnet with only a north or a south pole. If you break a two-inch magnet in half, the two one-inch halves will instantly possess their own unique north and south poles, but the magnetic flux of each magnet will be halved. If you were to shave off the last one-millionth of an inch of the magnet, that thin shaving would immediately exhibit both north and south poles of its own with one-millionth of the original magnet's flux density (strength). Gauss's law of magnetism captures this

664 https://www.sacred-texts.com/eso/sta/sta29.htm.

phenomenon mathematically by stating that lines of force begin on north poles and end on south poles, so the net flux emanating from any magnet is zero.

When we study phenomena at the quantum level, we enter a bewildering freak show of strangeness that nearly beggars belief that the inner structure of our reality could be this strange. But it is. It's stranger than we can imagine. But even deep within all this strangeness, there is still order. One of the most core fundamentals of mathematics is the principle that complex numbers come in conjugate pairs. The concept of the complex conjugate is one of the key bedrock concepts upon which all electrical engineering, optics, quantum physics, fluid dynamics, and many other scientific disciplines depend. Throughout all physics and engineering (throughout reality as we know it), this principle holds. Anyone interested in this topic should read up on *Hermitian conjugates*, which are attributed to the revolutionary work of French mathematician Charles Hermite. A fascinating video on complex numbers by a former schoolmate of mine named Eugene Khutoryansky is included as a footnote for the inquisitive reader.[665]

Hermite was born in Paris on December 24, 1822. Without his pioneering work in the field of complex analysis and linear algebra, we simply wouldn't be able to understand quantum physics.[666] A video introduction to Hermitian operators is provided in the footnote.[667]

In electricity, we have positive and negative charge. Electrical charges of one flavor can exist without the other out in free space—that is, infinitely far from other charged particles. However, the law of electric charge induction states that if you place a positive charge (say +10 coulombs of charge) in the vicinity of a neutral (zero charge) object, the positively charged object will induce an opposing negative charge of -10 coulombs on the surface of the previously neutral object where you created the charge deficit. The point is that if you create positive charge somewhere, it will simultaneously cause a negative charge to appear from an otherwise neutral object. In human life, there is a similar phenomenon. When you win the lottery, you've created a windfall of positive charge for your bank account, and now you've got a million people crawling out of the woodwork with negative energy that wasn't there before. They are envi-

665 https://www.youtube.com/watch?v=bIY6ahHVgqA
666 https://www.britannica.com/biography/Charles-Hermite
667 https://www.youtube.com/watch?v=0Q_KmTOy07E

ous and willing to do anything to get what you have. People you've never met can suddenly become enemies!

The moral of the story is that the total *amount* of charge in the universe has not changed since the moment of creation. Only the *distribution* has! The common axiom "opposites attract" is hard to actually prove when analyzing why dissimilar people tend to be attracted to one another, but it is a scientific fact that oppositely charged particles are electrically attracted to each other all the way down to the atomic level! When 23 female chromosomes chemically bond together with 23 male chromosomes to create a new human life, this is the result of positive charges and negative charges bonding together at the molecular level. All the material world boils down to chemistry, and all chemistry boils down to electrical charges. At the molecular level, male and female reproductive cells have something the other gender needs in order to be electrically complete with no net unbalanced charges.

In electrical signal processing theory, I encountered one of the most mysterious duality concepts of all, specifically the time-frequency duality. To the reader familiar with the Fourier- and Laplace transforms, it is well known that any signal can be reconstructed using nothing but sine waves of varying frequencies and amplitudes. The time-frequency duality statement goes like this: A time-limited signal such as the Dirac delta function (which models as a hammer blow to a church bell) will be composed of infinitely many frequencies, and a frequency-limited signal such as a pure sine wave will be infinite in time. The bell will only respond to the frequency that corresponds to its natural resonance. This becomes clear via example. Take the simple sine wave. It has one frequency and repeats on and on forever in the time domain. On the other hand, a square wave pulse is limited in time (just one pulse) but requires summing together infinitely many sine waves to construct it. In signal and system analysis, we use the Dirac delta function, which has infinite height and zero width, to elicit the behavior of a system that is mathematically analogous to a hammer sharply striking a bell for a fraction of a second, and then measure its natural frequency response. For the mathematically curious reader, please search for a video on "greens function PDE" and you'll see a sample of the level of difficulty in electrical engineering math at the graduate level.[668]

For something much lighter and interesting, go to YouTube, and search

668 https://www.youtube.com/watch?v=xNqLZnM-PPY

for a video titled "Fourier Series Animation (Square Wave)."[669] Then you can get a fantastic and enjoyable visual representation of what I'm talking about. Even if you completely hate math, I can guarantee you'll find the video pleasurable. Try me. The reason I took up the space for this challenging topic is that everything we see or hear can be saved as data if we can determine the fourier spectra of the sounds and sights, and it can stored digitally to be reconstructed later. This is what happens electronically when an event is video-recorded, saved on a disc, and then replayed at a later time.

Hot and cold is another duality that everyone understands intuitively, and thus, it requires little discussion. Bitter and sweet. Loud and soft. Our senses are loaded with data about the extremes of each sense. We remember the coldest and hottest objects we have ever touched and calibrate every other object we touch in terms of how hot or cold we perceive it based on our knowledge of these upper and lower limits. This is similar to how electronic sensors are calibrated. When calibrating a glass tube thermometer, the first mark would be the freezing point of water (0 degree Celsius) after placing it in a bath of ice water and letting it equilibrate. Similarly, the 100 degree Celsius mark would be inscribed at a higher point on the tube after being allowed to equalize to the temperature of a bath of boiling water. We would then correctly deduce that the 50 degree Celsius mark would be located exactly between the 0 and 100 marks. We actually built our own thermometers in eighth-grade chemistry lab class and used this procedure to calibrate our new instruments. Under the context of duality, it is also remarkable that chemistry has a fundamental principle of duality between acids and bases, which are opposites.

The concepts of north and south as well as east and west are directional dualities that we all understand intuitively. Similarly, we have up and down, in and out, black and white, and profit and loss. Our entire earthly existence is built upon understanding of these concepts of polarity.

In order to create beauty in one place, we humans must destroy beauty somewhere else. To build a beautiful log cabin, you must cut down pristine forest somewhere else. To mine gold, diamonds, oil, or other natural resources, we must rip up a portion of the Earth. Life is the noble exception. When we create life, we start with beauty and then create new beauty. The second law of thermodynamics states that the arrangement of

669 https://www.youtube.com/watch?v=k8FXF1KjzY0&t=87s

atoms in a gas always goes from a state of order toward disorder, due to entropy. Life seems to be in violation of this fundamental law, as our bodies create order out of disorder. The creative genius of nature is the only entity capable of turning ugliness into beauty and randomness into order. Humans have many great lessons to learn from this important concept. A wonderful, short book titled *What Is Life* was written by physicist Erwin Schrodinger, and I strongly recommend the readers add this to their reading lists. It's a very short but deeply inspiring read.

Heaven and hell is another duality, but it is a construct that the orthodox religions of Europe and the Middle East have created and taught for millennia. Hell is essentially the absence of connection to the Creator of the universe. Heaven is being connected to that source. It's as simple as that in my viewpoint. Our earthly experience is *the* great test. We are given the free will to pursue our lives in a way that either seeks or avoids connection to God. God did not create us as robots with a predetermined set of choices and outcomes. We get to play the parts of robot and programmer simultaneously, and through our webs of decisions and choices, we get to determine whether we will connect to or disconnect from God. When we are born, we are as close to the source as we can be. We have pure innocence. Then the corruptive forces of the world act to draw us away from that Eden-like state of perfection. Life is a protracted struggle between satisfying our earthly cravings and preserving our pure desire for God. In most cases, the problem points to the person being overly attached to pleasures of the world.

Probably the most common duality we see in everyday life is that of light and dark. On average, every part of Earth gets 12 hours of light and 12 hours of dark throughout the year. Depending on latitude, the seasonal swings intensify to the point of 24 hours of light in the polar regions during summer and 24 hours of darkness in winter, but it still averages out to 12 and 12 over the course of a year.

The concepts of light and dark often have correlations to the notions of good and evil. By means of education, religion, and other vestiges of modern culture, society has taught us to sort everything in terms of duality. Rather than accept everything in the universe for what it is, we have been conditioned to sort things into categories of good or evil. The spiritual awakening experience teaches us that everything *just is* and that we should not judge everything. We learn to accept that everything happening or being allowed to happen in the universe is happening because that's the way it was meant to play out in the grand scheme of the cosmos. When we judge everything in terms of good or evil, we place unnecessary stress upon ourselves. The awakening process is about accepting the current state of the universe and focusing on how you as an individual can direct your own thoughts and intentions toward effecting a more positive universe. The power of our thoughts and intentions is a tremendous force for change, and we must learn to focus them toward the greater good. Western religion teaches us to focus our prayers outward to appeal to an external God and to ask for his help. This book attempts to show that God has actually built himself deeply inside of every man and woman on Earth *as well as* being simultaneously everywhere else in the universe. Luke 17:21 states, "Neither shall they say, Lo here! or, lo there! for, behold, the kingdom of God is within you."[670] This changes the way we pray. Instead of appealing to a strictly external deity, we can learn to focus our intentions inwardly and channel our psychic/spiritual energy to effect the changes we want to see in the real world. I now view prayer as intentions directed by the power of my will and backed up by my faith that it will come to pass.

Life and death is another duality that absolutely everyone will come to terms with at some point—hopefully before the moment of earthly passing comes upon us. This is without a doubt the scariest of all the dualistic concepts that anyone ever has or ever will contemplate. Modern society treats life as something that comes to be at birth and expires at death. The world's mainstream religions attempt to give us relief from this doomed mindset by giving us a path to salvation and eternal life after passing. This requires faith, and this is why religions are often referred to as *faiths*. Spiritual faith gives the believer that precious sense of love and peace in knowing that there is something bigger going on than just the prospect of becoming a piece of meat dying, rotting, and expiring forever. The great message is that the divine Creator is infinitely intelligent and loving and he has a compassionate plan for us all after our earthly walks are complete.

You are a co-creator of this reality and this world! The fact that humans are able to reproduce and create life is direct evidence that we are indeed

670 https://www.biblegateway.com/verse/en/Luke%2017%3A21.

more than just passive participants and have the ability to access divine power within us.

Further Ponderings on God and Creation

No book that has ever existed can prove the existence of God, but this book hopes to give questioning and discerning minds enough evidence and empirical data to arrive at their own conclusions. How could all of this have happened simply by rolling the cosmic dice of chance? It is a virtual mathematical impossibility.

Having been raised with a Christian upbringing, I doubted and questioned the existence of God for the first forty years of my life. I needed proof and evidence. Early on, my studies in science caused me to lean toward science for all the answers and to further doubt the existence of God. But as I went deeper and explored the intricate complexities in nature, it became increasingly apparent to me that a higher intelligence had created the universe in its own image. The famous theoretical physicist and pioneer in quantum mechanics, Werner Heisenberg, said it eloquently, "The first gulp from the glass of natural sciences will turn you into an atheist, but at the bottom of the glass God is waiting for you."[671] I would have to agree.

In my primarily scientific education, the main narrative that was pushed was the doctrine of evolution. This runs in direct opposition to the biblical story of divine creation. But let's consider the evolutionary point of view for a moment and ask a few questions. Let's say that life on Earth did in fact begin when an amino acid or fungus spores from somewhere else in the universe hitched a ride in the core of a comet, landed on Earth, and began to mutate and form proteins and then cells and then basic life-forms? What if all life started out as single cell organisms, and then over the course of billions of years, continually mutated and improved itself and eventually evolved into all the known life-forms we have today, including humans? Wouldn't that be an even more amazing story, showcasing God's incredible power and genius in allowing DNA molecules to form? To my point of view, if this was the case, the original seed still had to be created somewhere by something intelligent. It in no way decreases God's greatness.

What if everything *did* start from a big bang event? If all the observable

671 https://en.wikiquote.org/wiki/Talk:Werner_Heisenberg

universe sprang forth from a singularity and blossomed out into the cosmos as we know it, is that still any proof that God doesn't exist? I think not. If everything we know as the universe and all the information contained in it sprung forth from a tiny particle, that in itself is evidence of a cosmic Creator. Interestingly, as technology capabilities have increased, the amount of information we can store on computer drives has gone up exponentially, to the point that we can fit gigabytes of information into volumes the size of a molecule. Eventually, we will have the ability to encode all known information into something the size of a DNA molecule. It is truly remarkable that if the DNA molecule was created 4.3 billion years ago, it took us that long for our technology to catch up to the technology from that long ago. Soon our information density will allow us to return to the singularity and be able to stuff all known information into the space of a pin head. I believe that the reason life exists is the result of infinite cosmic boredom. An infinite well of intelligence and energy may have been locked up in an infinitely dense, infinitely small space, and before time, the divine Creator realized the unbounded potential for it to experience itself and thus exploded into the universe as we know it and created life as a way of knowing itself. Physicist Carl Sagan said it best, "The cosmos is within us. We are made of star-stuff. We are a way for the universe to know itself."[672]

What is intelligence and consciousness? Are animals the only life-forms that possess these traits? As a child, I used to assume squirrels were inherently stupid because they would bury acorns and other tree nuts and then forget about them. But what if their actions are intentional with the conscious knowledge that they are planting future trees from which they will derive future acorns? What if the act of burying tree seed was a conscious way of giving back to the tree that sustained them? What if they consciously and purposely were planting seeds to ensure food supply for future generations of ostensibly dumb "tree rats"? I'm a great believer in inherent intelligence in nature.

Do life-forms in the plant and fungus kingdoms experience consciousness? Our brains are composed of billions of single, relatively "unsmart" cells. Intelligence is formed by the number and complexity of the connections between them. The largest living organism on the planet is not

672 https://www.goodreads.com/quotes/484665-the-cosmos-is-within-us-we-are-made-of-star-stuff

a whale or a redwood tree, but rather a mushroom—a honey fungus in Oregon that is 2.4 miles wide.[673]

I would offer that there is a very good chance these underground networks of living cells could constitute an infinitely intelligent living and conscious being. The same process could be abstracted to trees and other members of the plant kingdom. If true, then we could literally consider the planet Earth to be a living, sentient being as well. Anyone who has experienced traditional plant-based entheogenic medicines would tend to agree.

We truly live in a miraculous universe. My hope is that any scientific-minded person who has doubted the presence of God will have seen enough empirical evidence to conclude that we have never been alone, and God has always had a good and perfect plan.

Pascal's Wager

Pascal's wager is an interesting thought experiment whereby the French philosopher and mathematician Blaise Pascal weighed the outcomes of either believing in God and being right or wrong in comparison to the outcomes of not believing in God and being right or wrong. The logical best option, he argues, is to assume that God exists. Then if you're wrong, you haven't lost anything anyway. According to the Stanford Encyclopedia of Philosophy website, Pascal stated:

> God is, or He is not. But to which side shall we incline? Reason can decide nothing here. There is an infinite chaos which separated us. A game is being played at the extremity of this infinite distance where heads or tails will turn up … Which will you choose then? Let us see. Since you must choose, let us see which interests you least. You have two things to lose, the true and the good; and two things to stake, your reason and your will, your knowledge and your happiness; and your nature has two things to shun, error and misery. Your reason is no more shocked in choosing one rather than the other, since you must of necessity choose … But your happiness? Let us weigh the gain and the loss in wagering that God is … If you gain, you gain all; if you lose, you lose nothing. Wager, then, without hesitation that He is.[674]

Anywhere we see pentagons or pentagrams, we know that the golden

673 Michael Pollan, *How to Change Your Mind* (New York: Penguin Press, 2019).
674 https://plato.stanford.edu/entries/pascal-wager/.

ratio can be found lurking. The US military headquarters is housed in the Pentagon, the largest symbol of the military on the planet. Most sheriffs' badges are either 5- or 6-pointed stars—symbols of authority. Just the sight of a star-shaped badge instills fear in all but the most hardened criminal. Stars represent power and authority.

Revelation 2:9 states, "I know thy works, and tribulation, and poverty, (but thou art rich) and I know the blasphemy of them which say they are Jews, and are not, but are the synagogue of Satan."[675] The global cabal is rooted in a core group of evil forces who control the world and hide behind the guise of being Jews as wolves in sheep's clothing. Don't believe me? Check for yourself. Google "triple parenthesis," or go to the link in the footnotes.[676] Just as the Nazis misappropriated the swastika from the peaceful religion of Buddhism, rotated it 45 degrees, reversed the direction of rotation, and perverted it to mean evil, similar mischief has happened to both the 5-pointed and 6-pointed stars. Satanists have also attempted to hijack the cross of Christianity by rotating it 180 degrees for an upside-down cross as an emblem of their solidarity with darkness.

The 5-pointed star has been a core symbol of Christianity since antiquity, representing the 5 wounds of Christ as well as the 5 senses, but the evil forces have attempted to corrupt the pentagram by rotating it 36 degrees to point downward as an emblem of satanism. This simple rotation modified a good symbol in order to represent evil and the dark occult. Freemasonry uses the 5-pointed star as one of its emblems, representing the eastern star. The pentagram also has the golden ratio built into its proportions.

Just to make an interesting illustration, Islam uses the Kaaba as its holiest shrine at Mecca, Saudi Arabia, and it also contains a black cube. Similarly, Orthodox Jews may wear a small black cube affixed to the forehead called a tefillin, which can contain small notes of scripture as an aid to prayer and meditation. I observed this practice during my 2004 visit to the Western Wall in Jerusalem. A cubic box, when unfolded, is a figure composed of six sides in the form of a cross as seen here.

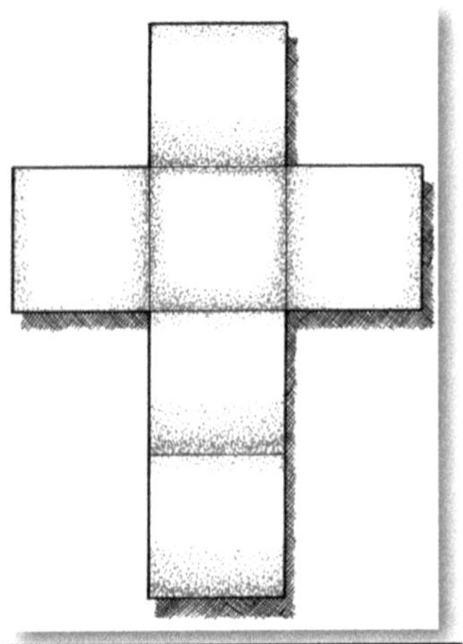

675 https://www.biblegateway.com/passage/?search=Revelation+2%3A9&version=NIV.
676 https://rationalwiki.org/wiki/Triple_parentheses.

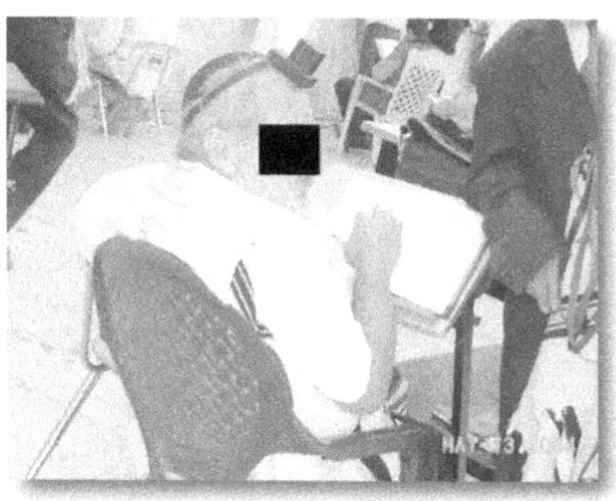

Man wearing a tefillin at the Western Wall in Jerusalem (face purposely obscured, for respect)

As can be seen below, the planet Saturn has a hexagon-shaped cloud system at its north pole and rotates counterclockwise. Similarly, pilgrims visiting Islam's most holy site, Mecca, promenade counterclockwise around their most holy shrine, the Kaaba. Note that when a cube is viewed at a compound angle or corner view where three sides can be seen at once, it has a hexagonal profile as seen in the yellow lines I superimposed in the following graphic:[677]

Understanding symbology is very important in comprehending religious concepts. Words and language operate at the conscious level, whereas symbols have meaning at the unconscious level, which is inaccessible to language and conscious thought. Symbols communicate deeper meanings to us, which go deeper than language alone can.

677 http://www.mostholyplace.com.

The day science begins to study non-physical phenomena, it will make more progress in one decade than in all the previous centuries of its existence.

—Nikola Tesla[678]

Each individual mind is a protrusion into the material world of one vast cosmic mind, and we must use the imagination to reach back into it and to engage with it.

—Mark Booth[679]

In the same way, let your light shine before others, that they may see your good deeds and glorify your Father in heaven.

—Matthew 5:16[680]

678 https://www.goodreads.com/quotes/139502-the-day-science-begins-to-study-non-physical-phenomena-it-will
679 Booth, Mark. The Secret History of the World. New York: The Overlook Press, 2008.
680 https://www.biblegateway.com/passage/?search=Matthew+5%3A16&version=NIV

CHAPTER 15

11:11 AS A CODE OF LIGHT

Welcome to the last chapter of *The 11:11 Code*. I've always said that I saved my very best material for last, so now we are getting into the really good stuff. Enjoy!

The Cosmic Serpent

The number 22 looks eerily similar to two parallel serpents or cobras in the strike-ready position. Jeremy Narby's book *The Cosmic Serpent* sets forth that humans have known for eons that life's fundamental structure was two intertwined serpents. He studied ancient cave drawings and other archeological relics of the past, noting that the intertwined snakes always represented life. (With the benefit of X-ray crystallography, we now know this to be true.) The DNA molecule is indeed two intertwined serpents in the form of the double helix!

Sperm cells are also in the form of microscopic serpents that themselves contain two intertwined snakes in the form of DNA. This is a most excellent treatise on the origins of life and intelligence, and it impressed me so much so that I booked a trip to take myself and my wife to Switzerland to interview Dr. Narby as a source for another book I'm working on. During our trip from Zurich to the Italian Alps, our GPS automatically routed us in such a way that about half of our trip took us along Highway 22, which took us through many quaint little towns that could have been taken straight from a children's storybook. The GPS seemed to be taking instructions directly from our higher power. We couldn't have planned a more beautiful trip. If you're reading this book, you obviously enjoy interesting things, so when you go to order a copy of *The Cosmic Serpent*, be sure and get a copy of one of the other books that helped me understand God through nature—Dr. Narby's other masterpiece is titled *Intelligence in Nature*. These two books will forever alter your perception of the world and your place in it.

Prior to meeting with Dr. Narby, I contacted him via email with an intriguing idea that all electromagnetic radiation, including ultraviolet, infrared, and visible light, radio, X-ray, gamma, and other forms of cosmic radiation, crosses the infinite vastness of space at the speed of light by means of the intermingling of a sine-wave-shaped magnetic field and a similarly shaped electric field. The two fields interact at trillions of cycles per second (terahertz) as two intertwined snakes. Dr. Narby was so intrigued by this proposal that he arrived at our meeting with the vector diagram from my email already printed out for us to discuss further. Here you have an anthropologist and an electrical engineer drawing parallels between serpents in human history and serpents within our entire electromagnetic spectrum. Both of us left the meeting just a bit smarter. Steel sharpens steel. Our separate observations were wonderful in their own right, but the union of the two points of view has value greater than the sum of their separate parts because it begs the question of why the universe seems to be using the serpent form to express virtually all the most fundamental concepts that underpin our existence and concept of reality. It is very interesting to think that in the process of photosynthesis, the energy of these two intertwined electric and magnetic *snakes* are processed within the leaves of the plant and used to produce sugars and starches that allow the plant to produce more cells and thus more coils of DNA, which is yet another set of twisted serpentine molecules!

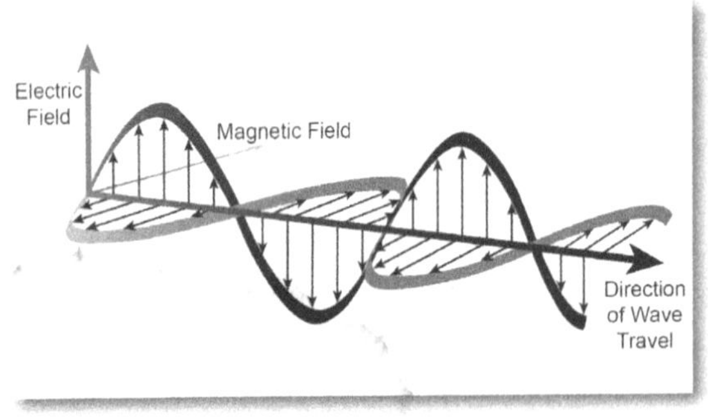

Diagram of the Poynting vector of a light wave. Electric field in black, magnetic field in gray, both at 90 degrees to each other. You can see that light is indeed composed of two intertwined serpents.

Fresnel Lens for Lighthouses

In the early nineteenth century, lighthouses in the United States were considered inferior to those in France and England. American mariners complained about the quality of light emanating from local lighthouse towers, arguing that European lighthouses were more effective at shining bright beams of light over long distances. While American lighthouses relied on lamps and mirrors to direct mariners, European lighthouses were equipped with compact lenses that could shine for miles.

In 1822, French scientist Augustin-Jean Fresnel was studying optics and light waves and discovered that by arranging a series of lenses and prisms into the shape of a beehive, the strength of lighthouse beams could be improved. His lens—known as the Fresnel lens—diffused light into beams that could be visible for miles. Fresnel designed his lenses in several different sizes, or orders. The first order lens, meant for use in coastal lighthouses, was the largest and strongest lens. The sixth order lens was the smallest, designed for use in small harbors and ports.[681] Here is an invention from 1822, where 22 is once again the 11 + 11 code manifesting itself as a source of light to guide humanity on our collective journey toward awakening.

The Birth of Photography

Hopefully by now, the reader has detected a pattern here—a preponderance of evidence seems to suggest that the 11:11 code has everything to do with a secret numerical cipher pointing to the light of the sun. As it turns out, photography as we know it began in 1822 and was originally called *heliography* (héliographie in French), which literally means *picture of the sun*.[682] The photographic process was invented by French inventor Joseph Nicéphore Niépce around 1822, which he used to make the earliest known surviving photograph from nature.[683] Niépce's process utilized bitumen, a tar-like substance that had to be exposed to the sun's light for several days in order to register a crude image.[684]

It wasn't until Niépce's death in 1833 that another French inventor named Louis Daguerre pioneered the daguerreotype process of photography after experimenting with the light-sensitive properties of silver salts. He be-

681 https://americanhistory.si.edu/collections/search/object/nmah_844143.
682 http://www.historyofinformation.com/detail.php?entryid=4121.
683 https://en.wikipedia.org/wiki/History_of_photography.
684 https://www.hrc.utexas.edu/exhibitions/permanent/firstphotograph/process/#top.

came known as one of the fathers of photography. Until this point in time, light, which travels at 671 million miles per hour, could not be stopped and recorded. Upon production of his first daguerreotype photograph, he exclaimed, "I have seized the light—I have arrested its flight!"[685] Daguerre's is one of 72 names inscribed on the Eiffel Tower in Paris. Here we have the numbers 22 and 33 showing up in the context of the invention of the photograph and the recording of optical energy for human enjoyment. This was a truly great achievement for all humankind.

The advent of color photography would not have been possible without James Clerk Maxwell's genius. The strategy for producing full-color projected images was outlined by Maxwell in a paper to the Royal Society of Edinburgh in 1855, published in detail in the *Society's Transactions* in 1857. In 1861, photographer Thomas Sutton, who worked with Maxwell, made three images of a tartan ribbon using red, green, and blue filters in front of the camera lens, and these became the first color photos in human history.[686] The set of Maxwell's black-and-white slides are on permanent display in the museum at Maxwell's birthplace.[687]

Albert Michelson and the Speed of Light

The pioneer of the modern measurement of the speed of light was Albert Michelson. In an effort to accurately measure the speed of light, he selected two mountain peaks in California between which a beam of light would be sent from one to the other and reflected back while the time of transit was measured. Using the relationship that distance equals speed times time, the speed of light could be calculated. Mount Wilson and Mt. San Antonio are located 22 (11+11) miles apart, and the surveying work began on October 16, 1922. In August of 1924, he performed his first experiment, which resulted in the calculated speed of 299,820 kilometers per second, accurate to about one part in ten thousand. Believing he could improve upon his results, he attempted the experiment in the summers of 1925 and 1926 again, yielding results that were what Michelson referred to as his "definitive measurements" and came within 0.00118 percent of the modern accepted value for the speed of light.[688] The new Beast Theater Works in collaboration with High Concept Laboratories produced a

685 https://en.wikipedia.org/wiki/Louis_Daguerre.
686 https://en.wikipedia.org/wiki/History_of_photography.
687 http://www.clerkmaxwellfoundation.org/html/first_colour_photographic_image.html.
688 http://www.otherhand.org/home-page/physics/historical-speed-of-light-measurements-in-southern-california/the-mount-wilson-mount-san-antonio-measurements-1922-1926/.

semi-opera about Michelson, his obsessive working style, and its effect on his family life. The production began on February 11, 2011, and ran through February 26, 2011, in Chicago, at the Building Stage.[689]

Recommended video: "Into the light" by Oase der Ruhe.

THE NUMBER OF LIGHT

The speed of light passing through free space is approximately 671 million miles per hour. If you take 671 divided by 666, these numbers are only 0.8 percent apart, which is stunningly close considering the Bible was written 2,000 years ago and they lacked the technology to accurately measure the speed of light.

The speed of light is so great that it could circumnavigate Earth seven times in one second![690]

Here's another gem of physics history: In 1666, Isaac Newton started experimenting with optical lenses and the refraction of light. In the year 1671, he published a technical paper on the subject. Here we have light and the number 671 again. He published his paper with the date 1671/72. According to Royal Society Publishing, prior to 1752, his native England was out of kilter with the rest of Europe because it followed the Julian rather than Gregorian calendar. When 11 days were removed in order to get the country and continent in sync, the first day of the year was shifted from March 25 to January 1.[691]

Could the number of the beast be the number of light? Could it be related to the number of a man because the perception of light is one of our most important sensory inputs? Could there be another incredibly cool occurrence of the number 671 that could give us the answer to the 11:11 code? When does a person usually ask a rhetorical question? In this case, when the answer is key to appreciating the punch line of *The 11:11 Code*.

ROBERT MILLIKAN'S 11:11 DISCOVERY

On 3/ 22/1868, physicist Robert Millikan was born. On November 11, 1925, Millikan was the first to discover cosmic rays impinging on Earth from the heavens. Here, once again, we see waves of energy from the

689 http://www.theinfolist.com/php/SummaryGet.php?FindGo=Albert%20A.%20Michelson.
690 Carl Sagan, *Cosmos* (New York: Ballantine Books, 2013).
691 http://rsta.royalsocietypublishing.org/content/373/2039/20140213.

heavens associated with the number 11.[692] Millikan received the Nobel Prize in physics in 1923 for his work on the famous oil drop experiment and the photoelectric effect,[693] the former established the value of the charge of an electron as 1.609 x 10^{-19} coulomb.[694] The base, 1.609, is within 0.5 percent of the value of the golden ratio.

Any quick internet search of the terms "11:11 awakening angel code" will turn up literally thousands of numerology sites that speak in glittering generalities about 11:11 being an awakening code, an enlightenment code, angel number, and countless other lofty descriptions. Instinctively, I always knew they were right, but I wasn't able to get to the root of the mystery until I was nearly done writing. Interestingly, this work provides a mathematically plausible background to support all these claims. It's as if humankind has intrinsically known about 11:11 being an enlightenment code all along, but no one could seem to put their finger on the connection to the speed of light. After reading the section on chromosome 22, you saw in the micrograph photo of the chromosomes that they indeed bear a striking resemblance to the number 11 in their physical form. It's almost as if the 11:11 code was written into the shape of our chromosomes as a reminder that we were created by an infinitely intelligent spirit that pervades every single aspect of our universe and every cell in our body. The Creator has left an infinite amount of Easter eggs for us to discover. While space doesn't permit inclusion here, the reader is encouraged to read about Millikan's religious and spiritual views on life, creation, and the universe.[695]

Lastly, I noticed another fundamental universal constant, the amount of electric charge possessed by a single electron. The magnitude of the elementary charge was first measured in Millikan's aforementioned oil drop experiment in 1909. The mantissa (the part to the left of the exponent term) is nearly equal to the golden ratio, phi, to an accuracy of almost exactly 1.0 percent. The elementary unit of charge was measured to be 1.6022 x 10^{-19} coulombs and is the standard in modern physics and electrical engineering.

Now let me massage the numbers a bit. At first, the base number 1.6022 doesn't seem that special. Notice our friend 22 is there. Also, a quick

692 https://www.onthisday.com/events/november/11.

693 https://www.nobelprize.org/prizes/physics/1923/summary/.

694 https://www.britannica.com/science/Millikan-oil-drop-experiment.

695 https://creation.com/robert-millikan.

calculation shows that it is within 0.998 percent of the golden ratio, phi (~1.618). The orthodox, purist mathematician would shake his head with a furrowed brow and call this nonsense, but my claim is stretching the truth of things no more than if I told you I would be there to see you in five minutes and arrived three seconds (1 percent) late. As an electrical engineer, I was trained under some of the most brutal mathematicians at a couple of the world's most challenging universities, and since then, I've learned to loosen my shoelaces a bit and actually enjoy the experience of looking into numbers and making connections like this. You don't always have to be exactly right as I wonder how many such missed connections were overlooked by perfection-minded people. Okay, but what were we talking about before I got sidetracked? Oh, yeah, electrons.

When humankind learned to master the electron, it heralded the beginning of one of the greatest revolutions in all of human history. Just imagine your life without any electricity whatsoever. Imagine a power outage that lasts the rest of your life. Life as we know it grinds to a screeching halt. This was life on Earth prior to electricity and prior to the discovery of the mathematics and physics necessary to understand how electrons behave. Life prior to understanding this elementary unit of charge was a very dark time in our collective history.

Light, Maxwell, Einstein, and the 11:11 Connection

To fully appreciate the following section, please
take the time to watch the one-hour video

Maxwell, The History of Electromagnetism—Documentary
by The King.

The other day I was just finishing putting the final touches on this project when it randomly occurred to me to calculate the number of minutes in 11 hours and 11 minutes (11:11). The answer wasn't very exciting—that is, not at first glance.

If you're unfamiliar with the worldwide obsession among people interested in numerology associated with the clock time 11:11, take a pause now and perform an internet search for the terms "11:11 enlightenment." Then read a few articles. Scour the websites to see what kinds of explanations you can find to explain why 11:11 is an enlightenment code. Most if not all use the circular reasoning that 11:11 is an enlightenment code because 11 has a high vibration, and it has a high vibration because it's an angel number or a master number. Natalia Kuna has some of the best material on the internet.[696]

But I have yet to find a website or a book that can truly answer the questions "why?" and "how?" Can we do better here in this book? I'm a big believer in saving the best for last. Here comes the climax of this book—the deep secret of *The 11:11 Code*.

Are you ready? You'll need to think about numbers like they did thousands of years ago in Babylon. Let's do this.

So, in order to decompose 11:11 from hours and minutes into strictly *minutes*, start by converting 11 hours to minutes, then add the remaining minutes on the right side of the colon. Knowing there are 60 minutes in an hour, we just multiply 60 times 11 hours to arrive at 660 minutes. Easy enough, yeah? Great! Now let's not forget our handsomely symmetric, two-legged friend to the right of the colon. Combining the 660 minutes with the remaining 11, we are left with 11hr:11min = 671 minutes.

Pretty mundane, huh? "Big deal!" you may say. "What's so special about that number?" That was my first impression as well, and I almost disregarded it. But then it dawned on me that I had already used the number 671 somewhere earlier in this book. Remember reading about the speed of light with the number 671 (as in 671 *million* miles per hour) being only 0.7 percent less than the number of the sun, 666, and I wrote about the striking proximity of these two numbers? I was really close to being on the cusp of a great discovery and didn't realize it until I was almost ready to send the manuscript off to my editor. This discovery was so shocking that I actually ended up completely changing the title of the book as well as its overall trajectory. Until this discovery, I was completely sold on titling this book *God Is a Mathematician* as a reply to the question in the book title *Is God a Mathematician?* by Mario Livio, PhD, one of my favorite authors. It was in this singular moment when reality hit me—the number 671 being both the total number of minutes in 11 hours and 11 minutes as well as the number of *millions of miles per hour* in the speed of light. The

696 http://www.nataliakuna.com/.

cosmic riddle was immediately clear. Google "speed of light MPH" and you'll instantly see that the speed of light is indeed 671,000,000 MPH!

By now, it should be no surprise that the number 22, or its expanded form 11+11, shows up wherever the topic of light is mentioned. We saw it in the production and transmission of light, but what about when light is received? As it turns out, if we ask the question, " How much energy does Earth and its atmosphere absorb from the sun in 24 hours?" the answer is very interesting. Starting with the easy stuff, we know there are 86,400 seconds in 24 hours. We also know that the sun emits about 1,368 watts per square meter of Earth's surface according to a study of solar irradiance by Harvard University.[697] Using simple high school geometry, we know that the area of Earth's disk being lit by the sun at any time is given by $A=\pi R^2$ where R is the radius of Earth in meters, $R=6.37 \times 10^9$ meters. We get the total energy in joules by multiplying the solar flux times Earth's cross sectional area, then times 86,400 seconds. Follow along with your own calculator.

$$E = (\text{sun flux}) \times (\text{earth disk area}) \times (86{,}400 \text{ sec.})$$

$$E=(1368\ J/s*m^2) \times (\pi \times (6.37 \times 10^9\ m)^2 \times (86{,}400\ sec) = 1.51 \times 10^{22}\ joules$$

To put this amount of energy into perspective, the amount of solar energy that impinges on Earth in 24 hours is the equivalent of 176 million nuclear reactors operating at 1,000 megawatts apiece. That's about one reactor for every 43 people on the planet.

NIMBY=Not In My Back Yard and BANANA=Build Absolutely Nothing Anywhere Near Anyone is what we would be hearing!

That's a truly astronomical amount of energy coming in from the central nuclear fusion engine of the solar system. Are you still convinced that mankind alone is causing climate change? Research the Milankovitch Cycle. Awesome stuff. A special thanks to Dr. David Porter, professor of Oceanography at Johns Hopkins University for opening my eyes to really big calculations to help me understand my home planet's physical processes in a very deep way. One of the best classes I have ever taken.

There you have it. We have 1.5 with 22 zeroes-to-the-right *joules* (or watt-seconds) of energy. The sun puts out 15 times a billion times a trillion watt-seconds of power into Earth's atmosphere and surface, every day, re-

697 http://articles.adsabs.harvard.edu//full/1984SSRv...38..203W/0000204.000.html page 204

gardless of the weather. That's 15 zettawatts. That just *sounds* completely badassed, doesn't it? But the sun's total output in all directions in space is a wiggy-wiggy-wicked 384.6 yottawatts, or 3.846 x 10^{26} watts equivalent to the energy hitting 25,470 Earths. The sun is incredibly productive.

Let this all sink in. We found 11+11 once again, associated with the flow of energy from the sun to Earth, via electromagnetic energy traveling at the speed of light, *as light*. This is the exact same energy that sustains every single living organism on the planet—past, present, and future. And that's just the tiny slice of the sun's energy that hits us. The University of Tennessee website has an interesting calculation for those who want more information like this.[698]

The reason 11:11 is widely considered to be the universal en***light***enment code is because *it secretly conceals the speed of light*. The secret for unlocking it was by using the ancient Babylonian sexagesimal (base-60) number thinking. Our system of timekeeping as well as for our system of angular measurement in degrees, minutes, and seconds are still based on the Babylonian system, whereby the circle is divided into 360 degrees (6 x 60), each degree subdivided into 60 minutes of arc, and each minute further divided into 60 seconds of arc. This was the absolute most pivotal and most unexpected "eureka!" moment that I experienced during the process of writing. I could even go so far as to say it was one of the most pivotal discoveries of my life, but the true measure will be how many people end up reading this.

If you look at the time 11:11, it is exactly 49 or 7x7 minutes before the noon (or midnight) when AM changes to PM (or vice-versa, respectively). Noon is when the sun is directly overhead, with maximum illumination, whereas midnight the sun is as far from view as possible, directly overhead on the other side of the planet. 11:11 really is a code of light and illumination.

I just showed you how 11:11 is a code of light at the macro scale, but what about at the micro-scale? Can we prove that 11:11 encodes light by digging into electromagnetic theory? Going back to the fundamentals of Maxwell's equations of electromagnetics from junior-year electrical engineering, one of the most striking results is the compact relation, as in $c = \frac{1}{\sqrt{\varepsilon_0 \mu_0}}$ where ε0 is the electric permittivity of free space (the vacuum

698 https://ag.tennessee.edu/solar/Pages/What%20Is%20Solar%20Energy/Sun's%20Energy.aspx

of space) and is equal to $\varepsilon_0 = \left(\frac{1}{36\pi}\right) \times 10^{-11}$ farads per meter (capacitance). This approximation is extremely accurate and is good enough for 99% of all engineering and scientific purposes, as confirmed by University of Illinois electrical engineering professor Jiang-Ming Jin, Ph.D. And $\mu 0$ is the magnetic permeability of free space and is equal to $\mu 0 = 4\pi \times 10^{-7}$ henries per meter (inductance). C is the speed of light. Plugging these numbers into $c = \frac{1}{\sqrt{\varepsilon_0 \mu_0}}$ to solve for the speed of light *based solely upon the electrical and magnetic properties of free space*, we get $c = \frac{1}{\sqrt{(1/36\pi \times 10^{-12})(4\pi \times 10^{-7})}}$. The pi's cancel out and this simplifies to exactly $c = \frac{1}{\sqrt{\frac{1}{9} \times 10^{-18}}}$ which simplifies further to: $c = \frac{1}{\sqrt{1111 \times 10^{-20}}}$ where you can see that "1111" is imbedded in the calculation of the speed of light! We get the truly amazing result of almost *exactly* 300 million meters per second or, equivalently, 300,000 kilometers per second. To convert from kilometers per hour to miles per hour, we multiply km/h times 2,236.9 to get miles per hour, as follows: $c_{MPH} = 2236.9 \times c_{kMH}$ which gives 671 million miles per hour, just as we derived from converting 11:11 from hours and minutes to purely minutes! I have demonstrated how the 11:11 code is a code of light at both the *macro* and *micro* scales. This is one of the most significant findings from the process of building this story, and I had absolutely no idea about this until almost the very end of the writing process. This is a prime example of something that I had no awareness of until I got deep into the writing process and it dawned on me. Interestingly, as I wrote this, I was deep in the throes of a graduate-level electromagnetics course for physicists and the textbook titled *Theory and Computation of Electromagnetic Fields* by Jian-Ming Jin ends on page 671, of all possible page numbers. Professor Jin at my alma mater, University of Illinois at Urbana-Champaign, was very cordial when I contacted him, and he confirmed my calculations and conclusions above.

The symbol *c* was chosen to represent the speed of light due to the Latin word *celeritas*, for *swiftness*.[699] It can be mathematically demonstrated that light travels 173 astronomical units in 24 hours. Think about that—during one full revolution of the planet, light travels 173 times the 92,700,000-mile distance from the sun to the earth or 1.608×10^{10} miles, or essentially ten-billion times the golden ratio of 1.618 within less than one percent. Who cares? I do, and you should too. If you're still with me this far into the book you probably understand where I am coming from when I say there truly are no coincidences.

699 https://www.cs.mcgill.ca/~rwest/wikispeedia/wpcd/wp/s/Speed_of_light.htm

Now that we have the speed of light in terms of the number 1111: $c=\frac{1}{1111\times10^{-20}}$. we can square both sides to get the speed of light squared as: $c^2=\frac{1}{1111\times10^{-20}}$. Bear with me one more second—now remember Einstein's little equation $e = mc^2$? Replace c^2 with the previous expression in terms of 1111 and you can re-write Einstein's equation as: $m = e(1111 \times 10^{-20})$. I leave the full development for the interested reader in Appendix 3. The point is that 1111 acts as a magic code that functions as a bridge between the realm of pure energy, and the amount of physical matter that has to be destroyed in order to create a specific quantity of energy. Think about it! This is pure, unadulterated magic! Sitting right under our noses all these years. All of these years I have simply fired numbers into my fancy engineering graphing calculator and let the number muncher do the hard work for me and I missed these intermediate steps and their results. Now, in graduate school I purposely work out all of my calculations manually, taking time to smell the roses as I work. This process has unfolded so many wonderful little gems like this. If that looked too complicated, just grab a calculator or an Excel spreadsheet and follow these simple steps:

1. Speed of light is 300,000,000 meters per second.
2. Multiply this number times itself once.
3. Take 1 divided by the answer in step 2.
4. You got 1111 with the decimal 17 places to the left, didn't you? If not, return to step 1.
5. Smile! It's really not as scary as it looks. *You* just proved that 1111 is in the speed of light.

Stop and admire what just happened: We just derived the speed of light mathematically by using only the fundamental electric and magnetic properties of free space, and within it, found the number 671 and made a direct connection to the 11:11 code by using ancient Babylonian sexagesimal calculations. Furthermore, 1.111×10^{-17} has the number 17 in the exponent, which is the position for the letter "Q" in the alphabet—perhaps a nice connection to the Qanon movement being a phenomenon of human enLIGHTenment. I have included deeper development of this concept in Appendix 2 for the mathematically inclined reader by working through the partial differential equation (PDE) for wave propagation, beginning with Maxwell's equations. PDEs are one of the highest levels of mathematics that I have ever studied, and Grant Sanderson, who owns the 3Blue1Brown YouTube channel, has a fascinating video which illustrates just how amazingly cool PDEs are.[700] A common misconception about PDEs is that they are somehow simpler than Ordinary Differential Equations, but nothing could be further from the truth. I digress... Grant Sanderson's channel has some of the best math lectures I've ever seen anywhere on the net.

Knowing that light travels at 671,000,000 miles per hour, we can compute how far light travels in a million years, just for curiosity. There are 365 days in a year and 24 hours in a day, and thus, we get 8,760 hours per year. The distance traveled by a photon in a million years is thus 671,000,000 x 8,760 x 1,000,000 = 5.88 x 10^{18} miles. Let's now multiply by 5,280, which is the number of feet in one mile, to obtain the distance that light travels in a million years in feet. We get 5,280 x 5.88 x 10^{18} = 3.11 x 10^{22} feet per million years. Light would travel three, followed by 22 zeroes miles in a million years. Here again, we have several of the core numbers that this book is built around: 3, 11, and 22 all tied to the phenomenon of light transmission.

Maxwell had committed Psalm 119 to memory by age eight. This is the longest chapter from the longest book in the Bible. The passage is composed of 22 sections, each with 8 lines, for a total of 8 x 22 = 176 lines. The first words of each line of the 22 verses start with each of the 22 Hebrew letters from aleph through tav. This psalm is all about praising, respecting, and understanding God's Word. The Word of God is a *lamp* to the world as stated in the well-known verse of the book of Psalms. "Thy Work is a lamp unto my feet and a *light* unto my path" (Psalm 119:105).[701] It's utterly fascinating to me to see how a child who meditated on scripture that spoke about light would later receive some of the greatest divine secrets ever given to man—the secret laws of electromagnetism that govern the physics of light.[702] Recall my earlier mention of this fact in the section on Egypt. Don't be intimidated by the math, just admire the beauty and elegance of these four equations that changed our world forever, as absolutely everything that uses electricity or light depends on an understanding of these laws of nature (Maxwell's equations in integral form):

700 https://www.youtube.com/watch?v=ly4S0oi3Yz8&t=734s.
701 https://www.biblegateway.com/passage/?search=Psalm+119%3A105&version=NIV
702 http://www.isee22.com/22_and_the_bible.html.

$$\oiint_{\partial\Omega} \overline{B} \bullet \overline{dS} = 0$$

If you add up all of the magnetic lines going out of a closed surface together with all of the magnetic lines going into the surface, you should get zero leftover arrows.

$$\oiint_{\partial\Omega} \overline{E} \bullet \overline{dS} = \frac{1}{\varepsilon_0} \iint_{\Omega} \rho dV$$

If you account for all of the electric field lines exiting out of a bag of electrical charges, then the strength of the electric field depends directly on how much charge you have stored inside the bag.

$$\oint_{\partial\Sigma} \overline{E} \bullet \overline{dl} = -\frac{d}{dt} \iint_{\Sigma} \overline{B} \bullet \overline{dS}$$

The electrical pressure inside a loop of wire depends on how quickly you change the magnetic field going through the loop. A bigger loop and higher magnetic field cause higher pressure.

$$\oint_{\partial\Sigma} \overline{B} \bullet \overline{dl} = \mu_0 \iint_{\Sigma} \overline{J} \bullet \overline{dS} + \mu_0 \varepsilon_0 \frac{d}{dt} \iint_{\Sigma} \overline{E} \bullet \overline{dS}$$

The current enclosed in a loop is equal to the surface current of the conductor plus the rate of change of the electric flux.

It is absolutely mind-blowing to consider that Maxwell came up with the mathematics of electromagnetism in 1861 utilizing vector calculus and complex analysis, many years before humankind physically measured radio waves. And it wasn't until 1922, when the speed of light was measured, that what Maxwell's equations predicted via pure mathematics was finally validated experimentally—61 years later![703]

I also noticed that the number of the beast is talked about in Revelation 13:18 and decided to see how many minutes would be in 11.11 hours, so I multiplied that number by 60 to convert to minutes and was shocked to see 666 come up. It's quite an interesting result as you get the number of the beast (666) if you multiply the number of light (11.11) by a unit of

703 https://www.otherhand.org/home-page/physics/historical-speed-of-light-measurements-in-southern-california/the-mount-wilson-station-1922-1928/ .

time (60 minutes). I literally have no idea what to make of this discovery other than to say "WOW."

What about the Great Pyramid of Giza, Egypt? The GPS coordinates for the Great Pyramid are: 29.976480 degrees north and 31.131302 east.[704] First off, 31 and the 13 in the longitude are mirror images, and the latitude, 29.976480 degrees, is almost exactly ten million times the speed of light, which is 299,792,458 meters per second.[705] You'll have to go out to the hundred-thousandths place to notice a difference when you divide the two numbers. That's about precise enough for me, for a structure that was built many thousands of years ago, don't you think? Working on nuclear power plants, accuracy to the nearest one-thousandth of an inch is close enough to operate the most powerful machines on the planet. Is this some sort of cosmic coincidence that the speed of light was built into the Great Pyramid's GPS latitude coordinate, or did an ancient civilization *purposely* put over two million car-sized blocks of stone at this exact location to send a message to future residents of the planet? By this stage of reading, I hope you're with me when I say there truly are no coincidences.

If you're reading this in paperback, you'll see that even my ISBN number has a 22 in it: 978-1-7346218-22 and if you're reading this electronically, you'll see a 77 in the ISBN: 978-1-7346218-77. My publishing company was named Lumanta Publications as the Esperanto language word for luminous. The power of numbers works from the spirit realm to the human realm, but it can be used the other direction as well. In electromagnetics, we have the reciprocity theorem which states that any antenna can function equally well as a transmitter or as a receiver of energy.[706] Once we learn to tune our spiritual antenna to the right frequency, we learn to receive energy. With enough practice, we learn how to transmit energy back to the universe. This is the raw physical essence of prayer and manifesting what we want in life. I think the harder we try to communicate with God, the harder he tries to listen and respond. That's some divine reciprocity right there!

Lightening of Enlightenment

As I type this, I am taking a graduate course on the Physics of Satellite Sensors. In the very first week, I read that the way satellites are set up to detect lightning strikes in Earth's atmosphere from space is quite

704 https://www.latlong.net/place/pyramids-of-giza-al-haram-giza-egypt-149.html
705 https://www.universetoday.com/38040/speed-of-light-2/
706 https://en.wikipedia.org/wiki/Reciprocity_(electromagnetism)

clever and, well, *en-lightening*. As it turns out, lightning is very hard to distinguish from daylight in the visible spectrum; however, lightning has a very special signature that is a tight triple-line emission spectrum centered around 777.40 nanometer wavelength. The three emission lines are located at 777.20, 777.42, and 777.54 nm, placing these signatures in the near-infrared band just below the visible spectrum.[707] The emission lines clustered at 777 nm are visible via satellite regardless of the amount of visible light. The cloud medium is optically opaque but absorbs very little energy at near-infrared frequencies.

In the Bible, Job 36:30-33 speaks about lightning and how God fills his hands with lightning and directs it where to strike. Could this be the foreshadowing of the electrical revolution?

Revelation 4:5 says:

> Out from the throne came flashes of **lightning** and sounds and peals of thunder. And there were **seven** lamps of fire burning before the throne, which are the **seven** spirits of God.[708]

Lots of seven's there, relating to lightning, huh! What about Psalm 77:18:

> Your thunder was heard in the whirlwind, your lightning lit up the world; the earth trembled and quaked.[709]

Job 37:3 says:

> Under the whole heaven He lets it loose, and His lightning to the ends of the earth.[710]

Again, is this spreading of lightning a metaphor for what we are doing by sending vast trillions of watts of electrical power through powerlines at voltages approaching a million volts? We have mastered lightning and have lit our planet up like a shimmering gem in the heavens. Industry is not an affront to nature; rather, it is but an expression of nature's intrinsic intelligence expressed through us in human form. We are but a conduit of heavenly knowledge—just messengers. Is it pure coincidence that lightning's three key signatures occur clustered at 777 nanometers, or is it a message from an intelligent creator that maybe there was a bit of careful consideration that went into creating our magical universe? God created us to be inquisitive, with an innate thirst for deep knowledge, and left

707 https://www.goes-r.gov/downloads/resources/documents/GOES-RSeriesDataBook.pdf
708 https://www.biblegateway.com/passage/?search=Revelation+4%3A5&version=NIV
709 https://www.biblegateway.com/passage/?search=Psalm+77%3A18&version=NIV
710 https://www.biblegateway.com/passage/?search=Job+37%3A3&version=NIV

fantastic little numerical gold nuggets like this for intellectual prospectors like me to find. Finds like this are what keep me coming back to the sluice and panning for more! I never imagined connecting God, 777, and lightening together from a physics class, but here we are. The wonders of physics never cease. Using our earlier work on dissecting 777, remember it is 7 x 111 and 111 = 3 x 37, and 37 is a star number. So 777 = (3x7) x 37 almost looks like two 37s, a double reference to stars, the original source of lightning's power—our sun.

Further Progress and Remarkable Number Connections

Thomas Edison began serious research into developing a practical incandescent lamp in 1878 and filed his first patent application for "Improvement in Electric Lights" on October 14, 1878. After many experiments, first with carbon in the early 1880s and then with platinum and other metals, Edison returned to a carbon filament in the end.

The following year, 1879, was indeed a momentous one. Note that Albert Einstein was born on pi day, 3/14/1879, another great source of enlightenment that was brought into the world in that same year. Sadly, James Clerk Maxwell, the pioneering physicist who discovered the laws of electromagnetism, died that same year. When God closes a door, he opens a window. With one great light turned off, another was immediately illuminated. In a cosmic changing of the guard, with the extinguishing of one great source of light, Maxwell, Edison would light the first viable light bulb on October 22, 1879 which wouldn't have been possible without Maxwell's sacred work that straddled the fence between science and religion.[711]

On the hundred-year anniversary of Maxwell's birthday, Albert Einstein described Maxwell's work as the "most profound and the most fruitful that physics has experienced since the time of Newton."[712] At the turn of the millennium, a poll of a hundred prominent physicists ranked Maxwell as the third most influential physicist of all time behind only Albert Einstein and Isaac Newton.[713]

As if that isn't enough evidence for how important the year 1879 was for human scientific progress, let's not forget that the first electric induction motor was demonstrated by Walter Baily in 1879.[714] Without the induction

711 https://en.m.wikipedia.org/wiki/Incandescent_light_bulb.
712 http://www.clerkmaxwellfoundation.org/html/about_maxwell.html.
713 http://news.bbc.co.uk/2/hi/science/nature/541840.stm.
714 http://waywiser.fas.harvard.edu/people/4613/walter-baily;jsessionid=039C6BA25236F745E7EFCBDDED0642C8.

motor, virtually every fan, blow dryer, washing machine, dryer, elevator, compressor, refrigerator, air conditioner, or most anything with an electric motor would not have been possible. Pretty much any electric motor under five horsepower is an induction motor.

Following is an electron microscope micrograph of a modern tungsten light bulb element. Note the similarity to the structure of DNA in terms of being a coil within a coil and a serpentine form. This invention took place 74 years or 37+37 years prior to Watson and Crick discovering that in fact our human DNA software is also a tightly wound spiral! Remembering that 37 is a star number, it seems appropriate that the invention of the light bulb and the discovery of DNA should both share the motif of the cosmic serpent along with the serpentine form of electromagnetic waves that propagate from the light bulb out into the vastness of space. God was the first to say "let there be light!" and then there was light—in the form of electromagnetic serpents. Now it was man's turn, and we used a serpent-wound filament of tungsten to produce still more serpentine electromagnetic waves of our own creation.

Edison was granted US Patent # 223,898 on January 27, 1880, for his invention of the incandescent light bulb. It is quite remarkable to see the number 22 showing up again in the context of bringing artificial light to the world.[715]

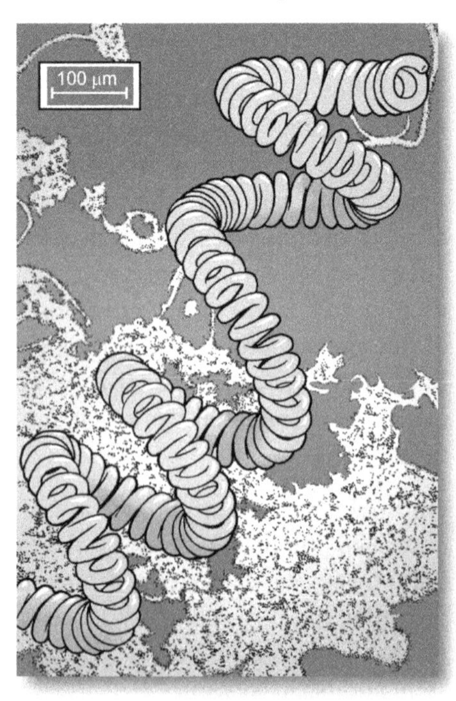

The coil-within-a-coil structure of a light bulb filament resembles the structure of DNA.[716]

715 https://www.uspto.gov/about-us/news-updates/uspto-museum-opens-new-exhibit-showcasing-american-ingenuity.
716 https://en.m.wikipedia.org/wiki/Incandescent_light_bulb#/media/File%3ATungsten_filament.JPG.

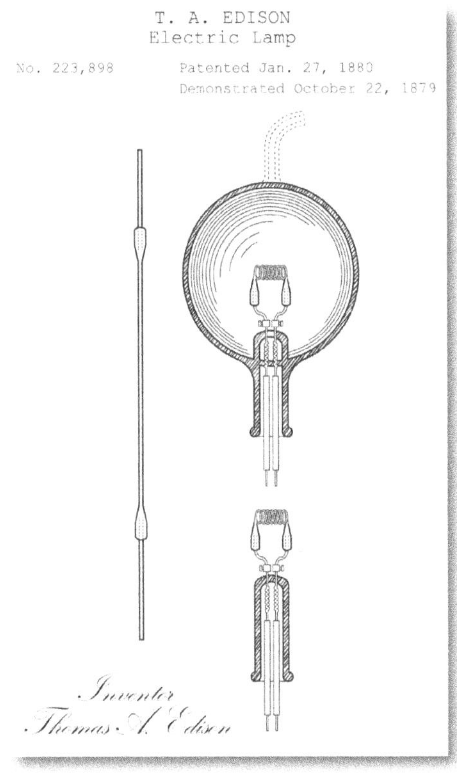

As long as we are on the topic of inventors who changed the world, Alexander Graham Bell, the father of the telephone, died on August 2, 1922. He was awarded a patent for his invention on 3/3/1876. The sum of the digits of 1876 add to 22, or 11 + 11. Furthermore, the Bell telephone system was composed of 22 local telephone service companies prior to the 1984 breakup of the monopoly.[717] And the year 1984 has digits that sum to 11 + 11. Think about it—the phone revolution began in a year whose digits sum to 22, and that inventor's monopoly on the phone system ended in a year that sums to 22. That's a whole lot of 11+11 action associated with one of the most influential inventions of all time that connected people all over the planet at the speed of light.

The Chicago 11:11 Connection

Samuel Insull was born in London, England, on November 11, 1859, and began his career as a real estate office clerk but was later fired. It was characteristic of him that he never forgave the man who fired him, thus sending him on his way to amazing success and riches. "My pride was hurt as it was never hurt before or since," Insull said years later. [718]

His next job in 1879 was as secretary to George E. Gouraud, the London representative of Thomas Alva Edison, who had shortly before invented the electric light. It wasn't long before twenty-year-old Insull had impressed Gouraud to the point that he decided to recommend him for a similar position with Edison. Interested in having Insull as his secretary,

717https://en.wikipedia.org/wiki/Bell_System#History.
718 https://chicagology.com/biographies/samuelinsull/

Edison met with him upon his arrival in New York City on 2/28/1881.[719] Insull would work with Edison and company for the next several years as they launched the nation's first central power station, Pearl Street Station in NYC, which began producing power on September 5, 1882. For the next 11 years, Insull became Edison's chief apostle of the central station concept, traveling across the country and selling various entrepreneurs on the idea of developing central power stations under the Edison franchise.

When he failed to get a promotion in 1892, Insull decided to quit.[720] He soon proved himself to be what Edison needed even more—an efficient businessman. He became manager of the Edison Machine Works in New York, helped to form General Electric, and became vice president of that company. Upon the formation of General Electric in 1881 in Schenectady, New York, Insull was given the position of vice president. Three years later, after finding out that the Chicago Edison company was seeking a new president, he would move to Chicago and assume that role in March of 1892. By 1907, all Chicago's power was being supplied by Insull's company, Commonwealth Edison (now shortened to simply ComEd), which is currently the largest electric utility in the state of Illinois.[721] The GE factory in Schenectady occupies ZIP code 12345, and I toured it in August 2019 during my career with GE.

> The Chicago World's Fair of 1893 was unique; there has never been anything quite like it before or since. In part, the spectacular architectural unity of the White City accounts for its singular impression on the American mind. Lavish displays of electrical technology also help explain why over 22 million people—one fifth of the nation—were attracted to the City of Light.[722]

Commonwealth Edison's first "big" power station to be constructed was the Fisk Street Generating Station located at 1111 West Cermak Road in the Pilsen area of Chicago. Fisk opened in 1903, the same year my great-grandmother was born, and at the time, it was the world's most powerful steam turbine at 5 million watts. The plant ran for an impressive 107 years

719 Harold Platt, *The Electric City: Energy and the Growth of the Chicago Area, 1880–1930* (Chicago: University of Chicago Press, 1991), 66.

720 https://chicagology.com/biographies/samuelinsull/.

721 https://www.britannica.com/biography/Samuel-Insull.

722 Harold Platt, *The Electric City: Energy and the Growth of the.Chicago Area, 1880–1930* (Chicago: University of Chicago Press, 1991), 59.

until finally ceasing operation in 2011.[723], [724] During the writing process, I made a day trip to Fisk Station to capture the photos below of one of planet Earth's oldest electric power generating stations. A true relic. As it turns out, the current-day Cermak Road was actually 22nd or 11 + 11 street until it was renamed in honor of a former Chicago mayor, Anton Cermak, whose career began in 1922 and ended with his assassination in 1933.[725],[726] Here are still more connections to the 11:11 Code.

Outside of Fisk station on August 27, 2019, showing the "1111 W Cermak Rd" address.

The electrification of Chicago wasn't the only accomplishment worthy of mention. By the fall of 1921, Westinghouse Electric and Manufacturing Company had inaugurated broadcasting services through KDKA in Pittsburgh, Pennsylvania; WBZ in Springfield, Massachusetts; and WJZ in Newark, New Jersey. This new form of mass communication combined with a great public service possibility had received widespread newspaper publicity, and accounts of these broadcasting stations were being read with interest throughout the United States.

At this period, the great Midwestern Insull Empire had reached its peak. Samuel Insull, the automatic head of the Insull interests, made his headquarters in Chicago, Illinois, and from his suite of offices in the Com-

723 For a reference point this is about the same power as a modern locomotive engine, and a nuclear power plant turbine can put out as much as 1,500,000 watts—about 300 times more than Fisk.

724 https://www.chicagoarchitecture.org/2019/01/29/shuttered-pilsen-power-plant-coming-back-as-data-center-and-more/.

725 https://en.wikipedia.org/wiki/Cermak_Road.

726 https://www.chipublib.org/mayor-anton-joseph-cermak-biography/.

monwealth Edison Company Building, he ruled the various public service enterprises that comprised his empire.

Mr. Insull had taken a great interest in the affairs of the Chicago Civic Opera and been financially underwriting it for several years. When the Westinghouse broadcasting activities were brought to the attention of Mr. Insull, he conceived the idea of establishing a radio station in Chicago to operate as an adjunct of the Chicago Opera Company so that the performances of the opera might be broadcast into the homes of the people of Chicago and the surrounding area. Through intermediaries, Mr. Insull contacted Mr. H. P. Davis, Westinghouse's vice president in charge of radio engineering and broadcasting, and an arrangement was made whereby Westinghouse would set up a broadcasting station in Chicago. It was agreed that the station would remain under the ownership and control of Westinghouse; however, it would be erected on the roof of the Commonwealth Edison Company Building and be operated jointly by Westinghouse and the Edison companies.

The original transmitter for the new station, KYW, was located on the elevator penthouse on the top of the Edison Building, and the studio was six floors below that on the sixteenth floor. Do the math: 6+16. The transmitter consisted of two 250-watt tubes used in a self-excited Hartley circuit, the output of which was Heising modulated by three 250-watt tubes. The plate supply was obtained from a 2,000-volt direct-current generator. The original antenna was a four-wire flat top supported by two fifty-foot steel poles mounted on top of the building. The operating frequency was 560 kilohertz. At four-thirty on the afternoon of 11/11/1921, a new broadcasting station, the first station in the Chicago area, KYW, went on the air with a program broadcast from the stage of the Chicago Civic Auditorium. Think about it, 11/11 was the dawning of the radio age in Chicago.

On January 18, 1922, KYW broadcast the first midnight revue from the studio on the sixteenth floor of the Edison Building. These revues brought the KYW audiences such entertainers as the Duncan Sisters, Dream Daddy Harry Davis, Uncle Bob, Wendell Hall, Herbie Mintz, Little Jack Little, Paul Ash, and many others who later climbed to fame as a result of their start at KYW. The feature on opening night was a scene from the *French Doll* with Irene Bordoni and several of her company.

Later in 1922, the news arrangement with the Chicago Evening American was expanded to a twenty-four-hour service under the title *World Crier*. News bulletins were read over the air on the hour and half hour twenty-four hours a day. Bulletins were delivered by messenger every few hours, and usually, there were sufficient bulletins to provide the announcer with enough material for five or six *World Crier* schedules.

The *World Crier* service started on December 27, 1922, and continued until 1927, when they discontinued it because of program scheduling.[727] I called my grandfather and explained these exciting discoveries to him immediately, and he said that he fondly remembered listening to Insull's radio station as a youth!

My career in the electric power industry started with Commonwealth Edison, where I began working as an engineering intern at the company's atomic power station in Byron, Illinois, and I went on to work for General Electric after graduating from university. My first interview with Commonwealth Edison took place in the Edison Building, where the radio station used to operate. The building seemed steeped in history, and I knew instinctively what an immeasurable impact the company had had by way of its role in supplying electric power to the great city of Chicago. When asked by the interviewer what qualifications made me suited for the job, I pulled out the following photo of myself building my first power plant from Legos at age four. The interviewer immediately knew that I had the right passion for the job, and I was hired. During my first summer internship at Byron, one of the 1,164 megawatt generator units tripped offline on an emergency due to a damaged hydrogen seal. Within hours, Westinghouse Electric Corporation had sent a generator specialist to the site to troubleshoot things and get the unit repaired and back online. When Michael Crislip arrived onsite, I latched onto him like a love-sick little puppy and never let him out of my sight while peppering him with questions to pick his brains. By the end of his second day, I had his promise to hire me after I graduate. I wanted this man's job. I'd finally met Dr. Who-Can-Fix-Nuclear-Machinery!

727 https://www.broadcastpioneers.com/kywstory.html.

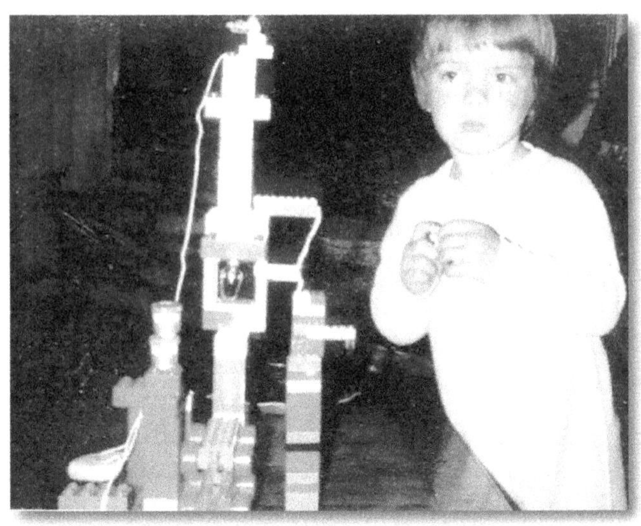

Age four, building my first power plant from Legos, light bulbs, and fuses. Photo credit: Mom!

So this is my tie-in to Chicago's great story of illumination, and what would later tie in to *The 11:11 Code*.

Let's review. Insull was born on 11/11 and was the pioneer in bringing light to the northeast quadrant of Illinois and the first to bring radio waves to the city of Chicago on 11/11. Both electricity and radio waves travel at the speed of light. Recalling from an earlier section, there are 671 minutes in 11 hours and 11 minutes, and the speed of light is 671 million miles per hour. Obviously, the same procedure works if you're dealing with 11min:11sec, which converts to 671 seconds. There could be no clearer proof that 11:11 is the secret code for all energy that travels at the speed of light. The number 11:11 represents the great illumination of humankind by means of electrical energy in all its conversions!

Growing up as a kid in the northern blue collar suburbs of Chicago, most kids watched the local PBS station, Channel 11 WTTW, whose call sign means "your Window to the World."

As a young boy, I took great delight in staying up until two in the morning to watch Doctor Who. One time on 11/22/1987, a person dressed up as Max Headroom stormed the WTTW studios and commandeered the broadcast for 90 seconds.[728] Why 11/22? Why Channel 11? I always loved

728 https://www.chicagotribune.com/business/ct-biz-wttw-max-headroom-30-years-20171122-story.html

and admired Dr. Who, as he zipped off to alien planets in his TARDIS space-time travel device to figure out all of their technical and social issues and then buzz off to the next place. In a surreal way, my wife thinks I am a lot like the doctor as I zip around the planet fixing huge power machines in foreign places and finding solutions to some of the power industry's most difficult problems. It's truly amazing how channel 11 programming really did act as a window to the world for me. God works in mysterious ways that often don't make sense until viewed in the rearview mirror from afar. In the case of channel 11, we have yet another example of 11 as a code of enlightenment. To boot, the channel 11 signal was broadcast from one of the two antenna masts radiating electromagnetic energy to our TV sets high atop the iconic John Hancock Center in downtown Chicago, which also appear to make a massive 11 in the sky. I never *metaphor* I didn't like!

Virtually every place we find 1111 in any form, whether it be 11:11, 11 + 11, 11.11, or 11 x 11, we have found unmistakable references to visible light and other frequencies of the electromagnetic spectrum, one of humankind's richest natural resources. The evidence is overwhelming, and the statistical probabilities are astronomical. The 11:11 Code really is a code of *illumination*, just like all those numerology websites and psychics have been telling us all along. If the 11:11 code is light and God is light, then is it God manifesting himself through occurrences of 11:11?

Mathematically, if we prove that X = Y, and also prove that Y = Z, then we can conclude by extension that X = Z.

Here's a very interesting idea for how all of us can try to combine our spiritual energy:

I propose that if you experience 11:11 synchronicity, pause and make a wish or say a prayer at 11:11 each day and wish for world peace, cures for all disease and human suffering, and for mass awakening for all humanity. You don't have to tell anyone, just make it a private personal habit. It could be as simple as setting an alarm for 11:11 to pause each day and silently say "thanks." The more of us that participate, the stronger the group intention becomes. Before we know it, as the movement spreads, I predict that we will start to see a positive shift in the group consciousness. As each of the world's 24 time zones passes through 11:11 each day, a wave of energy will go "up" from each zone of the planet. Who knows what we could accomplish if we all set our intentions toward a positive outcome simultaneously.

The good news is that if it fails, it didn't cost us anything; if it works, we got something for free. Make a difference in the world today by replacing all sources of negativity in your life with positivity and watch what happens.

CONCLUSIONS

Now that we have reached the conclusion of this endeavor, let's summarize some of the book's most profound concepts. Here are some of the most salient points:

- The number 22 (11 + 11) shows up in the basic alphabet of life in the 22 amino acids that are used to write the DNA code of *all* life-forms.
- Human DNA software is composed of 22 (11 + 11) chromosomes with the 23rd reserved strictly for determining gender.
- Chromosome 22 is composed of 11 million amino acids, each composed of 3 base pairs for a total of 33 million base pairs (11-22-33).
- The 22 (11 + 11) letters of the Hebrew alphabet were used to write the Book of Life, the Bible.
- All science is built upon 7 fundamental measurement units and 22 derived units.
- Robert Millikan discovered cosmic rays on 11/11/1925.
- Michelson measured the speed of light between two peaks 22 (11 + 11) miles apart, beginning in 1922.
- The time 11:11 works out to 671 minutes, and the speed of light is 671 million miles per hour.
- The 11:11 Code is found at the atomic level in electromagnetic computation of the speed of light by

multiplying the electric permittivity of free space, epsilon, by the magnetic permeability of free space, mu.

- Einstein's equation $e=mc^2$ contains 1111 in the reciprocal of c^2.
- Lightning contains three signatures of 777 nanometer wavelength energy pulses.
- The sun's activity cycles happen in multiples of 11 and 22 years.
- Edison demonstrated the first light bulb on October 22, 1879.
- Samuel Insull, Edison's British protege and the architect of Chicago's electrification, was born on 11/11, built his first major power station at 1111 W Cermak Rd, and launched Chicago's first radio station on 11/11. These achievements equate to light and enlightenment, respectively.
- The number of carbon atoms in a 1-carat diamond and the estimated number of stars in the universe are both approximately equal to one followed by 22 zeroes.

This book has endeavored to show that if humankind were left to our own devices without divine intervention, we would certainly have destroyed ourselves by now by the sinister plans of the elite evil few at the top. The plans were already in place for a hellish apocalypse. This book attempts to elucidate how the divine plan has been silently operating in the background and dropping numerical hints here, there, and everywhere.

As the old adage goes, putting 2 and 2 together, you get 22. This colloquialism means "to figure something out, to deduce or discern something."[729] This sounds awfully similar to the process that has unfolded while assembling this vast array of universal knowledge into the book you have nearly finished reading. In my opinion, the Word from John 1 could very well be a reference to DNA, the 3.5-billion letter *word* that spells out the software that underpins all life.

I hope you are able to see how just a handful of very special numbers can be found at the bottom of virtually any subject of human knowledge. This has been a whirlwind survey of many diverse topics, including astronomy, astrology, biology, chemistry, physics, mathematics, genetics, history,

729 https://en.m.wiktionary.org/wiki/put_two_and_two_together.

religion, spirituality, metaphysics, philosophy, geology, linguistics, language, engineering, and many others. Encountering numbers such as 3, 7, 11, 22, 33, 37, the golden ratio, φ, Euler's number, e, and Archimedes's constant, π at some of the deepest levels of virtually all areas of human knowledge seems to suggest that the same higher intellect was involved in creating all these bodies of knowledge. These numbers appear to be some sort of divine fingerprint of authenticity. Identifying these unmistakable and statistically significant pieces of empirical data scattered across all areas of human knowledge provides a clear message to me that the same omniscient, omnipresent cosmic entity was the common source of *all knowledge*. Evidence of intelligent creation can be found through the microscope and the telescope and at all scales in between. Just pick a power of ten. Or better yet, watch the video "Universe to Scale."[730] Toward the end of the video clip, doesn't it seem like the universe at a macro level looks oddly similar to the brain at a micro level? It sure makes me wonder if we all aren't just the gods of the atoms, and the atoms of the gods. The devil may be in the details, but God's fingerprints can be found in them as well. It all depends on what you're looking for! Intentions matter.

Isaiah 45:7 states, "I form the light and create darkness, I bring prosperity and create disaster; I, the LORD, do all these things."[731] Perhaps this explains why the magic numbers 11, 22, 33, and 11:11 are associated with so many of the wonderful *and* terrible events that punctuated the great human story.

Now you know the true secret concealed within the title *The 11:11 Code*, which has eluded humankind until now. The fact that 11 + 11 = 22 puts to rest the mystery of why the number 22 has been showing up in my life (and perhaps yours?) countless times through various synchronicities. It was as if a higher being was trying to communicate some sort of secret message to me throughout my life. I honestly believe that these coincidences and messages were literally hidden in our DNA as an awakening code that has been talked about for so long by so many. A proper regimen of high-quality music, meditation, literature, and healthy foods are important steps toward getting your spiritual radio tuned to the right station. The cosmic spiritual message has always been broadcasting, but it takes time and effort to get our spirit frequency tuned in.

730 https://www.youtube.com/watch?v=ZOKRPUx8soc.
731 https://biblehub.com/isaiah/45-7.htm.

In a nutshell, you can think of 11:11 as four of God's fingers patiently poking their way into your consciousness until they catch your attention. The four fingers on your hand make four numeral ones or 11:11. It is a code that was written so cleverly into our DNA code, containing a message of cosmic love and intelligence as a reminder to never forget that we were made with care by someone who was a mathematician of the highest degree and who loves surprises and mysteries. Mysteries are wonderful things to ponder as we look out into the heavens and ask why we are here.

Stop for a moment and perform an internet search for "meerkat galactic center image."[732] You'll see that at the heart of our galaxy is what appears to be a massive heart. God loves us all as sent in a message at least 25,000 years ago, the amount of time it takes light to travel from the center of our galaxy to our retina today.

Then God commanded,
"Let there be light"—and light appeared."

—Genesis 1:3[733]

The number 2 and its mirror image form a heart.

Suggested video: "Stunning New Universe Fly-Through"

Admittedly, this is a pretty serious book, so I thought I would end it with a bit of lighthearted fun. Virtually everyone on the planet has an opinion of which way the toilet paper roll should be oriented. Some people such as myself staunchly believe that the free end of the roll should be near the user, while still others believe the tail should be away from the user and near the wall. There is no middle ground in this debate, no neutral position. You're either with us or against us. Perhaps one of humankind's greatest lingering debates centers around which orientation is the correct

732 https://cosmosmagazine.com/space/the-centre-of-the-galaxy-in-radio-vision.
733 https://www.biblegateway.com/passage/?search=Genesis+1-3&version=NIV.

one. An internet search of US patent #465,588 turns up an invention by Seth Wheeler titled "Toilet Paper Roll," which has an illustration that clearly depicts the free end of the roll oriented away from the wall and toward the user.[734] Now if everyone could just mount the toilet roll with the free end away from the wall, that'd be great.

Why is this showing up in *The 11:11 Code*? The patent was awarded on December 22, 1891. There you have it. The number 22 (11 + 11) has shown up in the solution to one of humankind's greatest debates. See, aren't you glad you slogged through the section on mathematics? I didn't want my book to be relegated to the category of "good toilet reading material," but here we are.

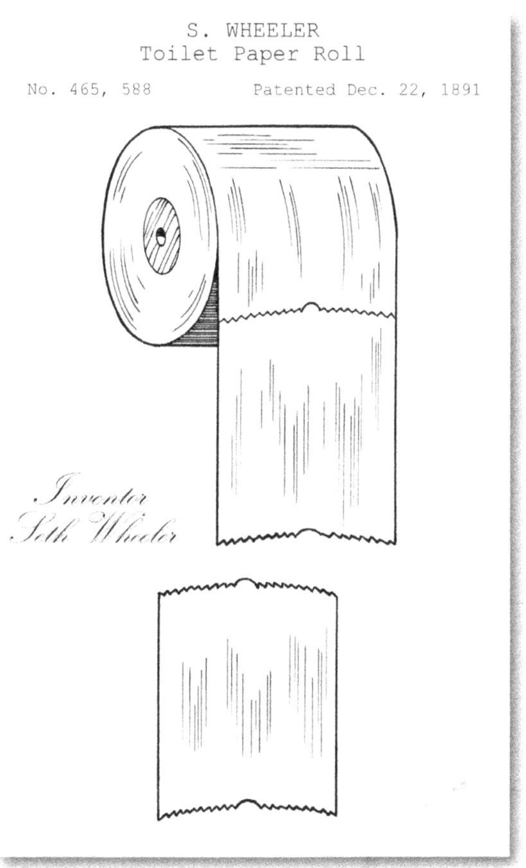

The toilet paper roll as depicted in Seth Wheeler's US patent

734 https://patents.google.com/patent/US465588A/en.

So, after reading all of this, you may still be asking, "What exactly is the 11:11 code?" I have reached the conclusion that it represents a small, permanent, and intentional tear in the veil that separates our human reality from the spiritual domain. Light can be shined either direction through the crack. We just have to be aware of it, and believe, and through this elevated consciousness we can become more connected to the great cosmic mind that created us and set the miracle of life in motion.

I hope you've enjoyed reading this as much as I enjoyed writing it. If you found this book enlightening, please recommend it to at least 6 friends so we can apply six degrees of separation, which is the concept that any two people on Earth are never more than 6 connections away from each other. By spreading the word, we can propagate this message of universal love, hope, and global awakening. You've probably heard catchy phrases such as "We're all connected," "Everything is connected," and "It's a small world," and this work is essentially proof of that by exhaustion using the universal, mystery-cloaked language of numbers.

This is the very first book I've ever published, so I have no earthly idea whether this will be a best seller or be relegated to the scrap heap of failed books or perhaps land somewhere in the middle. But I came out and swung for the parking lot, and where the ball lands is in God's capable hands (and yours!) at this point.

Did you know that the *New York Times* best-seller list made its debut on October 12 (my father's birthday) in 1931? And it was *and still is* a composite of the top-selling books in 22 of the largest cities in America.[735] The end outcome of this effort really is in the hands of you, the reader. You are the most important person on my sales team. If I've helped you learn a little something about your world and your universe, why not say thanks by referring your friends and family to my endeavor. Give someone the gift of enlightenment.

Parting Tune: Please visit YouTube and pull up the video "Beginning | Chill Out Mix" on the Chilloutdeer channel.[736] Sounds amazing in the car. Thank me later.

735 https://books.google.com/books?id=PEZkkbohbtoC&pg=PA290#v=onepage&q&f=false
736 https://www.youtube.com/watch?v=OVsCBmkEKTg&t=267s

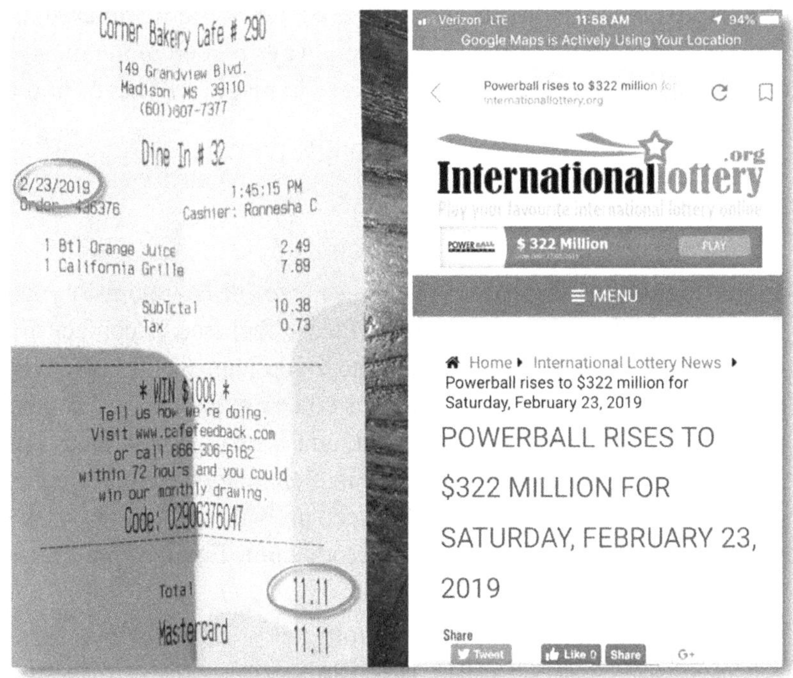

Lunch receipt and lottery announcement from February 23, 2019

Modern retake of the 1980 photo on the steps of my childhood home at 322 Hull Court, Waukegan, IL with my childhood friend and neighbor, Bob "Bobby" Kretz

And above all watch with glittering eyes the whole world around you because the greatest secrets are always hidden in the most unlikely places. Those who don't believe in magic will never find it.

—Roald Dahl[737]

***

I look forward to feedback from readers, so please return to your favorite retailer and write a review. Please feel free to contact me directly as well, especially to share how you happened to discover this book and/or any 1111 occurrences you've experienced. I can be reached at **the1111code@gmail.com**, and if enough new ideas are submitted, I'll include them along with a citation of the contributor in any future editions. You can also keep up with any news by visiting the book's website at **www.1111code.com**. Email is preferred, but letters can be addressed to:

Charles Wolfe
P.O. Box 486
Sturgeon Bay, WI
54235-0486

737 https://quotefancy.com/quote/757782/Roald-Dahl-And-above-all-watch-with-glittering-eyes-the-whole-world-around-you-because

ABOUT THE AUTHOR

Charles Wolfe was born in Waukegan, Illinois, and earned his bachelor of science degree at the University of Illinois at Urbana-Champaign, with a minor in mathematics. As an electrical engineering major, his specialty was in power systems and electromagnetics. During a year abroad at the University of Örebro in Sweden, he studied mathematics, the Swedish language, genealogy, and engineering, going on to earn his master of engineering degree from the University of Wisconsin at Madison in 2012. He speaks six languages at varying levels of fluency. In his work with Siemens Power Corporation, Mitsubishi Power Systems, and General Electric, Mr. Wolfe served project needs throughout the world. He is currently about halfway through his master of science degree in Applied Physics through Johns Hopkins University Applied Physics Laboratory.

Charles has dedicated his life to helping keep the lights on during his day job while using his nascent book-writing hobby as a way to bring spiritual light to the world. It is his sincere hope that, by reading this, people will be one large step closer to understanding their overall purpose in the universe and better appreciate their relationship and connection to the divine architect of the cosmos. Charles's motivation for writing is to share his vision of hope, peace, and freedom for all of humanity.

When not writing, the author's hobbies include hiking, camping, traveling, cooking, and reading in a wide array of topics.

If you're still reading, you deserve one last treat, courtesy of my lovely wife, Britta, who taught me the meaning of life. The nuclear plant referenced is the Byron nuclear plant where my career began. Enjoy. Search YouTube for: "Painting The Impossible" by Akiane Kramarik. I now understand the deep suffering that goes into a masterpiece, and the hard work that so many are quick to simply dismiss as genius.[738]

738 https://www.youtube.com/watch?v=Wm9BGxpf0hU&feature=youtu.be

ACKNOWLEDGMENTS

I want to take this moment to thank my wife, Britta, and son, Erik, for their for their tireless support, love, and patience during the last year as I changed careers, moved to another state, started a new business, and wrote this book while working on my masters in Physics and traveling the world for work. Writing a serious book such as this is an immense undertaking, and it has completely dominated any and all free space in my head for the last two years. The book is now done, and your husband and father are back now. I hope it will all be worth the sacrifice. I really gave it everything I had and much more, including three visits to the ER. I missed being involved in your lives the last two years.

I wanted to give a special thanks to all the people who took the time out of their own busy lives to review this monster of a book and provide me with invaluable feedback. Your careful and insightful feedback showed me just how important it is to solicit the help of others. My deepest gratitude goes to my wife, Britta, for her undying support and patience during the writing process and for her musical genius, which she used to help me find so many of the beautiful music selections included in the work. I would also like to thank the following:

Life is the most amazing thing to ever happen
to me, Thanks, Jennifer Fox, aka Mom.

James Wolfe, “Dad,” for teaching me to shoot
for the stars. I hope you’re proud up there.

Robert Maves, a.k.a. Grandpa, for teaching me to
be an intrepid explorer in search of truth.

Don Jones for helping me discover the joy of contented sobriety.

Steve & Teri Hupp for helping me recover from rock-bottom.

Donna Carlson for opening my mind to higher mathematics.

Traci Nathans-Kelly for your help in improving this book.

Doug Cunliffe-Owen for your friendship and feedback.

Diana Gomez, Cecilia Taylor, Christian Albert, Al Fossler, and Tony Orawiec for helping me jump-start my career with engineering internships with Commonwealth Edison.

Dr. Pete Sauer for being my senior advisor at UIUC.

Adam Medlin, David Ramey, and Daniel Steingraeber for sending around the world for GE.

Stephanie Knabel-Gracyalny for thirty years of friendship and all the book feedback.

Michael Crislip for introducing me to one of the most fascinating careers on Earth.

Wesley Hout for editing suggestions and a lifetime of friendship and laughs.

Mike Valdes for all the conversations that led me to dig into the 11:11 code.

My talented editors, Debra, Ginny, and Elizabeth for your professionalism.

Mary Kordys for helping get my Siemens career started out of college.

Toby Ward for your technical perspective and for all the physics lessons.

Ruth Telfer for encouraging me to write a book about my world travels.

Robert Bruce Powers for your friendship and rocket science tutelage.

Jon Wheeler for being the big brother I never had; I miss you, dude.

Christine Nicometo for challenging me to become a better writer.

Beth Nilsson for your feedback and advice.

EXTRAS

APPENDIX 1:

MORE REALLY COOL VIDEOS

For the curious reader who wants more, I advise searching YouTube for the following video titles:

A hole in a hole in a hole—Numberphile

Around the World in a Tea Daze—Shpongle

But what is a partial differential equation?—Grant Sanderson, who owns the 3Blue1Brown YouTube channel

Closer to You—Kaisaku

Fourier Series Animation (Square Wave)—Brek Martin

Fourier Series Animation (Saw Wave)—Brek Martin

Great Demo on Fibonacci Sequence Spirals in Nature—The Golden Ratio—Wise Wanderer

gyroscope nutation—CGS

How Earth Moves—vsauce

I am a soul—Nibana

Imaginary Numbers, Functions of Complex Variables—Eugene Khutoryansky

Into the light—Oase der Ruhe

Mandelbrot deep zoom to 10E+2431 at 60 fps—Needle Julia evolution—Fractal Universe A Year in the Life of the Sun—Douglas Nichols

Maxwell, The History of Electromagnetism—Documentary— The King

Odyssey—Olie Bassweight

Powers of Ten (1977)—Eames Office

Precession of the Earth—Steven Sanders

Stunning New Universe Fly-Through—(multiple sources)

Symphony of Science—We Are All Connected—(multiple sources)

The Hardest Mandelbrot Zoom Ever—Fractal Universe

The Mandelbrot Set—Numberphile (The only video you need to see)

Trollabundin 10.08.13—Eivor Palsdottir

Universe to Scale—Cosmic Portals

APPENDIX 2:

ELECTROMAGNETIC DERIVATION OF THE SPEED OF LIGHT

In Chapter 15, I mentioned that the interested reader could come here to see the complete derivation of how I arrived at finding the 11:11 code in the speed of light, beginning with Maxwell's equations. The remainder of that development is presented here. The development is limited to considering the electric field in free space for the sake of time and space within the book, but a nearly identical workup applies to the magnetic field.

Beginning with Maxwell's source-free field equations:
$\nabla \times \bar{E} = \text{curl}\,\bar{E} = -j\omega\mu_0\bar{H}$ and $\nabla \times \bar{H} = \text{curl}\,\bar{H} = -j\omega\varepsilon_0\bar{E}$

From the above equations, we find that both $\bar{E}$ & $\bar{H}$ satisfy the same Helmholtz equation
$\nabla^2\bar{E} - \gamma^2\bar{E} = 0$ and $\nabla^2\bar{H} - \gamma^2\bar{H} = 0$ where $\gamma^2 = -\omega^2\varepsilon_0\mu_0$ for free space and ∇^2 is the Laplacian operator.

Each component of the $\bar{E}$ and $\bar{H}$ vectors satisfies the same scalar Helmholtz equation for the x-component of the $\bar{E}$ vector which can be expressed in vector form as: $\nabla^2 E_x - \gamma^2 E_x = 0$, or as a partial differential equation (PDE) as follows:

$$\frac{\partial^2 E_x}{\partial x^2} + \frac{\partial^2 E_x}{\partial y^2} + \frac{\partial^2 E_x}{\partial z^2} + \omega^2\varepsilon_0\mu_0 E_x = 0$$

which is readily recognized as the Wave Equation whose velocity of wave propagation is: $V_p = \frac{1}{\sqrt{\varepsilon_0\mu_0}} = \frac{1}{\sqrt{1111 \times 10^{-20}}} = \ldots$

$\ldots = V_p = 300{,}000$ kilometers per second which is the speed of light in free space. The number 1111 is the base of the product of ε_0 and μ_0 where $\varepsilon_0\mu_0 = \left(\frac{1}{36\pi} \times 10^{-9}\right) \times \left(4\pi \times 10^{-7}\right)$ which reduces to $\varepsilon_0\mu_0 = \frac{4\pi}{36\pi} \times 10^{-16} = \frac{1}{9} \times 10^{-16} = 0.1111 \times 10^{-16}$ which is equivalent to 1111×10^{-20}.

Now we have proven that "1111" is the 11:11 Code manifested in the derivation of the speed of light using Maxwell's Equations.

APPENDIX 3:

WRITING EINSTEIN'S MASS-ENERGY EQUATION IN TERMS OF 1111

1111 is a bridge between mass and energy!

The speed of light is: $c = \frac{1}{\sqrt{\mu_0 \varepsilon_0}}$ (-1-)

Squaring both sides of (-1-) gives $c^2 = \frac{1}{\mu_0 \varepsilon_0}$

The electric permittivity of free space is $\varepsilon_0 = \frac{1}{36\pi} \times 10^{-9}$

The magnetic permeability of free space is $\mu_0 = 4\pi \times 10^{-7}$

Multiplying μ_0 by ε_0 gives;

$\mu_0 \times \varepsilon_0 = (4\pi \times 10^{-7}) \times (\frac{1}{36\pi} \times 10^{-9}) = \frac{4\pi}{36\pi} \times 10^{-7-9} = \ldots$

$= \mu_0 \times \varepsilon_0 = \frac{4\pi}{4 \times 9\pi} \times 10^{-16} = \frac{1}{9} \times 10^{-16} = 0.1111 \times 10^{-16}$

We can shift the deimal point 4 places to the right and change the exponent by 4, giving

$\mu_0 \varepsilon_0 = 1111 \times 10^{-20}$ ← Substitute this into (-1-)

gives us: $c = \frac{1}{\sqrt{1111 \times 10^{-20}}}$ and similarly,

we get $c^2 = \frac{1}{1111 \times 10^{-20}}$

Recalling Einsteins famous equation $e = mc^2$

$$e = m\left(\frac{1}{1111 \times 10^{-20}}\right)$$

Summing up, we see that when "m" Kilograms of mass is converted into energy, the amount of energy is equal to the mass destroyed divided by 1111×10^{-20} Joules.

APPENDIX 4:

LIST OF PEOPLE WHO HELPED DESIGN COVER ART

Andrew Fossler
Al & Charles Fossler
Bob Kretz
Brandy & Brian Turcotte
Brittany Keller
Carol and Dale Stewart
Chris Sawa
Christy Fruits
Cindy Klinefelter
Crystal & Matthew Siver
Danny "P.D." Newman
Debra Hartmann
Frank Cope
Hollie & Brent Owens
Jacque Brund
James Cantrell
James Meffen
Janice & Ken Albrecht
Janice & Bill Devore
Jeff Thompson
Jennifer Fox
Jill Vrchota
Johanna Glembo
Joy Williamson
Julie Vandersteen
Kajsa Ehmer
Kara Melchiorre
Kate McCrew
Kirsten Emmerson
Kim & Gary Richards
Kevin & Indi Cicona
Kristin Sowinski
Larseric Elestig
Lars Ehmer
Linda Knabel
Lin Lindemann
Luisa Velarde
Mark & Diane Ottersen
Marshall Troutman
Mary Kordys
Michael Killeen
Mike Valdes
Natalie Rompella
Nick Hannar
Peggy Steele
Rachel Tianhaara
Ruth Telfer
Spencer Lorenz
Stephanie Gracyalny
Wesley Hout
Wesley Manning

APPENDIX 5:

PLACES I'VE WORKED

If you live within 1,000 kilometers of any major blob in the picture above, or any of these places worldwide listed below, then I've worked on electric machines that supplies the lamp you're reading with or the charger that charged your tablet:

Algeria – Oran, Hassi Messaoud

Argentina - Tucuman

Aruba

Bahrain – Riffa

Belgium – Ghent

Canada – Sarnia, ON; Saskatoon, SK; Cold Lake, AB.

Chad – Doba (4 trips)

Chile – Talcahuano

China – Hangzhou, Shanghai, Dongguan, Jinhua…

China - Baochang, Ningbo, Foshan, Huizhou (17 trips)

Colombia – Cali (3 trips)

Dominican Republic – Los Mina, Monte Rio

Ecuador - Guayaquil

Egypt – Cairo North, Alexandria

England – Peterborough, Immingham, Basildon, Spalding

Germany – Duisburg

Ghana – Takoradi

Guatemala – El Estor

Hong Kong – Black Point

Indonesia – Palembang, Dumai

Israel – Netanya, Beer Sheva, Eilat

Jamaica – Montego Bay, Hunts Bay

Japan – Kimitsu, Tokyo, Hitachi, Kawasaki

Jordan – Samra

Kazakhstan – Zhangaozen, Tengiz, Almaty (5 trips)

Korea - Yeosu

Malaysia – Kota Kinabalu

Mexico – Bajio, Chihuahua, Merida, Tuxpan, Manzanillo…

Mexico - Loreto, Rio Bravo, Mexicali (20+)

Netherlands – Vlissingen

Nicaragua – San Jacinto

Nigeria – Ikot Abasi, Bonny Island (4 trips)

Oman – Salalah
Philippines – Ormoc City (3 trips)

Puerto Rico – San Juan, Ponce (4 trips)

Qatar – Doha, Ras Laffan, Messaieed Industrial City (6 trips)

Romania – Cernavoda

Saudi Arabia – Dammam, Jeddah, Riyadh (4 trips)

South Africa – Johannesburg

Spain – Oviedo, Santurtzi, Tarragona

Taiwan – Chia Yi, Hsin Tao

Thailand – Chon Buri

Trinidad – Point Lisas (3 trips)

Tunisia – Bouchemma (2 trips)

Turkey – Ankara, Mersin, Adana, Izmir, Eskisehir, Kemalpasa (13 trips)

Turkmenistan – Ashgabat, Turkmenbashi, Buzmein, Balkanabat (6 trips)

UAE – Dubai, Ajman, Abu Dhabi, Fujairah, Nakheel (11 trips)

USA - Every state but MT, SD, AK and WY.

Venezuela - Maracaibo

Vietnam – Vung Tau

SELECTED REFERENCES

Aldrin, Edwin. *Magnificent Desolation.* New York: Harmony Books, 2009.

Aldrin, Edwin. *Line of Sight Guidance Techniques for Manned Orbital Rendezvous*. Boston: Massachusetts Institute of Technology Library Archives, 1963.

Booth, Mark. *The Secret History of the World.* New York: The Overlook Press, 2008.

Bushby, Tony. *The Secret in the Bible*. Queensland, Australia: Joshua Books, 2003.

Cahn, Jonathan. *The Paradigm*. Lake Mary, FL: Charisma House Book Group, 2017.

Carey, George. *God-Man: The Word Made Flesh.* Mansfield Centre, CT: Martino Publishing, 2013.

Cernan, Eugene. *The Last Man on the Moon.* New York: St. Martin's Griffin, 1999.

DePillis, John. *777 Mathematical Conversation Starters*. Washington, DC: The Mathematical Association of America, 2002.

Dudley, Underwood. *Numerology: Or, What Pythagoras Wrought*. Washington, DC: The Mathematical Association of America, 1997.

Finch, Steven. *Mathematical Constants*. Cambridge: Cambridge University Press, 2003.

Gough, Richard. *The Bible Wheel: A Revelation of the Divine Unity of the Holy Bible*. Yakima, WA: Bible Wheel Book House, 2006.

Hancock, Graham. *Fingerprints of the Gods*. New York: Three Rivers Press, 1995.

Il Y'Viavia, Signet. *The Akshaya Patra Series*. Bloomington, IN: Xlibris, 2015.

Jin, Jiang-Ming. *Theory and Computation of Electromagnetic Fields*. Hoboken, NJ: John Wiley & Sons, 2015. (Quoted by permission of Professor Jiang-Ming Jin)

Knauss, John. *Introduction to Physical Oceanography.* Long Grove, IL: 2017.

Lanza, Robert. *Biocentrism*. Dallas: Benbella Books, 2009.

Limar, Igor. "Carl G. Jung's Synchronicity and Quantum Entanglement: Schrödinger's Cat 'Wanders' Between Chromosomes." *NeuroQuantology* 9, no. 2 (2011): 313.

Livio, Mario. *The Golden Ratio: The Story of Phi, the World's Most Astonishing Number*. New York: Broadway Books, 2003.

Livio, Mario. *Is God a Mathematician?* New York: Simon & Schuster Paperbacks, 2009.

McGough, Richard Amiel. *The Bible Wheel.* **https://www.biblewheel.com/Wheel/Spokes/tav_seal.php**. (Quoted by permission of Richard Amiel McGough)

Narby, Jeremy. *The Cosmic Serpent: DNA and the Origins of Knowledge*. New York: Jeremy P. Tarcher/Putnam, 1998. (Quoted by permission of Jeremy Narby)

Newman, P D. *Alchemically Stoned – The Psychedelic Secret of Freemasonry* (The Laudable Pursuit, 2017). (Quoted by permission of P. D. Newman)

Pickover, Clifford. *Sex, Drugs, Einstein, and Elves: Sushi, Psychedelics, Parallel Universes, and the Quest for Transcendence*. Petaluma, CA: Smart Publications, 2005.

Platt, Harold. *The Electric City: Energy and the Growth of the Chicago Area, 1880–1930*. Chicago: University of Chicago Press, 1991.

Ridley, Matt. *Genome: The Autobiography of a Species in 23 Chapters*. New York: Harper Perennial, 1999.

Sagan, Carl. *Cosmos*. New York: Ballantine Books, 2013.

Sams, Gregory. *Sun of gOd: Discover the Self-Organizing Consciousness That Underlies Everything*. San Francisco: Weiser Books, 2009.

Schimmel, Annemarie. *The Mystery of Numbers*. Oxford: Oxford University Press, 1993.

Schneider, Michael. *A Beginner's Guide to Constructing the Universe: The Mathematical Archetypes of Nature, Art, and Science*. New York: Harper Perennial, 1993.

Schrodinger, Erwin. *What Is Life?* Cambridge: Cambridge University Press, 2015.

Shanon, Benny. *Antipodes of the Mind: Charting the Phenomenology of the Ayahuasca Experience*. Oxford, UK: Oxford University Press, 2002.

Skinner, Stephen. *Sacred Geometry: Deciphering the Code*. (New York: Sterling Publishing Co., 2006.

Stein, William. *Elementary Number Theory: Primes, Congruences, and Secrets*. New York: Springer, 2009.

Stipp, David. *A Most Elegant Equation: Euler's Formula and the Beauty of Mathematics*. New York: Basic Books, 2017.

Wallace, Irving. *The Square Pegs: Some Americans Who Dared to Be Different*. New York: Borzoi Books, 1957.

Watson, James. *DNA: The Secret of Life*. London: Arrow Books, 2004.

Wilcock, David. *The Synchronicity Key: The Hidden Intelligence Guiding the Universe and You*. New York: Dutton, 2013.

Wood, Gillen D'Arcy. *Tambora: The Eruption That Changed the World*. Princeton, NJ: Princeton University Press, 2014.

COVER ART

During a work trip to Belgium in January 2020, I was in Frankfurt, Germany's international airport shopping when a three-dimensional puzzle model of the globe caught my eye. I gave it to my son as an early birthday present. As we reached about 75% completion, I had the idea to take the incomplete globe outside and take a picture of it sitting on top of about a foot of freshly fallen snow. The idea occurred to me to use this as my cover shot, and then I worked with graphic artist Jacque Brund to develop it into what it is today.

I crowdsourced some of the design process by uploading various versions of the cover shot onto my personal Facebook page and asking my friends to vote on which style they preferred. I tallied the votes and went with the majority, but not until I had asked all of the others what they didn't like about the majority choice. I was able to integrate the feedback of about 50 people in 21 US states and 5 countries worldwide. Think of it: a picture of the world, designed by the world. You guys did this! I deeply appreciate everyone's help in making the cover shot into something we can all feel proud of. (A complete list of those who helped is included in Appendix 4.)

The Ravensburger puzzle was the most interesting and enjoyable puzzles I have ever put together and my son really loved it too. The globe is made of hard plastic pieces which are all precision cut, and the overall quality is unbelievably good. I'd highly recommend it to anyone who might be interested. It was only about $45 US and makes a great gift for someone of virtually any age.

Here is a link to Ravensburger puzzles:

https://www.ravensburger.us/products/3d-puzzles/index.html

CPSIA information can be obtained
at www.ICGtesting.com
Printed in the USA
BVHW040950200320
575516BV00004B/6